The Editor

LARRY J. REYNOLDS is Thomas Franklin Mayo Professor in Liberal Arts and Professor of English at Texas A&M University, where he co-founded and served as first director of the Interdisciplinary Group for Historical Literary Study. He is author of *James Kirke Paulding* and *European Revolutions and the American Literary Renaissance* and co-editor of *"These Sad But Glorious Days": Dispatches from Europe, 1846–1850* and *New Historical Literary Study.*

WOMAN IN THE NINETEENTH CENTURY

AN AUTHORITATIVE TEXT

BACKGROUNDS

CRITICISM

A NORTON CRITICAL EDITION

Margaret Fuller

WOMAN IN THE NINETEENTH CENTURY

AN AUTHORITATIVE TEXT

BACKGROUNDS

CRITICISM

Edited by

LARRY J. REYNOLDS

TEXAS A&M UNIVERSITY

W • W • NORTON & COMPANY • *New York* • *London*

The text of this book is composed in Electra
with the display set in Bernhard Modern.
Composition by PennSet, Inc.
Manufacturing by R R Donnelley
Book design by Antonina Krass.

Library of Congress Cataloging-in-Publication Data

Fuller, Margaret, 1810–1850.
    Woman in the nineteenth century : an authoritative text,
backgrounds, criticism / edited by Larry J. Reynolds.
        p.   cm. — (A Norton critical edition)
    Includes bibliographical references (p.   ).
    ISBN 0-393-97157-0 (pbk.)
    1. Women—History—Modern period, 1600–   I. Reynolds,
Larry J. (Larry John), 1942–   . II. Title.
HQ1154.08   1997
305.4'09'034—dc21   96-40450
                                                     CIP

W. W. Norton & Company, Inc., 500 Fifth Avenue, New York, N.Y. 10110
http://www.wwnorton.com

W. W. Norton & Company Ltd., Castle House, 75/76 Wells Street, London W1T 3QT

7 8 9 0

Contents

vii

viii CONTENTS

Criticism

Editor's Preface

Margaret Fuller (1810–1850) has recently gained recognition as an important figure in American cultural history and is now regarded as America's first major female intellectual. During the past twenty years, there has been a surge of interest in Fuller and her writings, especially *Woman in the Nineteenth Century* (1845), which is now considered the foundational text of the women's rights movement in America. Leaders of this movement, including Elizabeth Cady Stanton and Susan B. Anthony, warmly acknowledged the inspiration Fuller provided.

Despite its straightforward title, *Woman in the Nineteenth Century* is an allusive, digressive, and challenging argument on behalf of the quest for human perfection, especially for women's full intellectual and spiritual development. First published in the July 1843 *Dial* as an essay titled "The Great Lawsuit: Man *versus* Men. Woman *versus* Women" (a title meant to suggest the tension between the ideal and the actual), it was transformed from essay to book in the fall of 1844, a transitional moment in Fuller's life and career. Having just accepted a job as literary critic and social commentator on the *New-York Daily Tribune*, Fuller was about to leave her circle of learned friends in New England and address a new mass audience in New York City.

Before she made this anxiety-producing move, she went to Fishkill Landing, a village on the east banks of the Hudson River, some sixty miles north of New York City, to finish the book. At the time, she was already an accomplished teacher, editor, and author. Eight years earlier, in 1836, she had taught at Bronson Alcott's progressive and controversial Temple School in Boston and, a year later, at the new Greene Street School in Providence, Rhode Island. After moving back to Boston in December 1838, she gave private language lessons, worked on a biography of Goethe, and became an active member of the Transcendental Club. During the winters of 1839–44, she held her series of classes, or "Conversations" as they were called, for prominent Boston women at Elizabeth Peabody's bookshop on West Street; and from January 1840 to March 1842, she edited the transcendentalist journal the *Dial*, with energy and skill. In the summer of 1843, she traveled to Chicago and the Great Lakes, acquiring new insights into the hardships of women on the frontier and into the injustices suffered by the American Indian. She wrote about her travels in *Summer on the Lakes, in*

1843 (1844), a book that caught the attention of Horace Greeley, the reform-minded editor of the *Tribune*, who asked her to work for his paper and offered to publish her next book. She accepted both offers.

At Fishkill Landing, as Fuller finished *Woman in the Nineteenth Century* (which Greeley would publish in February 1845), she felt exhilarated, and she credited the site with liberating her as a writer. In letters to friends, she emphasized the elevation of the place and made the high hills behind the town into lofty mountains. In her letters and in the book itself, she even used high ground as a metaphor to suggest the quality of her work and its elevating effects. "The boldness, sweetness, and variety here, just what I like," she wrote. "How idle to pretend that one could live and write so well amid fallow flat fields! This majesty, this calm splendor, could not but exhilarate the mind, and make it nobly free and plastic."[1]

The additions and revisions Fuller made at this time show her trying to negotiate between an emerging egalitarianism associated with her new job on the *Tribune* and a residual intellectual elitism associated with her former Boston-Cambridge-Concord milieu. Her reformist sentiments emerge in new passages that treat the problems of abused wives, female slaves, prostitutes, old maids, and female factory workers; her exclusive tastes, however, emerge in the abundant historical and literary materials she also added. Fuller sensed the apparent inconsistency, and she wrote her friend William Henry Channing, "The writing, though I have tried to make my meaning full and clear, requires, shall I say? too much culture in the reader to be quickly or extensively diffused."[2]

The annotations included in this Norton Critical Edition should go a long way toward solving this particular problem for today's readers of Fuller's text. The background materials included here should also help elucidate the difficult ideas Fuller developed and show how she arrived at them. Fuller drew heavily on her own experiences as she pondered the plight of woman in the nineteenth century; consequently, much of the background material I have included is autobiographical and biographical in nature.

The early reviews reprinted here are meant to place Fuller's book within its historical moment and reveal the strong reactions it evoked from its early readers. The six examples of modern criticism, selected for their explanatory power, show not only different approaches to Fuller's text but also why it is valued so highly today. Other excellent Fuller scholarship — bibliographies; biographies; critical articles and books; and recent editions of Fuller's letters, journals, dispatches, and other writings — can be found in the "Selected Bibliography."

The preparation of this edition was made possible through the help

1. *The Letters of Margaret Fuller*, ed. Robert N. Hudspeth (Ithaca, N.Y.: Cornell University Press, 1983–95), 3:232.
2. Ibid., 3:242.

of a number of people, whom I'm delighted to acknowledge here. My department head, J. Lawrence Mitchell, has been consistently supportive of the project; the members of the Interdisciplinary Group for Historical Literary Study have provided a stimulating intellectual environment in which to work; my colleagues Nancy Golsan, Melanie Hawthorne, Craig Kallendorf, and Howard Marchitello kindly helped me with difficult translations; my graduate research assistant Trent Masicki and my son Robin Reynolds obtained needed books, articles, and entries for me; Fuller scholars Bell Gale Chevigny and Joel Myerson generously sent me encouragement as well as rare materials from their files; and Jeffrey Steele graciously agreed to contribute an original essay to the volume. Finally, my wife and colleague, Susan Bolet Egenolf, provided wise counsel and invaluable harmony in difference.

The Text of
WOMAN IN THE
NINETEENTH CENTURY

"Frei durch Vernunft, stark durch Gesetze,
Durch Sanftmuth gross, und reich durch Schätze,
Die lange Zeit dein Busen dir verschwieg."[1]

"I meant the day-star should not brighter rise,
Nor lend like influence from its lucent seat;
   I meant she should be courteous, facile, sweet,
Free from that solemn vice of greatness, pride;
   I meant each softest virtue there should meet,
Fit in that softer bosom to reside;
   Only a (heavenward and instructed) soul
I purposed her, that should, with even powers,
   The rock, the spindle, and the shears control
Of destiny, and spin her own free hours."[2]

1. "Free through Reason, strong through Laws, / Through gentleness great, and rich through treasures, / This long time your breast has concealed you." Source unknown.
2. From "On Lucy, Countess of Bedford," by the English poet and playwright Ben Jonson (1572–1637), modified parenthetically by Fuller (see p. 23).

Preface

18:46

The following essay is a reproduction, modified and expanded, of an article published in "The Dial, Boston, July, 1843," under the title of "The Great Lawsuit. Man versus Men: Woman versus Women."

This article excited a good deal of sympathy, and still more interest. It is in compliance with wishes expressed from many quarters, that it is prepared for publication in its present form.

Objections having been made to the former title, as not sufficiently easy to be understood, the present has been substituted as expressive of the main purpose of the essay; though, by myself, the other is preferred, partly for the reason others do not like it, *i.e.*, that it requires some thought to see what it means, and might thus prepare the reader to meet me on my own ground. Beside, it offers a larger scope, and is, in that way, more just to my desire. I meant, by that title, to intimate the fact that, while it is the destiny of Man, in the course of the Ages, to ascertain and fulfil the law of his being, so that his life shall be seen, as a whole, to be that of an angel or messenger, the action of prejudices and passions, which attend, in the day, the growth of the individual, is continually obstructing the holy work that is to make the earth a part of heaven. By Man I mean both man and woman: these are the two halves of one thought. I lay no especial stress on the welfare of either. I believe that the development of the one cannot be effected without that of the other. My highest wish is that this truth should be distinctly and rationally apprehended, and the conditions of life and freedom recognized as the same for the daughters and the sons of time; twin exponents of a divine thought.

I solicit a sincere and patient attention from those who open the following pages at all. I solicit of women that they will lay it to heart to ascertain what is for them the liberty of law. It is for this, and not for any, the largest, extension of partial privileges that I seek. I ask them, if interested by these suggestions, to search their own experience and intuitions for better, and fill up with fit materials the trenches that hedge them in. From men I ask a noble and earnest attention to any thing that can be offered on this great and still obscure

5

subject, such as I have met from many with whom I stand in private relations.

And may truth, unpolluted by prejudice, vanity, or selfishness, be granted daily more and more, as the due inheritance, and only valuable conquest for us all!

November, 1844.

Woman in the Nineteenth Century

$\partial \Gamma \cdot 45$

"Frailty, thy name is WOMAN."[1]
"The Earth waits for her Queen."

The connection between these quotations may not be obvious, but it is strict. Yet would any contradict us, if we made them applicable to the other side, and began also

> Frailty, thy name is MAN.
> The Earth waits for its King.

Yet man, if not yet fully installed in his powers, has given much earnest of his claims. Frail he is indeed, how frail! how impure! Yet often has the vein of gold displayed itself amid the baser ores, and Man has appeared before us in princely promise worthy of his future.

If, oftentimes, we see the prodigal son feeding on the husks in the fair field no more his own, anon, we raise the eyelids, heavy from bitter tears, to behold in him the radiant apparition of genius and love, demanding not less than the all of goodness, power and beauty.[2] We see that in him the largest claim finds a due foundation. That claim is for no partial sway, no exclusive possession. He cannot be satisfied with any one gift of life, any one department of knowledge or telescopic peep at the heavens. He feels himself called to understand and aid nature, that she may, through his intelligence, be raised and interpreted; to be a student of, and servant to, the universe-spirit; and king of his planet, that as an angelic minister, he may bring it into conscious harmony with the law of that spirit.

In clear triumphant moments, many times, has rung through the spheres the prophecy of his jubilee, and those moments, though past in time, have been translated into eternity by thought; the bright signs they left hang in the heavens, as single stars or constellations, and, already, a thickly sown radiance consoles the wanderer in the darkest night. Other heroes since Hercules have fulfilled the zodiac of beneficent labors, and then given up their mortal part to the fire without a murmur; while no God dared deny that they should have their reward.

---

1. From *Hamlet* 1.2.146 by William Shakespeare (1564–1616). The source of the second quotation is unknown.
2. Fuller alludes to the story of the prodigal son (Luke 15.11–32) to emphasize the inspiration of spiritual growth.

Siquis tamen, Hercule, siquis
Forte Deo doliturus erit, data præmia nollet,
Sed meruise dari sciet, invitus que probabit,
Assensere Dei.[3]

⌊Sages and lawgivers have bent their whole nature to the search for truth, and thought themselves happy if they could buy, with the sacrifice of all temporal ease and pleasure, one seed for the future Eden. Poets and priests have strung the lyre with the heart-strings, poured out their best blood upon the altar, which, reared anew from age to age shall at last sustain the flame pure enough to rise to highest heaven. Shall we not name with as deep a benediction those who, if not so immediately, or so consciously, in connection with the eternal truth, yet, led and fashioned by a divine instinct, serve no less to develope and interpret the open secret of love passing into life, energy creating for the purpose of happiness; the artist whose hand, drawn by a pre-existent harmony to a certain medium, moulds it to forms of life more highly and completely organized than are seen elsewhere, and, by carrying out the intention of nature, reveals her meaning to those who are not yet wise enough to divine it; the philosopher who listens steadily for laws and causes, and from those obvious, infers those yet unknown; the historian who, in faith that all events must have their reason and their aim, records them, and thus fills archives from which the youth of prophets may be fed. The man of science dissects the statements, tests the facts, and demonstrates order, even where he cannot its purpose.⌋

Lives, too, which bear none of these names, have yielded tones of no less significance. The candlestick set in a low place has given light as faithfully, where it was needed, as that upon the hill.[4] In close alleys, in dismal nooks, the Word has been read as distinctly, as when shown by angels to holy men in the dark prison. Those who till a spot of earth scarcely larger than is wanted for a grave, have deserved that the sun should shine upon its sod till violets answer.

So great has been, from time to time, the promise, that, in all ages, men have said the gods themselves came down to dwell with them; that the All-Creating wandered on the earth to taste, in a limited nature, the sweetness of virtue; that the All-Sustaining incarnated himself to guard, in space and time, the destinies of this world; that heavenly

---

3. In "The Great Lawsuit," Fuller provided the following translation by John Gay (1685–1732): "If any God dissent, and judge too great / The sacred honors of the heavenly seat, / Even he shall own his deeds deserve the sky, / Even he, reluctant, shall at length comply. / Th' assembled powers assent." In book 9 of Ovid's *Metamorphoses*, Jove, the supreme god, makes this declaration after Hercules has been killed.
4. Fuller draws on Matthew 5.14–15: "Ye are the light of the world. A city that is set on a hill cannot be hid. Neither do men light a candle, and put it under a bushel, but on a candlestick; and it giveth light unto all that are in the house."

genius dwelt among the shepherds, to sing to them and teach them how to sing. Indeed

"Der stets den Hirten gnadig sich bewies."

"He has constantly shown himself favorable to shepherds."

And the dwellers in green pastures and natural students of the stars were selected to hail, first among men, the holy child, whose life and death were to present the type of excellence, which has sustained the heart of so large a portion of mankind in these later generations.

⚹ ⌊Such marks have been made by the footsteps of *man*, (still alas! to be spoken of as the *ideal* man,) wherever he has passed through the wilderness of *men*, and whenever the pigmies stepped in one of those they felt dilate within the breast somewhat that promised nobler stature and purer blood. They were impelled to forsake their evil ways of decrepit scepticism, and covetousness of corruptible possessions. Conviction flowed in upon them. They, too, raised the cry; God is living, now, to-day; and all beings are brothers, for they are his children. Simple words enough, yet which only angelic nature, can use or hear in their full free sense.⌋

These were the triumphant moments, but soon the lower nature took its turn, and the era of a truly human life was postponed.

Thus is man still a stranger to his inheritance, still a pleader, still a pilgrim. Yet his happiness is secure in the end. And now, no more a glimmering consciousness, but assurance begins to be felt and spoken, that the highest ideal man can form of his own powers, is that which he is destined to attain. Whatever the soul knows how to seek, it cannot fail to obtain. This is the law and the prophets. Knock and it shall be opened, seek and ye shall find.[5] It is demonstrated; it is a maxim. Man no longer paints his proper nature in some form and says, "Prometheus[6] had it; it is God-like;" but "Man must have it; it is human." However disputed by many, however ignorantly used, or falsified by those who do receive it, the fact of an universal, unceasing revelation has been too clearly stated in words to be lost sight of in thought, and sermons preached from the text, "Be ye perfect,"[7] are the only sermons of a pervasive and deep-searching influence.

But, among those who meditate upon this text, there is a great difference of view, as to the way in which perfection shall be sought.

Through the intellect, say some. Gather from every growth of life its seed of thought; look behind every symbol for its law; if thou canst *see* clearly, the rest will follow.

5. Matthew 7.12: "Therefore all things whatsoever ye would that men should do to you, do ye even so to them: for this is the law and the prophets." Matthew 7.8: "For every one that asketh receiveth; and he that seeketh findeth; and to him that knocketh it shall be opened."
6. Greek god who stole fire from the gods and gave it to humankind.
7. Matthew 5.48: "Be ye therefore perfect, even as your Father which is in heaven is perfect."

Through the life, say others. Do the best thou knowest to-day. Shrink not from frequent error in this gradual fragmentary state. Follow thy light for as much as it will show thee, be faithful as far as thou canst, in hope that faith presently will lead to sight. Help others, without blaming their need of thy help. Love much and be forgiven.

It needs not intellect, needs not experience, says a third. If you took the true way, your destiny would be accomplished in a purer and more natural order. You would not learn through facts of thought or action, but express through them the certainties of wisdom. In quietness yield thy soul to the causal soul. Do not disturb thy apprenticeship by premature effort; neither check the tide of instruction by methods of thy own. Be still, seek not, but wait in obedience. Thy commission will be given.

Could we indeed say what we want, could we give a description of the child that is lost, he would be found. As soon as the soul can affirm clearly that a certain demonstration is wanted, it is at hand. When the Jewish prophet described the Lamb,[8] as the expression of what was required by the coming era, the time drew nigh. But we say not, see not as yet, clearly, what we would. Those who call for a more triumphant expression of love, a love that cannot be crucified, show not a perfect sense of what has already been given. Love has already been expressed, that made all things new, that gave the worm its place and ministry as well as the eagle; a love to which it was alike to descend into the depths of hell, or to sit at the right hand of the Father.[9]

Yet, no doubt, a new manifestation is at hand, a new hour in the day of man.[1] We cannot expect to see any one sample of completed being, when the mass of men still lie engaged in the sod, or use the freedom of their limbs only with wolfish energy. The tree cannot come to flower till its root be free from the cankering worm, and its whole growth open to air and light. While any one is base, none can be entirely free and noble. Yet something new shall presently be shown of the life of man, for hearts crave, if minds do not know how to ask it.

Among the strains of prophecy, the following, by an earnest mind of a foreign land, written some thirty years ago, is not yet outgrown; and it has the merit of being a positive appeal from the heart, instead of a critical declaration what man should *not* do.

"The ministry of man implies, that he must be filled from the divine fountains which are being engendered through all eternity, so that, at

---

8. The Lamb, of course, is Jesus. The prophet is probably Isaiah. Isaiah 7.14 reads, "Therefore the Lord himself shall give you a sign; Behold, a virgin shall conceive, and bear a son, and shall call his name Immanuel."
9. Jesus, after his resurrection, "was received up into heaven, and sat on the right hand of God" (Mark 16.19).
1. During the early 1840s, radical social change seemed imminent to many observers, due to the wave of utopian and reform movements sweeping the country; abolitionism, Fourierism, mesmerism, spiritualism, Swedenborgianism, temperance, transcendentalism, vegetarianism, and women's rights were some of the most prominent ones.

the mere name of his master, he may be able to cast all his enemies into the abyss; that he may deliver all parts of nature from the barriers that imprison them; that he may purge the terrestrial atmosphere from the poisons that infect it; that he may preserve the bodies of men from the corrupt influences that surround, and the maladies that afflict them; still more, that he may keep their souls pure from the malignant insinuations which pollute, and the gloomy images that obscure them; that he may restore its serenity to the Word, which false words of men fill with mourning and sadness; that he may satisfy the desires of the angels, who await from him the development of the marvels of nature; that, in fine, his world may be filled with God, as eternity is."[2]

Another attempt we will give, by an obscure observer of our own day and country, to draw some lines of the desired image. It was suggested by seeing the design of Crawford's Orpheus,[3] and connecting with the circumstance of the American, in his garret at Rome, making choice of this subject, that of Americans here at home, showing such ambition to represent the character, by calling their prose and verse "Orphic sayings"[4]—"Orphics." We wish we could add that they have shown that musical apprehension of the progress of nature through her ascending gradations which entitled them so to do, but their attempts are frigid, though sometimes grand; in their strain we are not warmed by the fire which fertilized the soil of Greece.

Orpheus was a law-giver by theocratic commission. He understood nature, and made her forms move to his music. He told her secrets in the form of hymns, nature as seen in the mind of God. His soul went forth toward all beings, yet could remain sternly faithful to a chosen type of excellence. Seeking what he loved, he feared not death nor hell, neither could any shape of dread daunt his faith in the power of the celestial harmony that filled his soul.

It seemed significant of the state of things in this country, that the sculptor should have represented the seer at the moment when he was obliged with his hand to shade his eyes.

> Each Orpheus must to the depths descend,
> For only thus the Poet can be wise,
> Must make the sad Persephone[5] his friend,

2. St. Martin [Fuller's note]. From *The Ministry of Man and Spirit* (1802) by Louis Claude de Saint-Martin (1743–1803), a French mystic philosopher.

3. In Greek myth, Orpheus, a poet and musician, played such perfect music on his lyre that he charmed the trees, rocks, and wild beasts. After the death of his wife, Eurydice, he journeyed to the underworld to rescue her from Death. He almost succeeded but lost her again when he looked back at her just before they reached the upper air. Thomas Crawford (1814–1857), American sculptor, in his most famous statue, *Orpheus and Cerebus*, depicts Orpheus searching for Eurydice with the dog of Hades, Cerebus, at his side.

4. Written by Amos Bronson Alcott (1799–1888), transcendental teacher and philosopher, and published in the *Dial*, while Fuller was its editor (1840–42). The sayings were ridiculed by some readers as pretentious and unintelligible.

5. Greek goddess of fertility and queen of the underworld; moved by Orpheus's music, she helped reunite him with Eurydice.

And buried love to second life arise;
   Again his love must lose through too much love,
Must lose his life by living life too true,
   For what he sought below is passed above,
Already done is all that he would do;
   Must tune all being with his single lyre,
Must melt all rocks free from their primal pain,
   Must search all nature with his one soul's fire,
Must bind anew all forms in heavenly chain.
   If he already sees what he must do,
Well may he shade his eyes from the far-shining view.[6]

A better comment could not be made on what is required to perfect man, and place him in that superior position for which he was designed, than by the interpretation of Bacon upon the legends of the Syren coast. When the wise Ulysses[7] passed, says he, he caused his mariners to stop their ears with wax, knowing there was in them no power to resist the lure of that voluptuous song. But he, the much experienced man, who wished to be experienced in all, and use all to the service of wisdom, desired to hear the song that he might understand its meaning. Yet, distrusting his own power to be firm in his better purpose, he caused himself to be bound to the mast, that he might be kept secure against his own weakness. But Orpheus passed unfettered, so absorbed in singing hymns to the gods that he could not even hear those sounds of degrading enchantment.

⌊Meanwhile not a few believe, and men themselves have expressed the opinion, that the time is come when Eurydice is to call for an Orpheus, rather than Orpheus for Eurydice: that the idea of Man, however imperfectly brought out, has been far more so than that of Woman, that she, the other half of the same thought, the other chamber of the heart of life, needs now to take her turn in the full pulsation, and that improvement in the daughters will best aid in the reformation of the sons of this age.⌋

It should be remarked that, as the principle of liberty is better understood, and more nobly interpreted, a broader protest is made in behalf of Woman. As men become aware that few men have had a fair chance, they are inclined to say that no women have had a fair chance. The French Revolution, that strangely disguised angel, bore witness in favor of woman, but interpreted her claims no less ignorantly than those of man. Its idea of happiness did not rise beyond outward enjoyment, unobstructed by the tyranny of others. The title it gave was citoyen, citoyenne,[8] and it is not unimportant to woman that even this species

6. The poem is Fuller's.
7. Hero of Homer's epic poem the *Odyssey* (c. 700 B.C.). Francis Bacon (1561–1626), English essayist and philosopher. "Syren coast": the Sirens were sea-nymphs whose songs lured passing mariners to their deaths upon the rocky coast of the Sirens' island.
8. Masculine and feminine forms, respectively, of the French word for "citizen."

of equality was awarded her. Before, she could be condemned to perish on the scaffold for treason, not as a citizen, but as a subject. The right with which this title then invested a human being, was that of bloodshed and license. The Goddess of Liberty was impure. As we read the poem addressed to her not long since, by Beranger, we can scarcely refrain from tears as painful as the tears of blood that flowed when "such crimes were committed in her name."[9] Yes! man, born to purify and animate the unintelligent and the cold, can, in his madness, degrade and pollute no less the fair and the chaste. Yet truth was prophesied in the ravings of that hideous fever, caused by long ignorance and abuse. Europe is conning a valued lesson from the blood-stained page. The same tendencies, farther unfolded, will bear good fruit in this country.

Yet, by men in this country, as by the Jews, when Moses was leading them to the promised land, every thing has been done that inherited depravity could do, to hinder the promise of heaven from its fulfilment. The cross here as elsewhere, has been planted only to be blasphemed by cruelty and fraud. The name of the Prince of Peace has been profaned by all kinds of injustice toward the Gentile whom he said he came to save. But I need not speak of what has been done towards the red man, the black man. Those deeds are the scoff of the world; and they have been accompanied by such pious words that the gentlest would not dare to intercede with "Father, forgive them, for they know not what they do."[1]

Here, as elsewhere, the gain of creation consists always in the growth of individual minds, which live and aspire, as flowers bloom and birds sing, in the midst of morasses; and in the continual development of that thought, the thought of human destiny, which is given to eternity adequately to express, and which ages of failure only seemingly impede. Only seemingly, and whatever seems to the contrary, this country is as surely destined to elucidate a great moral law, as Europe was to promote the mental culture of man.

Though the national independence be blurred by the servility of individuals, though freedom and equality have been proclaimed only to leave room for a monstrous display of slave-dealing and slave-keeping; though the free American so often feels himself free, like the Roman, only to pamper his appetites and his indolence through the misery of his fellow beings, still it is not in vain, that the verbal statement has been made, "All men are born free and equal."[2] There it stands, a golden certainty wherewith to encourage the good, to shame the bad. The new world may be called clearly to perceive that it incurs the

9. The quotation alludes to the final words attributed to the French revolutionary leader Madame Roland (1754–1793) before she was guillotined: "O liberty: what crimes are committed in thy name!" Pierre-Jean de Béranger (1780–1857), French poet and song writer.
1. Luke 23.34.
2. Fuller alters the phrase "all men are created equal," from The Declaration of Independence.

utmost penalty, if it reject or oppress the sorrowful brother. And, if men are deaf, the angels hear. But men cannot be deaf. It is inevitable that an external freedom, an independence of the encroachments of other men, such as has been achieved for the nation, should be so also for every member of it. That which has once been clearly conceived in the intelligence cannot fail sooner or later to be acted out. It has become a law as irrevocable as that of the Medes in their ancient dominion; men will privately sin against it, but the law, as expressed by a leading mind of the age,

> "Tutti fatti a sembianza d'un Solo,
> Figli tutti d'un solo riscatto,
> In qual'ora, in qual parte del suolo
> Trascorriamo quest' aura vital,
> Siam fratelli, siam stretti ad un patto:
> Maladetto colui che lo infrange,
> Che s'innalza sul fiacco che piange
> Che contrista uno spirto immortal."[3]

> "All made in the likeness of the One,
> All children of one ransom,
> In whatever hour, in whatever part of the soil,
> We draw this vital air,
> We are brothers; we must be bound by one compact,
> Accursed he who infringes it,
> Who raises himself upon the weak who weep,
> Who saddens an immortal spirit."

ᒪThis law cannot fail of universal recognition. Accursed be he who willingly saddens an immortal spirit, doomed to infamy in later, wiser ages, doomed in future stages of his own being to deadly penance, only short of death. Accursed be he who sins in ignorance, if that ignorance be caused by sloth.ᒧ

We sicken no less at the pomp than the strife of words. We feel that never were lungs so puffed with the wind of declamation, on moral and religious subjects, as now. We are tempted to implore these "word-heroes," these word-Catos,[4] word-Christs, to beware of cant[5] above all things; to remember that hypocrisy is the most hopeless as well as the meanest of crimes, and that those must surely be polluted by it, who do not reserve a part of their morality and religion for private use.

3. Manzoni [Fuller's note]. Alessandro Manzoni (1785–1873), Italian poet and novelist.
4. Marcus Porcius Cato (234–149 B.C.), Roman statesman and orator, known for his moralistic denunciations of Greek culture.
5. Dr. Johnson's one piece of advice should be written on every door; "Clear your mind of cant." But Byron, to whom it was so acceptable, in clearing away the noxious vine, shook down the building. Sterling's emendation is worthy of honor: "Realize your cant, not cast it off" [Fuller's note]. "Cant" here means hypocritical, insincere talk. The English authors mentioned are Samuel Johnson (1709–1784), George, Lord Byron (1788–1824), and John Sterling (1806–1844).

Landor[6] says that he cannot have a great deal of mind who cannot afford to let the larger part of it lie fallow, and what is true of genius is not less so of virtue. The tongue is a valuable member, but should appropriate but a small part of the vital juices that are needful all over the body. We feel that the mind may "grow black and rancid in the smoke" even "of altars." We start up from the harangue to go into our closet and shut the door. There inquires the spirit, "Is this rhetoric the bloom of healthy blood or a false pigment artfully laid on?" And yet again we know where is so much smoke, must be some fire; with so much talk about virtue and freedom, must be mingled some desire for them; that it cannot be in vain that such have become the common topics of conversation among men, rather than schemes for tyranny and plunder, that the very newspapers see it best to proclaim themselves Pilgrims, Puritans, Heralds of Holiness. The king that maintains so costly a retinue cannot be a mere boast, or Carabbas[7] fiction. We have waited here long in the dust; we are tired and hungry, but the triumphal procession must appear at last.

Of all its banners, none has been more steadily upheld, and under none have more valor and willingness for real sacrifices been shown, than that of the champions of the enslaved African. And this band it is, which, partly from a natural following out of principles, partly because many women have been prominent in that cause, makes, just now, the warmest appeal in behalf of woman.

Though there has been a growing liberality on this subject, yet society at large is not so prepared for the demands of this party, but that they are and will be for some time, coldly regarded as the Jacobins[8] of their day.

"Is it not enough," cries the irritated trader, "that you have done all you could to break up the national union, and thus destroy the prosperity of our country, but now you must be trying to break up family union, to take my wife away from the cradle and the kitchen hearth to vote at polls, and preach from a pulpit? Of course, if she does such things, she cannot attend to those of her own sphere. She is happy enough as she is. She has more leisure than I have, every means of improvement, every indulgence."

"Have you asked her whether she was satisfied with these *indulgences?*"

"No, but I know she is. She is too amiable to wish what would make me unhappy, and too judicious to wish to step beyond the sphere of her sex. I will never consent to have our peace disturbed by any such discussions." 44:47

6. Walter Savage Landor (1775–1864), English poet.
7. The Marquess of Carabas is the fictional title the cat invents for his master in the French fairy tale "Le Chat Botté" (Puss in boots) by Charles Perrault (1628–1703).
8. Members of a group of radical republicans formed during the French Revolution, known for instituting the Reign of Terror (1793–94).

" 'Consent—you?' it is not consent from you that is in question, it is assent from your wife."

"Am not I the head of my house?"

"You are not the head of your wife. God has given her a mind of her own."

"I am the head and she the heart."

"God grant you play true to one another then. I suppose I am to be grateful that you did not say she was only the hand. If the head represses no natural pulse of the heart, there can be no question as to your giving your consent. Both will be of one accord, and there needs but to present any question to get a full and true answer. There is no need of precaution, of indulgence, or consent. But our doubt is whether the heart does consent with the head, or only obeys its decrees with a passiveness that precludes the exercise of its natural powers, or a repugnance that turns sweet qualities to bitter, or a doubt that lays waste the fair occasions of life. It is to ascertain the truth, that we propose some liberating measures."

Thus vaguely are these questions proposed and discussed at present. But their being proposed at all implies much thought and suggests more. Many women are considering within themselves, what they need that they have not, and what they can have, if they find they need it. Many men are considering whether women are capable of being and having more than they are and have, *and*, whether, if so, it will be best to consent to improvement in their condition.

This morning, I open the Boston "Daily Mail," and find in its "poet's corner," a translation of Schiller's[9] "Dignity of Woman." In the advertisement of a book on America, I see in the table of contents this sequence, "Republican Institutions. American Slavery. American Ladies."

I open the *"Deutsche Schnellpost,"*[1] published in New-York, and find at the head of a column, *Judenund Frauen-emancipation in Ungarn.* Emancipation of Jews and Women in Hungary.

The past year has seen action in the Rhode-Island legislature, to secure married women rights over their own property, where men showed that a very little examination of the subject could teach them much; an article in the Democratic Review on the same subject more largely considered,[2] written by a woman, impelled, it is said, by glaring wrong to a distinguished friend having shown the defects in the existing laws, and the state of opinion from which they spring; and an answer

9. Friedrich von Schiller (1759–1805), German poet and dramatist.
1. German-language newspaper.
2. "The Legal Wrongs of Women," *United States Magazine and Democratic Review* 14 (May 1844): 477–83.

from the revered old man, J. Q. Adams, in some respects the Phocion[3] of his time, to an address made him by some ladies. To this last I shall again advert in another place.

These symptoms of the times have come under my view quite accidentally: one who seeks, may, each month or week, collect more.

The numerous party, whose opinions are already labelled and adjusted too much to their mind to admit of any new light, strive, by lectures on some model-woman of bride-like beauty and gentleness, by writing and lending little treatises, intended to mark out with precision the limits of woman's sphere, and woman's mission, to prevent other than the rightful shepherd from climbing the wall, or the flock from using any chance to go astray.

Without enrolling ourselves at once on either side, let us look upon the subject from the best point of view which to-day offers. No better, it is to be feared, than a high house-top. A high hill-top, or at least a cathedral spire, would be desirable.

It may well be an Anti-Slavery party that pleads for woman, if we consider merely that she does not hold property on equal terms with men; so that, if a husband dies without making a will, the wife, instead of taking at once his place as head of the family, inherits only a part of his fortune, often brought him by herself, as if she were a child, or ward only, not an equal partner.

We will not speak of the innumerable instances in which profligate and idle men live upon the earnings of industrious wives; or if the wives leave them, and take with them the children, to perform the double duty of mother and father, follow from place to place, and threaten to rob them of the children, if deprived of the rights of a husband, as they call them, planting themselves in their poor lodgings, frightening them into paying tribute by taking from them the children, running into debt at the expense of these otherwise so overtasked helots. Such instances count up by scores within my own memory. I have seen the husband who had stained himself by a long course of low vice, till his wife was wearied from her heroic forgiveness, by finding that his treachery made it useless, and that if she would provide bread for herself and her children, she must be separate from his ill fame. I have known this man come to instal himself in the chamber of a woman who loathed him and say she should never take food without his company. I have known these men steal their children whom they knew they had no means to maintain, take them into dissolute company, expose them to bodily danger, to frighten the poor woman, to whom, it seems, the fact that she alone had borne the pangs of their birth, and nourished their in-

3. Athenian statesman and general (c. 402–318 B.C.), known for his great moderation and personal integrity; John Quincy Adams (1767–1848), sixth president of the United States; for his speech, see page 84.

fancy, does not give an equal right to them. I do believe that this mode of kidnapping, and it is frequent enough in all classes of society, will be by the next age viewed as it is by Heaven now, and that the man who avails himself of the shelter of men's laws to steal from a mother her own children, or arrogate any superior right in them, save that of superior virtue, will bear the stigma he deserves, in common with him who steals grown men from their mother land, their hopes, and their homes.

I said, we will not speak of this now, yet I have spoken, for the subject makes me feel too much. I could give instances that would startle the most vulgar and callous, but I will not, for the public opinion of their own sex is already against such men, and where cases of extreme tyranny are made known, there is private action in the wife's favor. But she ought not to need this, nor, I think, can she long. Men must soon see that, on their own ground, that woman is the weaker party, she ought to have legal protection, which would make such oppression impossible. But I would not deal with "atrocious instances" except in the way of illustration, neither demand from men a partial redress in some one matter, but go to the root of the whole. If principles could be established, particulars would adjust themselves aright. Ascertain the true destiny of woman, give her legitimate hopes, and a standard within herself; marriage and all other relations would by degrees be harmonized with these.

But to return to the historical progress of this matter. Knowing that there exists in the minds of men a tone of feeling towards women as towards slaves, such as is expressed in the common phrase, "Tell that to women and children," that the infinite soul can only work through them in already ascertained limits; that the gift of reason, man's highest prerogative, is allotted to them in much lower degree; that they must be kept from mischief and melancholy by being constantly engaged in active labor, which is to be furnished and directed by those better able to think, &c. &c.; we need not multiply instances, for who can review the experience of last week without recalling words which imply, whether in jest or earnest, these views or views like these; knowing this, can we wonder that many reformers think that measures are not likely to be taken in behalf of women, unless their wishes could be publicly represented by women?

That can never be necessary, cry the other side. All men are privately influenced by women; each has his wife, sister, or female friends, and is too much biased by these relations to fail of representing their interests, and, if this is not enough, let them propose and enforce their wishes with the pen. The beauty of home would be destroyed, the delicacy of the sex be violated, the dignity of halls of legislation degraded by an attempt to introduce them there. Such duties are inconsistent with those of a mother; and then we have ludicrous pictures of ladies in hysterics at the polls, and senate chambers filled with cradles.

But if, in reply, we admit as truth that woman seems destined by nature rather for the inner circle, we must add that the arrangements of civilized life have not been, as yet, such as to secure it to her. Her circle, if the duller, is not the quieter. If kept from "excitement," she is not from drudgery. Not only the Indian squaw carries the burdens of the camp, but the favorites of Louis the Fourteenth accompany him in his journeys, and the washerwoman stands at her tub and carries home her work at all seasons, and in all states of health. Those who think the physical circumstances of woman would make a part in the affairs of national government unsuitable, are by no means those who think it impossible for the negresses to endure field work, even during pregnancy, or the sempstresses to go through their killing labors.

As to the use of the pen, there was quite as much opposition to woman's possessing herself of that help to free agency, as there is now to her seizing on the rostrum or the desk; and she is likely to draw, from a permission to plead her cause that way, opposite inferences to what might be wished by those who now grant it.

As to the possibility of her filling with grace and dignity, any such position, we should think those who had seen the great actresses, and heard the Quaker preachers of modern times, would not doubt, that woman can express publicly the fulness of thought and creation, without losing any of the peculiar beauty of her sex. What can pollute and tarnish is to act thus from any motive except that something needs to be said or done. Women could take part in the processions, the songs, the dances of old religion; no one fancied their delicacy was impaired by appearing in public for such a cause.

As to her home, she is not likely to leave it more than she now does for balls, theatres, meetings for promoting missions, revival meetings, and others to which she flies, in hope of an animation for her existence, commensurate with what she sees enjoyed by men. Governors of ladies' fairs are no less engrossed by such a change, than the Governor of the state by his; presidents of Washingtonian societies no less away from home than presidents of conventions. If men look straitly to it, they will find that, unless their lives are domestic, those of the women will not be. A house is no home unless it contain food and fire for the mind as well as for the body. The female Greek, of our day, is as much in the street as the male to cry, What news? We doubt not it was the same in Athens of old. The women, shut out from the market place, made up for it at the religious festivals. For human beings are not so constituted that they can live without expansion. If they do not get it one way, they must another, or perish.

As to men's representing women fairly at present, while we hear from men who owe to their wives not only all that is comfortable or graceful, but all that is wise in the arrangement of their lives, the frequent remark, "You cannot reason with a woman," when from those of delicacy, nobleness, and poetic culture, the contemptuous phrase "women and children," and that in no light sally of the hour, but in works intended to give a permanent statement of the best experiences, when not one man, in the million, shall I say? no, not in the hundred million, can rise above the belief that woman was made *for man*, when such traits as these are daily forced upon the attention, can we feel that man will always do justice to the interests of woman? Can we think that he takes a sufficiently discerning and religious view of her office and destiny, *ever* to do her justice, except when prompted by sentiment, accidentally or transiently, that is, for the sentiment will vary according to the relations in which he is placed. The lover, the poet, the artist, are likely to view her nobly. The father and the philosopher have some chance of liberality; the man of the world, the legislator for expediency, none.

Under these circumstances, without attaching importance, in themselves, to the changes demanded by the champions of woman, we hail them as signs of the times. We would have every arbitrary barrier thrown down. We would have every path laid open to woman as freely as to man. Were this done and a slight temporary fermentation allowed to subside, we should see crystallizations more pure and of more various beauty. We believe the divine energy would pervade nature to a degree unknown in the history of former ages, and that no discordant collision, but a ravishing harmony of the spheres would ensue.

Yet, then and only then, will mankind be ripe for this, when inward and outward freedom for woman as much as for man shall be acknowledged as a right, not yielded as a concession. As the friend of the negro assumes that one man cannot by right, hold another in bondage, so should the friend of woman assume that man cannot, by right, lay even well-meant restrictions on woman. If the negro be a soul, if the woman be a soul, appareled in flesh, to one Master only are they accountable. There is but one law for souls, and if there is to be an interpreter of it, he must come not as man, or son of man, but as son of God.

Were thought and feeling once so far elevated that man should esteem himself the brother and friend, but nowise the lord and tutor of woman, were he really bound with her in equal worship, arrangements as to function and employment would be of no consequence. What woman needs is not as a woman to act or rule, but as a nature to grow, as an intellect to discern, as a soul to live freely and unimpeded, to unfold such powers as were given her when we left our common home. If fewer talents were given her, yet if allowed the free and full employment of these, so that she may render back to the giver his own with usury,[4] she will not complain; nay I dare to say she will bless and rejoice

---

4. Interest. In the parable of the talents (Matthew 25.14–30), the servant who buries his one talent is told by his lord, "Thou oughtest . . . to have put my money to the exchangers, and then at my coming I should have received mine own with usury."

in her earthly birth-place, her earthly lot. Let us consider what obstructions impede this good era, and what signs give reason to hope that it draws near.

I was talking on this subject with Miranda,[5] a woman, who, if any in the world could, might speak without heat and bitterness of the position of her sex. Her father was a man who cherished no sentimental reverence for woman, but a firm belief in the equality of the sexes. She was his eldest child, and came to him at an age when he needed a companion. From the time she could speak and go alone, he addressed her not as a plaything, but as a living mind. Among the few verses he ever wrote was a copy addressed to this child, when the first locks were cut from her head, and the reverence expressed on this occasion for that cherished head, he never belied. It was to him the temple of immortal intellect. He respected his child, however, too much to be an indulgent parent. He called on her for clear judgment, for courage, for honor and fidelity; in short, for such virtues as he knew. In so far as he possessed the keys to the wonders of this universe, he allowed free use of them to her, and by the incentive of a high expectation, he forbade, as far as possible, that she should let the privilege lie idle.

Thus this child was early led to feel herself a child of the spirit. She took her place easily, not only in the world of organized being, but in the world of mind. A dignified sense of self-dependence was given as all her portion, and she found it a sure anchor. Herself securely anchored, her relations with others were established with equal security. She was fortunate in a total absence of those charms which might have drawn to her bewildering flatteries, and in a strong electric nature, which repelled those who did not belong to her, and attracted those who did. With men and women her relations were noble, affectionate without passion, intellectual without coldness. The world was free to her, and she lived freely in it. Outward adversity came, and inward conflict, but that faith and self-respect had early been awakened which must always lead at last, to an outward serenity and an inward peace.

Of Miranda I had always thought as an example, that the restraints upon the sex were insuperable only to those who think them so, or who noisily strive to break them. She had taken a course of her own, and no man stood in her way. Many of her acts had been unusual, but excited no uproar. Few helped, but none checked her, and the many men, who knew her mind and her life, showed to her confidence, as to a brother, gentleness as to a sister. And not only refined, but very coarse men approved and aided one in whom they saw resolution and clearness of design. Her mind was often the leading one, always effective.

When I talked with her upon these matters, and had said very much

5. Miranda's experiences parallel Fuller's own; her name is that of the gifted, learned daughter of Prospero in Shakespeare's *The Tempest*.

what I have written, she smilingly replied: "and yet we must admit that I have been fortunate, and this should not be. My good father's early trust gave the first bias, and the rest followed of course. It is true that I have had less outward aid, in after years, than most women, but that is of little consequence. Religion was early awakened in my soul, a sense that what the soul is capable to ask it must attain, and that, though I might be aided and instructed by others, I must depend on myself as the only constant friend. This self dependence, which was honored in me, is deprecated as a fault in most women. They are taught to learn their rule from without, not to unfold it from within.

"This is the fault of man, who is still vain, and wishes to be more important to woman than, by right, he should be."

"Men have not shown this disposition toward you," I said.

"No! because the position I early was enabled to take was one of self-reliance. And were all women as sure of their wants as I was, the result would be the same. But they are so overloaded with precepts by guardians, who think that nothing is so much to be dreaded for a woman as originality of thought or character, that their minds are impeded by doubts till they lose their chance of fair free proportions. The difficulty is to get them to the point from which they shall naturally develope self-respect, and learn self-help.

"Once I thought that men would help to forward this state of things more than I do now. I saw so many of them wretched in the connections they had formed in weakness and vanity. They seemed so glad to esteem women whenever they could.

"The soft arms of affection," said one of the most discerning spirits, "will not suffice for me, unless on them I see the steel bracelets of strength."

But early I perceived that men never, in any extreme of despair, wished to be women. On the contrary they were ever ready to taunt one another at any sign of weakness, with,

"Art thou not like the women, who"—

The passage ends various ways, according to the occasion and rhetoric of the speaker. When they admired any woman they were inclined to speak of her as "above her sex." Silently I observed this, and feared it argued a rooted scepticism, which for ages had been fastening on the heart, and which only an age of miracles could eradicate. Ever I have been treated with great sincerity; and I look upon it as a signal instance of this, that an intimate friend of the other sex said, in a fervent moment, that I "deserved in some star to be a man." He was much surprised when I disclosed my view of my position and hopes, when I declared my faith that the feminine side, the side of love, of beauty, of holiness, was now to have its full chance, and that, if either were better, it was better now to be a woman, for even the slightest achievement of good was furthering an especial work of our time. He smiled incredulous. "She makes the best she can of it," thought he. "Let Jews believe the pride of Jewry, but I am of the better sort, and know better."

Another used as highest praise, in speaking of a character in literature, the words "a manly woman."

So in the noble passage of Ben Jonson:

> "I meant the day-star should not brighter ride,
>   Nor shed like influence from its lucent seat;
> I meant she should be courteous, facile, sweet,
>   Free from that solemn vice of greatness, pride;
> I meant each softest virtue there should meet,
>   Fit in that softer bosom to abide,
> Only a learned and a *manly* soul,
>   I purposed her, that should with even powers,
> The rock, the spindle, and the shears control
> Of destiny, and spin her own free hours."[6]

"Methinks," said I, "you are too fastidious in objecting to this. Jonson in using the word 'manly' only meant to heighten the picture of this, the true, the intelligent fate, with one of the deeper colors." 'And yet,' said she, 'so invariable is the use of this word where a heroic quality is to be described, and I feel so sure that persistence and courage are the most womanly no less than the most manly qualities, that I would exchange these words for others of a larger sense at the risk of marring the fine tissue of the verse. Read, 'a heavenward and instructed soul,' and I should be satisfied. Let it not be said, wherever there is energy or creative genius, 'She has a masculine mind.'

This by no means argues a willing want of generosity toward woman. Man is as generous toward her, as he knows how to be.

Wherever she has herself arisen in national or private history, and nobly shone forth in any form of excellence, men have received her, not only willingly, but with triumph. Their encomiums indeed, are always, in some sense, mortifying; they show too much surprise. Can this be you? he cries to the transfigured Cinderella; well I should never have thought it, but I am very glad. We will tell every one that you have "*surpassed your sex.*"

In every-day life the feelings of the many are stained with vanity. Each wishes to be lord in a little world, to be superior at least over one; and he does not feel strong enough to retain a life-long ascendancy over a strong nature. Only a Theseus could conquer before he wed the Amazonian Queen. Hercules wished rather to rest with Dejanira, and

6. "On Lucy, Countess of Bedford."

received the poisoned robe, as a fit guerdon.[7] The tale should be interpreted to all those who seek repose with the weak.

But not only is man vain and fond of power, but the same want of development, which thus affects him morally, prevents his intellectually discerning the destiny of woman. The boy wants no woman, but only a girl to play ball with him, and mark his pocket handkerchief.

Thus, in Schiller's Dignity of Woman, beautiful as the poem is, there is no "grave and perfect man," but only a great boy to be softened and restrained by the influence of girls. Poets, the elder brothers of their race, have usually seen farther; but what can you expect of every-day men, if Schiller was not more prophetic as to what women must be? Even with Richter,[8] one foremost thought about a wife was that she would "cook him something good." But as this is a delicate subject, and we are in constant danger of being accused of slighting what are called "the functions," let me say in behalf of Miranda and myself, that we have high respect for those who cook something good, who create and preserve fair order in houses, and prepare therein the shining raiment for worthy inmates, worthy guests. Only these "functions" must not be a drudgery, or enforced necessity, but a part of life. Let Ulysses drive the beeves home while Penelope[9] there piles up the fragrant loaves; they are both well employed if these be done in thought and love, willingly. But Penelope is no more meant for a baker or weaver solely, than Ulysses for a cattle-herd.

The sexes should not only correspond to and appreciate, but prophesy to one another. In individual instances this happens. Two persons love in one another the future good which they aid one another to unfold. This is imperfectly or rarely done in the general life. Man has gone but little way; now he is waiting to see whether woman can keep step with him, but instead of calling out, like a good brother, "you can do it, if you only think so," or impersonally; "any one can do what he tries to do;" he often discourages with school-boy brag: "Girls can't do that; girls can't play ball." But let any one defy their taunts, break through and be brave and secure, they rend the air with shouts.

This fluctuation was obvious in a narrative I have lately seen, the story of the life of Countess Emily Plater, the heroine of the last revolution in Poland.[1] The dignity, the purity, the concentrated resolve,

---

7. A badge. Hercules' jealous wife, Deianira, sent him a tunic she thought was permeated with a love potion, but instead it held a poison that consumed his flesh. In Greek myth, Theseus, king of Athens, attacked the Amazons and carried away their queen, Antiope.
8. Jean (Johann) Paul Friedrich Richter (1763–1825), German novelist and poet.
9. In Greek myth, Ulysses was the king of Ithaca and a heroic leader in the Trojan War. Penelope, Ulysses' wife, who shrewdly resisted suitors during her husband's twenty-year absence, became a model of fidelity.
1. Fuller refers to the article "Emily Plater, the Polish Heroine," United States Magazine and Democratic Review 11 (July 1842): 23–28. Plater (1806–1831), raised in Lithuania, became a Polish nationalist who fought against the Russians to free Poland. She died two months after the rebellion was put down.

the calm, deep enthusiasm, which yet could, when occasion called, sparkle up a holy, an indignant fire, make of this young maiden the figure I want for my frontispiece. Her portrait is to be seen in the book, a gentle shadow of her soul. Short was the career—like the maid of Orleans,[2] she only did enough to verify her credentials, and then passed from a scene on which she was, probably, a premature apparition.

When the young girl joined the army where the report of her exploits had preceded her, she was received in a manner that marks the usual state of feeling. Some of the officers were disappointed at her quiet manners; that she had not the air and tone of a stage-heroine. They thought she could not have acted heroically unless in buskins; had no idea that such deeds only showed the habit of her mind. Others talked of the delicacy of her sex, advised her to withdraw from perils and dangers, and had no comprehension of the feelings within her breast that made this impossible. The gentle irony of her reply to these self-constituted tutors, (not one of whom showed himself her equal in conduct or reason,) is as good as her indignant reproof at a later period to the general, whose perfidy ruined all.

But though, to the mass of these men, she was an embarrassment and a puzzle, the nobler sort viewed her with a tender enthusiasm worthy of her. "Her name," said her biographer, "is known throughout Europe. I paint her character that she may be as widely loved."

With pride, he shows her freedom from all personal affections; that, though tender and gentle in an uncommon degree, there was no room for a private love in her consecrated life. She inspired those who knew her with a simple energy of feeling like her own. We have seen, they felt, a woman worthy the name, capable of all sweet affections, capable of stern virtue.

It is a fact worthy of remark, that all these revolutions in favor of liberty have produced female champions that share the same traits, but Emily alone has found a biographer. Only a near friend could have performed for her this task, for the flower was reared in feminine seclusion, and the few and simple traits of her history before her appearance in the field could only have been known to the domestic circle. Her biographer has gathered them up with a brotherly devotion.

No! man is not willingly ungenerous. He wants faith and love, because he is not yet himself an elevated being. He cries, with sneering skepticism, Give us a sign. But if the sign appears, his eyes glisten, and he offers not merely approval, but homage.

The severe nation[3] which taught that the happiness of the race was forfeited through the fault of a woman, and showed its thought of what sort of regard man owed her, by making him accuse her on the first

2. Joan of Arc (c. 1412–1431).
3. The Jewish nation.

question to his God;[4] who gave her to the patriarch as a handmaid, and by the Mosaical law, bound her to allegiance like a serf; even they greeted, with solemn rapture, all great and holy women as heroines, prophetesses, judges in Israel; and if they made Eve listen to the serpent, gave Mary as a bride to the Holy Spirit.[5] In other nations it has been the same down to our day. To the woman who could conquer, a triumph was awarded. And not only those whose strength was recommended to the heart by association with goodness and beauty, but those who were bad, if they were steadfast and strong, had their claims allowed. In any age a Semiramis, an Elizabeth of England, a Catharine of Russia,[6] makes her place good, whether in a large or small circle. How has a little wit, a little genius, been celebrated in a woman! What an intellectual triumph was that of the lonely Aspasia,[7] and how heartily acknowledged! She, indeed, met a Pericles. But what annalist, the rudest of men, the most plebeian of husbands, will spare from his page one of the few anecdotes of Roman women—Sappho! Eloisa![8] The names are of threadbare celebrity. Indeed they were not more suitably met in their own time than the Countess Colonel Plater on her first joining the army. They had much to mourn, and their great impulses did not find due scope. But with time enough, space enough, their kindred appear on the scene. Across the ages, forms lean, trying to touch the hem of their retreating robes. The youth here by my side cannot be weary of the fragments from the life of Sappho. He will not believe they are not addressed to himself, or that he to whom they were addressed could be ungrateful. A recluse of high powers devotes himself to understand and explain the thought of Eloisa; he asserts her vast superiority in soul and genius to her master; he curses the fate that cast his lot in another age than hers. He could have understood her: he would have been to her a friend, such as Abelard never could. And this one woman he could have loved and reverenced, and she, alas! lay cold in her grave hundreds of years ago. His sorrow is truly pathetic. These responses that come too late to give joy are as tragic as any thing we know, and yet the tears of later ages glitter as they fall on Tasso's prison bars.[9] And we know how elevating to the captive is the security that somewhere an intelligence must answer to his.

4. In Genesis 3.12, Adam tells God, "The woman whom thou gavest to be with me, she gave me of the tree, and I did eat."
5. In Luke 1.35, the angel Gabriel tells Mary that "the Holy Ghost shall come upon thee."
6. Known as Catherine the Great (1729–1796), she reigned from 1762 to 1796. Semiramis (ninth century B.C.), an Assyrian queen and the legendary founder of Babylon. Queen Elizabeth I (1533–1603) ruled England from 1558 to 1603.
7. A controversial figure in Athenian society (c. 470–410 B.C.), who presided over a lively circle of intellectuals and statesmen, including Pericles (495–429 B.C.), whose mistress she became.
8. Or Héloïse (c. 1098–1164), French abbess of the Paraclete community, famous for her letters to her teacher and lover, Peter Abelard (1079–1142). Sappho (seventh century), Greek lyric poet from the isle of Lesbos.
9. Torquato Tasso (1544–1595), Italian epic poet, was imprisoned for insanity for seven years after verbally abusing his former patron, Duke Alfonso II of Ferrara.

The man habitually most narrow towards women will be flushed, as by the worst assault on Christianity, if you say it has made no improvement in her condition. Indeed, those most opposed to new acts in her favor, are jealous of the reputation of those which have been done.

We will not speak of the enthusiasm excited by actresses, improvisatrici, female singers, for here mingles the charm of beauty and grace; but female authors, even learned women, if not insufferably ugly and slovenly, from the Italian professor's daughter, who taught behind the curtain, down to Mrs. Carter and Madame Dacier,[1] are sure of an admiring audience, and what is far better, chance to use what they have learned, and to learn more, if they can once get a platform on which to stand.

But how to get this platform, or how to make it of reasonably easy access is the difficulty. Plants of great vigor will almost always struggle into blossom, despite impediments. But there should be encouragement, and a free genial atmosphere for those of more timid sort, fair play for each in its own kind. Some are like the little, delicate flowers which love to hide in the dripping mosses, by the sides of mountain torrents, or in the shade of tall trees. But others require an open field, a rich and loosened soil, or they never show their proper hues.

It may be said that man does not have his fair play either; his energies are repressed and distorted by the interposition of artificial obstacles. Ay, but he himself has put them there; they have grown out of his own imperfections. If there *is* a misfortune in woman's lot, it is in obstacles being interposed by men, which do *not* mark her state; and, if they express her past ignorance, do not her present needs. As every man is of woman born, she has slow but sure means of redress, yet the sooner a general justness of thought makes smooth the path, the better.

Man is of woman born, and her face bends over him in infancy with an expression he can never quite forget. Eminent men have delighted to pay tribute to this image, and it is an hacknied observation, that most men of genius boast some remarkable development in the mother. The rudest tar[2] brushes off a tear with his coat-sleeve at the hallowed name. The other day, I met a decrepit old man of seventy, on a journey, who challenged the stage-company to guess where he was going. They guessed aright, "To see your mother." "Yes," said he, "she is ninety-two, but has good eye-sight still, they say. I have not seen her these forty years, and I thought I could not die in peace without." I should have liked his picture painted as a companion piece to that of a boisterous little boy, whom I saw attempt to declaim at a school exhibition—

1. Anne Lefevre Dacier (1647–1720), French classical scholar and translator. Elizabeth Carter (1717–1806), English poet and translator.
2. Sailor.

"O that those lips had language. Life has passed
With me but roughly since I heard thee last."[3]

He got but very little way before sudden tears shamed him from the stage.

Some gleams of the same expression which shone down upon his infancy, angelically pure and benign, visit man again with hopes of pure love, of a holy marriage. Or, if not before, in the eyes of the mother of his child they again are seen, and dim fancies pass before his mind, that woman may not have been born for him alone, but have come from heaven, a commissioned soul, a messenger of truth and love; that she can only make for him a home in which he may lawfully repose, in so far as she is

"True to the kindred points of Heaven and home."[4]

In gleams, in dim fancies, this thought visits the mind of common men. It is soon obscured by the mists of sensuality, the dust of routine, and he thinks it was only some meteor, or ignis fatuus that shone. But, as a Rosicrucian lamp, it burns unwearied, though condemned to the solitude of tombs;[5] and to its permanent life, as to every truth, each age has in some form borne witness. For the truths, which visit the minds of careless men only in fitful gleams, shine with radiant clearness into those of the poet, the priest, and the artist.

Whatever may have been the domestic manners of the ancients, the idea of woman was nobly manifested in their mythologies and poems, where she appears as Sita in the Ramayana, a form of tender purity, as the Egyptian Isis,[6] of divine wisdom never yet surpassed. In Egypt, too, the Sphynx, walking the earth with lion tread, looked out upon its marvels in the calm, inscrutable beauty of a virgin's face, and the Greek could only add wings to the great emblem. In Greece, Ceres and Proserpine,[7] significantly termed "the great goddesses," were seen seated, side by side. They needed not to rise for any worshipper or any change; they were prepared for all things, as those initiated to their mysteries knew. More obvious is the meaning of these three forms, the Diana,

3. From "On the Receipt of My Mother's Picture out of Norfolk" by William Cowper (1731–1800).
4. From "To a Skylark" (1842) by William Wordsworth (1770–1850), English Romantic poet.
5. The Rosicrucians, an occult religious order founded in the seventeenth century in northern Europe, supposedly possessed the art of maintaining lamps that burned indefinitely, using an oil obtained from liquid gold. "Ignis fatuus": a phosphorescent light seen at night near marshes and swamps.
6. For an adequate description of the Isis, see Appendix A [Fuller's note]. In Egyptian myth, Isis is the goddess of fertility, mother of the god-kings of Egypt, and both sister and consort of the god Osiris. In the Hindu epic poem of India, the *Ramayana* or *Life of Rama* (ca. 300 B.C.), Sita is an earth goddess and the consort of Rama, the god Vishnu incarnate.
7. Ceres (in Greek myth, Demeter) was the Roman goddess of agriculture; Proserpine was her daughter. The Sphynx was a legendary creature, with the body of a lion and the head of a woman.

Minerva, and Vesta.[8] Unlike in the expression of their beauty, but alike in this,—that each was self-sufficing. Other forms were only accessories and illustrations, none the complement to one like these. Another might, indeed, be the companion, and the Apollo and Diana set off one another's beauty. Of the Vesta, it is to be observed, that not only deep-eyed, deep-discerning Greece, but ruder Rome, who represents the only form of good man, (the always busy warrior,) that could be indifferent to woman, confided the permanence of its glory to a tutelary goddess, and her wisest legislator spoke of meditation as a nymph.

Perhaps in Rome the neglect of woman was a reaction on the manners of Etruria,[9] where the priestess Queen, warrior Queen, would seem to have been so usual a character.

An instance of the noble Roman marriage, where the stern and calm nobleness of the nation was common to both, we see in the historic page through the little that is told us of Brutus and Portia.[1] Shakspeare has seized on the relation in its native lineaments, harmonizing the particular with the universal; and, while it is conjugal love, and no other, making it unlike the same relation, as seen in Cymbeline, or Othello, even as one star differeth from another in glory.

> "By that great vow
> Which did incorporate and make us one,
> Unfold to me, yourself, your half,
> Why you are heavy. •   •   •
>   Dwell I but in the suburbs
> Of your good pleasure? If it be no more,
> Portia is Brutus' harlot, not his wife."

Mark the sad majesty of his tone in answer. Who would not have lent a life-long credence to that voice of honor?

> "You are my true and honorable wife,
> As dear to me as are the ruddy drops
> That visit this sad heart."

It is the same voice that tells the moral of his life in the last words—

> "Countrymen,
> My heart doth joy, that yet in all my life,
> I found no man but he was true to me."

8. Roman goddesses of the moon and the hunt; of war, wisdom, and the arts; and of fire and the hearth, respectively. All were virgins and thus "self-sufficing" in Fuller's terms.
9. A portion of northern Italy, from the Tiber to the Alps, where the ancient Etruscan civilization flourished between 700 and 100 B.C.
1. Marcus Junius Brutus (c. 84–42 B.C.), ardent Roman republican and chief assassin of Julius Caesar, was supported in his actions by his wife, Portia. The quotations that follow are from Shakespeare's *Julius Caesar* 2.1.272–75, 285–87, 288–90; 5.4.33–35; 2.1.292–97; 4.2.119–24.

It was not wonderful that it should be so.

Shakspeare, however, was not content to let Portia rest her plea for confidence on the essential nature of the marriage bond;

> "I grant I am a woman; but withal,
> A woman that lord Brutus took to wife.
> I grant I am a woman; but withal,
> A woman well reputed—Cato's[2] daughter.
> Think you I am *no stronger than my sex*,
> Being so fathered and so husbanded?"

And afterwards in the very scene where Brutus is suffering under that "insupportable and touching loss," the death of his wife, Cassius pleads—

> "Have you not love enough to bear with me,
> When that rash humor which my mother gave me
> Makes me forgetful?
> *Brutus.*—Yes, Cassius; and henceforth,
> When you are over-earnest with your Brutus,
> He'll think your mother chides and leave you so."

As indeed it was a frequent belief among the ancients, as with our Indians, that the *body* was inherited from the mother, the *soul* from the father. As in that noble passage of Ovid,[3] already quoted, where Jupiter, as his divine synod are looking down on the funeral pyre of Hercules, thus triumphs—

> Nic nisi *maternâ* Vulcanum parte potentem.
> Sentiet. Aeternum est, à me quod traxit, et expers
> At que immune necis, nullaque domabile flamma
> Idque ego defunctum terrâ cœlestibus oris
> Accipiam, cunctisque meum lætabile factum
> Dis fore confido.
> "The part alone of gross *maternal* frame
> Fire shall devour, while that from me he drew
> Shall live immortal and its force renew;
> That, when he's dead, I'll raise to realms above;
> Let all the powers the righteous act approve."

It is indeed a god speaking of his union with an earthly woman, but it expresses the common Roman thought as to marriage, the same which permitted a man to lend his wife to a friend, as if she were a chattel.

---

2. Portia's father was Cato, Marcus Porcius ("Cato the Younger") (95–46 B.C.), Roman statesman and philosopher.
3. *Metamorphoses* 9.

"She dwelt but in the suburbs of his good pleasure."[4]

Yet the same city as I have said leaned on the worship of Vesta, the Preserver, and in later times was devoted to that of Isis. In Sparta,[5] thought, in this respect as in all others, was expressed in the characters of real life, and the women of Sparta were as much Spartans as the men. The citoyen, citoyenne of France was here actualized. Was not the calm equality they enjoyed as honorable as the devotion of chivalry? They intelligently shared the ideal life of their nation.

Like the men they felt

> "Honor gone, all's gone,
> Better never have been born."[6]

They were the true friends of men. The Spartan, surely, would not think that he received only his body from his mother. The sage, had he lived in that community, could not have thought the souls of "vain and foppish men will be degraded after death, to the forms of women, and, if they do not there make great efforts to retrieve themselves, will become birds."

(By the way it is very expressive of the hard intellectuality of the merely *mannish* mind, to speak thus of birds, chosen always by the *feminine* poet as the symbols of his fairest thoughts.)

We are told of the Greek nations in general, that woman occupied there an infinitely lower place than man. It is difficult to believe this when we see such range and dignity of thought on the subject in the mythologies, and find the poets producing such ideals as Cassandra, Iphiginia, Antigone, Macaria, where Sibylline priestesses told the oracle of the highest god, and he could not be content to reign with a court of fewer than nine muses. Even victory wore a female form.[7]

But whatever were the facts of daily life, I cannot complain of the age and nation, which represents its thought by such a symbol as I see before me at this moment. It is a zodiac of the busts of gods and goddesses, arranged in pairs. The circle breathes the music of a heavenly order. Male and female heads are distinct in expression, but equal in beauty, strength and calmness. Each male head is that of a brother and a king—each female of a sister and a queen. Could the thought,

---

4. In Shakespeare's *Julius Caesar* 2.1.285–86, Portia asks her husband, Brutus, "Dwell I but in the suburbs / Of your good pleasure?"
5. Ancient Greek city whose citizens were known for self-discipline and fortitude.
6. Unidentified.
7. Nike was the winged Greek goddess of victory. Cassandra, daughter of Priam, the last king of Troy, possessed the gift of prophecy, though no one believed her. Iphigenia, daughter of King Agamemnon, was to be sacrificed by her father (to obtain favorable winds for the fleet sailing to Troy), but she was rescued by the goddess Artemis. Antigone, daughter of Oedipus, buried the corpse of her brother, Polyneices, against the orders of her uncle Creon and was sentenced to death for it. Macaria, the daughter of Hercules, sacrificed herself to save Athens. Sibylline priestesses, worshipers of the god Apollo, delivered his messages to the oracle at Delphi in ancient Greece. The muses were nine goddesses who presided over literature and the arts and sciences.

thus expressed, be lived out, there would be nothing more to be desired. There would be unison in variety, congeniality in difference.

Coming nearer our own time, we find religion and poetry no less true in their revelations. The rude man, just disengaged from the sod, the Adam, accuses woman to his God, and records her disgrace to their posterity. He is not ashamed to write that he could be drawn from heaven by one beneath him, one made, he says, from but a small part of himself. But in the same nation, educated by time, instructed by a succession of prophets, we find woman in as high a position as she has ever occupied. No figure that has ever arisen to greet our eyes has been received with more fervent reverence than that of the Madonna. Heine calls her the *Dame du Comptoir* of the Catholic church,[8] and this jeer well expresses a serious truth.

And not only this holy and significant image was worshipped by the pilgrim, and the favorite subject of the artist, but it exercised an immediate influence on the destiny of the sex. The empresses who embraced the cross, converted sons and husbands. Whole calendars of female saints, heroic dames of chivalry, binding the emblem of faith on the heart of the best-beloved, and wasting the bloom of youth in separation and loneliness, for the sake of duties they thought it religion to assume, with innumerable forms of poesy, trace their lineage to this one. Nor, however imperfect may be the action, in our day, of the faith thus expressed, and though we can scarcely think it nearer this ideal, than that of India or Greece was near their ideal, is it in vain that the truth has been recognized, that woman is not only a part of man, bone of his bone, and flesh of his flesh, born that men might not be lonely, but that women are in themselves possessors of and possessed by immortal souls. This truth undoubtedly received a greater outward stability from the belief of the church that the earthly parent of the Saviour of souls was a woman.

The assumption of the Virgin,[9] as painted by sublime artists, Petrarch's Hymn to the Madonna,[1] cannot have spoken to the world wholly without result, yet, oftentimes those who had ears heard not.

See upon the nations the influence of this powerful example. In Spain look only at the ballads. Woman in these is "very woman"; she is the betrothed, the bride, the spouse of man, there is on her no hue of the philosopher, the heroine, the savante, but she looks great and noble; why? because she is also, through her deep devotion, the betrothed of heaven. Her up-turned eyes have drawn down the light that

---

8. Heinrich Heine (1797–1856), German poet, journalist, and literary critic. His jeer translates from the French as "saleswoman," implying that the Madonna helps sell the Catholic religion.
9. Taking up of the Virgin Mary into heaven.
1. Appendix, B [Fuller's note]. Italian poet Francesco Petrarca (1304–1374).

casts a radiance round her. See only such a ballad as that of "Lady Teresa's Bridal."[2]

Where the Infanta,[3] given to the Moorish bridegroom, calls down the vengeance of Heaven on his unhallowed passion, and thinks it not too much to expiate by a life in the cloister, the involuntary stain upon her princely youth.[4] It was this constant sense of claims above those of earthly love or happiness that made the Spanish lady who shared this spirit, a guerdon to be won by toils and blood and constant purity, rather than a chattel to be bought for pleasure and service.

Germany did not need to *learn* a high view of woman; it was inborn in that race. Woman was to the Teuton warrior his priestess, his friend, his sister, in truth, a wife. And the Christian statues of noble pairs, as they lie above their graves in stone, expressing the meaning of all the by-gone pilgrimage by hands folded in mutual prayer, yield not a nobler sense of the place and powers of woman, than belonged to the altvater day. The holy love of Christ which summoned them, also, to choose "the better part, that which could not be taken from them," refined and hallowed in this nation a native faith, thus showing that it was not the warlike spirit alone that left the Latins so barbarous in this respect.

But the Germans, taking so kindly to this thought, did it the more justice. The idea of woman in their literature is expressed both to a greater height and depth than elsewhere.

I will give as instances the themes of three ballads.

One is upon a knight who had always the name of the Virgin on his lips. This protected him all his life through, in various and beautiful modes, both from sin and other dangers, and, when he died, a plant sprang from his grave, which so gently whispered the Ave Maria that none could pass it by with an unpurified heart.

Another is one of the legends of the famous Drachenfels.[5] A maiden, one of the earliest converts to Christianity, was carried by the enraged populace to this dread haunt of "the dragon's fabled brood," to be their prey. She was left alone, but unafraid, for she knew in whom she trusted. So, when the dragons came rushing towards her, she showed them a crucifix and they crouched reverently at her feet. Next day the people came, and seeing these wonders, are all turned to the faith which exalts the lowly.

The third I have in mind is another of the Rhine legends. A youth

2. This ballad, published in *Ancient Spanish Ballads* (1823) by John Gibson Lockhart (1794–1854), indicates that Lady Teresa was sister of King Alphonso V of León (994–1028).
3. Princess.
4. Appendix, C [Fuller's note].
5. A mountain peak in western Germany on the Rhine. Its name means dragon's rock.

is sitting with the maid he loves on the shore of an isle, her fairy kingdom, then perfumed by the blossoming grape vines, which draped its bowers. They are happy; all blossoms with them, and life promises its richest wine. A boat approaches on the tide; it pauses at their feet. It brings, perhaps, some joyous message, fresh dew for their flowers, fresh light on the wave. No! it is the usual check on such great happiness. The father of the Count departs for the crusade; will his son join him, or remain to rule their domain, and wed her he loves? Neither of the affianced pair hesitate a moment. "I must go with my father." "Thou must go with thy father." It was one thought, one word. "I will be here again," he said, "when these blossoms have turned to purple grapes." "I hope so," she sighed, while the prophetic sense said "no."

And there she waited, and the grapes ripened, and were gathered into the vintage, and he came not. Year after year passed thus, and no tidings; yet still she waited.

He, meanwhile, was in a Moslem prison. Long he languished there without hope, till, at last, his patron saint appeared in vision and announced his release, but only on condition of his joining the monastic order for the service of the saint.

And so his release was effected, and a safe voyage home given. And once more he sets sail upon the Rhine. The maiden, still watching beneath the vines, sees at last the object of all this patient love approach. Approach, but not to touch the strand to which she, with outstretched arms, has rushed. He dares not trust himself to land, but in low, heart-broken tones, tells her of heaven's will; and that he, in obedience to his vow, is now on his way to a convent on the river bank, there to pass the rest of his earthly life in the service of the shrine. And then he turns his boat, and floats away from her and hope of any happiness in this world, but urged, as he believes, by the breath of heaven.

The maiden stands appalled, but she dares not murmur, and cannot hesitate long. She also bids them prepare her boat. She follows her lost love to the convent gate, requests an interview with the abbot, and devotes her Elysian isle, where vines had ripened their ruby fruit in vain for her, to the service of the monastery where her love was to serve. Then, passing over to the nunnery opposite, she takes the veil, and meets her betrothed at the altar; and for a life long union, if not the one they had hoped in earlier years.

Is not this sorrowful story of a lofty beauty? Does it not show a sufficiently high view of woman, of marriage? This is commonly the chivalric, still more the German view.

Yet, wherever there was a balance in the mind of man of sentiment, with intellect, such a result was sure. The Greek Xenophon has not only painted as a sweet picture of the domestic woman, in his Economics, but in the Cyropedia has given, in the picture of Panthea,[6] a view of woman which no German picture can surpass, whether lonely and quiet with veiled lids, the temple of a vestal loveliness, or with eyes flashing, and hair flowing to the free wind, cheering on the hero to fight for his God, his country, or whatever name his duty might bear at the time. This picture I shall copy by and by. Yet Xenophon grew up in the same age with him who makes Iphigenia say to Achilles—

> "Better a thousand women should perish than one man cease to see the light."[7]

This was the vulgar Greek sentiment. Xenophon, aiming at the ideal man, caught glimpses of the ideal woman also. From the figure of a Cyrus, the Pantheas stand not afar. They do not in thought; they would not in life.

I could swell the catalogue of instances far beyond the reader's patience. But enough have been brought forward to show that, though there has been great disparity betwixt the nations as between individuals in their culture on this point, yet the idea of woman has always cast some rays and often been forcibly represented.

Far less has woman to complain that she has not had her share of power. This, in all ranks of society, except the lowest, has been hers to the extent that vanity would crave, far beyond what wisdom would accept. In the very lowest, where man, pressed by poverty, sees in woman only the partner of toils and cares, and cannot hope, scarcely has an idea of, a comfortable home, he often maltreats her, and is less influenced by her. In all ranks, those who are gentle and uncomplaining, too candid to intrigue, too delicate to encroach, suffer much. They suffer long, and are kind; verily, they have their reward. But wherever man is sufficiently raised above extreme poverty or brutal stupidity, to care for the comforts of the fireside, or the bloom and ornament of life, woman has always power enough, if she choose to exert it, and is usually disposed to do so, in proportion to her ignorance and childish vanity. Unacquainted with the importance of life and its purposes, trained to a selfish coquetry and love of petty power, she does not look beyond the pleasure of making herself felt at the moment, and governments are shaken and commerce broken up to gratify the pique of a female favorite. The English shopkeeper's wife does not vote, but it is for her interest that the politician canvasses by the coarsest flattery. France suffers no woman on her throne, but her proud nobles kiss the

---

6. For the story of Panthea, see p. 50. Xenophon (c. 431–c. 350 B.C.), Greek historian and essayist and author of *Economics*, a fictitious dialogue about estate management (which features a dutiful wife), and *Cyropedia*, a historical novel about the education of Cyrus the Great (which emphasizes the importance of the family).
7. From Euripedes' play *Iphigenia at Aulis*, discussed by Fuller in Appendix G (see p. 123).

dust at the feet of Pompadour and Dubarry;[8] for such flare in the lighted foreground where a Roland would modestly aid in the closet. Spain, (that same Spain which sang of Ximena and the Lady Teresa,) shuts up her women in the care of duennas, and allows them no book but the Breviary,[9] but the ruin follows only the more surely from the worthless favorite of a worthless queen.[1] Relying on mean precautions, men indeed cry peace, peace, where there is no peace.

It is not the transient breath of poetic incense that women want; each can receive that from a lover. It is not life-long sway; it needs but to become a coquette, a shrew, or a good cook, to be sure of that. It is not money, nor notoriety, nor the badges of authority that men have appropriated to themselves. If demands, made in their behalf, lay stress on any of these particulars, those who make them have not searched deeply into the need. It is for that which at once includes these and precludes them; which would not be forbidden power, lest there be temptation to steal and misuse it; which would not have the mind perverted by flattery from a worthiness of esteem. It is for that which is the birthright of every being capable to receive it,—the freedom, the religious, the intelligent freedom of the universe, to use its means; to learn its secret as far as nature has enabled them, with God alone for their guide and their judge.

Ye cannot believe it, men; but the only reason why women ever assume what is more appropriate to you, is because you prevent them from finding out what is fit for themselves. Were they free, were they wise fully to develop the strength and beauty of woman; they would never wish to be men, or man-like. The well-instructed moon flies not from her orbit to seize on the glories of her partner. No; for she knows that one law rules, one heaven contains, one universe replies to them alike. It is with women as with the slave.

"Vor dem Sklaven, wenn er die Kette bricht,
Vor dem freien Menschen erzittert nicht."[2]

Tremble not before the free man, but before the slave who has chains to break.

In slavery, acknowledged slavery, women are on a par with men. Each is a work-tool, an article of property, no more! In perfect freedom, such as is painted in Olympus, in Swedenborg's angelic state, in the

8. Jeanne Antoinette Poisson, marquise de Pompadour (1721–1764) and Marie Jeanne Bécu, comtesse du Barry (1743–1793) were influencial mistresses of Louis XV of France.
9. A book of hymns and prayers. Ximena was the wife of the legendary Spanish soldier El Cid. "Lady Teresa": see n. 2, p. 33. "Duennas": governesses.
1. Probably Manuel de Godoy (1767–1851), corrupt Spanish statesman, lover of Queen Maria Louisa, and chief minister of Charles IV of Spain. His alliance with Napoléon against England led to the Spanish naval defeat at Trafalgar (1805) and the invasion of Spain by Napoléon's forces.
2. From "Words of Faith" (1798) by Friedrich von Schiller.

heaven where there is no marrying nor giving in marriage, each is a purified intelligence, an enfranchised[3] soul,—no less!

> Jene himmlische Gestalten
> Sie fragen nicht nach Mann und Weib,
> Und keine kleider, keine Falten
> Umgeben den verklarten Leib.[4]

The child who sang this was a prophetic form, expressive of the longing for a state of perfect freedom, pure love. She could not remain here, but was transplanted to another air. And it may be that the air of this earth will never be so tempered that such can bear it long. But, while they stay, they must bear testimony to the truth they are consti-tuted to demand.

That an era approaches which shall approximate nearer to such a temper than any has yet done, there are many tokens, indeed so many, that only a few of the most prominent can here be enumerated.

The reigns of Elizabeth of England and Isabella of Castile[5] foreboded this era. They expressed the beginning of the new state, while they forwarded its progress. These were strong characters and in harmony with the wants of their time. One showed that this strength did not unfit a woman for the duties of a wife and a mother, the other that it could enable her to live and die alone, a wide energetic life, a coura-geous death. Elizabeth is certainly no pleasing example. In rising above the weakness, she did not lay aside the weaknesses ascribed to her sex; but her strength must be respected now, as it was in her own time.

Elizabeth and Mary Stuart[6] seem types, moulded by the spirit of the time, and placed upon an elevated platform to show to the coming ages, woman such as the conduct and wishes of man in general is likely to make her, lovely even to allurement, quick in apprehension and weak in judgment, with grace and dignity of sentiment, but no prin-ciple; credulous and indiscreet, yet artful; capable of sudden greatness or of crime, but not of a steadfast wisdom, or self-restraining virtue; and woman half-emancipated and jealous of her freedom, such as she has figured before and since in many a combative attitude, mannish, not equally manly, strong and prudent more than great or wise; able to control vanity, and the wish to rule through coquetry and passion, but not to resign these dear deceits, from the very foundation, as unworthy

---

3. Liberated. In Greek myth, mount Olympus was the home of the gods. Emanuel Swedenborg (1688–1772), Swedish theologian and mystic. In Matthew 22.30, Jesus says, "For in the res-urrection they neither marry, nor are given in marriage."
4. "Those heavenly forms, / Do not wonder about man and woman, / And no clothes, no folds / Surround the transfigured body." From *Wilhelm Meister's Apprenticeship* by Johann Wolf-gang von Goethe (1749–1832).
5. Queen Isabella I (1451–1504) of Castille and León established the unified Spanish kingdom by her marriage to Ferdinand V of Aragon.
6. Known as Mary Queen of Scots (1542–1587), she was involved in several ill-fated plots against Queen Elizabeth I, who imprisoned and eventually executed her.

a being capable of truth and nobleness. Elizabeth, taught by adversity, put on her virtues as armor, more than produced them in a natural order from her soul. The time and her position called on her to act the wise sovereign, and she was proud that she could do so, but her tastes and inclinations would have led her to act the weak woman. She was without magnanimity of any kind.

We may accept as an omen for ourselves, that it was Isabella who furnished Columbus with the means of coming hither. This land must pay back its debt to woman, without whose aid it would not have been brought into alliance with the civilized world.

A graceful and meaning figure is that introduced to us by Mr. Prescott, in the Conquest of Mexico,[7] in the Indian girl Marina, who accompanied Cortes, and was his interpreter in all the various difficulties of his career. She stood at his side, on the walls of the besieged palace, to plead with her enraged countrymen. By her name he was known in New Spain, and, after the conquest, her gentle intercession was often of avail to the conquered. The poem of the Future may be read in some features of the story of "Malinche."[8]

The influence of Elizabeth on literature was real, though, by sympathy with its finer productions, she was no more entitled to give name to an era than Queen Anne.[9] It was simply that the fact of having a female sovereign on the throne affected the course of a writer's thoughts. In this sense, the presence of a woman on the throne always makes its mark. Life is lived before the eyes of men, by which their imaginations are stimulated as to the possibilities of woman. "We will die for our King, Maria Theresa,"[1] cry the wild warriors, clashing their swords, and the sounds vibrate through the poems of that generation. The range of female character in Spenser alone might content us for one period. Britomart and Belphœbe have as much room on the canvass as Florimel; and where this is the case, the haughtiest amazon will not murmur that Una should be felt to be the fairest type.[2]

Unlike as was the English Queen to a fairy queen, we may yet conceive that it was the image of *a* queen before the poet's mind, that called up this splendid court of women. Shakspeare's range is also great; but he has left out the heroic characters, such as the Macaria of Greece, the Britomart of Spenser. Ford and Massinger[3] have, in this respect,

7. *History of the Conquest of Mexico* (1843) by the American historian William Hickling Prescott (1796–1859).
8. The Aztec princess who became Cortés's slave and interpreter; he baptized her "Marina."
9. During the reign of Anne (1665–1714), queen of Great Britain and Ireland (1702–14), the arts and architecture flourished.
1. Maria Theresa (1717–1780), archduchess of Austria and queen of Hungary and Bohemia (1740–80).
2. In *The Faerie Queene* (1590–96) by Edmund Spenser (c. 1552–1599), Britomart is the female knight of chastity; Belphœbe is a chaste huntress, symbolizing Queen Elizabeth; Florimell is a model of chastity and virtue; and Una is the embodiment of Truth, or the true religion.
3. John Ford (1586–c. 1639) and Philip Massinger (1583–1640), English playwrights.

soared to a higher flight of feeling than he. It was the holy and heroic woman they most loved, and if they could not paint an Imogen, a Desdemona, a Rosalind, yet, in those of a stronger mould, they showed a higher ideal, though with so much less poetic power to embody it, than we see in Portia or Isabella. The simple truth of Cordelia,[4] indeed, is of this sort. The beauty of Cordelia is neither male nor female; it is the beauty of virtue.

The ideal of love and marriage rose high in the mind of all the Christian nations who were capable of grave and deep feeling. We may take as examples of its English aspect, the lines,

> "I could not love thee, dear, so much,
> Loved I not honor more."[5]

Or the address of the Commonwealth's man to his wife,[6] as she looked out from the Tower window to see him for the last time, on his way to the scaffold. He stood up in the cart, waved his hat, and cried, "To Heaven, my love, to Heaven, and leave you in the storm?"

Such was the love of faith and honor, a love which stopped, like Colonel Hutchinson's, "on this side idolatry," because it was religious. The meeting of two such souls Donne describes as giving birth to an "abler soul."[7]

Lord Herbert wrote to his love,

> "Were not our souls immortal made,
> Our equal loves can make them such."[8]

In the "Broken Heart" of Ford, Penthea, a character which engages my admiration even more deeply than the famous one of Calanthe,[9] is made to present to the mind the most beautiful picture of what these relations should be in their purity. Her life cannot sustain the violation of what she so clearly felt.

Shakspeare, too, saw that, in true love as in fire, the utmost ardor is coincident with the utmost purity. It is a true lover that exclaims in the agony of Othello,

> "If thou art false, O then Heaven mocks itself."[1]

4. Imogen, Desdemona, Rosalind, Portia, Isabella, and Cordelia are female characters in Shakespeare's plays *Cymbeline*, *Othello*, *As You Like It*, *Julius Caesar*, *Measure for Measure*, and *King Lear*, respectively.
5. From "To Locasta, Going to the Wars" by the English poet Richard Lovelace (1618–1658).
6. Colonel John Hutchinson (1615–1664) supported the Commonwealth during the English Civil War and signed the death warrant of King Charles I. His wife, Lucy, described their love for one another in her *Memoirs of the Life of Colonel Hutchinson*.
7. From "The Exstacie" by the English poet John Donne (1572–1631).
8. From "An Ode upon a Question Moved, Whether Love Should Continue Forever?" by the English poet Edward Herbert (1583–1648).
9. In Ford's tragedy *The Broken Heart* (1633), Penthea is forced by her brother to marry the jealous and contemptible Bassanes, who makes her so miserable she dies. Calanthe, another female character in the play, also dies brokenhearted.
1. *Othello* 3.3.278.

The son, framed like Hamlet, to appreciate truth in all the beauty of relations, sinks into deep melancholy, when he finds his natural expectations disappointed. He has no mother. She to whom he gave the name, disgraces from his heart's shrine all the sex.

"Frailty, thy name is woman."

It is because a Hamlet could find cause to say so, that I have put the line, whose stigma has never been removed, at the head of my work. But, as a lover, surely a Hamlet would not have so far mistook, as to have finished with such a conviction. He would have felt the faith of Othello, and that faith could not, in his more dispassionate mind, have been disturbed by calumny.

In Spain, this thought is arrayed in a sublimity, which belongs to the sombre and passionate genius of the nation. Calderon's Justina[2] resists all the temptation of the Demon, and raises her lover, with her, above the sweet lures of mere temporal happiness. Their marriage is vowed at the stake; their souls are liberated together by the martyr flame into "a purer state of sensation and existence."

In Italy, the great poets wove into their lives an ideal love which answered to the highest wants. It included those of the intellect and the affections, for it was a love of spirit for spirit. It was not ascetic, or superhuman, but, interpreting all things, gave their proper beauty to details of the common life, the common day; the poet spoke of his love, not as a flower to place in his bosom, or hold carelessly in his hand, but as a light towards which he must find wings to fly, or "a stair to heaven." He delighted to speak of her, not only as the bride of his heart, but the mother of his soul; for he saw that, in cases where the right direction had been taken, the greater delicacy of her frame, and stillness of her life, left her more open to spiritual influx than man is. So he did not look upon her as betwixt him and earth, to serve his temporal needs, but, rather, betwixt him and heaven, to purify his affections and lead him to wisdom through love. He sought, in her, not so much the Eve, as the Madonna.

In these minds the thought, which gleams through all the legends of chivalry, shines in broad intellectual effulgence, not to be misinterpreted, and their thought is reverenced by the world, though it lies so far from the practice of the world as yet, so far, that it seems as though a gulf of death yawned between.

Even with such men, the practice was, often, widely different from the mental faith. I say mental, for if the heart were thoroughly alive with it, the practice could not be dissonant. Lord Herbert's was a

---

2. The beautiful Justina saves herself and her lover, the philosopher Cyprian, from the Devil, in the play *El Magico Prodigioso* (The mighty magician) (1637) by Pedro Calderón de la Barca (1600–1681), Spanish dramatist.

marriage of convention, made for him at fifteen; he was not discontented with it, but looked only to the advantages it brought of perpetuating his family on the basis of a great fortune. He paid, in act, what he considered a dutiful attention to the bond; his thoughts travelled elsewhere; and while forming a high ideal of the companionship of minds in marriage, he seems never to have doubted that its realization must be postponed to some other state of being. Dante, almost immediately after the death of Beatrice, married a lady chosen for him by his friends, and Boccaccio,[3] in describing the miseries that attended, in this case,

"The form of an union where union is none,"

speaks as if these were inevitable to the connection, and the scholar and poet, especially, could expect nothing but misery and obstruction in a domestic partnership with woman.

Centuries have passed since, but civilized Europe is still in a transition state about marriage; not only in practice, but in thought. It is idle to speak with contempt of the nations where polygamy is an institution, or seraglios[4] a custom, when practices far more debasing haunt, well nigh fill, every city and every town. And so far as union of one with one is believed to be the only pure form of marriage, a great majority of societies and individuals are still doubtful whether the earthly bond must be a meeting of souls, or only supposes a contract of convenience and utility. Were woman established in the rights of an immortal being, this could not be. She would not, in some countries, be given away by her father, with scarcely more respect for her feelings than is shown by the Indian chief, who sells his daughter for a horse, and beats her if she runs away from her new home. Nor, in societies where her choice is left free, would she be perverted, by the current of opinion that seizes her, into the belief that she must marry, if it be only to find a protector, and a home of her own.

Neither would man, if he thought the connection of permanent importance, form it so lightly. He would not deem it a trifle, that he was to enter into the closest relations with another soul, which, if not eternal in themselves, must eternally affect his growth.

Neither, did he believe woman capable of friendship,[5] would he, by rash haste, lose the chance of finding a friend in the person who might, probably, live half a century by his side. Did love, to his mind, stretch forth into infinity, he would not miss his chance of its revelations, that he might, the sooner, rest from his weariness by a bright fireside, and

3. Giovanni Boccaccio (1313–1375), Italian poet, storyteller, and scholar. The great Italian poet Dante Alighieri (1265–1321) married Gemma Donati after the death of his exalted muse Beatrice Portinari (1266–1290).
4. Harems.
5. See Appendix D, Spinoza's view [Fuller's note].

secure a sweet and graceful attendant "devoted to him alone." Were
he a step higher, he would not carelessly enter into a relation where
he might not be able to do the duty of a friend, as well as a protector from external ill, to the other party, and have a being in his
power pining for sympathy, intelligence and aid, that he could not
give.

What deep communion, what real intercourse is implied by the sharing the joys and cares of parentage, when any degree of equality is
admitted between the parties! It is true that, in a majority of instances,
the man looks upon his wife as an adopted child, and places her to the
other children in the relation of nurse or governess, rather than of
parent. Her influence with them is sure, but she misses the education
which should enlighten that influence, by being thus treated. It is the
order of nature that children should complete the education, moral
and mental, of parents, by making them think what is needed for the
best culture of human beings, and conquer all faults and impulses that
interfere with their giving this to these dear objects, who represent the
world to them. Father and mother should assist one another to learn
what is required for this sublime priesthood of nature. But, for this, a
religious recognition of equality is required.

Where this thought of equality begins to diffuse itself, it is shown in
four ways.

The household partnership. In our country, the woman looks for a
"smart but kind" husband; the man for a "capable, sweet-tempered"
wife.

The man furnishes the house; the woman regulates it. Their relation
is one of mutual esteem, mutual dependence. Their talk is of business,
their affection shows itself by practical kindness. They know that life
goes more smoothly and cheerfully to each for the other's aid; they are
grateful and content. The wife praises her husband as a "good provider;"
the husband, in return, compliments her as a "capital housekeeper."
This relation is good, as far as it goes.

Next comes a closer tie, which takes the two forms, either of mutual
idolatry, or of intellectual companionship. The first, we suppose, is to
no one a pleasing subject of contemplation. The parties weaken and
narrow one another; they lock the gate against all the glories of the
universe, that they may live in a cell together. To themselves they seem
the only wise, to all others steeped in infatuation; the gods smile as
they look forward to the crisis of cure; to men, the woman seems an
unlovely syren; to women, the man an effeminate boy.

The other form, of intellectual companionship, has become more
and more frequent. Men engaged in public life, literary men, and artists, have often found in their wives companions and confidants in
thought no less than in feeling. And as the intellectual development of
woman has spread wider and risen higher, they have, not unfrequently,

shared the same employment. As in the case of Roland and his wife,[6] who were friends in the household and in the nation's councils, read, regulated home affairs, or prepared public documents together, indifferently.

It is very pleasant, in letters begun by Roland, and finished by his wife, to see the harmony of mind, and the difference of nature; one thought, but various ways of treating it.

This is one of the best instances of a marriage of friendship. It was only friendship, whose basis was esteem; probably neither party knew love, except by name.

Roland was a good man, worthy to esteem, and be esteemed; his wife as deserving of admiration, as able to do without it. Madame Roland is the fairest specimen we have yet of her class, as clear to discern her aim, as valiant to pursue it, as Spenser's Britomart; austerely set apart from all that did not belong to her, whether as woman or as mind. She is an antetype of a class to which the coming time will afford a field, the Spartan matron, brought by the culture of the age of Books to intellectual consciousness and expansion.

Self-sufficingness, strength, and clear-sightedness were, in her, combined with a power of deep and calm affection. She, too, would have given a son or husband the device for his shield, "Return with it or upon it;" and this, not because she loved little, but much. The page of her life is one of unsullied dignity.

Her appeal to posterity is one against the injustice of those who committed such crimes in the name of Liberty. She makes it in behalf of herself and her husband. I would put beside it, on the shelf, a little volume, containing a similar appeal from the verdict of contemporaries to that of mankind, made by Godwin in behalf of his wife, the celebrated, the, by most men, detested, Mary Wolstonecraft.[7] In his view, it was an appeal from the injustice of those who did such wrong in the name of virtue.

Were this little book interesting for no other cause, it would be so for the generous affection evinced under the peculiar circumstances. This man had courage to love and honor this woman in the face of the world's sentence, and of all that was repulsive in her own past history. He believed he saw of what soul she was, and that the impulses she had struggled to act out were noble, though the opinions to which they had led might not be thoroughly weighed. He loved her, and he

6. Jean-Marie Roland de la Platière (1734–1793) and his wife, Jeanne-Marie Roland, French intellectuals and revolutionaries, sided with the Girondists against the Jacobins during the French Revolution. He committed suicide upon learning of his wife's execution during the Reign of Terror (see also n. 9, p. 13).
7. William Godwin (1756–1836), novelist and English political philosopher, married Mary Wollstonecraft (1759–1797), feminist author of A Vindication of the Rights of Woman (1792). The year after her death, Godwin published a memoir of his wife, revealing her 1793–95 love affair with the American Gilbert Imlay, by whom she had a daughter out of wedlock.

defended her for the meaning and tendency of her inner life. It was a good fact.

Mary Wolstonecraft, like Madame Dudevant, (commonly known as George Sand,[8]) in our day, was a woman whose existence better proved the need of some new interpretation of woman's rights, than any thing she wrote. Such beings as these, rich in genius, of most tender sympathies, capable of high virtue and a chastened harmony, ought not to find themselves, by birth, in a place so narrow, that, in breaking bonds, they become outlaws. Were there as much room in the world for such, as in Spenser's poem for Britomart, they would not run their heads so wildly against the walls, but prize their shelter rather. They find their way, at last, to light and air, but the world will not take off the brand it has set upon them. The champion of the Rights of Woman found, in Godwin, one who would plead that cause like a brother. He who delineated with such purity of traits the form of woman in the Marguerite, of whom the weak St. Leon[9] could never learn to be worthy, a pearl indeed whose price was above rubies, was not false in life to the faith by which he had hallowed his romance. He acted as he wrote, like a brother. This form of appeal rarely fails to touch the basest man. "Are you acting towards other women in the way you would have men act towards your sister?" George Sand smokes, wears male attire, wishes to be addressed as "Mon frère";[1]—perhaps, if she found those who were as brothers, indeed, she would not care whether she were brother or sister.[2]

8. George Sand, pseudonym of the French Romantic novelist Amandine Lucile Aurore Dudevant (1804–1876), whose male attire and series of love affairs scandalized many Americans.
9. Marguerite and St. Leon are characters in Godwin's novel *St. Leon* (1799).
1. My brother (French).
2. Since writing the above, I have read with great satisfaction, the following sonnets addressed to George Sand by a woman who has precisely the qualities that the author of Simon and Indiana lacks. It is such a woman, so unblemished in character, so high in aim, and pure in soul, that should address this other, as noble in nature, but clouded by error, and struggling with circumstances. It is such women that will do such justice. They are not afraid to look for virtue and reply to aspiration, among those who have *not* "dwelt in decencies forever." It is a source of pride and happiness to read this address from the heart of Elizabeth Barrett.

To George Sand

A DESIRE

Thou large-brained woman and large-hearted man,
    Self-called George Sand! whose soul, amid the lions
    Of thy tumultuous senses moans defiance,
And answers roar for roar, as spirits can:
I would some mild miraculous thunder ran
    Above the applauded circus, in appliance
    Of thine own nobler nature's strength and science,
    Drawing two pinions, white as wings of swan,
From the strong shoulders, to amaze the place
    With holier light! that thou to woman's claim,
And man's might join, beside, the angel's grace
    Of a pure genius sanctified from blame;
Till child and maiden pressed to thine embrace,
    To kiss upon thy lips a stainless fame.

We rejoice to see that she, who expresses such a painful contempt for men in most of her works, as shows she must have known great wrong from them, depicting in "La Roche Mauprat,"[3] a man raised by the workings of love, from the depths of savage sensualism, to a moral and intellectual life. It was love for a pure object, for a steadfast woman, one of those who, the Italian said, could make the stair to heaven.

This author, beginning like the many in assault upon bad institutions, and external ills, yet deepening the experience through comparative freedom, sees at last, that the only efficient remedy must come from individual character. These bad institutions, indeed, it may always be replied, prevent individuals from forming good character, therefore we must remove them. Agreed, yet keep steadily the higher aim in view. Could you clear away all the bad forms of society, it is vain, unless the individual begin to be ready for better. There must be a parallel movement in these two branches of life. And all the rules left by Moses availed less to further the best life than the living example of one Messiah.

Still, still the mind of the age struggles confusedly with these problems, better discerning as yet the ill it can no longer bear, than the good by which it may supersede it. But women, like Sand, will speak now and cannot be silenced; their characters and their eloquence alike foretell an era when such as they shall easier learn to lead true lives. But though such forebode, not such shall be the parents of it.[4] Those who would reform the world must show that they do not speak in the heat of wild impulse; their lives must be unstained by passionate error; they must be severe lawgivers to themselves. They must be religious students of the divine purpose with regard to man, if they would not

---

To the Same

A RECOGNITION

True genius, but true woman! dost deny
      Thy woman's nature with a manly scorn,
And break away the gauds and armlets worn
      By weaker women in captivity?
Ah, vain denial! that revolted cry
      Is sobbed in by a woman's voice forlorn:—
Thy woman's hair, my sister, all unshorn,
      Floats back dishevelled strength in agony,
Disproving thy man's name, and while before
      The world thou burnest in a poet-fire,
We see thy woman-heart beat evermore
      Through the large flame. Beat purer, heart, and higher,
Till God unsex thee on the spirit-shore;
      To which alone unsexing, purely aspire.

This last sonnet seems to have been written after seeing the picture of Sand, which represents her in a man's dress, but with long loose hair, and an eye whose mournful fire is impressive even in the caricatures [Fuller's note]. After meeting Sand in person in Paris in 1847, Fuller declared she "never liked a woman better."
3. Published in 1837.
4. Appendix, E [Fuller's note].

confound the fancies of a day with the requisitions of eternal good. Their liberty must be the liberty of law and knowledge. But, as to the transgressions against custom which have caused such outcry against those of noble intention, it may be observed, that the resolve of Eloisa to be only the mistress of Abelard, was that of one who saw in practice around her, the contract of marriage made the seal of degradation. Shelley[5] feared not to be fettered, unless so to be was to be false. Wherever abuses are seen, the timid will suffer; the bold will protest. But society has a right to outlaw them till she has revised her law; and this she must be taught to do, by one who speaks with authority, not in anger or haste.

If Godwin's choice of the calumniated authoress of the "Rights of Woman,"[6] for his honored wife, be a sign of a new era, no less so is an article to which I have alluded some pages back, published five or six years ago in one of the English Reviews, where the writer, in doing full justice to Eloisa, shows his bitter regret that she lives not now to love him, who might have known better how to prize her love than did the egotistical Abelard.

These marriages, these characters, with all their imperfections, express an onward tendency. They speak of aspiration of soul, of energy of mind, seeking clearness and freedom. Of a like promise are the tracts lately published by Goodwyn Barmby, (the European Pariah,[7] as he calls himself,) and his wife Catharine. Whatever we may think of their measures, we see in them wedlock; the two minds are wed by the only contract that can permanently avail, of a common faith and a common purpose.

We might mention instances, nearer home, of minds, partners in work and in life, sharing together, on equal terms, public and private interests, and which wear not, on any side, the aspect of offence shown by those last-named: persons who steer straight onward, yet, in our comparatively free life, have not been obliged to run their heads against any wall. But the principles which guide them might, under petrified and oppressive institutions, have made them warlike, paradoxical, and in some sense, Pariahs. The phenomena are different, the law is the same, in all these cases. Men and women have been obliged to build up their house anew from the very foundation. If they found stone ready in the quarry, they took it peaceably, other wise they alarmed the country by pulling down old towers to get materials.

These are all instances of marriage as intellectual companionship. The parties meet mind to mind, and a mutual trust is produced, which can buckler them against a million. They work together for a common

5. Percy Bysshe Shelley (1792–1822), English poet, married Harriet Westbrook in 1811; but three years later, he eloped with Mary Godwin, whom he later married after Harriet committed suicide.
6. Mary Wollstonecraft.
7. An outcast. John Goodwyn Barmby (1820–1881), Unitarian minister and Christian socialist.

purpose, and, in all these instances, with the same implement, the pen. The pen and the writing-desk furnish forth as naturally the retirement of woman as of man.

A pleasing expression, in this kind, is afforded by the union in the names of the Howitts. William and Mary Howitt[8] we heard named together for years, supposing them to be brother and sister; the equality of labors and reputation, even so, was auspicious; more so, now we find them man and wife. In his late work on Germany,[9] Howitt mentions his wife, with pride, as one among the constellation of distinguished English-women, and in a graceful simple manner.

Our pleasure, indeed, in this picture, is marred by the vulgar apparition which has of late displaced the image, which we had from her writings cherished of a pure and gentle Quaker poetess. The surprise was painful as that of the little sentimentalist in the tale of "L'Amie Inconnue" when she found her correspondent, the poetess, the "adored Araminta," scolding her servants in Welsh, and eating toasted cheese and garlic. Still, we cannot forget what we have thought of the partnership in literature and affection between the Howitts, the congenial pursuits and productions, the pedestrian tours where the married pair showed that marriage, on a wide enough basis, does not destroy the "inexhaustible" entertainment which lovers found in one another's company.

In naming these instances, I do not mean to imply that community of employment is essential to union of husband and wife, more than to the union of friends. Harmony exists in difference, no less than in likeness, if only the same key-note govern both parts. Woman the poem, man the poet! Woman the heart, man the head! Such divisions are only important when they are never to be transcended. If nature is never bound down, nor the voice of inspiration stifled, that is enough. We are pleased that women should write and speak, if they feel the need of it, from having something to tell; but silence for ages would be no misfortune, if that silence be from divine command, and not from man's tradition.

While Goetz Von Berlichingen rides to battle, his wife is busy in the kitchen; but difference of occupation does not prevent that community of inward life, that perfect esteem, with which he says—

"Whom God loves, to him gives he such a wife."[1]

Manzoni thus dedicates his "Adelchi."[2]

"To his beloved and venerated wife, Enrichetta Luigia Blondel, who, with conjugal affection and maternal wisdom, has preserved a virgin

8. Mary Botham Howitt (1799–1888) married William Howitt (1792–1879) in 1821; they pursued a joint career as writers, editors, and social reformers.
9. *The Rural and Domestic Life of Germany* (1842).
1. From the play *Goetz von Berlichingen* (1773) by Goethe about a German knight.
2. A tragedy published in 1822.

mind, the author dedicates this "Adelchi," grieving that he could not, by a more splendid and more durable monument, honor the dear name, and the memory of so many virtues."

The relation could not be fairer, or more equal, if she, too, had written poems. Yet the position of the parties might have been the reverse as well; the woman might have sung the deeds, given voice to the life of the man, and beauty would have been the result, as we see, in pictures of Arcadia,[3] the nymph singing to the shepherds, or the shepherd, with his pipe, alluring the nymphs; either makes a good picture. The sounding lyre requires, not muscular strength, but energy of soul to animate the hand which would control it. Nature seems to delight in varying the arrangements, as if to show that she will be fettered by no rule, and we must admit the same varieties that she admits.

The fourth and highest grade of marriage union, is the religious, which may be expressed as pilgrimage towards a common shrine. This includes the others; home sympathies and household wisdom, for these pilgrims must know how to assist each other along the dusty way; intellectual communion, for how sad it would be on such a journey to have a companion to whom you could not communicate thoughts and aspirations as they sprang to life; who would have no feeling for the prospects that open, more and more glorious as we advance; who would never see the flowers that may be gathered by the most industrious traveller. It must include all these. Such a fellow-pilgrim Count Zinzendorf[4] seems to have found in his Countess, of whom he thus writes:

"Twenty-five years' experience has shown me that just the help-mate whom I have, is the only one that could suit my vocation. Who else could have so carried through my family affairs? Who lived so spotlessly before the world? Who so wisely aided me in my rejection of a dry morality? Who so clearly set aside the Pharisaism[5] which, as years passed, threatened to creep in among us? Who so deeply discerned as to the spirits of delusion, which sought to bewilder us? Who would have governed my whole economy so wisely, richly, and hospitably, when circumstances commanded? Who have taken indifferently the part of servant or mistress, without, on the one side, affecting an especial spirituality; on the other, being sullied by any worldly pride? Who, in a community where all ranks are eager to be on a level, would, from wise and real causes, have known how to maintain inward and outward distinctions? Who, without a murmur, have seen her husband encounter such dangers by land and sea? Who undertaken with him, and *sustained* such astonishing pilgrimages? Who, amid such difficulties, always held up her head and supported me? Who found such vast sums

3. Pastoral region of ancient Greece.
4. Nicolaus Ludwig von Zinzendorf (count of Zinzendorf and Pottendorf) (1700–1760), German religious and social reformer who directed the missionary program of the Moravian Church.
5. Hypocritical self-righteousness.

of money, and acquitted them on her own credit? And, finally, who, of all human beings, could so well understand and interpret to others my inner and outer being as this one, of such nobleness in her way of thinking, such great intellectual capacity, and free from the theological perplexities that enveloped me!"

Let any one peruse, with all their power, the lineaments of this portrait, and see if the husband had not reason, with this air of solemn rapture and conviction, to challenge comparison? We are reminded of the majestic cadence of the line whose feet step in the just proportions of Humanity,

"Daughter of God and Man, accomplished Eve!"[6]

An observer[7] adds this testimony:

"We may, in many marriages, regard it as the best arrangement, if the man has so much advantage over his wife, that she can, without much thought of her own, be, by him, led and directed as by a father. But it was not so with the Count and his consort. She was not made to be a copy; she was an original; and, while she loved and honored him, she thought for herself, on all subjects, with so much intelligence, that he could and did look on her as sister and friend also."

Compare with this refined specimen of a religiously civilized life, the following imperfect sketch of a North American Indian, and we shall see that the same causes will always produce the same results. The Flying Pigeon (Ratchewaine) was the wife of a barbarous chief, who had six others, but she was his only true wife, because the only one of a strong and pure character, and, having this, inspired a veneration, as like as the mind of the man permitted, to that inspired by the Countess Zinzendorf. She died when her son was only four years old, yet left on his mind a feeling of reverent love worthy the thought of Christian chivalry. Grown to manhood, he shed tears on seeing her portrait.

THE FLYING PIGEON[8]

"Ratchewaine was chaste, mild, gentle in her disposition, kind, generous, and devoted to her husband. A harsh word was never known to proceed from her mouth; nor was she ever known to be in a passion. Mahaskah used to say of her, after her death, that her hand was shut, when those, who did not want, came into her presence; but when the really poor came in, it was like a strainer full of holes, letting all she held in it pass through. In the exercise

6. *Paradise Lost* (1667) 4.660 by the English poet John Milton (1608–1674).
7. Spangenberg [Fuller's note]. August Gotlieb Spangenberg (1704–1792) succeeded Count Zinzendorf as bishop of the Moravian Church.
8. The two-paragraph quotation comes from *History of the Indian Tribes of North America* (1836–44) by Thomas McKenney and James Hall.

of generous feeling she was uniform. It was not indebted for its
exercise to whim, or caprice, or partiality. No matter of what nation
the applicant for her bounty was, or whether at war or peace with
her nation; if he were hungry, she fed him; if naked, she clothed
him; and if houseless, she gave him shelter. The continued exercise of this generous feeling kept her poor. And she has been
known to give away her last blanket—all the honey that was in the
lodge, the last bladder of bear's oil, and the last piece of dried
meat.

"She was scrupulously exact in the observance of all the religious rites which her faith imposed upon her. Her conscience is
represented to have been extremely tender. She often feared that
her acts were displeasing to the Great Spirit, when she would
blacken her face, and retire to some lone place, and fast and pray."

To these traits should be added, but for want of room, anecdotes
which show the quick decision and vivacity of her mind. Her face was
in harmony with this combination. Her brow is as ideal and the eyes
and lids as devout and modest as the Italian pictures of the Madonna,
while the lower part of the face has the simplicity and childish strength
of the Indian race. Her picture presents the finest specimen of Indian
beauty we have ever seen.

Such a woman is the sister and friend of all beings, as the worthy
man is their brother and helper.

With like pleasure we survey the pairs wedded on the eve of missionary effort. They, indeed, are fellow pilgrims on a well-made road,
and whether or no they accomplish all they hope for the sad Hindoo,
or the nearer savage, we feel that, in the burning waste, their love is
like to be a healing dew, in the forlorn jungle, a tent of solace to one
another. They meet, as children of one Father, to read together one
book of instruction.

We must insert in this connection the most beautiful picture presented by ancient literature of wedded love under this noble form.

It is from the romance in which Xenophon, the chivalrous Greek,
presents his ideal of what human nature should be.[9]

The generals of Cyrus had taken captive a princess, a woman of
unequalled beauty, and hastened to present her to the prince as the
part of the spoil he would think most worthy of his acceptance.

Cyrus visits the lady, and is filled with immediate admiration by the
modesty and majesty with which she receives him. He finds her name
is Panthea, and that she is the wife of Abradatus, a young king whom
she entirely loves. He protects her as a sister, in his camp, till he can
restore her to her husband.

After the first transports of joy at this re-union, the heart of Panthea

9. *Cyropaedia* by Xenophon (c. 430–c. 355 B.C.), Greek historian.

is bent on showing her love and gratitude to her magnanimous and delicate protector. And as she has nothing so precious to give as the aid of Abradatus, that is what she most wishes to offer. Her husband is of one soul with her in this, as in all things.

The description of her grief and self-destruction, after the death which ensued upon this devotion, I have seen quoted, but never that of their parting when she sends him forth to battle. I shall copy both. If they have been read by any of my readers, they may be so again with profit in this connexion, for never were the heroism of a true woman, and the purity of love, in a true marriage, painted in colors more delicate or more lively.

"The chariot of Abradatus, that had four perches and eight horses, was completely adorned for him; and when he was going to put on his linen corslet, which was a sort of armor used by those of his country, Panthea brought him a golden helmet, and arm-pieces, broad bracelets for his wrists, a purple habit that reached down to his feet, and hung in folds at the bottom, and a crest dyed of a violet color. These things she had made unknown to her husband, and by taking the measure of his armor. He wondered when he saw them, and inquired thus of Panthea: "And have you made me these arms, woman, by destroying your own ornaments?" "No by Jove," said Panthea, "not what is the most valuable of them; for it is you, if you appear to others to be what I think you, that will be my greatest ornament." And, saying that, she put on him the armor, and, though she endeavored to conceal it, the tears poured down her cheeks. When Abradatus, who was before a man of fine appearance, was set out in those arms, he appeared the most beautiful and noble of all, especially, being likewise so by nature. Then, taking the reins from the driver, he was just preparing to mount the chariot, when Panthea, after she had desired all that were there to retire, thus said:

'O Abradatus! if ever there was a woman who had a greater regard to her husband than to her own soul, I believe you know that I am such an one; what need I therefore speak of things in particular? for I reckon that my actions have convinced you more than any words I can now use. And yet, though I stand thus affected towards you, as you know I do, I swear by this friendship of mine and yours, that I certainly would rather choose to be put under ground jointly with you, approving yourself a brave man, than to live with you in disgrace and shame; so much do I think you and myself worthy of the noblest things. Then I think that we both lie under great obligations to Cyrus, that, when I was a captive, and chosen out for himself, he thought fit to treat me neither as a slave, nor, indeed, as a woman of mean account, but he took and kept me for you, as if I were his brother's wife. Besides, when Araspes, who was my guard, went away from him, I promised him, that, if he would allow me to send for you, you would come to him, and approve yourself a much better and more faithful friend than Araspes.'

"Thus she spoke; and Abradatus being struck with admiration at her discourse, laying his hand gently on her head, and lifting up his eyes to heaven, made this prayer: 'Do thou, O greatest Jove! grant me to appear a husband worthy of Panthea, and a friend worthy of Cyrus, who has done us so much honor!'

"Having said this, he mounted the chariot by the door of the driver's seat; and, after he had got up, when the driver shut the door, Panthea, who had now no other way to salute him, kissed the seat of the chariot. The chariot then moved, and she, unknown to him, followed, till Abradatus turning about, and seeing her, said: 'Take courage, Panthea! Fare you happily and well, and now go your ways.' On this her women and servants carried her to her conveyance, and, laying her down, concealed her by throwing the covering of a tent over her. The people, though Abradatus and his chariot made a noble spectacle, were not able to look at him till Panthea was gone."

After the battle—

"Cyrus calling to some of his servants, 'Tell me,' said he, 'has any one seen Abradatus? for I admire that he now does not appear.' One replied, 'My sovereign, it is because he is not living, but died in the battle as he broke in with his chariot on the Egyptians. All the rest, except his particular companions, they say, turned off when they saw the Egyptians' compact body. His wife is now said to have taken up his dead body, to have placed it in the carriage that she herself was conveyed in, and to have brought it hither to some place on the river Pactolus, and her servants are digging a grave on a certain elevation. They say that his wife, after setting him out with all the ornaments she has, is sitting on the ground with his head on her knees.' Cyrus, hearing this, gave himself a blow on the thigh, mounted his horse at a leap, and taking with him a thousand horse, rode away to this scene of affliction; but gave orders to Gadatas and Gobryas to take with them all the rich ornaments proper for a friend and an excellent man deceased, and to follow after him; and whoever had herds of cattle with him, he ordered them to take both oxen, and horses, and sheep in good number, and to bring them away to the place where, by inquiry, they should find him to be, that he might sacrifice these to Abradatus.

"As soon as he saw the woman sitting on the ground, and the dead body there lying, he shed tears at the afflicting sight, and said: 'Alas! thou brave and faithful soul, hast thou left us, and art thou gone?' At the same time he took him by the right hand, and the hand of the deceased came away, for it had been cut off, with a sword, by the Egyptians. He, at the sight of this, became yet much more concerned than before. The woman shrieked out in a lamentable manner, and, taking the hand from Cyrus, kissed it, fitted it to its proper place again, as well as she could, and said, 'The rest, Cyrus, is in the same condition, but what need you see it? And I know that I was not one of the least concerned in these his sufferings, and, perhaps, you were not less so, for I, fool that I was! frequently exhorted him to behave in such a manner as to appear a friend to you, worthy of notice; and I know he never thought of what he himself should suffer, but of what he should do to please you. He is dead, therefore,' said she, 'without reproach, and I, who urged him on, sit here alive.' Cyrus, shedding tears for some time in silence, then spoke—'He has died, woman, the noblest death; for he has died victorious! do you adorn him with these things that I furnish you with.' (Gobryas and Gadatas were then come up and had brought rich ornaments in great abundance with them.) 'Then,' said he, 'be assured that he shall not want respect and honor in all other things: but, over and above, multitudes shall concur in raising him a monument that shall be worthy of us, and all the sacrifices shall be made him that are proper to be made in honor of a brave man. You shall not be left destitute, but, for the sake of your modesty and every other virtue, I will pay you all other honors, as well as place those about you who will conduct you wherever you please. Do you but make it known to me where it is that you desire to be conveyed to.' And Panthea replied, 'Be confident, Cyrus,' said she, 'I will not conceal from you to whom it is that I desire to go.'

"He, having said this, went away with great pity for her that she should have lost such a husband, and for the man that he should have left such a wife behind him, never to see her more. Panthea then gave orders for her servants to retire, 'Till such time,' said she, 'as I shall have lamented my husband, as I please.' Her nurse she bid to stay, and gave orders that, when she was dead, she would wrap her and her husband up in one mantle together. The nurse, after having repeatedly begged her not to do this, and meeting with no success, but observing her to grow angry, sat herself down, breaking out into tears. She, being before-hand provided with a sword, killed herself, and, laying her head down on her husband's breast, she died. The nurse set up a lamentable cry, and covered them both as Panthea had directed.

"Cyrus, as soon as he was informed of what the woman had done, being struck with it, went to help her if he could. The servants, three in number, seeing what had been done, drew their swords and killed themselves, as they stood at the place where she had ordered them. And the monument is now said to have been raised by continuing the mount on to the servants; and on a pillar above, they say, the names of the man and woman were written in Syriac letters.

"Below were three pillars, and they were inscribed thus, "Of the servants." Cyrus, when he came to this melancholy scene, was struck with admiration of the woman, and, having lamented over her, went away. He took care, as was proper, that all the funeral rites should be

paid them in the noblest manner, and the monument, they say, was
raised up to a very great size."

These be the ancients, who, so many assert had no idea of the dignity
of woman, or of marriage. Such love Xenophon could paint as subsist-
ing between those who after death "would see one another never
more." Thousands of years have passed since, and with the reception
of the cross, the nations assume the belief that those who part thus,
may meet again and forever, if spiritually fitted to one another, as Abradatus and Panthea were, and yet do we see such marriages among
them? If at all, how often?

I must quote two more short passages from Xenophon, for he is a
writer who pleases me well.

Cyrus receiving the Armenians whom he had conquered.

"Tigranes," said he, "at what rate would you purchase the regaining
of your wife?" Now Tigranes happened to be *but lately married*, and
had a very great love for his wife," (that clause perhaps sounds *modern*).

"Cyrus," said he, "I would ransom her at the expense of my life."

"Take then your own to yourself," said he. •   •   •

When they came home, one talked of Cyrus' wisdom, another of his
patience and resolution, another of his mildness. One spoke of his
beauty and the smallness of his person, and, on that, Tigranes asked
his wife, "And do you, Armenian dame, think Cyrus handsome?"
"Truly," said she, "I did not look at him." "At whom, then, did you
look?" said Tigranes. "At him who said that, to save me from servitude,
he would ransom me at the expense of his own life."

From the Banquet.[1]—

Socrates, who observed her with pleasure, said, "This young girl has
confirmed me in the opinion I have had, for a long time, that the
female sex are nothing inferior to ours, excepting only in strength of
body, or, perhaps, in steadiness of judgment."

In the Economics,[2] the manner in which the husband gives counsel
to his young wife, presents the model of politeness and refinement.
Xenophon is thoroughly the gentleman, gentle in breeding and in soul.
All the men he describes are so, while the shades of manner are distinctly marked. There is the serene dignity of Socrates, with gleams of
playfulness thrown across its cool religious shades, the princely mildness
of Cyrus, and the more domestic elegance of the husband in the
Economics.

There is no way that men sin more against refinement, as well as
discretion, than in their conduct towards their wives. Let them look at

1. A reference to Plato's *Symposium*, which Fuller called by its French title, having read it in
French.
2. By Xenophon.

the men of Xenophon. Such would know how to give counsel, for they would know how to receive it. They would feel that the most intimate relations claimed most, not least, of refined courtesy. They would not suppose that confidence justified carelessness, nor the reality of affection want of delicacy in the expression of it.

Such men would be too wise to hide their affairs from the wife and then expect her to act as if she knew them. They would know that if she is expected to face calamity with courage, she must be instructed and trusted in prosperity, or, if they had failed in wise confidence such as the husband shows in the Economics, they would be ashamed of anger or querulous surprise at the results that naturally follow.

Such men would not be exposed to the bad influence of bad wives, for all wives, bad or good, loved or unloved, inevitably influence their husbands, from the power their position not merely gives, but necessitates, of coloring evidence and infusing feelings in hours when the patient, shall I call him? is off his guard. Those who understand the wife's mind, and think it worth while to respect her springs of action, know better where they are. But to the bad or thoughtless man who lives carelessly and irreverently so near another mind, the wrong he does daily back upon himself recoils. A Cyrus, an Abradatus knows where he stands.

But to return to the thread of my subject.

Another sign of the times is furnished by the triumphs of female authorship. These have been great and constantly increasing. Women have taken possession of so many provinces for which men had pronounced them unfit, that though these still declare there are some inaccessible to them, it is difficult to say just *where* they must stop.

The shining names of famous women have cast light upon the path of the sex, and many obstructions have been removed. When a Montague[3] could learn better than her brother, and use her lore afterward to such purpose, as an observer, it seemed amiss to hinder woman from preparing themselves to see, or from seeing all they could, when prepared. Since Somerville[4] has achieved so much, will any young girl be prevented from seeking a knowledge of the physical sciences, if she wishes it? De Stael's[5] name was not so clear of offence; she could not forget the woman in the thought; while she was instructing you as a mind, she wished to be admired as a woman; sentimental tears often dimmed the eagle glance. Her intellect too, with all its splendor, trained in a drawing-room, fed on flattery, was tainted and flawed; yet its beams make the obscurest school-house in New-England warmer and lighter

3. Lady Mary Wortley Montagu (1689–1762), English travel writer.
4. Mary Fairfax Somerville (1780–1872), Scottish mathematician and science writer.
5. Anne Louise Germaine Necker, Baroness de Staël (1766–1817), French critic, novelist, historian, and playwright.

to the little rugged girls, who are gathered together on its wooden bench. They may never through life hear her name, but she is not the less their benefactress.

The influence has been such, that the aim certainly is, now, in arranging school instruction for girls, to give them as fair a field as boys. As yet, indeed, these arrangements are made with little judgment or reflection; just as the tutors of Lady Jane Grey,[6] and other distinguished women of her time, taught them Latin and Greek, because they knew nothing else themselves, so now the improvement in the education of girls is to be made by giving them young men as teachers, who only teach what has been taught themselves at college, while methods and topics need revision for these new subjects, which could better be made by those who had experienced the same wants. Women are, often, at the head of these institutions, but they have, as yet, seldom been thinking women, capable to organize a new whole for the wants of the time, and choose persons to officiate in the departments. And when some portion of instruction is got of a good sort from the school, the far greater proportion which is infused from the general atmosphere of society contradicts its purport. Yet books and a little elementary instruction are not furnished, in vain. Women are better aware how great and rich the universe is, not so easily blinded by narrowness or partial views of a home circle. "Her mother did so before her," is no longer a sufficient excuse. Indeed, it was never received as an excuse to mitigate the severity of censure, but was adduced as a reason, rather, why there should be no effort made for reformation.

Whether much or little has been done or will be done, whether women will add to the talent of narration, the power of systematizing, whether they will carve marble, as well as draw and paint, is not important. But that it should be acknowledged that they have intellect which needs developing; that they should not be considered complete, if beings of affection and habit alone, is important.

Yet even this acknowledgment, rather conquered by woman than proffered by man, has been sullied by the usual selfishness. So much is said of women being better educated, that they may become better companions and mothers *for men*. They should be fit for such companionship, and we have mentioned, with satisfaction, instances where it has been established. Earth knows no fairer, holier relation than that of a mother. It is one which, rightly understood, must both promote and require the highest attainments. But a being of infinite scope must not be treated with an exclusive view to any one relation. Give the soul free course, let the organization, both of body and mind, be freely developed, and the being will be fit for any and every relation to which it may be called. The intellect, no more than the sense of hearing, is

6. Lady Jane Grey (1537–1554), brilliant great-granddaughter of Henry VII of England, was queen of England for nine days in 1553; she was later executed by Mary Tudor.

to be cultivated merely that she may be a more valuable companion to man, but because the Power who gave a power, by its mere existence, signifies that it must be brought out towards perfection.

In this regard of self-dependence, and a greater simplicity and fulness of being, we must hail as a preliminary the increase of the class contemptuously designated as old maids.

We cannot wonder at the aversion with which old bachelors and old maids have been regarded. Marriage is the natural means of forming a sphere, of taking root on the earth; it requires more strength to do this without such an opening; very many have failed, and their imperfections have been in every one's way. They have been more partial, more harsh, more officious and impertinent than those compelled by severer friction to render themselves endurable. Those, who have a more full experience of the instincts, have a distrust, as to whether they can be thoroughly human and humane, such as is hinted in the saying, "Old maids' and bachelors' children are well cared for," which derides at once their ignorance and their presumption.

Yet the business of society has become so complex, that it could now scarcely be carried on without the presence of these despised auxiliaries; and detachments from the army of aunts and uncles are wanted to stop gaps in every hedge. They rove about, mental and moral Ishmaelites,[7] pitching their tents amid the fixed and ornamented homes of men.

In a striking variety of forms, genius of late, both at home and abroad, has paid its tribute to the character of the Aunt, and the Uncle, recognizing in these personages the spiritual parents, who had supplied defects in the treatment of the busy or careless actual parents.

They also gain a wider, if not so deep experience. Those who are not intimately and permanently linked with others, are thrown upon themselves, and, if they do not there find peace and incessant life, there is none to flatter them that they are not very poor and very mean.

A position which so constantly admonishes, may be of inestimable benefit. The person may gain, undistracted by other relationships, a closer communion with the one. Such a use is made of it by saints and sybils. Or she may be one of the lay sisters of charity, a Canoness, bound by an inward vow! Or the useful drudge of all men, the Martha,[8] much sought, little prized! Or the intellectual interpreter of the varied life she sees; the Urania[9] of a half-formed world's twilight.

Or she may combine all these. Not "needing to care that she may please a husband," a frail and limited being, her thoughts may turn to the centre, and she may, by steadfast contemplation entering into the secret of truth and love, use it for the use of all men, instead of a

---

7. Wanderers. In Genesis 21.14–21, Ishmael and his mother, Hagar, Abraham's concubine, are cast out by Abraham after the birth of Isaac, Abraham's legitimate son.
8. In Luke 10.40, she does household chores while her sister sits at Jesus's feet.
9. The Greek muse of astronomy and celestial forces.

chosen few, and interpret through it all the forms of life. It is possible, perhaps, to be at once a priestly servant, and a loving muse.

Saints and geniuses have often chosen a lonely position in the faith that if, undisturbed by the pressure of near ties, they would give themselves up to the inspiring spirit, it would enable them to understand and reproduce life better than actual experience could.

How many old maids take this high stand, we cannot say: it is an unhappy fact, that too many who have come before the eye are gossips rather, and not always good-natured gossips. But if these abuse, and none make the best of their vocation, yet it has not failed to produce some good results. It has been seen by others, if not by themselves, that beings, likely to be left alone, need to be fortified and furnished within themselves, and education and thought have tended more and more to regard these beings as related to absolute Being, as well as to other men. It has been seen that, as the breaking of no bond ought to destroy a man, so ought the missing of none to hinder him from growing. And thus a circumstance of the time, which springs rather from its luxury than its purity, has helped to place women on the true platform.

Perhaps the next generation, looking deeper into this matter, will find that contempt is put upon old maids, or old women at all, merely because they do not use the elixir which would keep them always young. Under its influence a gem brightens yearly which is only seen to more advantage through the fissures Time makes in the casket.[1] No one thinks of Michael Angelo's Persican Sibyl, or St. Theresa, or Tasso's Leonora, or the Greek Electra, as an old maid, more than of Michael Angelo or Canova[2] as old bachelors, though all had reached the period in life's course appointed to take that degree.

See a common woman at forty; scarcely has she the remains of beauty, of any soft poetic grace which gave her attraction as woman, which kindled the hearts of those who looked on her to sparkling thoughts, or diffused round her a roseate air of gentle love. See her, who was, indeed, a lovely girl, in the coarse full-blown dahlia flower of what is commonly called matron-beauty, fat, fair, and forty, showily dressed, and with manners as broad and full as her frill or satin cloak. People observe, "how well she is preserved;" "she is a fine woman still," they say. This woman, whether as a duchess in diamonds, or one of our city dames in mosaics, charms the poet's heart no more, and would look much out of place kneeling before the Madonna. She "does well

1. Appendix, F [Fuller's note].
2. Antonio Canova (1757–1822), Italian sculptor. The Persican Sibyl, the oldest of the Sibyls, was one of the five ancient prophetesses depicted by Michelangelo Buonorati (1475–1564) on the ceiling of the Sistine Chapel. St. Theresa of Ávila (1515–1582), Spanish mystic. Leonora d'Este, patroness of the Italian poet Torquato Tasso, who loved her. In Greek myth, Electra, daughter of Agamemnon and Clytemnestra, helps her brother avenge the murder of their father.

the honors of her house," "leads society," is, in short, always spoken and thought of upholstery-wise.

Or see that care-worn face, from which every soft line is blotted, those faded eyes from which lonely tears have driven the flashes of fancy, the mild white beam of a tender enthusiasm. This woman is not so ornamental to a tea party; yet she would please better, in picture. Yet surely she, no more than the other, looks as a human being should at the end of forty years. Forty years! have they bound those brows with no garland? shed in the lamp no drop of ambrosial oil?

Not so looked the Iphigenia in Aulis.[3] Her forty years had seen her in anguish, in sacrifice, in utter loneliness. But those pains were borne for her father and her country; the sacrifice she had made pure for herself and those around her. Wandering alone at night in the vestal solitude of her imprisoning grove, she has looked up through its "living summits" to the stars, which shed down into her aspect their own lofty melody. At forty she would not misbecome the marble.

Not so looks the Persica.[4] She is withered, she is faded; the drapery that enfolds her has, in its dignity an angularity, too, that tells of age, of sorrow, of a stern composure to the *must*. But her eye, that torch of the soul, is untamed, and in the intensity of her reading, we see a soul invincibly young in faith and hope. Her age is her charm, for it is the night of the Past that gives this beacon fire leave to shine. Wither more and more, black Chrysalid![5] thou dost but give the winged beauty time to mature its splendors.

Not so looked Victoria Colonna,[6] after her life of a great hope, and of true conjugal fidelity. She had been, not merely a bride, but a wife, and each hour had helped to plume the noble bird. A coronet of pearls will not shame her brow; it is white and ample, a worthy altar for love and thought.

Even among the North American Indians, a race of men as completely engaged in mere instinctive life as almost any in the world, and where each chief, keeping many wives as useful servants, of course looks with no kind eye on celibacy in woman, it was excused in the following instance mentioned by Mrs. Jameson.[7] A woman dreamt in youth that she was betrothed to the Sun. She built her a wigwam apart, filled it with emblems of her alliance, and means of an independent life. There

3. Iphigenia, the daughter of Agamemnon and Clytemnestra, after being saved from sacrifice by the virgin goddess Artemis, is taken to the island of Tauris, where she served as priestess to the goddess (see n. 7, p. 31). The story is told in the plays *Iphigenia in Aulis* and *Iphigenia in Tauris* by Euripedes (c. 484–406 B.C.).
4. Or Persican Sibyl (see n. 2, p. 58).
5. The pupa or cacoon stage of a butterfly.
6. Vittoria Colonna (1492–1547), Italian poet, wrote over a hundred sonnets commemorating her husband after his death.
7. Anna Brownell Jameson (1794–1860), Irish-born English essayist, critic, and travel writer, tells the story of this Chippewa woman in *Winter Studies and Summer Rambles in Canada* (1838).

she passed her days, sustained by her own exertions, and true to her supposed engagement.

In any tribe, we believe, a woman, who lived as if she was betrothed to the Sun, would be tolerated, and the rays which made her youth blossom sweetly, would crown her with a halo in age.

There is, on this subject, a nobler view than heretofore, if not the noblest, and improvement here must coincide with that in the view taken of marriage.

We must have units before we can have union, says one of the ripe thinkers of the times.

If larger intellectual resources begin to be deemed needful to woman, still more is a spiritual dignity in her, or even the mere assumption of it, looked upon with respect. Joanna Southcote and Mother Anne Lee are sure of a band of disciples; Ecstatica, Dolorosa,[8] of enraptured believers who will visit them in their lowly huts, and wait for days to revere them in their trances. The foreign noble traverses land and sea to hear a few words from the lips of the lowly peasant girl, whom he believes especially visited by the Most High. Very beautiful, in this way, was the influence of the invalid of St. Petersburg, as described by De Maistre.[9]

Mysticism, which may be defined as the brooding soul of the world, cannot fail of its oracular promise as to woman. "The mothers"—"The mother of all things," are expressions of thought which lead the mind towards this side of universal growth. Whenever a mystical whisper was heard, from Behmen down to St. Simon,[1] sprang up the thought, that, if it be true, as the legend says, that humanity withers through a fault committed by and a curse laid upon woman, through her pure child, or influence, shall the new Adam, the redemption, arise. Innocence is to be replaced by virtue, dependence by a willing submission, in the heart of the Virgin Mother of the new race.

The spiritual tendency is towards the elevation of woman, but the intellectual by itself is not so. Plato sometimes seems penetrated by that high idea of love, which considers man and woman as the two-fold expression of one thought. This the angel of Swedenborg, the angel of the coming age, cannot surpass, but only explain more fully. But then again Plato, the man of intellect, treats woman in the Republic as property, and, in the Timæus, says that man, if he misuse the privileges of one life, shall be degraded into the form of woman, and then, if he

8. Ecstatica and Dolorosa are female types of religious ecstacy and grief. The Virgin Mary, as she weeps over the body of Christ, is often called Dolorosa. Joanna Southcott (1750–1814), English prophetic writer and religious leader, predicted she would give birth to the second Christ. Mother Anne Lee (1736–1784), English religious leader and co-founder of the American Shaker movement, saw Christ's Second Coming embodied within her.
9. Joseph de Maistre (1754–1821), French philosopher and mystic, author of *Soirées de St. Petersbourg*.
1. Claude-Henri de Rouvroy, comte de Saint-Simon (1760–1825), French socialist and religious thinker. Jakob Boehme (1575–1624), German mystic.

do not redeem himself, into that of a bird. This, as I said above, expresses most happily how anti-poetical is this state of mind. For the poet, contemplating the world of things, selects various birds as the symbols of his most gracious and ethereal thoughts, just as he calls upon his genius, as muse, rather than as God. But the intellect, cold, is ever more masculine than feminine; warmed by emotion, it rushes towards mother earth, and puts on the forms of beauty.

The electrical, the magnetic element in woman has not been fairly brought out at any period. Every thing might be expected from it; she has far more of it than man. This is commonly expressed by saying that her intuitions are more rapid and more correct. You will often see men of high intellect absolutely stupid in regard to the atmospheric changes, the fine invisible links which connect the forms of life around them, while common women, if pure and modest, so that a vulgar self do not overshadow the mental eye, will seize and delineate these with unerring discrimination.

Women who combine this organization with creative genius, are very commonly unhappy at present. They see too much to act in conformity with those around them, and their quick impulses seem folly to those who do not discern the motives. This is an usual effect of the apparition of genius, whether in man or woman, but is more frequent with regard to the latter, because a harmony, an obvious order and self-restraining decorum, is most expected from her.

Then women of genius, even more than men, are likely to be enslaved by an impassioned sensibility. The world repels them more rudely, and they are of weaker bodily frame.

Those, who seem overladen with electricity, frighten those around them. "When she merely enters the room, I am what the French call *herissé*,"[2] said a man of petty feelings and worldly character of such a woman, whose depth of eye and powerful motion announced the conductor of the mysterious fluid.

Wo to such a woman who finds herself linked to such a man in bonds too close. It is the cruellest of errors. He will detest her with all the bitterness of wounded self-love. He will take the whole prejudice of manhood upon himself, and to the utmost of his power imprison and torture her by its imperious rigors.

Yet, allow room enough, and the electric fluid will be found to invigorate and embellish, not destroy life. Such women are the great actresses, the songsters. Such traits we read in a late searching, though too French analysis of the character of Mademoiselle Rachel, by a modern La Rochefoucoult.[3] The Greeks thus represent the muses; they

2. Defensive or ruffled.
3. François, Duc de la Rochefoucauld (1613–1680), French writer, known for his moral maxims. The "modern La Rochefoucoult" is unidentified. Mademoiselle Rachel (1820–1858), famous French actress, known for her highly emotional performances.

have not the golden serenity of Apollo; they are *over*-flowed with thought; there is something tragic in their air. Such are the Sibyls of Guercino,[4] the eye is over-full of expression, dilated and lustrous; it seems to have drawn the whole being into it.

Sickness is the frequent result of this over-charged existence. To this region, however misunderstood, or interpreted with presumptuous carelessness, belong the phenomena of magnetism, or mesmerism, as it is now often called, where the trance of the Ecstatica purports to be produced by the agency of one human being on another, instead of, as in her case, direct from the spirit.

The worldling has his sneer at this as at the services of religion. "The churches can always be filled with women." "Show me a man in one of your magnetic states, and I will believe."

Women are, indeed, the easy victims both of priest-craft and self-delusion, but this would not be, if the intellect was developed in proportion to the other powers. They would, then, have a regulator, and be more in equipoise, yet must retain the same nervous susceptibility, while their physical structure is such as it is.

It is with just that hope, that we welcome every thing that tends to strengthen the fibre and develope the nature on more sides. When the intellect and affections are in harmony; when intellectual consciousness is calm and deep; inspiration will not be confounded with fancy.

> Then, "she who advances
>   With rapturous, lyrical glances,
> Singing the song of the earth, singing
>   Its hymn to the Gods,"[5]

will not be pitied, as a madwoman, nor shrunk from as unnatural.

The Greeks, who saw every thing in forms, which we are trying to ascertain as law, and classify as cause, embodied all this in the form of Cassandra. Cassandra was only unfortunate in receiving her gift too soon. The remarks, however, that the world still makes in such cases, are well expressed by the Greek dramatist.

In the Trojan Dames, there are fine touches of nature with regard to Cassandra. Hecuba[6] shows that mixture of shame and reverence that prosaic kindred always do towards the inspired child, the poet, the elected sufferer for the race.

When the herald announces that Cassandra is chosen to be the mistress of Agamemnon, Hecuba answers, with indignation, betraying the pride and faith she involuntarily felt in this daughter.

4. I.e., Giovanni Francesco Barbieri (1591–1666), Italian painter.
5. Source unidentified.
6. In Euripedes's drama *The Trojan Women* (415 B.C.), Troy has been conquered by the Greeks; Hecuba, queen of Troy, is to become a Greek slave; and her daughter, Cassandra, a holy virgin, is to become the mistress of King Agamemnon, leader of the Greeks.

Hec. 'The maiden of Phoebus, to whom the golden haired
    Gave as a privilege a virgin life!
Tal. Love of the inspired maiden hath pierced him.
Hec. Then cast away, my child, the sacred keys, and from thy person
    The consecrated garlands which thou wearest.'

Yet, when a moment after, Cassandra appears, singing, wildly, her
inspired song, Hecuba calls her, "My *frantic* child."
Yet how graceful she is in her tragic *raptus*,[7] the chorus shows.

    Chor. 'How sweetly at thy house's ills thou smil'st,
        Chanting what, haply, thou wilt not show true.'

If Hecuba dares not trust her highest instinct about her daughter,
still less can the vulgar mind of the herald Talthybius, a man not without feeling, but with no princely, no poetic blood, abide the wild prophetic mood which insults all his prejudices.

    Tal. 'The venerable, and that accounted wise,
        Is nothing better than that of no repute,
        For the greatest king of all the Greeks,
        The dear son of Atreus, is possessed with the love
        Of this madwoman. I, indeed, am poor,
        Yet, I would not receive her to my bed.'

The royal Agamemnon could see the beauty of Cassandra, HE was
not afraid of her prophetic gifts.
The best topic for a chapter on this subject in the present day, would
be the history of the Seeress of Prevorst, the best observed subject of
magnetism in our present times, and who, like her ancestresses of
Delphos, was roused to ecstacy or phrenzy by the touch of the laurel.[8]
I observe in her case, and in one known to me here, that, what might
have been a gradual and gentle disclosure of remarkable powers, was
broken and jarred into disease by an unsuitable marriage. Both these
persons were unfortunate in not understanding what was involved in
this relation, but acted ignorantly as their friends desired. They thought
that this was the inevitable destiny of woman. But when engaged in
the false position, it was impossible for them to endure its dissonances,
as those of less delicate perceptions can, and the fine flow of life was
checked and sullied. They grew sick, but, even so, learnt and disclosed
more than those in health are wont to do.
In such cases, worldlings sneer, but reverent men learn wondrous
news, either from the person observed, or by thoughts caused in them-

---

7. Rapture, mystical trance.
8. The oracle at Delphi was the most famous in ancient Greece; the prophetess chewed laurel
   leaves during her trance. The Seeress of Prevorst was Friederike Hauffe (1801–1827), a young
   woman from the rural German hamlet of Prevorst, who at age nineteen sank into a depression
   and began to experience prophetic dreams and trances as her body wasted away from a
   mysterious illness. Fuller discusses the Seeress at length in chapter 5 of *Summer on the Lakes.*

selves by the observation. Fenelon learns from Guyon, Kerner, from his Seeress,[9] what we fain would know. But to appreciate such disclosures one must be a child, and here the phrase, "women and children" may, perhaps, be interpreted aright, that only little children shall enter into the kingdom of heaven.

All these motions of the time, tides that betoken a waxing moon, overflow upon our land. The world, at large, is readier to let woman learn and manifest the capacities of her nature than it ever was before, and here is a less encumbered field and freer air than any where else. And it ought to be so; we ought to pay for Isabella's jewels.[1]

The names of nations are feminine—religion, virtue, and victory are feminine. To those who have a superstition, as to outward reigns, it is not without significance that the name of the queen of our motherland should at this crisis be Victoria—Victoria the First. Perhaps to us it may be given to disclose the era thus outwardly presaged.

Another Isabella[2] too at this time ascends the throne. Might she open a new world to her sex! But, probably, these poor little women are, least of any, educated to serve as examples or inspirers for the rest. The Spanish queen is younger; we know of her that she sprained her foot the other day, dancing in her private apartments; of Victoria, that she reads aloud, in a distinct voice and agreeable manner, her addresses to parliament on certain solemn days, and, yearly, that she presents to the nation some new prop of royalty. These ladies have, very likely, been trained more completely to the puppet life than any other. The queens, who have been queens indeed, were trained by adverse circumstances to know the world around them and their own powers.

It is moving, while amusing, to read of the Scottish peasant measuring the print left by the queen's foot as she walks, and priding himself on its beauty. It is so natural to wish to find what is fair and precious in high places, so astonishing to find the Bourbon a glutton, or the Guelpha[3] a dullard or gossip.

In our own country, women are, in many respects, better situated than men. Good books are allowed, with more time to read them. They are not so early forced into the bustle of life, nor so weighed down by demands for outward success. The perpetual changes, incident to our society, make the blood circulate freely through the body politic, and,

9. Justinus Kerner (1786–1862) was Friederike Hauffe's German physician; his *Die Seherin von Prevorst* (The seeress of Prevorst) (1829) details her illness. François Fénélon (1651–1715), French theologian, defended the activities of Jeanne-Marie Guyon (1648–1717), religious mystic and founder of the controversial doctrine of quietism, passive contemplation of divine things.
1. Isabella I supposedly sold her jewels to help finance Christopher Columbus's famous expedition (see also n. 5, p. 37).
2. Isabella II (1830–1904), queen of Spain from 1843 to 1870.
3. The Guelphs were a German dynasty of the Middle Ages who eventually became the dukes of Bavaria and Saxony. The Bourbons were the French royal family.

if not favorable at present to the grace and bloom of life, they are so to activity, resource, and would be to reflection, but for a low materialist tendency, from which the women are generally exempt in themselves, though its existence, among the men, has a tendency to repress their impulses and make them doubt their instincts, thus, often, paralyzing their action during the best years.

But they have time to think, and no traditions chain them, and few conventionalities compared with what must be met in other nations. There is no reason why they should not discover that the secrets of nature are open, the revelations of the spirit waiting for whoever will seek them. When the mind is once awakened to this consciousness, it will not be restrained by the habits of the past, but fly to seek the seeds of a heavenly future.

Their employments are more favorable to meditation than those of men.

Woman is not addressed religiously here, more than elsewhere. She is told she should be worthy to be the mother of a Washington, or the companion of some good man. But in many, many instances, she has already learnt that all bribes have the same flaw; that truth and good are to be sought solely for their own sakes. And, already, an ideal sweetness floats over many forms, shines in many eyes.

Already deep questions are put by young girls on the great theme: What shall I do to enter upon the eternal life?[4]

Men are very courteous to them. They praise them often, check them seldom. There is chivalry in the feeling towards "the ladies," which gives them the best seats in the stage-coach, frequent admission, not only to lectures of all sorts, but to courts of justice, halls of legislature, reform conventions. The newspaper editor "would be better pleased that the Lady's Book[5] should be filled up exclusively by ladies. It would then, indeed, be a true gem, worthy to be presented by young men to the mistresses of their affections." Can gallantry go further?

In this country is venerated, wherever seen, the character which Goethe spoke of an Ideal, which he saw actualized in his friend and patroness, the Grand Duchess Amelia. "The excellent woman is she, who, if the husband dies, can be a father to the children." And this, if read aright, tells a great deal.

Women who speak in public, if they have a moral power, such as has been felt from Angelina Grimke and Abby Kelly;[6] that is, if they speak for conscience' sake, to serve a cause which they hold sacred,

---

4. In Matthew 19.16, a young man asks Jesus, "Good Master, what good thing shall I do, that I may have eternal life?"
5. Godey's Lady's Book, a popular magazine of the period.
6. Abbey Kelley (1811–1887), Quaker abolitionist and women's rights lecturer. Grimké (1805–1879), essayist and abolitionist, whose An Appeal to the Women of the Nominally Free States (1837) makes the connection between women and slaves.

invariably subdue the prejudices of their hearers, and excite an interest proportionate to the aversion with which it had been the purpose to regard them.

A passage in a private letter so happily illustrates this, that it must be inserted here.

Abby Kelly in the Town-House of _____.

"The scene was not unheroic—to see that woman, true to humanity and her own nature, a centre of rude eyes and tongues, even gentlemen feeling licensed to make part of a species of mob around a female out of her sphere. As she took her seat in the desk amid the great noise, and in the throng, full, like a wave, of something to ensue, I saw her humanity in a gentleness and unpretension, tenderly open to the sphere around her, and, had she not been supported by the power of the will of genuineness and principle, she would have failed. It led her to prayer, which, in woman especially, is childlike; sensibility and will going to the side of God and looking up to him; and humanity was poured out in aspiration.

"She acted like a gentle hero, with her mild decision and womanly calmness. All heroism is mild and quiet and gentle, for it is life and possession, and combativeness and firmness show a want of actualness. She is as earnest, fresh, and simple as when she first entered the crusade. I think she did much good, more than the men in her place could do, for woman feels more as being and reproducing, this brings the subject more into home relations. Men speak through, and mostly from intellect, and this addresses itself in others, which creates and is combative."

Not easily shall we find elsewhere, or before this time, any written observations on the same subject, so delicate and profound.

The late Dr. Channing,[7] whose enlarged and tender and religious nature, shared every onward impulse of his time, though his thoughts followed his wishes with a deliberative caution, which belonged to his habits and temperament, was greatly interested in these expectations for women. His own treatment of them was absolutely and thoroughly religious. He regarded them as souls, each of which had a destiny of its own, incalculable to other minds, and whose leading it must follow, guided by the light of a private conscience. He had sentiment, delicacy, kindness, taste; but they were all pervaded and ruled by this one thought, that all beings had souls, and must vindicate their own inheritance. Thus all beings were treated by him with an equal, and sweet, though solemn, courtesy. The young and unknown, the woman and the child, all felt themselves regarded with an infinite expectation, from which there was no reaction to vulgar prejudice. He demanded of all he met, to use his favorite phrase, "great truths."

7. William Ellery Channing (1780–1842), liberal Unitarian minister whose progressive ideas inspired Fuller and her circle of friends.

His memory, every way dear and reverend, is, by many, especially cherished for this intercourse of unbroken respect.

At one time, when the progress of Harriet Martineau[8] through this country, Angelina Grimke's appearance in public, and the visit of Mrs. Jameson had turned his thoughts to this subject, he expressed high hopes as to what the coming era would bring to woman. He had been much pleased with the dignified courage of Mrs. Jameson in taking up the defence of her sex, in a way from which women usually shrink, because, if they express themselves on such subjects with sufficient force and clearness to do any good, they are exposed to assaults whose vulgarity makes them painful. In intercourse with such a woman, he had shared her indignation at the base injustice, in many respects, and in many regions, done to the sex; and been led to think of it far more than ever before. He seemed to think that he might some time write upon the subject. That his aid is withdrawn from the cause is a subject of great regret, for, on this question as on others, he would have known how to sum up the evidence and take, in the noblest spirit, middle ground. He always furnished a platform on which opposing parties could stand, and look at one another under the influence of his mildness and enlightened candor.

Two younger thinkers, men both, have uttered noble prophecies, auspicious for woman. Kinmont,[9] all whose thoughts tended towards the establishment of the reign of love and peace, thought that the inevitable means of this would be an increased predominance given to the idea of woman. Had he lived longer, to see the growth of the peace party, the reforms in life and medical practice which seek to substitute water for wine and drugs, pulse for animal food, he would have been confirmed in his view of the way in which the desired changes are to be effected.

In this connection, I must mention Shelley,[1] who, like all men of genius, shared the feminine development, and, unlike many, knew it. His life was one of the first pulse-beats in the present reform-growth. He, too, abhorred blood and heat, and, by his system and his song, tended to reinstate a plant-like gentleness in the development of energy. In harmony with this, his ideas of marriage were lofty, and, of course, no less so of woman, her nature, and destiny.

For woman, if, by a sympathy as to outward condition she is led to aid the enfranchisement of the slave, must be no less so, by inward tendency, to favor measures which promise to bring the world more

8. Harriet Martineau (1802–1876), English travel writer, toured the United States in 1835 and wrote *Society in America* (1837).
9. Alexander Kinmont (1799–1838), Scottish educator, came to America in 1823 and established Kinmont's Academy of Classics and Mathematics in Cincinnati. His *Twelve Lectures on the Natural History of Man, and the Rise and Progress of Philosophy* (1839) was published after his death to aid his family.
1. Percy Bysshe Shelley (1792–1822), English Romantic poet.

thoroughly and deeply into harmony with her nature. When the lamb takes place of the lion as the emblem of nations, both women and men will be as children of one spirit, perpetual learners of the word and doers thereof, not hearers only.

A writer in the New-York Pathfinder, in two articles headed "Femality,"[2] has uttered a still more pregnant word than any we have named. He views woman truly from the soul, and not from society, and the depth and leading of his thoughts are proportionably remarkable. He views the feminine nature as a harmonizer of the vehement elements, and this has often been hinted elsewhere; but what he expresses most forcibly is the lyrical, the inspiring, and inspired apprehensiveness of her being.

This view being identical with what I have before attempted to indicate, as to her superior susceptibility to magnetic or electric influence, I will now try to express myself more fully.

There are two aspects of woman's nature, represented by the ancients as Muse and Minerva.[3] It is the former to which the writer in the Pathfinder looks. It is the latter which Wordsworth has in mind, when he says—

"With a placid brow,
Which woman ne'er should forfeit, keep thy vow."[4]

The especial genius of woman I believe to be electrical in movement, intuitive in function, spiritual in tendency. She excels not so easily in classification, or re-creation, as in an instinctive seizure of causes, and a simple breathing out of what she receives that has the singleness of life, rather than the selecting and energizing of art.

More native is it to her to be the living model of the artist than to set apart from herself any one form in objective reality; more native to inspire and receive the poem, than to create it. In so far as soul is in her completely developed, all soul is the same; but as far as it is modified in her as woman, it flows, it breathes, it sings, rather than deposits soil, or finishes work, and that which is especially feminine flushes, in blossom, the face of earth, and pervades, like air and water, all this seeming solid globe, daily renewing and purifying its life. Such may be the especially feminine element, spoken of as Femality. But it is no more the order of nature that it should be incarnated pure in any form, than that the masculine energy should exist unmingled with it in any form.

Male and female represent the two sides of the great radical dualism. But, in fact, they are perpetually passing into one another. Fluid hard-

2. By "V.," *Pathfinder*, Mar. 18, 1843, pp. 35–36, 51–52.
3. The goddess of wisdom.
4. Altered from "Liberty" (1835) by William Wordsworth.

ens to solid, solid rushes to fluid. There is no wholly masculine man, no purely feminine woman.

History jeers at the attempts of physiologists to bind great original laws by the forms which flow from them. They make a rule; they say from observation, what can and cannot be. In vain! Nature provides exceptions to every rule. She sends women to battle, and sets Hercules spinning;[5] she enables women to bear immense burdens, cold, and frost; she enables the man, who feels maternal love, to nourish his infant like a mother. Of late she plays still gayer pranks. Not only she deprives organizations, but organs, of a necessary end. She enables people to read with the top of the head, and see with the pit of the stomach. Presently she will make a female Newton, and a male Syren.[6]

Man partakes of the feminine in the Apollo, woman of the masculine as Minerva.

What I mean by the Muse is the unimpeded clearness of the intuitive powers which a perfectly truthful adherence to every admonition of the higher instincts would bring to a finely organized human being. It may appear as prophecy or as poesy. It enabled Cassandra to foresee the results of actions passing round her; the Seeress to behold the true character of the person through the mask of his customary life. (Sometimes she saw a feminine form behind the man, sometimes the reverse.) It enabled the daughter of Linnæus to see the soul of the flower exhaling from the flower.[7] It gave a man, but a poet man, the power of which he thus speaks: "Often in my contemplation of nature, radiant intimations, and as it were sheaves of light appear before me as to the facts of cosmogony in which my mind has, perhaps, taken especial part." He wisely adds, "but it is necessary with earnestness to verify the knowledge we gain by these flashes of light." And none should forget this. Sight must be verified by life before it can deserve the honors of piety and genius. Yet sight comes first, and of this sight of the world of causes, this approximation to the region of primitive motions, women I hold to be especially capable. Even without equal freedom with the other sex, they have already shown themselves so, and should these faculties have free play, I believe they will open new, deeper and purer sources of joyous inspiration than have as yet refreshed the earth.

Let us be wise and not impede the soul. Let her work as she will. Let us have one creative energy, one incessant revelation. Let it take what form it will, and let us not bind it by the past to man or woman,

5. In Greek myth, Hercules fell in love with Omphale, queen of Lydia, and led a submissive life spinning wool; she wore his lion's skin, and he dressed as a woman.
6. See n. 7, p. 12. Sir Isaac Newton (1642–1727), English mathematician.
7. The daughter of Linnaeus states, that, while looking steadfastly at the red lily, she saw its spirit hovering above it, as a red flame. It is true, this, like many fair spirit-stories, may be explained away as an optical illusion, but its poetic beauty and meaning would, even then, make it valuable, as an illustration of the spiritual fact [Fuller's note]. Carolus Linnaeus (later von Linné) (1707–1778), Swedish botanist who founded the scientific system of plant and animal classification.

black or white. Jove sprang from Rhea, Pallas[8] from Jove. So let it be.

If it has been the tendency of these remarks to call woman rather to the Minerva side,—if I, unlike the more generous writer, have spoken from society no less than the soul,—let it be pardoned! It is love that has caused this, love for many incarcerated souls, that might be freed, could the idea of religious self-dependence be established in them, could the weakening habit of dependence on others be broken up.

Proclus[9] teaches that every life has, in its sphere, a totality or wholeness of the animating powers of the other spheres; having only, as its own characteristic, a predominance of some one power. Thus Jupiter comprises, within himself, the other twelve powers, which stand thus: The first triad is *demiurgic or fabricative*, i.e., Jupiter, Neptune, Vulcan; the second, *defensive*, Vesta, Minerva, Mars; the third, *vivific*, Ceres, Juno, Diana; and the fourth, Mercury, Venus, Apollo, *elevating and harmonic*. In the sphere of Jupiter, energy is predominant—with Venus, beauty; but each comprehends and apprehends all the others.

When the same community of life and consciousness of mind begins among men, humanity will have, positively and finally, subjugated its brute elements and Titanic childhood; criticism will have perished; arbitrary limits and ignorant censure be impossible; all will have entered upon the liberty of law, and the harmony of common growth.

Then Apollo will sing to his lyre what Vulcan forges on the anvil, and the Muse weave anew the tapestries of Minerva.

It is, therefore, only in the present crisis that the preference is given to Minerva. The power of continence must establish the legitimacy of freedom, the power of self-poise the perfection of motion.

Every relation, every gradation of nature is incalculably precious, but only to the soul which is poised upon itself, and to whom no loss, no change, can bring dull discord, for it is in harmony with the central soul.

If any individual live too much in relations, so that he becomes a stranger to the resources of his own nature, he falls, after a while, into a distraction, or imbecility, from which he can only be cured by a time of isolation, which gives the renovating fountains time to rise up. With a society it is the same. Many minds, deprived of the traditionary or instinctive means of passing a cheerful existence, must find help in self-impulse, or perish. It is therefore that, while any elevation, in the view of union, is to be hailed with joy, we shall not decline celibacy as the great fact of the time. It is one from which no vow, no arrangement, can at present save a thinking mind. For now the rowers are pausing on their oars; they wait a change before they can pull together. All

---

8. Greek goddess (also known as Athena and Minerva), who was born from the head of her father, Jove (also known as Zeus and Jupiter), who was the supreme god.
9. Greek Neoplatonist philosopher (c. 412–485).

tends to illustrate the thought of a wise cotemporary.[1] Union is only possible to those who are units. To be fit for relations in time, souls, whether of man or woman, must be able to do without them in the spirit.

It is therefore that I would have woman lay aside all thought, such as she habitually cherishes, of being taught and led by men. I would have her, like the Indian girl, dedicate herself to the Sun, the Sun of Truth, and go no where if his beams did not make clear the path. I would have her free from compromise, from complaisance, from help-lessness, because I would have her good enough and strong enough to love one and all beings, from the fulness, not the poverty of being.

Men, as at present instructed, will not help this work, because they also are under the slavery of habit. I have seen with delight their poetic impulses. A sister is the fairest ideal, and how nobly Wordsworth, and even Byron,[2] have written of a sister.

There is no sweeter sight than to see a father with his little daughter. Very vulgar men become refined to the eye when leading a little girl by the hand. At that moment the right relation between the sexes seems established, and you feel as if the man would aid in the noblest purpose, if you ask him in behalf of his little daughter. Once two fine figures stood before me, thus. The father of very intellectual aspect, his falcon eye softened by affection as he looked down on his fair child, she the image of himself, only more graceful and brilliant in expression. I was reminded of Southey's Kehama;[3] when lo, the dream was rudely bro-ken. They were talking of education, and he said,

"I shall not have Maria brought too forward. If she knows too much, she will never find a husband; superior women hardly ever can."

"Surely," said his wife, with a blush, "you wish Maria to be as good and wise as she can, whether it will help her to marriage or not."

"No," he persisted, "I want her to have a sphere and a home, and some one to protect her when I am gone."

It was a trifling incident, but made a deep impression. I felt that the holiest relations fail to instruct the unprepared and perverted mind. If this man, indeed, could have looked at it on the other side, he was the last that would have been willing to have been taken himself for the home and protection he could give, but would have been much more likely to repeat the tale of Alcibiades[4] with his phials.

1. Or contemporary; probably Fuller's friend Ralph Waldo Emerson (1803–1882), the transcen-dentalist philosopher whose essay "Friendship" (1844) expresses these thoughts.
2. Byron wrote the poem "Epistle to Augusta" to his half-sister, Augusta Leigh (1783–1851). Wordsworth addressed several poems to his sister, Dorothy Wordsworth (1771–1855), includ-ing "To My Sister" and "Tintern Abbey."
3. The Curse of Kehama (1810), an epic poem by the English poet Robert Southey (1774–1843), features a humble and patient peasant who protects his daughter from various dangers that threaten her.
4. An Athenian politician and general (c. 450–404 B.C.), who stole the gold and silver cups, or phials, of his admirer, Anytus.

But men do *not* look at both sides, and women must leave off asking them and being influenced by them, but retire within themselves, and explore the groundwork of life till they find their peculiar secret. Then, when they come forth again, renovated and baptized, they will know how to turn all dross to gold, and will be rich and free though they live in a hut, tranquil, if in a crowd. Then their sweet singing shall not be from passionate impulse, but the lyrical overflow of a divine rapture, and a new music shall be evolved from this many-chorded world.

Grant her, then, for a while, the armor and the javelin. Let her put from her the press of other minds and meditate in virgin loneliness. The same idea shall re-appear in due time as Muse, or Ceres,[5] the all-kindly patient Earth-Spirit.

Among the throng of symptoms which denote the present tendency to a crisis in the life of woman, which resembles the change from girlhood with its beautiful instincts, but unharmonized thoughts, its blind pupilage and restless seeking, to self-possessed, wise, and graceful womanhood, I have attempted to select a few.

One of prominent interest is the unison of three male minds, upon the subject, which, for width of culture, power of self-concentration and dignity of aim, take rank as the prophets of the coming age, while their histories and labors are rooted in the past.

Swedenborg came, he tells us, to interpret the past revelation and unfold a new. He announces the new church that is to prepare the way for the New Jerusalem, a city built of precious stones, hardened and purified by secret processes in the veins of earth through the ages.

Swedenborg approximated to that harmony between the scientific and poetic lives of mind, which we hope from the perfected man. The links that bind together the realms of nature, the mysteries that accompany her births and growths, were unusually plain to him. He seems a man to whom insight was given at a period when the mental frame was sufficiently matured to retain and express its gifts.

His views of woman are, in the main, satisfactory. In some details, we may object to them as, in all his system, there are still remains of what is arbitrary and seemingly groundless; fancies that show the marks of old habits, and a nature yet not thoroughly leavened with the spiritual leaven. At least so it seems to me now. I speak reverently, for I find such reason to venerate Swedenborg, from an imperfect knowledge of his mind, that I feel one more perfect might explain to me much that does not now secure my sympathy.

His idea of woman is sufficiently large and noble to interpose no obstacle to her progress. His idea of marriage is consequently sufficient.

---

5. Roman goddess of agriculture.

Man and woman share an angelic ministry, the union is from one to one, permanent and pure.

As the New Church extends its ranks, the needs of woman must be more considered.

Quakerism[6] also establishes woman on a sufficient equality with man. But though the original thought of Quakerism is pure, its scope is too narrow, and its influence, having established a certain amount of good and made clear some truth, must, by degrees, be merged in one of wider range.[7] The mind of Swedenborg appeals to the various nature of man and allows room for æsthetic culture and the free expression of energy.

As apostle of the new order, of the social fabric that is to rise from love, and supersede the old that was based on strife, Charles Fourier[8] comes next, expressing, in an outward order, many facts of which Swedenborg saw the secret springs. The mind of Fourier, though grand and clear, was, in some respects, superficial. He was a stranger to the highest experiences. His eye was fixed on the outward more than the inward needs of man. Yet he, too, was a seer of the divine order, in its musical expression, if not in its poetic soul. He has filled one department of instruction for the new era, and the harmony in action, and freedom for individual growth he hopes shall exist; and if the methods he proposes should not prove the true ones, yet his fair propositions shall give many hints, and make room for the inspiration needed for such.

He, too, places woman on an entire equality with man, and wishes to give to one as to the other that independence which must result from intellectual and practical development.

Those who will consult him for no other reason, might do so to see how the energies of woman may be made available in the pecuniary way. The object of Fourier was to give her the needed means of self help, that she might dignify and unfold her life for her own happiness, and that of society. The many, now, who see their daughters liable to destitution, or vice to escape from it, may be interested to examine the means, if they have not yet soul enough to appreciate the ends he proposes.

On the opposite side of the advancing army, leads the great apostle of individual culture, Goethe. Swedenborg makes organization and union the necessary results of solitary thought. Fourier, whose nature was, above all, constructive, looked to them too exclusively. Better institutions, he thought, will make better men. Goethe expressed, in every

6. The Quakers, or the Religious Society of Friends, originated in England in the seventeenth century under the leadership of George Fox (1624–1691).
7. In worship at stated periods, in daily expression, whether by word or deed, the Quakers have placed woman on the same platform with man. Can any one assert that they have reason to repent this? [Fuller's note].
8. French philosopher and socialist (1772–1837), whose writings inspired a number of utopian communities, including Brook Farm (1841–1847) at West Roxbury, Massachusetts.

way, the other side. If one man could present better forms, the rest could not use them till ripe for them.

Fourier says, As the institutions, so the men! All follies are excusable and natural under bad institutions.

Goethe thinks, As the man, so the institutions! There is no excuse for ignorance and folly. A man can grow in any place, if he will.

Ay! but Goethe, bad institutions are prison walls and impure air that make him stupid, so that he does not will.

And thou, Fourier, do not expect to change mankind at once, or even "in three generations" by arrangement of groups and series, or flourish of trumpets for attractive industry.[9] If these attempts are made by unready men, they will fail.

Yet we prize the theory of Fourier no less than the profound suggestion of Goethe. Both are educating the age to a clearer consciousness of what man needs, what man can be, and better life must ensue.

Goethe, proceeding on his own track, elevating the human being in the most imperfect states of society, by continual efforts at self-culture, takes as good care of women as of men. His mother, the bold, gay Frau Aja, with such playful freedom of nature; the wise and gentle maiden, known in his youth, over whose sickly solitude "the Holy Ghost brooded as a dove;" his sister, the intellectual woman *par excellence*: the Duchess Amelia; Lili,[1] who combined the character of the woman of the world with the lyrical sweetness of the shepherdess, on whose chaste and noble breast flowers and gems were equally at home; all these had supplied abundant suggestions to his mind, as to the wants and the possible excellencies of woman. And, from his poetic soul, grew up forms new and more admirable than life has yet produced, for whom his clear eye marked out paths in the future.

In Faust, we see the redeeming power, which, at present, upholds woman, while waiting for a better day, in Margaret.[2] The lovely little girl, pure in instinct, ignorant in mind, is misled and profaned by man abusing her confidence.[3] To the Mater *Dolorosa*[4] she appeals for aid. It is given to the soul, if not against outward sorrow; and the maiden, enlightened by her sufferings, refusing to receive temporal salvation by the aid of an evil power, obtains the eternal in its stead.

In the second part, the intellectual man, after all his manifold strivings, owes to the interposition of her whom he had betrayed *his* sal-

---

9. One of Fourier's ideas was that each laborer should choose his or her own work and thus engage in industry found attractive.
1. Goethe was briefly engaged to Lili Schöneman in 1775.
2. In Goethe's verse drama *Faust* (1808), Margaret personifies innocence and love. At the instigation of the Devil, Faust seduces her, bringing about her miserable death.
3. As Faust says, her only fault was a "Kindly delusion,"—"ein guter wahn" [Fuller's note].
4. The Virgin Mary, Mother of Sorrows.

vation. She intercedes, this time herself a glorified spirit, with the Mater Gloriosa.[5]

Leonora,[6] too, is woman, as we see her now, pure, thoughtful, refined by much acquaintance with grief.

Iphigenia[7] he speaks of in his journals as his "daughter," and she is the daughter[8] whom a man will wish, even if he has chosen his wife from very mean motives. She is the virgin, steadfast soul, to whom falsehood is more dreadful than any other death.

But it is to Wilhelm Meister's Apprenticeship and Wandering Years that I would especially refer, as these volumes contain the sum of the Sage's observations during a long life, as to what man should do, under present circumstances, to obtain mastery over outward, through an initiation into inward life, and severe discipline of faculty.

As Wilhelm advances in the upward path he becomes acquainted with better forms of woman by knowing how to seek, and how to prize them when found. For the weak and immature man will, often, admire a superior woman, but he will not be able to abide by a feeling, which is too severe a tax on his habitual existence. But, with Wilhelm, the gradation is natural and expresses ascent in the scale of being. At first he finds charm in Mariana and Philina, very common forms of feminine character, not without redeeming traits, no less than charms, but without wisdom or purity. Soon he is attended by Mignon, the finest expression ever yet given to what I have called the lyrical element in woman. She is a child, but too full-grown for this man; he loves, but cannot follow her; yet is the association not without an enduring influence. Poesy has been domesticated in his life, and, though he strives to bind down her heavenward impulse, as art or apothegm, these are only the tents, beneath which he may sojourn for a while, but which may be easily struck, and carried on limitless wanderings.

Advancing into the region of thought, he encounters a wise philanthropy in Natalia, (instructed, let us observe, by an *uncle*,) practical judgment and the outward economy of life in Theresa, pure devotion in the Fair Saint.

Farther and last he comes to the house of Macaria, the soul of a star,

---

5. The Virgin Mary, Mother of Glory.
6. The beloved of Tasso in Goethe's play *Torquato Tasso* (1790).
7. Appears in Goethe's verse drama *Iphigenia auf Tauris* (1787). See also n. 3, p. 59.
8. Goethe was as false to his ideas in practice, as Lord Herbert. And his punishment was the just and usual one of connections formed beneath the standard of right, from the impulses of the baser self. Iphigenia was the worthy daughter of his mind, but the son, child of his degrading connection in actual life, corresponded with that connection. This son, on whom Goethe vainly lavished so much thought and care, was like his mother, and like Goethe's attachment for his mother. "This young man," says a late well informed writer, (M. Henri Blaze,) "Wieland, with good reason, called the son of the servant, *der Sohn der Magd*. He inherited from his father only his name and his *physique*" [Fuller's note]. Christiane Vulpius, Goethe's social inferior, was his common-law wife from 1788 until their marriage in 1806. Henri Blaze (1813–1888), French music critic.

i.e. a pure and perfected intelligence embodied in feminine form, and the centre of a world whose members revolve harmoniously round her. She instructs him in the archives of a rich human history, and introduces him to the contemplation of the heavens.

From the hours passed by the side of Mariana to these with Macaria, is a wide distance for human feet to traverse. Nor has Wilhelm travelled so far, seen and suffered so much in vain. He now begins to study how he may aid the next generation; he sees objects in harmonious arrangement, and from his observations deduces precepts by which to guide his course as a teacher and a master, "help-full, comfort-full."

In all these expressions of woman, the aim of Goethe is satisfactory to me. He aims at a pure self-subsistence, and free development of any powers with which they may be gifted by nature as much for them as for men. They are units, addressed as souls. Accordingly the meeting between man and woman, as represented by him, is equal and noble, and, if he does not depict marriage, he makes it possible.

In the Macaria, bound with the heavenly bodies in fixed revolutions, the centre of all relations, herself unrelated, he expresses the Minerva side of feminine nature. It was not by chance that Goethe gave her this name. Macaria, the daughter of Hercules, who offered herself as a victim for the good of her country, was canonized by the Greeks, and worshipped as the Goddess of true Felicity. Goethe has embodied this Felicity as the Serenity that arises from Wisdom, a Wisdom, such as the Jewish wise man venerated, alike instructed in the designs of heaven, and the methods necessary to carry them into effect upon earth.

Mignon is the electrical, inspired, lyrical nature. And wherever it appears we echo in our aspirations that of the child,

> "So let me seem until I be:—
> Take not the *white robe* away."
>
> •   •   •   •   •
>
> "Though I lived without care and toil,
> Yet felt I sharp pain enough,
> Make me again forever young."[9]

All these women, though we see them in relations, we can think of as unrelated. They all are very individual, yet seem, nowhere, restrained. They satisfy for the present, yet arouse an infinite expectation.

The economist Theresa, the benevolent Natalia, the fair Saint, have chosen a path, but their thoughts are not narrowed to it. The functions of life to them are not ends, but suggestions.

Thus, to them, all things are important, because none is necessary. Their different characters have fair play, and each is beautiful in its minute indications, for nothing is enforced or conventional, but every thing, however slight, grows from the essential life of the being.

9. From *Wilhelm Meister's Apprenticeship* (1795–96), book 8, chapter 2.

Mignon and Theresa wear male attire when they like, and it is graceful for them to do so, while Macaria is confined to her arm-chair behind the green curtain, and the Fair Saint could not bear a speck of dust on her robe.

All things are in their places in this little world, because all is natural and free, just as "there is room for everything out of doors." Yet all is rounded in by natural harmony, which will always arise where Truth and Love are sought in the light of Freedom.

Goethe's book bodes an era of freedom like its own of "extraordinary generous seeking," and new revelations. New individualities shall be developed in the actual world, which shall advance upon it as gently as the figures come out upon his canvass.

I have indicated on this point the coincidence between his hopes and those of Fourier, though his are directed by an infinitely higher and deeper knowledge of human nature. But, for our present purpose, it is sufficient to show how surely these different paths have conducted to the same end two earnest thinkers. In some other place I wish to point out similar coincidences between Goethe's model school and the plans of Fourier, which may cast light upon the page of prophecy.

Many women have observed that the time drew nigh for a better care of the sex, and have thrown out hints that may be useful. Among these may be mentioned—

Miss Edgeworth,[1] who, although restrained by the habits of her age and country, and belonging more to the eighteenth than the nineteenth century, has done excellently as far as she goes. She had a horror of sentimentalism, and the love of notoriety, and saw how likely women, in the early stages of culture, were to aim at these. Therefore she bent her efforts to recommending domestic life. But the methods she recommends are such as will fit a character for any position to which it may be called. She taught a contempt of falsehood, no less in its most graceful, than in its meanest apparitions; the cultivation of a clear, independent judgment, and adherence to its dictates; habits of various and liberal study and employment, and a capacity for friendship. Her standard of character is the same for both sexes. Truth, honor, enlightened benevolence, and aspiration after knowledge. Of poetry, she knows nothing, and her religion consists in honor and loyalty to obligations once assumed, in short, in "the great idea of duty which holds us upright." Her whole tendency is practical.

Mrs. Jameson[2] is a sentimentalist, and, therefore, suits us ill in some respects, but she is full of talent, has a just and refined perception of the beautiful, and a genuine courage when she finds it necessary. She does not appear to have thought out, thoroughly, the subject on which

---

1. Maria Edgeworth (1767–1849), Anglo-Irish novelist, coauthored with her father, Richard Lovell Edgeworth (1744–1817), the nonfiction *Practical Education* (1798).
2. See n. 7, p. 59.

we are engaged, and her opinions, expressed as opinions, are sometimes inconsistent with one another. But from the refined perception of character, admirable suggestions are given in her "Women of Shakspeare," and "Loves of the Poets."

But that for which I most respect her is the decision with which she speaks on a subject which refined women are usually afraid to approach, for fear of the insult and scurril jest they may encounter; but on which she neither can nor will restrain the indignation of a full heart. I refer to the degradation of a large portion of women into the sold and polluted slaves of men, and the daring with which the legislator and man of the world lifts his head beneath the heavens, and says "this must be; it cannot be helped; it is a necessary accompaniment of *civilization.*"

So speaks the *citizen.* Man born of woman, the father of daughters, declares that he will and must buy the comforts and commercial advantages of his London, Vienna, Paris, New-York, by conniving at the moral death, the damnation, so far as the action of society can insure it, of thousands of women for each splendid metropolis.

O men! I speak not to you. It is true that your wickedness (for you must not deny that, at least, nine thousand out of the ten fall through the vanity you have systematically flattered, or the promises you have treacherously broken;) yes, it is true that your wickedness is its own punishment. Your forms degraded and your eyes clouded by secret sin; natural harmony broken and fineness of perception destroyed in your mental and bodily organization; God and love shut out from your hearts by the foul visitants you have permitted there; incapable of pure marriage; incapable of pure parentage; incapable of worship; oh wretched men, your sin is its own punishment! You have lost the world in losing yourselves. Who ruins another has admitted the worm to the root of his own tree, and the fuller ye fill the cup of evil, the deeper must be your own bitter draught. But I speak not to you—you need to teach and warn one another. And more than one voice rises in earnestness. And all that *women* say to the heart that has once chosen the evil path, is considered prudery, or ignorance, or perhaps, a feebleness of nature which exempts from similar temptations.

But to you, women, American women, a few words may not be addressed in vain. One here and there may listen.

You know how it was in the Oriental clime. One man, if wealth permitted, had several wives and many hand-maidens. The chastity and equality of genuine marriage, with "the thousand decencies that flow," from its communion, the precious virtues that gradually may be matured, within its enclosure, were unknown.

But this man did not wrong according to his light. What he did, he might publish to God and Man; it was not a wicked secret that hid in vile lurking-places and dens, like the banquets of beasts of prey. Those women were not lost, not polluted in their own eyes, nor those of others. If they were not in a state of knowledge and virtue, they were at least in one of comparative innocence.

You know how it was with the natives of this continent. A chief had many wives whom he maintained and who did his household work; those women were but servants, still they enjoyed the respect of others and their own. They lived together in peace. They knew that a sin against what was in their nation esteemed virtue, would be as strictly punished in man as in woman.

Now pass to the countries where marriage is between one and one. I will not speak of the Pagan nations, but come to those which own the Christian rule. We all know what that enjoins; there is a standard to appeal to.

See now, not the mass of the people, for we all know that it is a proverb and a bitter jest to speak of the "down-trodden million." We know that, down to our own time, a principle never had so fair a chance to pervade the mass of the people, but that we must solicit its illustration from select examples.

Take the Paladin, take the Poet.[3] Did *they* believe purity more impossible to man than to woman? Did they wish woman to believe that man was less amenable to higher motives, that pure aspirations would not guard him against bad passions, that honorable employments and temperate habits would not keep him free from slavery to the body. O no! Love was to them a part of heaven, and they could not even wish to receive its happiness, unless assured of being worthy of it. Its highest happiness to them was, that it made them wish to be worthy. They courted probation. They wished not the title of knight, till the banner had been upheld in the heats of battle, amid the rout of cowards.

I ask of you, young girls—I do not mean *you*, whose heart is that of an old coxcomb, though your locks have not yet lost their sunny tinge. Not of you whose whole character is tainted with vanity, inherited or taught, who have early learnt the love of coquettish excitement, and whose eyes rove restlessly in search of a "conquest" or a "beau." You who are ashamed *not* to be seen by others the mark of the most contemptuous flattery or injurious desire. To such I do not speak. But to thee, maiden, who, if not so fair, art yet of that unpolluted nature which Milton saw when he dreamed of Comus[4] and the Paradise. Thou, child of an unprofaned wedlock, brought up amid the teachings of the woods and fields, kept fancy-free by useful employment and a free flight into the heaven of thought, loving to please only those whom thou wouldst not be ashamed to love; I ask of thee, whose cheek has not forgotten

3. Paladin, originally one of the twelve legendary champions of the emperor Charlemagne (742–814), but later any heroic knight. Fuller here uses "the Paladin" and "the Poet" as representatives of the medieval romantic tradition.
4. In Milton's *Comus* (1684), a lady, waylaid by the pagan god Comus, resists his charms and preserves her chastity.

its blush nor thy heart its lark-like hopes, if he whom thou mayst hope the Father will send thee, as the companion of life's toils and joys, is not to thy thought pure? Is not manliness to thy thought purity, *not* lawlessness? Can his lips speak falsely? Can he do, in secret, what he could not avow to the mother that bore him? O say, dost thou not look for a heart free, open as thine own, all whose thoughts may be avowed, incapable of wronging the innocent, or still farther degrading the fallen. A man, in short, in whom brute nature is entirely subject to the impulses of his better self.

Yes! it was thus that thou didst hope, for I have many, many times seen the image of a future life, of a destined spouse, painted on the tablets of a virgin heart.

It might be that she was not true to these hopes. She was taken into what is called "the world," froth and scum as it mostly is on the social caldron. There, she saw fair woman carried in the waltz close to the heart of a being who appeared to her a Satyr.[5] Being warned by a male friend that he was in fact of that class, and not fit for such familiar nearness to a chaste being, the advised replied that "women should know nothing about such things." She saw one fairer given in wedlock to a man of the same class. "Papa and mamma said that 'all men were faulty, at some time in their lives; they had a great many temptations. Frederick would be so happy at home; he would not want to do wrong.' " She turned to the married women; they, oh tenfold horror! laughed at her supposing "men were like women." Sometimes, I say, she was not true and either sadly accommodated herself to "woman's lot," or acquired a taste for satyr-society, like some of the Nymphs, and all the Bacchanals[6] of old. But to these who could not and would not accept a mess of pottage, or a Circe cup,[7] in lieu of their birthright, and to these others who have yet their choice to make, I say, Courage! I have some words of cheer for you. A man, himself of unbroken purity, reported to me the words of a foreign artist, that "the world would never be better till men subjected themselves to the same laws they had imposed on women"; that artist, he added, was true to the thought. The same was true of Canova, the same of Beethoven. "Like each other demi-god, they kept themselves free from stain," and Michael Angelo, looking over here from the loneliness of his century, might meet some eyes that need not shun his glance.

In private life, I am assured by men who are not so sustained and occupied by the worship of pure beauty, that a similar consecration is possible, is practiced. That many men feel that no temptation can be too strong for the will of man, if he invokes the aid of the Spirit instead

5. A lecherous man.
6. Wild and licentious worshipers of the Roman god of wine and fertility, Bachus. "Nymphs": young, beautiful goddesses associated with nature.
7. In Greek myth, Circe was an enchantress who turned men into swine; to reject her cup was to foil the transformation.

of seeking extenuation from the brute alliances of his nature. In short, what the child fancies is really true, though almost the whole world declares it a lie. Man is a child of God; and if he seek His guidance to keep the heart with diligence, it will be so given that all the issues of life may be pure. Life will then be a temple.

The temple round
Spread green the pleasant ground;
The fair colonnade
Be of pure marble pillars made;
Strong to sustain the roof,
Time and tempest proof,
Yet, amidst which, the lightest breeze
Can play as it please;
The audience hall
Be free to all
Who revere
The Power worshipped here,
Sole guide of youth
Unswerving Truth:
In the inmost shrine
Stands the image divine,
Only seen
By those whose deeds have worthy been—
Priestlike clean.
Those, who initiated are,
Declare,
As the hours
Usher in varying hopes and powers;
It changes its face,
It changes its age,
Now a young beaming Grace,
Now Nestorian Sage:[8]
But, to the pure in heart,
This shape of primal art
In age is fair,
In youth seems wise,
Beyond compare,
Above surprise;
What it teaches native seems
Its new lore our ancient dreams;
Incense rises from the ground,
Music flows around,
Firm rest the feet below, clear gaze the eyes above,
When Truth to point the way through Life assumes the wand of Love;

8. Nestor, king of Pylos, was in old age a wise counselor to the Greeks at Troy. The poem is Fuller's.

But, if she cast aside the robe of green,
Winter's silver sheen,
White, pure as light,
Makes gentle shroud as worthy weed as bridal robe had been.[9]

We are now in a transition state, and but few steps have yet been taken. From polygamy, Europe passed to the marriage *de convenance*.[1] This was scarcely an improvement. An attempt was then made to substitute genuine marriage, (the mutual choice of souls inducing a permanent union,) as yet baffled on every side by the haste, the ignorance, or the impurity of man.

Where man assumes a high principle to which he is not yet ripened; it will happen, for a long time, that the few will be nobler than before; the many worse. Thus now. In the country of Sidney and Milton, the metropolis is a den of wickedness, and a stye of sensuality; in the country of Lady Russell,[2] the custom of English Peeresses, of selling their daughters to the highest bidder, is made the theme and jest of fashionable novels by unthinking children who would stare at the idea of sending them to a Turkish slave dealer, though the circumstances of the bargain are there less degrading, as the will and thoughts of the person sold are not so degraded by it, and it is not done in defiance of an acknowledged law of right in the land and the age.

I must here add that I do not believe there ever was put upon record more depravation of man, and more despicable frivolity of thought and aim in woman, than in the novels which purport to give the picture of English fashionable life, which are read with such favor in our drawing rooms, and give the tone to the manners of some circles. Compared with the hard-hearted cold folly there described, crime is hopeful, for it, at least, shows some power remaining in the mental constitution.

To return: Attention has been awakened among men to the stains of celibacy, and the profanations of marriage. They begin to write about it and lecture about it. It is the tendency now to endeavor to help the erring by showing them the physical law. This is wise and excellent; but forget not the better half. Cold bathing and exercise will not suffice to keep a life pure, without an inward baptism and noble and exhilarating employment for the thoughts and the passions. Early marriages

9. *(As described by the historian.)*
    The temple of Juno is like what the character of woman should be.
    Columns! graceful decorums, attractive yet sheltering.
    Porch! noble inviting aspect of the life.
    Kaos! receives the worshippers. See here the statue of the Divinity.
    Ophistodomos! Sanctuary where the most precious possessions were
    kept safe from the hand of the spoiler and the eye of the world
        [Fuller's note].
1. Of convenience, arranged (French).
2. Lady Rachel Russell (1636–1723), highly respected wife of the statesman Lord William Russell.

are desirable, but if, (and the world is now so out of joint that there
are a hundred thousand chances to one against it,) a man does not
early, or at all, find the person to whom he can be united in the marriage of souls, will you give him in the marriage *de convenance*, or if
not married, can you find no way for him to lead a virtuous and happy
life? Think of it well, ye who think yourselves better than pagans, for
many of *them* knew this sure way.[3]

To you, women of America, it is more especially my business to
address myself on this subject, and my advice may be classed under
three heads:

Clear your souls from the taint of vanity.

Do not rejoice in conquests, either that your power to allure may be
seen by other women, or for the pleasure of rousing passionate feelings
that gratify your love of excitement.

It must happen, no doubt, that frank and generous women will excite
love they do not reciprocate, but, in nine cases out of ten, the woman
has, half consciously, done much to excite. In this case she shall not
be held guiltless, either as to the unhappiness or injury to the lover.
Pure love, inspired by a worthy object, must ennoble and bless, whether
mutual or not; but that which is excited by coquettish attraction of any
grade of refinement, must cause bitterness and doubt, as to the reality
of human goodness, so soon as the flush of passion is over. And that
you may avoid all taste for these false pleasures

"Steep the soul
In one pure love, and it will last thee long."[4]

The love of truth, the love of excellence, which, whether you clothe
them in the person of a special object or not, will have power to save
you from following Duessa, and lead you in the green glades where
Una's[5] feet have trod.

It was on this one subject that a venerable champion of good, the
last representative of the spirit which sanctified the revolution and gave
our country such a sunlight of hope in the eyes of the nations, the same
who lately in Boston offered anew to the young men the pledge taken
by the young men of his day, offered, also, his counsel, on being addressed by the principal of a girl's school, thus:

3. The Persian sacred books, the Desatir, describe the great and holy prince Ky Khosrou, as
being "an angel, and the son of an angel," one to whom the Supreme says, "Thou art not
absent from before me for one twinkling of an eye. I am never out of thy heart. And I am
nearer unto thee than thou art to thyself." This Prince had in his Golden Seraglio three ladies
of surpassing beauty, and all four, in this royal monastery, passed their lives, and left the world,
as virgins.
   The Persian people had no scepticism when the history of such a mind was narrated. They
were Catholics [Fuller's note].
4. Unidentified.
5. In Spenser's *The Faerie Queene*, Duessa is an evil enchantress and Una, a virginal young
woman representing truth.

REPLY OF MR. ADAMS[6]

Mr. Adams was so deeply affected by the address of Miss Foster,[7] as to be for some time inaudible. When heard, he spoke as follows:

"This is the first instance in which a lady has thus addressed me personally; and I trust that all the ladies present will be able sufficiently to enter into my feelings to know, that I am more affected by this honor, than by any other I could have received.

"You have been pleased, Madam, to allude to the character of my father,[8] and the history of my family, and their services to the country. It is indeed true, that from the existence of the Republic as an independent nation, my father and myself have been in the public service of the country, almost without interruption. I came into the world, as a person having personal responsibilities, with the Declaration of Independence, which constituted us a nation. I was a child at that time, and had then perhaps the greatest of blessings that can be bestowed on man—a mother[9] who was anxious and capable to form her children to what they ought to be. From that mother I derived whatever instruction—religious especially, and moral—has pervaded a long life; I will not say perfectly, and as it ought to be; but I will say, because it is justice only to the memory of her whom I revere, that if, in the course of my life, there has been any imperfection, or deviation from what she taught me, the fault is mine, and not hers.

"With such a mother, and such other relations with the sex, of sister, wife, and daughter, it has been the perpetual instruction of my life to love and revere the female sex. And in order to carry that sentiment of love and reverence to its highest degree of perfection, I know of nothing that exists in human society better adapted to produce that result, than institutions of the character that I have now the honor to address.

"I have been taught, as I have said, through the course of my life, to love and to revere the female sex; but I have been taught, also—and that lesson has perhaps impressed itself on my mind even more strongly, it may be, than the other—I have been taught not to flatter them. It is not unusual in the intercourse of man with the other sex—and especially for young men—to think, that the way to win the hearts of ladies is by flattery.—To love and to revere the sex, is what I think the duty of man; but *not to flatter them*; and this I would say to the young ladies here; and if they, and others present, will allow me, with all the authority which nearly four score years may have with those who have

6. See n. 3, p. 17.
7. Hannah Foster (1759–1840), novelist and educator, author of *The Coquette* (1797) and *The Boarding School; or, Lessons of a Preceptress to her Pupils* (1798).
8. John Adams (1735–1826), second president of the United States.
9. Abigail Smith Adams (1744–1818), known as one of the most distinguished and influential of American first ladies.

not yet attained one score—I would say to them what I have no doubt they say to themselves, and are taught here, not to take the flattery of men as proof of perfection.

"I am now, however, I fear, assuming too much of a character that does not exactly belong to me. I therefore conclude, by assuring you, Madam, that your reception of me has affected me, as you perceive, more than I can express in words; and that I shall offer my best prayers, till my latest hour, to the Creator of us all, that this institution especially, and all others of a similar kind, designed to form the female mind to wisdom and virtue, may prosper to the end of time."

It will be interesting to add here the character of Mr. Adams's mother, as drawn by her husband, the first John Adams, in a family letter[1] written just before his death.

"I have reserved for the last the life of Lady Russell. This I have not yet read, because I read it more than forty years ago. On this hangs a tale which you ought to know and communicate it to your children. I bought the life and letters of Lady Russell, in the year 1775, and sent it to your grandmother, with an express intent and desire, that she should consider it a mirror in which to contemplate herself; for, at that time, I thought it extremely probable, from the daring and dangerous career I was determined to run, that she would one day find herself in the situation of Lady Russell, her husband without a head.[2] This lady was more beautiful than Lady Russell, had a brighter genius, more information, a more refined taste, and, at least, her equal in the virtues of the heart; equal fortitude and firmness of character, equal resignation to the will of Heaven, equal in all the virtues and graces of the christian life. Like Lady Russell, she never, by word or look, discouraged me from running all hazards for the salvation of my country's liberties; she was willing to share with me, and that her children should share with us both, in all the dangerous consequences we had to hazard."

Will a woman who loves flattery or an aimless excitement, who wastes the flower of her mind on transitory sentiments, ever be loved with a love like that, when fifty years trial have entitled to the privileges of "the golden marriage?"

Such was the love of the iron-handed warrior for her, not his hand-maid, but his help-meet:

"Whom God loves, to him gives he such a wife."

I find the whole of what I want in this relation, in the two epithets by which Milton makes Adam address *his* wife.

In the intercourse of every day he begins:

---

1. Journal and Correspondence of Miss Adams, vol. i. p. 246 [Fuller's note]. This edition was published in New York by Wiley & Putnam in 1841. John Adams's letter is dated July 12, 1820.
2. Sir William Russell was beheaded for treason in 1683.

"Daughter of God and man, *accomplished* Eve."[3]

In a moment of stronger feeling,

"Daughter of God and man, IMMORTAL Eve."

What majesty in the cadence of the line; what dignity, what reverence in the attitude, both of giver and receiver!

The woman who permits, in her life, the alloy of vanity; the woman who lives upon flattery, coarse or fine, shall never be thus addressed. She is *not* immortal as far as her will is concerned, and every woman who does so creates miasma,[4] whose spread is indefinite. The hand, which casts into the waters of life a stone of offence, knows not how far the circles thus caused, may spread their agitations.

A little while since, I was at one of the most fashionable places of public resort. I saw there many women, dressed without regard to the season or the demands of the place, in apery, or, as it looked, in mockery of European fashions. I saw their eyes restlessly courting attention. I saw the way in which it was paid, the style of devotion, almost an open sneer, which it pleased those ladies to receive from men whose expression marked their own low position in the moral and intellectual world. Those women went to their pillows with their heads full of folly, their hearts of jealousy, or gratified vanity: those men, with the low opinion they already entertained of woman confirmed. These were American *ladies*; i.e., they were of that class who have wealth and leisure to make full use of the day, and confer benefits on others. They were of that class whom the possession of external advantages makes of pernicious example to many, if these advantages be misused.

Soon after, I met a circle of women, stamped by society as among the most degraded of their sex. "How," it was asked of them, "did you come here?" for, by the society that I saw in the former place, they were shut up in a prison.[5] The causes were not difficult to trace: love of dress, love of flattery, love of excitement. They had not dresses like the other ladies, so they stole them; they could not pay for flattery by distinctions, and the dower of a worldly marriage, so they paid by the profanation of their persons. In excitement, more and more madly sought from day to day, they drowned the voice of conscience.

Now I ask you, my sisters, if the women at the fashionable house be not answerable for those women being in the prison?

As to position in the world of souls, we may suppose the women of the prison stood fairest, both because they had misused less light, and because loneliness and sorrow had brought some of them to feel the

3. See Appendix, H [Fuller's note]. This quotation and the one below are from *Paradise Lost* 4.660 and 9.291, respectively.
4. A pervasive unhealthful vapor.
5. During her writing of *Woman in the Nineteenth Century*, Fuller visited female inmates at Sing Sing Prison on the Hudson River.

need of better life, nearer truth and good. This was no merit in them, being an effect of circumstance, but it was hopeful. But you, my friends, (and some of you I have already met,) consecrate yourselves without waiting for reproof, in free love and unbroken energy, to win and to diffuse a better life. Offer beauty, talents, riches, on the altar; thus shall ye keep spotless your own hearts, and be visibly or invisibly the angels to others.

I would urge upon those women who have not yet considered this subject, to do so. Do not forget the unfortunates who dare not cross your guarded way. If it do not suit you to act with those who have organized measures of reform, then hold not yourself excused from acting in private. Seek out these degraded women, give them tender sympathy, counsel, employment. Take the place of mothers, such as might have saved them originally.

If you can do little for those already under the ban of the world, and the best considered efforts have often failed, from a want of strength in those unhappy ones to bear up against the sting of shame and the prejudices of the world, which makes them seek oblivion again in their old excitements, you will at least leave a sense of love and justice in their hearts that will prevent their becoming utterly imbittered and corrupt. And you may learn the means of prevention for those yet uninjured. There will be found in a diffusion of mental culture, simple tastes, best taught by your example, a genuine self-respect, and above all, what the influence of man tends to hide from woman, the love and fear of a divine, in preference to a human tribunal.

But suppose you save many who would have lost their bodily innocence (for as to mental, the loss of that is incalculably more general,) through mere vanity and folly; there still remain many, the prey and spoil of the brute passions of man. For the stories frequent in our newspapers outshame antiquity, and vie with the horrors of war.

As to this, it must be considered that, as the vanity and proneness to seduction of the imprisoned women represented a general degradation in their sex; so do these acts a still more general and worse in the male. Where so many are weak it is natural there should be many lost, where legislators admit that ten thousand prostitutes are a fair proportion to one city, and husbands tell their wives that it is folly to expect chastity from men, it is inevitable that there should be many monsters of vice.

I must in this place mention, with respect and gratitude, the conduct of Mrs. Child in the case of Amelia Norman.[6] The action and speech of this lady was of straight-forward nobleness, undeterred by custom or cavil from duty towards an injured sister. She showed the case and the arguments the counsel against the prisoner had the assurance to use in

---

6. A young woman acquitted of charges after stabbing her seducer. Lydia Maria Child (1802–1880), American author, abolitionist, and women's rights advocate, publicly supported Norman.

their true light to the public. She put the case on the only ground of religion and equity. She was successful in arresting the attention of many who had before shrugged their shoulders, and let sin pass as necessarily a part of the company of men. They begin to ask whether virtue is not possible, perhaps necessary, to man as well as to woman. They begin to fear that the perdition of a woman must involve that of a man. This is a crisis. The results of this case will be important.

In this connection I must mention Eugene Sue,[7] the French novelist, several of whose works have been lately transplanted among us, as having the true spirit of reform as to women. Like every other French writer, he is still tainted with the transmissions of the old regime. Still falsehood may be permitted for the sake of advancing truth, evil as the way to good. Even George Sand, who would trample on every graceful decorum, and every human law for the sake of a sincere life, does not see that she violates it by making her heroines able to tell falsehoods in a good cause. These French writers need ever to be confronted by the clear perception of the English and German mind, that the only good man, consequently the only good reformer, is he

> "Who bases good on good alone, and owes
> To virtue every triumph that he knows."[8]

Still, Sue has the heart of a reformer, and especially towards women, he sees what they need, and what causes are injuring them. From the histories of Fleur de Marie and La Louve, from the lovely and independent character of Rigolette,[9] from the distortion given to Matilda's mind, by the present views of marriage, and from the truly noble and immortal character of the "hump-backed Sempstress"[1] in the "Wandering Jew," may be gathered much that shall elucidate doubt and direct inquiry on this subject. In reform, as in philosophy, the French are the interpreters to the civilized world. Their own attainments are not great, but they make clear the past, and break down barriers to the future.

Observe that the good man of Sue is pure as Sir Charles Grandison.[2]

Apropos to Sir Charles, women are accustomed to be told by men that the reform is to come *from them*. "You," say the men, "must frown upon vice, you must decline the attentions of the corrupt, you must not submit to the will of your husband when it seems to you unworthy, but give the laws in marriage, and redeem it from its present sensual and mental pollutions."

This seems to us hard. Men have, indeed, been, for more than a

7. French author of sensational novels about the Parisian underworld (1804–1857).
8. Unidentified.
9. Characters in Sue's novel *Mysteries of Paris* (1842–43).
1. Appears in Sue's *The Wandering Jew* (1844–45).
2. High-minded protagonist of the novel *The History of Sir Charles Grandison* (1753–54) by the English author Samuel Richardson (1689–1761).

hundred years, rating women for countenancing vice. But at the same time, they have carefully hid from them its nature, so that the preference often shown by women for bad men, arises rather from a confused idea that they are bold and adventurous, acquainted with regions which women are forbidden to explore, and the curiosity that ensues, than a corrupt heart in the woman. As to marriage it has been inculcated on women for centuries, that men have not only stronger passions than they, but of a sort that it would be shameful for them to share or even understand. That, therefore, they must "confide in their husbands," i.e., submit implicitly to their will. That the least appearance of coldness or withdrawal, from whatever cause, in the wife is wicked, because liable to turn her husband's thoughts to illicit indulgence; for a man is so constituted that he must indulge his passions or die!

Accordingly a great part of women look upon men as a kind of wild beasts, but "suppose they are all alike"; the unmarried are assured by the married that, "if they knew men as they do," i.e., by being married to them, "they would not expect continence or self-government from them."

I might accumulate illustrations on this theme, drawn from acquaintance with the histories of women, which would startle and grieve all thinking men, but I forbear. Let Sir Charles Grandison preach to his own sex, or if none there be, who feels himself able to speak with authority from a life unspotted in will or deed, let those who are convinced of the practicability and need of a pure life, as the foreign artist was, advise the others, and warn them by their own example, if need be.

The following passage from a female writer on female affairs, expresses a prevalent way of thinking on this subject.

"It may be that a young woman, exempt from all motives of vanity, determines to take for a husband a man who does not inspire her with a very decided inclination. Imperious circumstances, the evident interest of her family, or the danger of a suffering celibacy, may explain such a resolution. If, however, she were to endeavor to surmount a personal repugnance, we should look upon this as *injudicious*. Such a rebellion of nature marks the limit that the influence of parents, or the self-sacrifice of the young girl, should never pass. *We shall be told that this repugnance is an affair of the imagination*; it may be so; but imagination is a power which it is temerity to brave; and its antipathy is more difficult to conquer than its preference."[3]

Among ourselves, the exhibition of such a repugnance from a woman who had been given in marriage "by advice of friends," was treated by an eminent physician as sufficient proof of insanity. If he had said sufficient cause for it, he would have been nearer right.

3. Madame Necker de Saussure [Fuller's note]. Albertine Adrienne Necker de Saussure (1766–1841).

It has been suggested by men who were pained by seeing bad men admitted, freely, to the society of modest women, thereby encouraged to vice by impunity, and corrupting the atmosphere of homes; that there should be a senate of the matrons in each city and town, who should decide what candidates were fit for admission to their houses and the society of their daughters.[4]

Such a plan might have excellent results, but it argues a moral dignity and decision, which does not yet exist, and needs to be induced by knowledge and reflection. It has been the tone to keep women ignorant on these subjects, or when they were not, to command that they should seem so. "It is indelicate," says the father or husband, "to inquire into the private character of such an one. It is sufficient that I do not think him unfit to visit you." And so, this man, who would not tolerate these pages in his house, "unfit for family reading," because they speak plainly, introduces there a man whose shame is written on his brow, as well as the open secret of the whole town, and, presently, if *respectable* still, and rich enough, gives him his daughter to wife. The mother affects ignorance, "supposing he is no worse than most men." The daughter *is* ignorant; something in the mind of the new spouse seems strange to her, but she supposes it is "woman's lot" not to be perfectly happy in her affections; she has always heard, "men could not understand women," so she weeps alone, or takes to dress and the duties of the house. The husband, of course, makes no avowal, and dreams of no redemption.

"In the heart of every young woman," says the female writer, above quoted, addressing herself to the husband, "depend upon it, there is a fund of exalted ideas; she conceals, represses, without succeeding in smothering them. *So long as these ideas in your wife are directed to* YOU, *they are, no doubt, innocent,* but take care that they be not accompanied with *too much* pain. In other respects, also, spare her delicacy. Let all the antecedent parts of your life, if there are such, which would give her pain, be concealed from her; *her happiness and her respect for you would suffer from this misplaced confidence.* Allow her to retain that flower of purity, *which should distinguish her in your eyes from every other woman.*" We should think so, truly, under this canon. Such a man must esteem purity an exotic that could only be preserved by the greatest care. Of the degree of mental intimacy possible, in such a marriage, let every one judge for himself!

On this subject, let every woman, who has once begun to think, examine herself, see whether she does not suppose virtue possible and necessary to man, and whether she would not desire for her son a virtue which aimed at a fitness for a divine life, and involved, if not asceticism, that degree of power over the lower self, which shall "not exterminate

---

4. See Goethe's Tasso. "A synod of good women should decide,"—if the golden age is to be restored [Fuller's note].

the passions, but keep them chained at the feet of reason." The passions, like fire, are a bad master; but confine them to the hearth and the altar, and they give life to the social economy, and make each sacrifice meet for heaven.

When many women have thought upon this subject, some will be fit for the Senate, and one such Senate in operation would affect the morals of the civilized world.

At present I look to the young. As preparatory to the Senate, I should like to see a society of novices, such as the world has never yet seen, bound by no oath, wearing no badge. In place of an oath they should have a religious faith in the capacity of man for virtue; instead of a badge, should wear in the heart a firm resolve not to stop short of the destiny promised him as a son of God. Their service should be action and conservatism, not of old habits, but of a better nature, enlightened by hopes that daily grow brighter.

If sin was to remain in the world, it should not be by their connivance at its stay, or one moment's concession to its claims.

They should succor the oppressed, and pay to the upright the reverence due in hero-worship by seeking to emulate them. They would not denounce the willingly bad, but they could not be with them, for the two classes could not breathe the same atmosphere.

They would heed no detention from the time-serving, the worldly and the timid.

They could love no pleasures that were not innocent and capable of good fruit.

I saw, in a foreign paper, the title now given to a party abroad, "Los Exaltados."[5] Such would be the title now given these children by the world: Los Exaltados, Las Exaltadas; but the world would not sneer always, for from them would issue a virtue by which it would, at last, be exalted too.

I have in my eye a youth and a maiden whom I look to as the nucleus of such a class. They are both in early youth, both as yet uncontaminated, both aspiring, without rashness, both thoughtful, both capable of deep affection, both of strong nature and sweet feelings, both capable of large mental development. They reside in different regions of earth, but their place in the soul is the same. To them I look, as, perhaps, the harbingers and leaders of a new era, for never yet have I known minds so truly virgin, without narrowness or ignorance.

When men call upon women to redeem them, they mean such maidens. But such are not easily formed under the present influences of society. As there are more such young men to help give a different tone, there will be more such maidens.

5. The exalted ones; a Spanish political party formed in the 1820s by urban radicals. *Las Exaltadas* is the feminine form.

The English novelist, D'Israeli,[6] has, in his novel of the "Young Duke," made a man of the most depraved stock be redeemed by a woman who despises him when he has only the brilliant mask of fortune and beauty to cover the poverty of his heart and brain, but knows how to encourage him when he enters on a better course. But this woman was educated by a father who valued character in women.

Still there will come now and then, one who will, as I hope of my young Exaltada, be example and instruction to the rest. It was not the opinion of woman current among Jewish men that formed the character of the mother of Jesus.

Since the sliding and backsliding men of the world, no less than the mystics declare that, as through woman man was lost, so through woman must man be redeemed, the time must be at hand. When she knows herself indeed as "accomplished," still more as "immortal Eve," this may be.

As an immortal, she may also know and inspire immortal love, a happiness not to be dreamed of under the circumstances advised in the last quotation. Where love is based on concealment, it must, of course, disappear when the soul enters the scene of clear vision!

And, without this hope, how worthless every plan, every bond, every power!

"The giants," said the Scandinavian Saga, "had induced Loke, (the spirit that hovers between good and ill,) to steal for them Iduna, (Goddess of Immortality,) and her apples of pure gold. He lured her out, by promising to show, on a marvellous tree he had discovered, apples beautiful as her own, if she would only take them with her for a comparison. Thus, having lured her beyond the heavenly domain, she was seized and carried away captive by the powers of misrule.

As now the gods could not find their friend Iduna, they were confused with grief; indeed they began visibly to grow old and gray. Discords arose, and love grew cold. Indeed, Odur, spouse of the goddess of love and beauty, wandered away and returned no more. At last, however, the gods, discovering the treachery of Loke, obliged him to win back Iduna from the prison in which she sat mourning. He changed himself into a falcon, and brought her back as a swallow, fiercely pursued by the Giant King, in the form of an eagle. So she strives to return among us, light and small as a swallow. We must welcome her form as the speck on the sky that assures the glad blue of Summer. Yet one swallow does not make a summer. Let us solicit them in flights and flocks!

Returning from the future to the present, let us see what forms Iduna takes, as she moves along the declivity of centuries to the valley where the lily flower may concentrate all its fragrance.

6. Benjamin Disraeli (1804–1881), author of the autobiographical novel *The Young Duke* (1831) and later prime minister of England.

It would seem as if this time were not very near to one fresh from books, such as I have of late been—no: *not* reading, but sighing over. A crowd of books having been sent me since my friends knew me to be engaged in this way, on Woman's "Sphere," Woman's "Mission," and Woman's "Destiny," I believe that almost all that is extant of formal precept has come under my eye. Among these I read with refreshment, a little one called "The Whole Duty of Woman,"[7] "indited by a noble lady at the request of a noble lord," and which has this much of nobleness, that the view it takes is a religious one. It aims to fit woman for heaven, the main bent of most of the others is to fit her to please, or, at least, not to disturb a husband.

Among these I select as a favorable specimen, the book I have already quoted, "The Study[8] of the Life of Woman, by Madame Necker de Saussure, of Geneva, translated from the French." This book was published at Philadelphia, and has been read with much favor here. Madame Necker is the cousin of Madame de Stael, and has taken from her works the motto prefixed to this.

"Cette vie n'a quelque prix que si elle sert a' l'education morale de notre cœur."[9]

Mde. Necker is, by nature, capable of entire consistency in the application of this motto, and, therefore, the qualifications she makes, in the instructions given to her own sex, show forcibly the weight which still paralyzes and distorts the energies of that sex.

The book is rich in passages marked by feeling and good suggestions, but taken in the whole the impression it leaves is this:

Woman is, and *shall remain* inferior to man and subject to his will, and, in endeavoring to aid her, we must anxiously avoid any thing that can be misconstrued into expression of the contrary opinion, else the men will be alarmed, and combine to defeat our efforts.

The present is a good time for these efforts, for men are less occupied about women than formerly. Let us, then, seize upon the occasion, and do what we can to make our lot tolerable. But we must sedulously avoid encroaching on the territory of man. If we study natural history, our observations may be made useful, by some male naturalist; if we draw well, we may make our services acceptable to the artists. But our names must not be known, and, to bring these labors to any result, we must take some man for our head, and be his hands.

The lot of woman is sad. She is constituted to expect and need a happiness that cannot exist on earth. She must stifle such aspirations within her secret heart, and fit herself, as well as she can, for a life of resignations and consolations.

7. Probably *The Whole Duty of a Woman; or, A guide to the female sex, written by a lady* (1709) by Richard Allestree (1619–1681), English chaplain and Regius professor of divinity.
8. This title seems to be incorrectly translated from the French. I have not seen the original [Fuller's note].
9. This life only has value if it promotes the moral education of our heart (French).

She will be very lonely while living with her husband. She must not expect to open her heart to him fully, or that, after marriage, he will be capable of the refined service of love. The man is not born for the woman, only the woman for the man. "Men cannot understand the hearts of women." The life of woman must be outwardly a well-intentioned, cheerful dissimulation of her real life.

Naturally, the feelings of the mother, at the birth of a female child, resemble those of the Paraguay woman, described by Southey as lamenting in such heart-breaking tones that her mother did not kill her the hour she was born. "Her mother, who knew what the life of a woman must be;"—or those women seen at the north by Sir A. Mackenzie,[1] who performed this pious duty towards female infants whenever they had an opportunity.

"After the first delight, the young mother experiences feelings a little different, according as the birth of a son or a daughter has been announced.

"Is it a son? A sort of glory swells at this thought the heart of the mother; she seems to feel that she is entitled to gratitude. She has given a citizen, a defender to her country. To her husband an heir of his name, to herself a protector. And yet the contrast of all these fine titles with this being, so humble, soon strikes her. At the aspect of this frail treasure, opposite feelings agitate her heart; she seems to recognize in him *a nature superior to her own,* but subjected to a low condition, and she honors a future greatness in the object of extreme compassion. Somewhat of that respect and adoration for a feeble child, of which some fine pictures offer the expression in the features of the happy Mary, seem reproduced with the young mother who has given birth to a son.

"Is it a daughter? There is usually a slight degree of regret; so deeply rooted is the idea of the superiority of man in happiness and dignity, and yet, as she looks upon this child, she is more and more *softened* towards it—a deep sympathy—a sentiment of identity with this delicate being takes possession of her; an extreme pity for so much weakness, a more pressing need of prayer stirs her heart. Whatever sorrows she may have felt, she dreads for her daughter; but she will guide her to become much wiser, much better than herself. And then the gayety, the frivolity of the young woman have their turn. This little creature is a flower to cultivate, a doll to decorate."

Similar sadness at the birth of a daughter I have heard mothers express not unfrequently.

As to this living so entirely for men, I should think when it was proposed to women they would feel, at least, some spark of the old spirit of races allied to our own. If he is to be my bridegroom *and lord,*

1. Sir Alexander Mackenzie (c. 1755–1820), Scottish fur trader and explorer of northwestern Canada.

cries Brunhilda,[2] he must first be able to pass through fire and water. I will serve at the banquet, says the Valkyrie, but only him who, in the trial of deadly combat, has shown himself a hero.

If women are to be bond-maids, let it be to men superior to women in fortitude, in aspiration, in moral power, in refined sense of beauty! You who give yourselves "to be supported," or because "one must love something," are they who make the lot of the sex such that mothers are sad when daughters are born.

It marks the state of feeling on this subject that it was mentioned, as a bitter censure on a woman who had influence over those younger than herself. "She makes those girls want to see heroes?"

"And will that hurt them?"

"Certainly; how *can* you ask? They will find none, and so they will never be married."

"*Get* married" is the usual phrase, and the one that correctly indicates the thought, but the speakers, on this occasion, were persons too outwardly refined to use it. They were ashamed of the word, but not of the thing. Madame Necker, however, sees good possible in celibacy.

Indeed, I know not how the subject could be better illustrated, than by separating the wheat from the chaff in Madame Necker's book; place them in two heaps and then summon the reader to choose; giving him first a near-sighted glass to examine the two; it might be a christian, an astronomical, or an artistic glass, any kind of good glass to obviate acquired defects in the eye. I would lay any wager on the result.

But time permits not here a prolonged analysis. I have given the clues for fault-finding.

As a specimen of the good take the following passage, on the phenomena of what I have spoken of, as the lyrical or electric element in woman.

"Women have been seen to show themselves poets in the most pathetic pantomimic scenes, where all the passions were depicted full of beauty; and these poets used a language unknown to themselves, and the performance once over, their inspiration was a forgotten dream. Without doubt there is an interior development to beings so gifted, but their sole mode of communication with us is their talent. They are, in all besides, the inhabitants of another planet."

Similar observations have been made by those who have seen the women at Irish wakes, or the funeral ceremonies of modern Greece or Brittany, at times when excitement gave the impulse to genius; but, apparently, without a thought that these rare powers belonged to no other planet, but were a high development of the growth of this, and might by wise and reverent treatment, be made to inform and embellish the scenes of every day. But, when woman has her fair chance, they

---

2. See the Nibelungen Lays [Fuller's note]. In the Medieval Nibelungen epic, Brünnehilde is queen of Iceland, defeated by Siegfried, whose death she contrives.

will do so, and the poem of the hour will vie with that of the ages. I come now with satisfaction to my own country, and to a writer, a female writer, whom I have selected as the clearest, wisest, and kindliest, who has as yet, used pen here on these subjects. This is Miss Sedgwick.[3]

Miss Sedgwick, though she inclines to the private path, and wishes that, by the cultivation of character, might should vindicate right, sets limits nowhere, and her objects and inducements are pure. They are the free and careful cultivation of the powers that have been given, with an aim at moral and intellectual perfection. Her speech is moderate and sane, but never palsied by fear or sceptical caution.

Herself a fine example of the independent and beneficent existence that intellect and character can give to woman, no less than man, if she know how to seek and prize it; also that the intellect need not absorb or weaken, but rather will refine and invigorate the affections, the teachings of her practical good sense come with great force, and cannot fail to avail much. Every way her writings please me both as to the means and the ends. I am pleased at the stress she lays on observance of the physical laws, because the true reason is given. Only in a strong and clean body can the soul do its message fitly.

She shows the meaning of the respect paid to personal neatness both in the indispensable form of cleanliness, and of that love of order and arrangement, that must issue from a true harmony of feeling.

The praises of cold water seem to me an excellent sign in the age. They denote a tendency to the true life. We are now to have, as a remedy for ills, not orvietan, or opium, or any quack medicine, but plenty of air and water, with due attention to warmth and freedom in dress, and simplicity of diet.

Every day we observe signs that the natural feelings on these subjects are about to be reinstated, and the body to claim care as the abode and organ of the soul, not as the tool of servile labor, or the object of voluptuous indulgence.

A poor woman who had passed through the lowest grades of ignominy, seemed to think she had never been wholly lost, "for," said she, "I would always have good under-clothes;" and, indeed, who could doubt that this denoted the remains of private self-respect in the mind?

A woman of excellent sense said, "it might seem childish, but to her one of the most favorable signs of the times, was that the ladies had been persuaded to give up corsets."

Yes! let us give up all artificial means of distortion. Let life be healthy, pure, all of a piece. Miss Sedgwick, in teaching that domestics must have the means of bathing as much as their mistresses, and time, too, to bathe, has symbolized one of the most important of human rights.

Another interesting sign of the time is the influence exercised by two

3. Catharine Maria Sedgwick (1789–1867), American novelist and essayist.

women, Miss Martineau and Miss Barrett,[4] from their sick rooms. The lamp of life which, if it had been fed only by the affections, depended on precarious human relations, would scarce have been able to maintain a feeble glare in the lonely prison, now shines far and wide over the nations, cheering fellow sufferers and hallowing the joy of the healthful.

These persons need not health or youth, or the charms of personal presence, to make their thoughts available. A few more such, and old woman[5] shall not be the synonyme for imbecility, nor old maid a term of contempt, nor woman be spoken of as a reed shaken in the wind.

It is time, indeed, that men and women both should cease to grow old in any other way than as the tree does, full of grace and honor. The hair of the artist turns white, but his eye shines clearer than ever, and we feel that age brings him maturity, not decay. So would it be with all were the springs of immortal refreshment but unsealed within the soul, then like these women they would see, from the lonely chamber window, the glories of the universe; or, shut in darkness, be visited by angels.

I now touch on my own place and day, and, as I write, events are occurring that threaten the fair fabric approached by so long an avenue. Week before last the Gentile was requested to aid the Jew to return to Palestine, for the Millennium, the reign of the Son of Mary, was near. Just now, at high and solemn mass, thanks were returned to the Virgin for having delivered O'Connell[6] from unjust imprisonment, in requital of his having consecrated to her the league formed in behalf of Liberty on Tara's Hill. But, last week brought news which threatens that a cause identical with the enfranchisement of Jews, Irish, women, ay, and of Americans in general, too, is in danger, for the choice of the people threatens to rivet the chains of slavery and the leprosy of sin permanently on this nation, through the annexation of Texas![7]

Ah! if this should take place, who will dare again to feel the throb of heavenly hope, as to the destiny of this country? The noble thought that gave unity to all our knowledge, harmony to all our designs;—the thought that the progress of history had brought on the era, the tissue of prophecies pointed out the spot, where humanity was, at last, to have a fair chance to know itself, and all men be born free and equal for the eagle's flight, flutters as if about to leave the breast, which, deprived of it, will have no more a nation, no more a home on earth.

4. Elizabeth Barrett (1806–1891), English poet, was an invalid before her marriage to Robert Browning in 1846. Harriet Martineau was an invalid between 1839 and 1844.
5. An apposite passage is quoted in Appendix F [Fuller's note].
6. Daniel O'Connell (1775–1847), Irish Catholic political leader, was imprisoned in 1844 for fourteen weeks on charges of sedition, after he demanded repeal of the union between Great Britain and Ireland.
7. U.S. annexation of the Republic of Texas was viewed by many in the North as a means to extend slavery territory. Annexation occurred in December 1845, shortly after Fuller had completed *Woman in the Nineteenth Century*.

Women of my country!—Exaltadas! if such there be,—Women of English, old English nobleness, who understand the courage of Boadicea, the sacrifice of Godiva, the power of Queen Emma to tread the red hot iron unharmed. Women who share the nature of Mrs. Hutchinson, Lady Russell,[8] and the mothers of our own revolution: have you nothing to do with this? You see the men, how they are willing to sell shamelessly, the happiness of countless generations of fellow-creatures, the honor of their country, and their immortal souls, for a money market and political power. Do you not feel within you that which can reprove them, which can check, which can convince them? You would not speak in vain; whether each in her own home, or banded in unison.

Tell these men that you will not accept the glittering baubles, spacious dwellings, and plentiful service, they mean to offer you through these means. Tell them that the heart of women demands nobleness and honor in man, and that, if they have not purity, have not mercy, they are no longer fathers, lovers, husbands, sons of yours.

This cause is your own, for as I have before said, there is a reason why the foes of African slavery seek more freedom for women; but put it not upon that ground, but on the ground of right.

If you have a power, it is a moral power. The films of interest are not so close around you as around the men. If you will but think, you cannot fail to wish to save the country from this disgrace. Let not slip the occasion, but do something to lift off the curse incurred by Eve.

You have heard the women engaged in the abolition movement accused of boldness, because they lifted the voice in public, and lifted the latch of the stranger. But were these acts, whether performed judiciously or no, so bold as to dare before God and man to partake the fruits of such offence as this?

You hear much of the modesty of your sex. Preserve it by filling the mind with noble desires that shall ward off the corruptions of vanity and idleness. A profligate woman, who left her accustomed haunts and took service in a New-York boarding-house, said "she had never heard talk so vile at the Five Points,[9] as from the ladies at the boarding-house." And why? Because they were idle; because, having nothing worthy to engage them, they dwelt, with unnatural curiosity, on the ill they dared not go to see.

It will not so much injure your modesty to have your name, by the unthinking, coupled with idle blame, as to have upon your soul the

---

8. See n. 2, p. 82. Boadice (1st century A.D.), warrior queen of the Iceni and leader of resistance to the Roman conquest of Britain. Lady Godiva (c. 1140–c. 1080), wife of Leofic, earl of Mercia, rode naked through Coventry to persuade her husband to remit a heavy tax levied on his subjects. Emma (d. 1052), queen of England who allegedly agreed to be tortured by hot iron to prove her fidelity. Anne Hutchinson (1591–1643), English colonist, banished from the Massachusetts Bay Colony for challenging the authority of the Puritan magistrates.
9. Notorious vice-ridden section of New York City.

weight of not trying to save a whole race of women from the scorn that is put upon *their* modesty.

Think of this well! I entreat, I conjure you, before it is too late. It is my belief that something effectual might be done by women, if they would only consider the subject, and enter upon it in the true spirit, a spirit gentle, but firm, and which feared the offence of none, save One who is of purer eyes than to behold iniquity.

And now I have designated in outline, if not in fulness, the stream which is ever flowing from the heights of my thought.

In the earlier tract,[1] I was told, I did not make my meaning sufficiently clear. In this I have consequently tried to illustrate it in various ways, and may have been guilty of much repetition. Yet, as I am anxious to leave no room for doubt, I shall venture to retrace, once more, the scope of my design in points, as was done in old-fashioned sermons.

Man is a being of two-fold relations, to nature beneath, and intelligences above him. The earth is his school, if not his birth-place: God his object: life and thought, his means of interpreting nature, and aspiring to God.

Only a fraction of this purpose is accomplished in the life of any one man. Its entire accomplishment is to be hoped only from the sum of the lives of men, or man considered as a whole.

As this whole has one soul and one body, any injury or obstruction to a part, or to the meanest member, affects the whole. Man can never be perfectly happy or virtuous, till all men are so.

To address man wisely, you must not forget that his life is partly animal, subject to the same laws with nature.

But you cannot address him wisely unless you consider him still more as soul, and appreciate the conditions and destiny of soul.

The growth of man is two-fold, masculine and feminine.

As far as these two methods can be distinguished they are so as

Energy and Harmony.

Power and Beauty.

Intellect and Love.

Or by some such rude classification, for we have not language primitive and pure enough to express such ideas with precision.

These two sides are supposed to be expressed in man and woman, that is, as the more and less, for the faculties have not been given pure to either, but only in preponderance. There are also exceptions in great number, such as men of far more beauty than power, and the reverse. But as a general rule, it seems to have been the intention to give a preponderance on the one side, that is called masculine, and on the other, one that is called feminine.

1. "The Great Lawsuit."

There cannot be a doubt that, if these two developments were in perfect harmony, they would correspond to and fulfil one another, like hemispheres, or the tenor and bass in music.

But there is no perfect harmony in human nature; and the two parts answer one another only now and then, or, if there be a persistent consonance, it can only be traced, at long intervals, instead of discoursing an obvious melody.

What is the cause of this?

Man, in the order of time, was developed first; as energy comes before harmony; power before beauty.

Woman was therefore under his care as an elder. He might have been her guardian and teacher.

But as human nature goes not straight forward, but by excessive action and then reaction in an undulated course, he misunderstood and abused his advantages, and became her temporal master instead of her spiritual sire.

On himself came the punishment. He educated woman more as a servant than a daughter, and found himself a king without a queen.

The children of this unequal union showed unequal natures, and, more and more, men seemed sons of the hand-maid, rather than princes.

At last there were so many Ishmaelites that the rest grew frightened and indignant. They laid the blame on Hagar,[2] and drove her forth into the wilderness.

But there were none the fewer Ishmaelites for that.

At last men became a little wiser, and saw that the infant Moses was, in every case, saved by the pure instincts of woman's breast. For, as too much adversity is better for the moral nature than too much prosperity, woman, in this respect, dwindled less than man, though in other respects, still a child in leading strings.

So man did her more and more justice, and grew more and more kind.

But yet, his habits and his will corrupted by the past, he did not clearly see that woman was half himself, that her interests were identical with his, and that, by the law of their common being, he could never reach his true proportions while she remained in any wise shorn of hers.

And so it has gone on to our day; both ideas developing, but more slowly than they would under a clearer recognition of truth and justice, which would have permitted the sexes their due influence on one another, and mutual improvement from more dignified relations.

Wherever there was pure love, the natural influences were, for the time, restored.

2. See n. 7, p. 57.

Wherever the poet or artist gave free course to his genius, he saw the truth, and expressed it in worthy forms, for these men especially share and need the feminine principle. The divine birds need to be brooded into life and song by mothers.

Wherever religion (I mean the thirst for truth and good, not the love of sect and dogma,) had its course, the original design was apprehended in its simplicity, and the dove presaged sweetly from Dodona's oak.[3]

I have aimed to show that no age was left entirely without a witness of the equality of the sexes in function, duty and hope.

Also that, when there was unwillingness or ignorance, which prevented this being acted upon, women had not the less power for their want of light and noble freedom. But it was power which hurt alike them and those against whom they made use of the arms of the servile; cunning, blandishment, and unreasonable emotion.

That now the time has come when a clearer vision and better action are possible. When man and woman may regard one another as brother and sister, the pillars of one porch, the priests of one worship.

I have believed and intimated that this hope would receive an ampler fruition, than ever before, in our own land.

And it will do so if this land carry out the principles from which sprang our national life.

I believe that, at present, women are the best helpers of one another.

Let them think; let them act; till they know what they need.

We only ask of men to remove arbitrary barriers. Some would like to do more. But I believe it needs for woman to show herself in her native dignity, to teach them how to aid her; their minds are so encumbered by tradition.

When Lord Edward Fitzgerald[4] travelled with the Indians, his manly heart obliged him at once, to take the packs from the squaws and carry them. But we do not read that the red men followed his example, though they are ready enough to carry the pack of the white woman, because she seems to them a superior being.

Let woman appear in the mild majesty of Ceres, and rudest churls will be willing to learn from her.

You ask, what use will she make of liberty, when she has so long been sustained and restrained?

I answer; in the first place, this will not be suddenly given. I read yesterday a debate of this year on the subject of enlarging women's rights over property. It was a leaf from the class-book that is preparing for the needed instruction. The men learned visibly as they spoke. The champions of woman saw the fallacy of arguments, on the opposite

3. Dodona, in ancient Greece, was the site of the oracle of Zeus. The god revealed himself through the rustlings and markings of the leaves of a sacred oak.
4. Irishman (1763–1798) who traveled to the Great Lakes and down the Mississippi River; he served in the British Army during the American Revolution and later became a famous rebel, trying to arrange a French invasion of Ireland.

side, and were startled by their own convictions. With their wives at home, and the readers of the paper, it was the same. And so the stream flows on; thought urging action, and action leading to the evolution of still better thought.

But, were this freedom to come suddenly, I have no fear of the consequences. Individuals might commit excesses, but there is not only in the sex a reverence for decorums and limits inherited and enhanced from generation to generation, which many years of other life could not efface, but a native love, in woman as woman, of proportion, of "the simple art of not too much," a Greek moderation, which would create immediately a restraining party, the natural legislators and instructors of the rest, and would gradually establish such rules as are needed to guard, without impeding, life.

The Graces would lead the choral dance, and teach the rest to regulate their steps to the measure of beauty.

But if you ask me what offices they may fill; I reply—any. I do not care what case you put; let them be sea-captains, if you will. I do not doubt there are women well fitted for such an office, and, if so, I should be glad to see them in it, as to welcome the maid of Saragossa, or the maid of Missolonghi, or the Suliote heroine, or Emily Plater.[5]

I think women need, especially at this juncture, a much greater range of occuption than they have, to rouse their latent powers. A party of travellers lately visited a lonely hut on a mountain. There they found an old woman that told them she and her husband had lived there forty years. "Why," they said, "did you choose so barren a spot?" She "did not know; *it was the man's notion.*"

And, during forty years, she had been content to act, without knowing why, upon "the man's notion." I would not have it so.

In families that I know, some little girls like to saw wood, others to use carpenters' tools. Where these tastes are indulged, cheerfulness and good humor are promoted. Where they are forbidden, because "such things are not proper for girls," they grow sullen and mischievous.

Fourier had observed these wants of women, as no one can fail to do who watches the desires of little girls, or knows the ennui that haunts grown women, except where they make to themselves a serene little world by art of some kind. He, therefore, in proposing a great variety of employments, in manufactures or the care of plants and animals, allows for one third of woman, as likely to have a taste for masculine pursuits, one third of men for feminine.

Who does not observe the immediate glow and serenity that is diffused over the life of women, before restless or fretful, by engaging in

5. Fuller here refers to women who fought on behalf of liberty. Saragossa is a Spanish city invaded by the French in 1808–09. Missolonghi is a Greek town besieged by the Turks in 1822–23 and 1825–26. Suli is a Greek island that rebelled against the Turks in 1820. In the late 1820s, Plater led the Polish rebellion against Russian rule (see also n. 1, p. 24).

gardening, building, or the lowest department of art. Here is something that is not routine, something that draws forth life toward the infinite.

I have no doubt, however, that a large proportion of women would give themselves to the same employments as now, because there are circumstances that must lead them. Mothers will delight to make the nest soft and warm. Nature would take care of that; no need to clip the wings of any bird that wants to soar and sing, or finds in itself the strength of pinion for a migratory flight unusual to its kind. The difference would be that *all* need not be constrained to employments, for which *some* are unfit.

I have urged upon the sex self-subsistence in its two forms of self-reliance and self-impulse, because I believe them to be the needed means of the present juncture.

I have urged on woman independence of man, not that I do not think the sexes mutually needed by one another, but because in woman this fact has led to an excessive devotion, which has cooled love, degraded marriage, and prevented either sex from being what it should be to itself or the other.

I wish woman to live, *first* for God's sake. Then she will not make an imperfect man her god, and thus sink to idolatry. Then she will not take what is not fit for her from a sense of weakness and poverty. Then, if she finds what she needs in man embodied, she will know how to love, and be worthy of being loved.

By being more a soul, she will not be less woman, for nature is perfected through spirit.

Now there is no woman, only an overgrown child.

That her hand may be given with dignity, she must be able to stand alone. I wish to see men and women capable of such relations as are depicted by Landor in his Pericles and Aspasia, where grace is the natural garb of strength, and the affections are calm, because deep. The softness is that of a firm tissue, as when

> "The gods approve
> The depth, but not the tumult of the soul,
> A fervent, not ungovernable love."[6]

A profound thinker has said, "no married woman can represent the female world, for she belongs to her husband. The idea of woman must be represented by a virgin."

But that is the very fault of marriage, and of the present relation between the sexes, that the woman does belong to the man, instead of forming a whole with him. Were it otherwise, there would be no such limitation to the thought.

Woman, self-centred, would never be absorbed by any relation; it

6. From Wordsworth's "Laodamia."

would be only an experience to her as to man. It is a vulgar error that love, *a* love to woman is her whole existence; she also is born for Truth and Love in their universal energy. Would she but assume her inheritance, Mary would not be the only virgin mother. Not Manzoni alone would celebrate in his wife the virgin mind with the maternal wisdom and conjugal affections. The soul is ever young, ever virgin.

And will not she soon appear? The woman who shall vindicate their birthright for all women; who shall teach them what to claim, and how to use what they obtain? Shall not her name be for her era Victoria,[7] for her country and life Virginia? Yet predictions are rash; she herself must teach us to give her the fitting name.

An idea not unknown to ancient times has of late been revived, that, in the metamorphoses of life, the soul assumes the form, first of man, then of woman,[8] and takes the chances, and reaps the benefits of either lot. Why then, say some, lay such emphasis on the rights or needs of woman? What she wins not, as woman, will come to her as man.

That makes no difference. It is not woman, but the law of right, the law of growth, that speaks in us, and demands the perfection of each being in its kind, apple as apple, woman as woman. Without adopting your theory I know that I, a daughter, live through the life of man; but what concerns me now is, that my life be a beautiful, powerful, in a word, a complete life in its kind. Had I but one more moment to live, I must wish the same.

Suppose, at the end of your cycle, your great world-year, all will be completed, whether I exert myself or not (and the supposition is *false,*) but suppose it true, am I to be indifferent about it? Not so! I must beat my own pulse true in the heart of the world; for *that* is virtue, excellence, health.

Thou, Lord of Day! didst leave us to-night so calmly glorious, not dismayed that cold winter is coming, not postponing thy beneficence to the fruitful summer! Thou didst smile on thy day's work when it was done, and adorn thy down-going as thy up-rising, for thou art loyal, and it is thy nature to give life, if thou canst, and shine at all events!

I stand in the sunny noon of life. Objects no longer glitter in the dews of morning, neither are yet softened by the shadows of evening. Every spot is seen, every chasm revealed. Climbing the dusty hill, some fair effigies that once stood for symbols of human destiny have been broken; those I still have with me, show defects in this broad light. Yet enough is left, even by experience, to point distinctly to the glories of that destiny; faint, but not to be mistaken streaks of the future day. I can say with the bard,

7. Queen Victoria (1819–1901) began her English reign in 1837; it would be the longest in English history, lasting until her death.
8. Emerson expresses this idea in his essay "Friendship."

"Though many have suffered shipwreck, still beat noble hearts."[9]

Always the soul says to us all: Cherish your best hopes as a faith, and abide by them in action. Such shall be the effectual fervent means to their fulfilment,

> For the Power to whom we bow
> Has given its pledge that, if not now,
> They of pure and stedfast mind,
> By faith exalted, truth refined,
> *Shall* hear all music loud and clear,
> Whose first notes they ventured here.
> Then fear not thou to wind the horn,
> Though elf and gnome thy courage scorn;
> Ask for the Castle's King and Queen;
> Though rabble rout may rush between,
> Beat thee senseless to the ground,
> In the dark beset thee round;
> Persist to ask and it will come,
> Seek not for rest in humbler home;
> So shalt thou see what few have seen,
> The palace home of King and Queen.[1]

15th November, 1844.

---

9. Unidentified.
1. The poem is Fuller's.

Appendix

A

Apparition of the goddess Isis to her votary, from Apuleius.[2]

"Scarcely had I closed my eyes, when behold (I saw in a dream) a divine form emerging from the middle of the sea, and raising a countenance venerable, even to the gods themselves. Afterwards, the whole of the most splendid image seemed to stand before me, having gradually shaken off the sea. I will endeavor to explain to you its admirable form, if the poverty of human language will but afford me the power of an appropriate narration; or if the divinity itself, of the most luminous form, will supply me with a liberal abundance of fluent diction. In the first place, then, her most copious and long hairs, being gradually intorted, and promiscuously scattered on her divine neck, were softly defluous. A multiform crown, consisting of various flowers, bound the sublime summit of her head. And in the middle of the crown, just on her forehead, there was a smooth orb resembling a mirror, or rather a white refulgent light, which indicated that she was the moon. Vipers rising up after the manner of furrows, environed the crown on the right hand and on the left, and Cerealian ears of corn were also extended from above. Her garment was of many colors, and woven from the finest flax, and was at one time lucid with a white splendor, at another yellow from the flower of crocus, and at another flaming with a rosy redness. But that which most excessively dazzled my sight, was a very black robe, fulgid with a dark splendor, and which, spreading round and passing under her right side, and ascending to her left shoulder, there rose protuberant, like the centre of a shield, the dependent part of her robe falling in many folds, and having small knots of fringe, gracefully flowing in its extremities. Glittering stars were dispersed through the embroidered border of the robe, and through the whole of its surface, and the full moon, shining in the middle of the stars, breathed forth flaming fires. A crown, wholly consisting of flowers and fruits of every kind, adhered with indivisible connexion to the border of the conspicuous robe, in all its undulating motions.

"What she carried in her hands also consisted of things of a very different nature. Her right hand bore a brazen rattle, through the narrow lamina of which, bent like a belt, certain rods passing, produced a sharp triple sound through the vibrating motion of her arm. An oblong vessel, in the shape of a boat, depended from her left hand, on the handle of which, in that part which was conspicuous, an asp raised its erect head and largely swelling neck. And shoes, woven from the leaves

---

2. Lucias Apuleius (2nd century), Roman writer, satirist, and rhetorician, quoted from his *Metamorphoses* or *The Golden Ass*, book 11.

of the victorious palm tree, covered her immortal feet. Such, and so great a goddess, breathing the fragrant odour of the shores of Arabia the happy, deigned thus to address me."

The foreign English of the translator, Thomas Taylor,[3] gives the description the air of being, itself, a part of the Mysteries. But its majestic beauty requires no formal initiation to be enjoyed.

B

I give this, in the original, as it does not bear translation. Those who read Italian will judge whether it is not a perfect description of a perfect woman.

Lodi e Preghiere a Maria[4]

Vergine bella che di sol vestita,
Coronata di stelle, al sommo Sole
   Piacesti si, che'n te sua luce ascose;
Amor mi spinge a dir di te parole:
   Ma non so 'ncominciar senza tu' aita,   5
E di Colui che amando in te si pose.
   Invoco lei che ben sempre rispose,
Chi la chiamò con fede.
   Vergine, s'a mercede
Miseria extrema dell' smane cose   10
   Giammai ti volse, al mio prego t'inchina:
Soccorri alla mia guerra;
Bench' i' sia terra, e tu del ciel Regina.

Vergine saggia, e del bel numero una
Delle beate vergini prudenti;   15
   Anzi la prima, e con più chiara lampa;
O saldo scudo dell' afflitte gente
   Contra colpi di Morte e di Fortuna,
Sotto' l qual si trionfa, non pur scampa:
   O refrigerio alcieco ardor ch' avvampa   20
Qui fra mortali sciocchi,
   Vergine, que' begli occhi
Che vider tristi la spietata stampa
   Ne' dolci membri del tuo caro figlio,
Volgi al mio dnbbio stato;   25
   Che sconsigliato a te vien per consiglio.

3. English classical scholar, mathematician, and neoplatonist philosopher (1758–1835).
4. Written by Francesco Petrarca (1304–1374), this poem is a celebration of and prayer to the Virgin Mary.

Vergine pura, d'ogni parte intera,
Del tuo parto gentil figliuola e madre;
   Che allumi questa vita, e l'altra adorni;
Per te il tuo Figlio e quel del sommo Padre,   30
   O finestra del ciel lucente altera,
Venne a salvarne in su gli estremi giorni,
   E fra tutt' i terreni altri soggiorni
Sola tu fusti eletta,
   Vergine benedetta;   35
Che 'l pianto d' Eva in allegrezza torni';
   Fammi; che puoi; della sua grazia degno,
Senza fine o beata,
   Già coronata nel superno regno.

Vergine santa d'ogni grazia piena;   40
Che per vera e altissima umiltate
   Salisti al ciel, onde miei preghi ascolti;
Tu partoristi il fonte di pietate,
   E di giustizia il Sol, che rasserena
Il secol pien d'errori oscuri e folti: 45
   Tre dolci e eari nomi ha' in te raccolti,
Madre, Figliuola, e Sposa;
   Vergine gloriosa,
Donna del Re che nostri lacci ha sciolti,
   E fatto 'l mondo libero e felice;   50
Nelle cui sante piaghe
   Prego ch'appaghe il cor, vera beatrice.

Vergine sola al mondo senza esempio,
Che 'l ciel di tue bellezze innamorasti,
   Cui nè prima fu simil, nè seconda;   55
Santi pensieri, atti pietosi e casti
   Al vero Dio sacrato, e vivo tempio
Fecero in tua virginita feconda.
   Per te può la mia vita esser gioconda,
S' a' tuoi preghi, o MARIA   60
   Vergine dolce, e pia,
Ove 'l fallo abbondo, la grazia abbonda.
   Con le ginocchia della mente inchine
Prego che sia mia scorta;
   E la mia torta via drizzi a buon fine.   65

Vergine chiara, e stabile in eterno,
Di questo tempestoso mare stella;
   D'ogni fedel nocchier fidata guida;
Pon mente in che terribile procella
   I mi ritrovo sol senza governo,   70
Ed ho gia' da vicin l'ultime strida:

Ma pur' in te l'anima mia si fida;
Peccatrice; i' nol nego,
  Vergine: ma te prego
Che 'l tuo nemico del mia mal non rida: 75
  Ricorditi che fece il peccar nostro
Prender Dio, per scamparne,
  Umana carne al tuo virginal christro.

Vergine, quante lagrime ho già sparte,
Quante lusinghe, e quanti preghi indarno,   80
  Pur per mia pena, e per mio grave danno!
Da poi ch' i nacqui in su la riva d' Arno;
  Cercando or questa ed or quell altra parte,
Non è stata mia vita altro ch' affanno.
  Mortal bellezza, atti, e parole m' hanno   85
Tutta ingombrata l'alma.
  Vergine sacra, ed alma,
Non tardar; ch' i' non forse all' ultim 'ann,
  I di miei piu correnti che saetta,
Fra miserie e peccati   90
  Sonsen andati, e sol Morte n'aspetta.

Vergine, tale è terra, eposto ha in doglia
Lo mio cor; che vivendo in pianto il tenne;
  E di mille miei mali un non sapea;
E per saperlo, pur quel che n'avvenne,   95
  Fora avvenuto: ch' ogni altra sua voglia
Era a me morte, ed a lei fama rea
  Or tu, donna del ciel, tu nostra Dea,
Se dir lice, e conviensi;
  Vergine d'alti sensi,   100
Tu vedi il tutto; e quel che non potea
  Far altri, è nulla a e la tua gran virtute;
Pon fine al mio dolore;
  Ch'a te onore ed a me fia salute.

Vergine, in cui ho tutta mia speranza   105
Che possi e vogli al gran bisogno aitarme;
  Non mi lasciare in su l'estremo passo.
Non guardar me, ma chi degnò crearme;
  No'l mio valor, ma l'alta sua sembianza;
Che in me ti mova a curar d'uorm si basso.   110
  Medusa, e l'error mio io han fatto un sasso
D'umor vano stillante;
  Vergine, tu di sante
Lagrime, e pie adempi 'l mio cor lasso;
  Ch' almen l'ultimo pianto sia divoto,   115

Senza terrestro limo;
Come fu'l primo non d'insania voto.

Vergine umana, e nemica d'orgoglio,
Del comune principio amor t'induca;
   Miserere d' un cor contrito umile;   120
Che se poca mortal terra caduca
   Amar con si mirabil fede soglio;
Che devro far di te cosa gentile?
   Se dal mio stato assai misero, e vile
Per le tue man resurgo,   125
   Vergine; è' sacro, e purgo
Al tuo nome e pens ieri e'ngegno, e stile;
   La lingua, e'l cor, le lagrime, e i sospiri,
Scorgimi al miglior guado;
   E prendi in grado i cangiati desiri.   130

Il di s'appressa, e non pote esser lunge;
   Si corre il tempo, e vola,
Vergine uuica, e sola;
   E'l cor' or conscienza, or morte punge.
Raccommandami al tuo Figliuol, verace   135
   Uomo, e verace Dio;
Ch accolga l mio spirto ultimo in pace.

As the Scandinavian represented Frigga[5] the Earth, or World mother, knowing all things, yet never herself revealing them, though ready to be called to counsel by the gods. It represents her in action, decked with jewels and gorgeously attended. But, says the Mythos, when she ascended the throne of Odin, her consort (Haaven) she left with mortals, her friend, the Goddess of Sympathy, to protect them in her absence.

Since, Sympathy goes about to do good. Especially she devotes herself to the most valiant and the most oppressed. She consoled the Gods in some degree even for the death of their darling Baldur. Among the heavenly powers she has no consort.

5. Goddess of Norse mythology, wife of the supreme god, Odin, and mother of Balder, god of light. Associated with fertility and childbirth.

C

"The Wedding of the Lady Theresa"

FROM LOCKHART'S SPANISH BALLADS[6]

" 'Twas when the fifth Alphonso in Leon held his sway,
  King Abdalla of Toledo an embassy did send;
He asked his sister for a wife, and in an evil day
  Alphonso sent her, for he feared Abdalla to offend;
He feared to move his anger, for many times before   5
He had received in danger much succor from the Moor.

Sad heart had fair Theresa, when she their paction knew;
  With streaming tears she heard them tell she 'mong the
        Moors must go;
That she, a Christian damsel, a Christian firm and true,
  Must wed a Moorish husband, it well might cause her wo;   10
But all her tears and all her prayers they are of small avail;
  At length she for her fate prepares, a victim sad and pale.

The king hath sent his sister to fair Toledo town,
  Where then the Moor Abdalla his royal state did keep;
When she drew near, the Moslem from his golden throne
        came down,   15
  And courteously received her, and bade her cease to weep;
With loving words he pressed her to come his bower within;
  With kisses he caressed her, but still she feared the sin.

"Sir King, Sir King, I pray thee,"—'twas thus Theresa spake,
  "I pray thee, have compassion, and do to me no wrong;   20
For sleep with thee I may not, unless the vows I break,
  Whereby I to the holy church of Christ my Lord belong;
For thou hast sworn to serve Mahoun, and if this thing should
        be,
The curse of God it must bring down upon thy realm and
        thee.

"The angel of Christ Jesu, to whom my heavenly Lord   25
  Hath given my soul in keeping, is ever by my side;
If thou dost me dishonor, he will unsheath his sword,
  And smite thy body fiercely, at the crying of thy bride;
Invisible he standeth; his sword like fiery flame,
Will penetrate thy bosom, the hour that sees my shame."   30

6. John Gibson Lockhart (1794–1854), Scottish author, translator and editor of *Ancient Spanish Ballads: Historical and Romantic* (1823).

The Moslem heard her with a smile; the earnest words she
    said,
    He took for bashful maiden's wile, and drew her to his
        bower:
In vain Theresa prayed and strove,—she pressed Abdalla's
    bed,
    Perforce received his kiss of love, and lost her maiden
        flower.
A woful woman there she lay, a loving lord beside,   35
And earnestly to God did pray, her succor to provide.

The angel of Christ Jesu her sore complaint did hear,
    And plucked his heavenly weapon from out his sheath
        unseen,
He waved the brand in his right hand, and to the King came
    near,
    And drew the point o'er limb and joint, beside the weeping
        Queen: 40
A mortal weakness from the stroke upon the King did fall;
He could not stand when daylight broke, but on his knees
    must crawl.

Abdalla shuddered inly, when he this sickness felt,
    And called upon his barons, his pillow to come nigh;
"Rise up," he said "my liegemen," as round his bed they
    knelt,   45
    "And take this Christian lady, else certainly I die;
Let gold be in your girdles, and precious stones beside,
    And swiftly ride to Leon, and render up my bride."

When they were come to Leon, Theresa would not go
    Into her brother's dwelling, where her maiden years were
        spent;   50
But o'er her downcast visage a white veil she did throw,
    And to the ancient nunnery of Las Huelgas went.
There, long, from worldly eyes retired, a holy life she led;
There she, an aged saint, expired; there sleeps she with the
    dead."

D

The following extract from Spinoza[7] is worthy of attention, as expressing the view which a man of the largest intellectual scope may
take of woman, if that part of his life to which her influence appeals,
has been left unawakened.

7. Benedict Spinoza (1632–1677), Dutch philsopher and theologian.

He was a man of the largest intellect, of unsurpassed reasoning powers, yet he makes a statement false to history, for we well know how often men and women have ruled together without difficulty, and one in which very few men even at the present day, I mean men who are thinkers, like him, would acquiesce.

I have put in contrast with it three expressions of the latest literature.

1st. From the poems of W. E. Channing,[8] a poem called "Reverence," equally remarkable for the deep wisdom of its thought and the beauty of its utterance, and containing as fine a description of one class of women as exists in literature.

In contrast with this picture of woman, the happy Goddess of Beauty, the wife, the friend, "the summer queen," I add one by the author of "Festus,"[9] of a woman of the muse, the sybil kind, which seems painted from living experience.

And thirdly, I subjoin Eugene Sue's description of a wicked, but able woman of the practical sort, and appeal to all readers whether a species that admits of three such varieties is so easily to be classed away, or kept within prescribed limits, as Spinoza, and those who think like him, believe.

Spinoza. Tractatus Politici, de Democratia, Caput XI

"Perhaps some one will here ask, whether the supremacy of man over woman is attributable to nature or custom? For if it be human institutions alone to which this fact is owing, there is no reason why we should exclude women from a share in government. Experience, however, most plainly teaches that it is woman's weakness which places her under the authority of man. Since it has nowhere happened that men and women ruled together; but wherever men and women are found the world over, there we see the men ruling and the women ruled, and in this order of things men and women live together in peace and harmony. The Amazons, it is true, are reputed formerly to have held the reins of government, but they drove men from their dominions; the male of their offspring they invariably destroyed, permitting their daughters alone to live. Now if women were by nature upon an equality with men, if they equalled men in fortitude, in genius (qualities which give to men might, and consequently, right) it surely would be the case, that among the numerous and diverse nations of the earth, some would be found where both sexes ruled conjointly, and others where the men were ruled by the women, and so educated as to be mentally inferior: since this state of things no where exists, it is perfectly fair to infer that the rights of women are not equal to those of men;

8. William Ellery Channing (1810–1901), transcendental poet, Fuller's brother-in-law, and author of *Poems* (1843).
9. A dramatic poem (1839) based on the Faust legend by Philip James Bailey (1816–1902), English author.

but that women must be subordinate, and therefore cannot have an equal, far less a superior place in the government. If, too, we consider the passions of men—how the love men feel towards women is seldom any thing but lust and impulse, and much less a reverence for qualities of soul than an admiration of physical beauty, observing, too, how men are afflicted when their sweethearts favor other wooers, and other things of the same character,—we shall see at a glance that it would be, in the highest degree, detrimental to peace and harmony, for men and women to possess an equal share in government."

"Reverence"

"As an ancestral heritage revere
All learning, and all thought. The painter's fame
Is thine, whate'er thy lot, who honorest grace.
And need enough in this low time, when they,
Who seek to captivate the fleeting notes   5
Of heaven's sweet beauty, must despair almost,
So heavy and obdurate show the hearts
Of their companions. Honor kindly then
Those who bear up in their so generous arms
The beautiful ideas of matchless forms;   10
For were these not portrayed, our human fate,—
Which is to be all high, majestical,
To grow to goodness with each coming age,
Till virtue leap and sing for joy to see
So noble, virtuous men,—would brief decay;   15
And the green, festering slime, oblivious, haunt
About our common fate. Oh honor them!

But what to all true eyes has chiefest charm,
And what to every breast where beats a heart
Framed to one beautiful emotion,—to   20
One sweet and natural feeling, lends a grace
To all the tedious walks of common life,
This is fair woman,—woman, whose applause
Each poet sings,—woman the beautiful.
Not that her fairest brow, or gentlest form   25
Charm us to tears; not that the smoothest cheek,
Where ever rosy tints have made their home,
So rivet us on her; but that she is
The subtle, delicate grace,—the inward grace,
For words too excellent; the noble, true,   30
The majesty of earth; the summer queen:
In whose conceptions nothing but what's great
Has any right. And, O! her love for him,
Who does but his small part in honoring her;

Discharging a sweet office, sweeter none,   35
Mother and child, friend, counsel and repose;—
Nought matches with her, nought has leave with her
To highest human praise. Farewell to him
Who reverences not with an excess
Of faith the beauteous sex; all barren he   40
Shall live a living death of mockery.

Ah! had but words the power, what could we say
Of woman! We, rude men, of violent phrase,
Harsh action, even in repose inwardly harsh;
Whose lives walk blustering on high stilts, removed   45
From all the purely gracious influence
Of mother earth. To single from the host
Of angel forms one only, and to her
Devote our deepest heart and deepest mind
Seems almost contradiction. Unto her   50
We owe our greatest blessings, hours of cheer,
Gay smiles, and sudden tears, and more than these
A sure perpetual love. Regard her as
She walks along the vast still earth; and see!
Before her flies a laughing troop of joys,   55
And by her side treads old experience,
With never-failing voice admonitory;
The gentle, though infallible, kind advice,
The watchful care, the fine regardfulness,
Whatever mates with what we hope to find,   60
All consummate in her—the summer queen.

To call past ages better than what now
Man is enacting on life's crowded stage,
Cannot improve our worth; and for the world
Blue is the sky as ever, and the stars   65
Kindle their crystal flames at soft-fallen eve
With the same purest lustre that the east
Worshipped. The river gently flows through fields
Where the broad-leaved corn spreads out, and loads
Its ear as when the Indian tilled the soil.   70
The dark green pine,—green in the winter's cold,
Still whispers meaning emblems, as of old;
The cricket chirps, and the sweet, eager birds
In the sad woods crowd their thick melodies;
But yet, to common eyes, life's poetry   75
Something has faded, and the cause of this
May be that man, no longer at the shrine
Of woman, kneeling with true reverence,
In spite of field, wood, river, stars and sea

Goes most disconsolate. A babble now,   80
A huge and wind-swelled babble, fills the place
Of that great adoration which of old
Man had for woman. In these days no more
Is love the pith and marrow of man's fate.

Thou who in early years feelest awake   85
To finest impulses from nature's breath,
And in thy walk hearest such sounds of truth
As on the common ear strike without heed,
Beware of men around thee. Men are foul,
With avarice, ambition and deceit;   90
The worst of all, ambition. This is life
Spent in a feverish chase for selfish ends,
Which has no virtue to redeem its toil
But one long, stagnant hope to raise the self.
The miser's life to this seems sweet and fair;   95
Better to pile the glittering coin, than seek
To overtop our brothers and our loves.
Merit in this? Where lies it, though thy name
Ring over distant lands, meeting the wind
Even on the extremest verge of the wide world.   100
Merit in this? Better be hurled abroad
On the vast whirling tide, than in thyself
Concentred, feed upon thy own applause.
Thee shall the good man yield no reverence;
But, while the idle, dissolute crowd are loud   105
In voice to send thee flattery, shall rejoice
That he has scaped thy fatal doom, and known
How humble faith in the good soul of things
Provides amplest enjoyment. O my brother,
If the Past's counsel any honor claim   110
From thee, go read the history of those
Who a like path have trod, and see a fate
Wretched with fears, changing like leaves at noon,
When the new wind sings in the white birch wood.
Learn from the simple child the rule of life,   115
And from the movements of the unconscious tribes
Of animal nature, those that bend the wing
Or cleave the azure tide, content to be,
What the great frame provides,—freedom and grace.
Thee, simple child, do the swift winds obey,   120
And the white waterfalls with their bold leaps
Follow thy movements. Tenderly the light
Thee watches, girding with a zone of radiance,
And all the swinging herbs love thy soft steps."

Description of Angela, from "Festus"

"I loved her for that she was beautiful,
And that to me she seemed to be all nature
And all varieties of things in one;
Would set at night in clouds of tears, and rise
All light and laughter in the morning; fear   5
No petty customs nor appearances,
But think what others only dreamed about;
And say what others did but think; and do
What others would but say; and glory in
What others dared but do; it was these which won me;   10
And that she never schooled within her breast
One thought or feeling, but gave holiday
To all; and that she told me all her woes
And wrongs and ills; and so she made them mine
In the communion of love; and we   15
Grew like each other, for we loved each other;
She, mild and generous as the sun in spring;
And I, like earth, all budding out with love.
     •   •   •
    The beautiful are never desolate:
For some one alway loves them; God or man;   20
If man abandons, God Himself takes them:
And thus it was. She whom I once loved died,
The lightning loathes its cloud; the soul its clay.
Can I forget that hand I took in mine,
Pale as pale violets; that eye, where mind   25
And matter met alike divine?—ah, no!
May God that moment judge me when I do!
Oh! she was fair; her nature once all spring
And deadly beauty, like a maiden sword,
Startlingly beautiful. I see her now!   30
Wherever thou art thy soul is in my mind;
Thy shadow hourly lengthens o'er my brain
And peoples all its pictures with thyself;
Gone, not forgotten; passed, not lost; thou wilt shine
In heaven like a bright spot in the sun!   35
She said she wished to die, and so she died,
For, cloudlike, she poured out her love, which was
Her life, to freshen this parched heart. It was thus;
I said we were to part, but she said nothing;
There was no discord; it was music ceased,   40
Life's thrilling, bursting, bounding joy. She sate,
Like a house-god, her hands fixed on her knee,
And her dark hair lay loose and long behind her,
Through which her wild bright eye flashed like a flint;

She spake not, moved not, but she looked the more,   45
As if her eye were action, speech, and feeling.
I felt it all, and came and knelt beside her,
The electric touch solved both our souls together;
Then came the feeling which unmakes, undoes;
Which tears the sealike soul up by the roots,   50
And lashes it in scorn against the skies.
     •   •   •

It is the saddest and the sorest sight,
One's own love weeping. But why call on God?
But that the feeling of the boundless bounds
All feeling; as the welkin does the world;   55
It is this which ones us with the whole and God.
Then first we wept; then closed and clung together;
And my heart shook this building of my breast
Like a live engine booming up and down:
She fell upon me like a snow-wreath thawing.   60
Never were bliss and beauty, love and wo,
Ravelled and twined together into madness,
As in that one wild hour to which all else
The past, is but a picture. That alone
Is real, and forever there in front.   65
     •   •   •

• • •   After that I left her,
And only saw her once again alive."

"Mother Saint Perpetua, the superior of the convent, was a tall woman, of about forty years, dressed in dark gray serge, with a long rosary hanging at her girdle; a white mob cap, with a long black veil, surrounded her thin wan face with its narrow hooded border. A great number of deep transverse wrinkles plowed her brow, which resembled yellowish ivory in color and substance. Her keen and prominent nose was curved like the hooked beak of a bird of prey; her black eye was piercing and sagacious; her face was at once intelligent, firm, and cold.

"For comprehending and managing the material interests of the society, Mother Saint Perpetua could have vied with the shrewdest and most wily lawyer. When women are possessed of what is called *business talent,* and when they apply thereto the sharpness of perception, the indefatigable perseverance, the prudent dissimulation, and above all, the correctness and rapidity of judgment at first sight, which are peculiar to them, they arrive at prodigious results.

"To Mother Saint Perpetua, a woman of a strong and solid head, the vast monied business of the society was but child's play. None better than she understood how to buy depreciated properties, to raise them to their original value, and sell them to advantage; the average purchase of rents, the fluctuations of exchange, and the current prices of shares in all the leading speculations, were perfectly familiar to her. Never had she directed her agents to make a single false speculation, when it had been the question how to invest funds, with which good souls were constantly endowing the society of Saint Mary. She had established in the house a degree of order, of discipline, and, above all, of economy, that were indeed remarkable; the constant aim of all her exertions being, not to enrich herself, but the community over which she presided; for the spirit of association, when it is directed to an object of *collective selfishness*, gives to corporations all the faults and vices of individuals."

E

The following is an extract from a letter addressed to me by one of the monks of the 19th century.[1] A part I have omitted, because it does not express my own view, unless with qualifications which I could not make, except by full discussion of the subject.

"Woman in the 19th century should be a pure, chaste, holy being.

This state of being in woman is no more attained by the expansion of her intellectual capacity, than by the augmentation of her physical force.

Neither is it attained by the increase or refinement of her love for man, or for any object whatever, or for all objects collectively; but

This state of being is attained by the reference of all her powers and all her actions to the source of Universal Love, whose constant requisition is a pure, chaste and holy life.

So long as woman looks to man (or to society) for that which she needs, she will remain in an indigent state, for he himself is indigent of it, and as much needs it as she does.

So long as this indigence continues, all unions or relations constructed between man and woman are constructed in indigence, and can produce only indigent results or unhappy consequences.

The unions now constructing, as well as those in which the parties constructing them were generated, being based on self-delight, or lust, can lead to no more happiness in the 20th, than is found in the 19th century.

It is not amended institutions, it is not improved education, it is not another selection of individuals for union, that can meliorate the sad result, but the *basis* of the union must be changed.

If in the natural order Woman and Man would adhere strictly to physiological or natural laws, in physical chastity, a most beautiful

1. Possibly by Fuller's acquaintance Charles Lane (1800–1870), English transcendentalist and social reformer, who joined the Shaker community at Harvard, Massachusetts, in 1844. For Lane's review of *Woman in the Nineteenth Century*, see p. 227.

amendment of the human race, and human condition, would in a few
generations adorn the world.

Still, it belongs to Woman in the spiritual order, to devote herself
wholly to her eternal husband, and become the Free Bride of the One
who alone can elevate her to her true position, and reconstruct her a
pure, chaste, and holy being."

F

I have mislaid an extract from "The Memoirs of an American Lady"[2]
which I wished to use on this subject, but its import is, briefly, this:

Observing of how little consequence the Indian women are in youth,
and how much in age, because in that trying life, good counsel and
sagacity are more prized than charms, Mrs. Grant expresses a wish that
Reformers would take a hint from observation of this circumstance.

In another place she says: "The misfortune of our sex is, that young
women are not regarded as the material from which old women must
be made."

I quote from memory, but believe the weight of the remark is
retained.

G

Euripides. Sophocles

As many allusions are made in the foregoing pages to characters of
women drawn by the Greek dramatists, which may not be familiar to
the majority of readers, I have borrowed from the papers of Miranda,[3]
some notes upon them. I trust the girlish tone of apostrophizing rapture
may be excused. Miranda was very young at the time of writing, compared with her present mental age. *Now*, she would express the same
feelings, but in a worthier garb—if she expressed them at all.

"Iphigenia! Antigone! you were worthy to live! We are fallen on evil
times, my sisters! our feelings have been checked; our thoughts questioned; our forms dwarfed and defaced by a bad nurture. Yet hearts,
like yours, are in our breasts, living, if unawakened; and our minds are
capable of the same resolves. You, we understand at once, those who
stare upon us pertly in the street, we cannot—could never understand.

You knew heroes, maidens, and your fathers were kings of men. You

---

2. Published in 1808, it was written by Anne Grant (1755–1838), the daughter of a captain in
the Scottish regiment who was stationed near Albany, New York, from 1758 to 1768.
3. One of Fuller's names for herself.

believed in your country, and the gods of your country. A great occasion was given to each, whereby to test her character.

You did not love on earth; for the poets wished to show us the force of woman's nature, virgin and unbiassed. You were women; not wives, or lovers, or mothers. Those are great names, but we are glad to see *you* in untouched flower.

Were brothers so dear, then, Antigone? We have no brothers. We see no men into whose lives we dare look steadfastly, or to whose destinies we look forward confidently. We care not for their urns; what inscription could we put upon them? They live for petty successes; or to win daily the bread of the day. No spark of kingly fire flashes from their eyes.

None! are there *none*?

It is a base speech to say it. Yes! there are some such; we have sometimes caught their glances. But rarely have they been rocked in the same cradle as we, and they do not look upon us much; for the time is not yet come.

Thou art so grand and simple! we need not follow thee; thou dost not need our love.

But, sweetest Iphigenia; who knew *thee*, as to me thou art known. I was not born in vain, if only for the heavenly tears I have shed with thee. She will be grateful for them. I have understood her wholly; as a friend should, better than she understood herself.

With what artless art the narrative rises to the crisis. The conflicts in Agamemnon's mind, and the imputations of Menelaus give us, at once, the full image of him, strong in will and pride, weak in virtue, weak in the noble powers of the mind that depend on imagination. He suffers, yet it requires the presence of his daughter to make him feel the full horror of what he is to do.

"Ah me! that breast, those cheeks, those golden tresses!"[4]

It is her beauty, not her misery, that makes the pathos. This is noble. And then, too, the injustice of the gods, that she, this creature of unblemished loveliness, must perish for the sake of a worthless woman.[5] Even Menelaus feels it, the moment he recovers from his wrath.

> "What hath she to do,
> The virgin daughter, with my Helena!
> •   •   Its former reasonings now
> My soul foregoes. •   •   •   •
>   For it is not just
> That thou shouldst groan, but my affairs go pleasantly,
> That those of thy house should die, and mine see the light."

4. This quotation and those that follow are from Euripides' *Iphigenia in Aulis*; see n. 3, p. 59).
5. Helen, wife of Menelaus, eloped with Paris to Troy and precipitated the famous Trojan war.

Indeed the overwhelmed aspect of the king of men might well move him.

> *Men.* "Brother, give me to take thy right hand,
> *Aga.* I give it, *for* the victory is thine, and I am wretched.
> I am, indeed, ashamed to drop the tear,
> And not to drop the tear I am ashamed."

How beautifully is Iphigenia introduced; beaming more and more softly on us with every touch of description. After Clytemnestra has given Orestes (then an infant,) out of the chariot, she says:

> "Ye females, in your arms,
> Receive her, for she is of tender age.
> Sit here by my feet, my child,
> By thy mother, Iphigenia, and show
> These strangers how I am blessed in thee,
> And here address thee to thy father.
> *Iphi.* Oh mother, should I run, wouldst thou be angry?
> And embrace my father breast to breast?"

With the same sweet timid trust she prefers the request to himself, and as he holds her in his arms, he seems as noble as Guido's Archangel; as if he never could sink below the trust of such a being!

The Achilles, in the first scene, is fine. A true Greek hero; not too good; all flushed with the pride of youth; but capable of god-like impulses. At first, he thinks only of his own wounded pride, (when he finds Iphigenia has been decoyed to Aulis under the pretext of becoming his wife;) but the grief of the queen soon makes him superior to his arrogant chafings. How well he says:—

> "*Far as a young man may*, I will repress
> So great a wrong."

By seeing him here, we understand why he, not Hector, was the hero of the Iliad. The beautiful moral nature of Hector was early developed by close domestic ties, and the cause of his country. Except in a purer simplicity of speech and manner, he might be a modern and a christian. But Achilles is cast in the largest and most vigorous mould of the earlier day: his nature is one of the richest capabilities, and therefore less quickly unfolds its meaning. The impression it makes at the early period is only of power and pride; running as fleetly with his armor on, as with it off; but sparks of pure lustre are struck, at moments, from the mass of ore. Of this sort is his refusal to see the beautiful virgin he has promised to protect. None of the Grecians must have the right to doubt his motives. How wise and prudent, too, the advice he gives as to the queen's conduct! He will not show himself, unless needed. His pride is the farthest possible remote from vanity. His thoughts are as free as any in our own time.

> "The prophet? what is he? a man
> Who speaks 'mong many falsehoods, but few truths,
> Whene'er chance leads him to speak true; when false,
> The prophet is no more."

Had Agamemnon possessed like clearness of sight, the virgin would not have perished, but also, Greece would have had no religion and no national existence.

When, in the interview with Agamemnon, the Queen begins her speech, in the true matrimonial style, dignified though her gesture be, and true all she says, we feel that truth, thus sauced with taunts, will not touch his heart, nor turn him from his purpose. But when Iphigenia begins her exquisite speech, as with the breathings of a lute,

> "Had I, my father, the persuasive voice
> Of Orpheus, &c.
>   Compel me not
> What is beneath to view. I was the first
> To call thee father; me thou first didst call
> Thy child: I was the first that on thy knees
> Fondly caressed thee, and from thee received
> The fond caress: this was thy speech to me:—
> 'Shall I, my child, e'er see thee in some house
> Of splendor, happy in thy husband, live
> And flourish, as becomes my dignity?'
> My speech to thee was, leaning 'gainst thy cheek,
> (Which with my hand I now caress:) 'And what
> Shall I then do for thee? shall I receive
> My father when grown old, and in my house
> Cheer him with each fond office, to repay
> The careful nurture which he gave my youth?'
> These words are in my memory deep impressed,
> Thou hast forgot them and will kill thy child."

Then she adjures him by all the sacred ties, and dwells pathetically on the circumstance which had struck even Menelaus.

> "If Paris be enamored of his bride,
> His Helen, what concerns it me? and how
> Comes he to my destruction?
>   Look upon me;
> Give me a smile, give me a kiss, my father;
> That if my words persuade thee not, in death
> I may have this memorial of thy love."

Never have the names of father and daughter been uttered with a holier tenderness than by Euripides, as in this most lovely passage, or in the "Supplicants," after the voluntary death of Evadne; Iphis says[6]

> "What shall this wretch now do? Should I return
> To my own house?—sad desolation there
> I shall behold, to sink my soul with grief.
> Or go I to the house of Capaneus?
> That was delightful to me, when I found
> My daughter there; but she is there no more:
> Oft would she kiss my cheek, with fond caress
> Oft soothe me. To a father, waxing old,
> Nothing is dearer than a daughter! sons
> Have spirits of higher pitch, but less inclined
> To sweet endearing fondness. Lead me then,
> Instantly lead me to my house, consign
> My wretched age to darkness, there to pine
> And waste away.
>   Old age,
> Struggling with many griefs, O how I hate thee!"

But to return to Iphigenia,—how infinitely melting is her appeal to Orestes, whom she holds in her robe.

> "My brother, small assistance canst thou give
> Thy friends; yet for thy sister with thy tears
> Implore thy father that she may not die:
> Even infants have a sense of ills; and see,
> My father! silent though he be, he sues
> To thee: be gentle to me; on my life
> Have pity: thy two children by this beard
> Entreat thee, thy dear children: one is yet
> An infant, one to riper years arrived."

The mention of Orestes, then an infant, all through, though slight, is of a domestic charm that prepares the mind to feel the tragedy of his after lot. When the Queen says

> "Dost thou sleep,
> My son? The rolling chariot hath subdued thee;
> Wake to thy sister's marriage happily."

---

6. In Euripides' play *Suppliant Woman* (c. 420–15 B.C.), Evadne throws herself on the funeral pyre of her slain husband. Iphis, her father, grieves.

We understand the horror of the doom which makes this cherished child a parricide. And so when Iphigenia takes leave of him after her fate is by herself accepted.

Iphi. "To manhood train Orestes,
Cly. Embrace him, for thou ne'er shalt see him more.
Iphi. (*To Orestes.*) Far as thou couldst, thou didst assist thy friends."

We know not how to blame the guilt of the maddened wife and mother. In her last meeting with Agamemnon, as in her previous expostulations and anguish, we see that a straw may turn the balance, and make her his deadliest foe. Just then, came the the suit of Ægisthus, then, when every feeling was uprooted or lacerated in her heart.

Iphigenia's moving address has no further effect than to make her father turn at bay and brave this terrible crisis. He goes out, firm in resolve; and she and her mother abandon themselves to a natural grief.

Hitherto nothing has been seen in Iphigenia, except the young girl, weak, delicate, full of feeling and beautiful as a sunbeam on the full green tree. But, in the next scene, the first impulse of that passion which makes and unmakes us, though unconfessed even to herself, though hopeless and unreturned, raises her at once into the heroic woman, worthy of the goddess who demands her.

Achilles appears to defend her, whom all others clamorously seek to deliver to the murderous knife. She sees him, and fired with thoughts, unknown before, devotes herself at once for the country which has given birth to such a man.

> "To be too fond of life
> Becomes not me; nor for myself alone,
> But to all Greece, a blessing didst thou bear me.
> Shall thousands, when their country's injured, lift
> Their shields; shall thousands grasp the oar, and dare,
> Advancing bravely 'gainst the foe, to die
> For Greece? And shall my life, my single life,
> Obstruct all this? Would this be just? What word
> Can we reply? Nay more, it is not right
> That he with all the Grecians should contest
> In fight, should die, *and for a woman.* No:
> More than a thousand women is one man
> Worthy to see the light of day.
> •   •   •   for Greece I give my life.
> Slay me; demolish Troy: for these shall be
> Long time my monuments, my children these,
> My nuptials and my glory."

This sentiment marks woman, when she loves enough to feel what a creature of glory and beauty a true *man* would be, as much in our own time as that of Euripides. Cooper makes the weak Hetty[7] say to her beautiful sister:

"Of course, I don't compare you with Harry. A handsome man is always far handsomer than any woman." True, it was the sentiment of the age, but it was the first time Iphigenia had felt it. In Agamemnon she saw *her father*, to him she could prefer her claim. In Achilles she saw *a man*, the crown of creation, enough to fill the world with his presence, were all other beings blotted from its spaces.[8]

The reply of Achilles is as noble. Here is his bride, he feels it now, and all his vain vauntings are hushed.

> "Daughter of Agamemnon, highly blessed
> Some god would make me, if I might attain
> Thy nuptials. Greece in thee I happy deem,
> And thee in Greece.   •   •
> •   •   •   in thy thought
> Revolve this well; death is a dreadful thing."

How sweet is her reply, and then the tender modesty with which she addresses him here and elsewhere as "*stranger.*"

> "Reflecting not on any, thus I speak:
> Enough of wars and slaughters from the charms
> Of Helen rise; but die not thou for me,
> O Stranger, nor distain thy sword with blood,
> But let me save my country if I may."
>
> *Achilles.* "O glorious spirit! nought have I 'gainst this
> To urge, since such thy will, for what thou sayst
> Is generous. Why should not the truth be spoken?"

But feeling that human weakness may conquer yet, he goes to wait at the altar, resolved to keep his promise of protection thoroughly.

In the next beautiful scene she shows that a few tears might overwhelm her in his absence. She raises her mother beyond weeping them, yet her soft purity she cannot impart.

> *Iphi.* "My father, and thy husband do not hate:
> *Cly.* For thy dear sake fierce contests must he bear.
> *Iphi.* For Greece reluctant me to death he yields;
> *Cly.* Basely, with guile unworthy Atreus' son."

7. In *The Deerslayer* (1841) by James Fenimore Cooper (1789–1851), Hetty Hutter is a somewhat feebleminded young woman and Hurry Harry March is a frontier scout in love with Hetty's beautiful sister, Judith.
8. Men do not often reciprocate this pure love.

> "Her prentice han' she tried on man,
> And then she made the lasses o',"

Is a fancy, not a feeling, in their more frequently passionate and strong, than noble or tender natures [Fuller's note]. The quotation is from "Green Grow the Rashes" by the Scottish poet Robert Burns (1759–1796).

This is truth incapable of an answer and Iphigenia attempts none. She begins the hymn which is to sustain her,

> "Lead me; mine the glorious fate,
> To o'erturn the Phrygian state."

After the sublime flow of lyric heroism, she suddenly sinks back into the tenderer feeling of her dreadful fate.

> "O my country, where these eyes
> Opened on Pelasgic skies!
> O ye virgins, once my pride,
> In Mycenæ who abide!
>
> CHORUS.
> Why of Perseus name the town,
> Which Cyclopean ramparts crown?
>
> IPHIGENIA.
> Me you rear'd a beam of light,
> Freely now I sink in night."

Freely; as the messenger afterwards recounts it.

> •   •   •

> "Imperial Agamemnon, when he saw
> His daughter, as a victim to the grave,
> Advancing, groan'd, and bursting into tears,
> Turned from the sight his head, before his eyes,
> Holding his robe. The virgin near him stood,
> And thus addressed him: 'Father, I to thee
> Am present; for my country, and for all
> The land of Greece, I freely give myself
> A victim: to the altar let them lead me,
> Since such the oracle. If aught on me
> Depends, be happy, and obtain the prize
> Of glorious conquest, and revisit safe
> Your country. Of the Grecians, for this cause,
> Let no one touch me; with intrepid spirit
> Silent will I present my neck.' She spoke,
> And all that heard revered the noble soul
> And virtue of the virgin."

How quickly had the fair bud bloomed up into its perfection. Had she lived a thousand years, she could not have surpassed this. Goethe's Iphigenia, the mature woman, with its myriad delicate traits, never surpasses, scarcely equals what we know of her in Euripides.

Can I appreciate this work in a translation? I think so, impossible as it may seem to one who can enjoy the thousand melodies, and words in exactly the right place and cadence of the original. They say you can see the Apollo Belvidere[9] in a plaster cast, and I cannot doubt it, so great the benefit conferred on my mind, by a transcript thus imperfect. And so with these translations from the Greek. I can divine the original through this veil, as I can see the movements of a spirited horse by those of his coarse grasscloth muffler. Beside, every translator who feels his subject is inspired, and the divine Aura informs even his stammering lips.

Iphigenia is more like one of the women Shakespeare loved than the others; she is a tender virgin, ennobled and strengthened by sentiment more than intellect, what they call a woman *par excellence*.

Macaria is more like one of Massinger's women. She advances boldly, though with the decorum of her sex and nation:

> *Macaria.* "Impute not boldness to me that I come
> Before you, strangers; this my first request
> I urge; for silence and a chaste reserve
> Is woman's genuine praise, and to remain
> Quiet within the house. But I come forth,
> Hearing thy lamentations, Iolaus:
> Though charged with no commission, yet perhaps,
> I may be useful."   •   •

Her speech when she offers herself as the victim, is reasonable, as one might speak to-day. She counts the cost all through. Iphigenia is too timid and delicate to dwell upon the loss of earthly bliss, and the due experience of life, even as much as Jeptha's daughter did,[1] but Macaria is explicit, as well befits the daughter of Hercules.

> "Should *these* die, myself
> Preserved, of prosperous future could I form
> One cheerful hope?
> A poor forsaken virgin who would deign
> To take in marriage? Who would wish for sons
> From one so wretched? Better then to die,
> Than bear such undeserved miseries:
> One less illustrious this might more beseem.
>   •   •   •
> I have a soul that unreluctantly
> Presents itself, and I proclaim aloud
> That for my brothers and myself I die.
> I am not fond of life, but think I gain
> An honorable prize to die with glory."

9. Famous marble statue of the god Apollo, a Roman copy of the original Greek bronze.
1. In Judges 11.30–39, Jeptha vows that if the Lord gives him victory in battle, he will sacrifice whatever greets him upon his return home. His virgin daughter is the unfortunate victim, and she asks for and receives two months to bewail her fate before she dies.

Still nobler when Iolaus proposes rather that she shall draw lots with
her sisters.

> "*By lot* I will not die, for to such death
> No thanks are due, or glory—name it not.
> If you accept me, if my offered life
> Be grateful to you, willingly I give it
> For these, but by constraint I will not die."

Very fine are her parting advice and injunctions to them all:

> "Farewell! revered old man, farewell! and teach
> These youths in all things to be wise, like thee,
> Naught will avail them more."

Macaria has the clear Minerva eye: Antigone's is deeper, and more
capable of emotion, but calm. Iphigenia's, glistening, gleaming with
angel truth, or dewy as a hidden violet.

I am sorry that Tennyson, who spoke with such fitness of all the
others in his "Dream of fair women," has not of Iphigenia. Of her
alone he has not made a fit picture, but only of the circumstances of
the sacrifice. He can never have taken to heart this work of Euripides,
yet he was so worthy to feel it. Of Jeptha's daughter, he has spoken as
he would of Iphigenia, both in her beautiful song, and when

> "I heard Him, for He spake, and grief became
>   A solemn scorn of ills.
>
> It comforts me in this one thought to dwell
>   That I subdued me to my father's will;
> Because the kiss he gave me, ere I fell,
>   Sweetens the spirit still.
>
> Moreover it is written, that my race
>   Hewed Ammon, hip and thigh from Arroer
> Or Arnon unto Minneth. Here her face
>   Glow'd as I look'd on her.
>
> She locked her lips; she left me where I stood;
>   "Glory to God," she sang, and past afar,
> Thridding the sombre boskage of the woods,
>   Toward the morning-star."[2]

In the "Trojan dames" there are fine touches of nature with regard
to Cassandra. Hecuba shows that mixture of shame and reverence, that
prose kindred always do, towards the inspired child, the poet, the
elected sufferer for the race.

When the herald announces that she is chosen to be the mistress of

2. From "A Dream of Fair Women" by the English poet Alfred, Lord Tennyson (1801–1892).

Agamemnon, Hecuba answers indignant, and betraying the involuntary pride and faith she felt in this daughter.

> "The virgin of Apollo, whom the God,
> Radiant with golden locks, allowed to live
> In her pure vow of maiden chastity?
> *Tal.* With love the raptured virgin smote his heart.
> *Hec.* Cast from thee, O my daughter, cast away
> Thy sacred wand, rend off the honored wreaths,
> The splendid ornaments that grace thy brows."

Yet the moment Cassandra appears, singing wildly her inspired song, Hecuba calls her

> "My *frantic* child."

Yet how graceful she is in her tragic phrenzy, the chorus shows—

> "How sweetly at thy house's ills thou smil'st,
> Chanting what haply thou wilt not show true?"

But if Hecuba dares not trust her highest instinct about her daughter, still less can the vulgar mind of the herald (a man not without tenderness of heart, but with no princely, no poetic blood,) abide the wild prophetic mood which insults his prejudices both as to country and decorums of the sex. Yet Agamemnon, though not a noble man, is of large mould and could admire this strange beauty which excited distaste in common minds.

> *Tal.* "What commands respect, and is held high
> As wise, is nothing better than the mean
> Of no repute: for this most potent king
> Of all the Grecians, the much honored son
> Of Atreus, is enamored with his prize,
> This frantic raver. I am a poor man,
> Yet would I not receive her to my bed."

Cassandra answers with a careless disdain,

> "This is a busy slave."

With all the lofty decorum of manners among the ancients, how free was their intercourse, man to man, how full the mutual understanding between prince and "busy slave!" Not here in adversity only, but in the pomp of power, it was so. Kings were approached with ceremonious obeisance, but not hedged round with etiquette, they could see and know their fellows.

The Andromache here is just as lovely as that of the Iliad.

To her child whom they are about to murder, the same that was frightened at the "glittering plume."

"Dost thou weep,
My son? Hast thou a sense of thy ill fate?
Why dost thou clasp me with thy hands, why hold
My robes, and shelter thee beneath my wings,
Like a young bird? No more my Hector comes,
Returning from the tomb; he grasps no more
His glittering spear, bringing protection to thee."
    •   •   •
        •   •   "O soft embrace,
And to thy mother dear. O fragrant breath!
In vain I swathed thy infant limbs, in vain
I gave thee nurture at this breast, and toiled,
Wasted with care. *If ever*, now embrace,
Now clasp thy mother; throw thine arms around
My neck and join thy cheek, thy lips to mine."

As I look up I meet the eyes of Beatrice Cenci.[3] Beautiful one, these woes, even, were less than thine, yet thou seemest to understand them all. Thy clear melancholy gaze says, they, at least, had known moments of bliss, and the tender relations of nature had not been broken and polluted from the very first. Yes! the gradations of wo are all but infinite: only good can be infinite.

Certainly the Greeks knew more of real home intercourse, and more of woman than the Americans. It is in vain to tell me of outward observances. The poets, the sculptors always tell the truth. In proportion as a nation is refined, women *must* have an ascendancy, it is the law of nature.

Beatrice! thou wert not "fond of life," either, more than those princesses. Thou wert able to cut it down in the full flower of beauty, as an offering to *the best* known to thee. Thou wert not so happy as to die for thy country or thy brethren, but thou wert worthy of such an occasion.

In the days of chivalry woman was habitually viewed more as an ideal, but I do not know that she inspired a deeper and more home-felt reverence than Iphigenia in the breast of Achilles, or Macaria in that of her old guardian, Iolaus.

We may, with satisfaction, add to these notes the words to which Haydn has adapted his magnificent music in "The Creation."[4]

"In native worth and honor clad, with beauty, courage, strength adorned, erect to heaven, and tall, he stands, a Man!—the lord and king of all! The large and arched front sublime of wisdom deep declares the seat, and in his eyes with brightness shines the soul, the breath and

---

3. Youngest daughter (1577–1599) of a wealthy Italian nobleman, who forced her to have incestuous relations with him. Beatrice conspired with one of her brothers and her stepmother to murder him; all three were beheaded by order of Pope Clement VIII.
4. The 1798 oratorio by Austrian composer Franz Joseph Haydn (1732–1809).

image of his God. With fondness leans upon his breast the partner for him formed, a woman fair, and graceful spouse. Her softly smiling virgin looks, of flowery spring the mirror, bespeak him love, and joy and bliss."

Whoever has heard this music must have a mental standard as to what man and woman should be. Such was marriage in Eden, when "erect to heaven *he* stood," but since, like other institutions, this must be not only reformed, but revived, may be offered as a picture of something intermediate,—the seed of the future growth,—

H

The Sacred Marriage

And has another's life as large a scope?
It may give due fulfillment to thy hope,
And every portal to the unknown may ope.

If, near this other life, thy inmost feeling
Trembles with fateful prescience of revealing
The future Deity, time is still concealing.

If thou feel thy whole force drawn more and more
To launch that other bark on seas without a shore;
And no still secret must be kept in store;

If meannesses that dim each temporal deed,
The dull decay that mars the fleshly weed,
And flower of love that seems to fall and leave no seed—

Hide never the full presence from thy sight
Of mutual aims and tasks, ideals bright,
Which feed their roots to-day on all this seeming blight.

Twin stars that mutual circle in the heaven,
Two parts for spiritual concord given,
Twin Sabbaths that inlock the Sacred Seven;

Still looking to the centre for the cause,
Mutual light giving to draw out the powers,
And learning all the other groups by cognizance of one
        another's laws:

The parent love the wedded love includes,
The one permits the two their mutual moods,
The two each other know mid myriad multitudes;

With child-like intellect discerning love,
And mutual action energizing love,
In myriad forms affiliating love.

A world whose seasons bloom from pole to pole,
A force which knows both starting-point and goal,
A Home in Heaven,—the Union in the Soul.[5]

5. The poem is Fuller's.

Note on the Text

This Norton Critical Edition is based on the first edition of *Woman in the Nineteenth Century*, published by the firm of Greeley & McElrath in New York City in 1845. The book was priced at fifty cents, and according to Horace Greeley, fifteen hundred copies were printed.[1] They went quickly. Fuller wrote to her brother Eugene on March 9, 1845 that the whole edition had been sold off in a week to booksellers and that she had received eighty-five dollars as her share.[2] Her plan at first was to bring out subsequent revised editions of the work, for she regarded it as an organic, ongoing project. When she had completed the manuscript in November 1844, she wrote William Henry Channing that she wished to give it to a publisher "only for one edition," adding "I should hope to be able to make it constantly better while I live and should wish to retain full command of it, in case of subsequent editions."[3] A year later, in the fall of 1845, Fuller saw a pirated copy of her book that had been republished in England in Clarke's Cabinet Library. "I had never heard a word about it from England," she wrote her brother Richard, "and am very glad to find it will be read by women there." She added that she hoped to get her own revised second edition out "before long" and asked him to send her other parts of the story of Panthea he thought she might like to add.[4] By February 1846, however, no progress had been made on a second edition, and Fuller blamed Thomas McElrath, Horace Greeley's cautious partner, for the delay. "Entre nous [between us], *strictly*," she wrote Richard, "Greeley and McElrath have not acted as I could wish the last few weeks. The blame lies wholly with the latter. He has devoted no attention to the 2d edition of my book, he delays making me a proposition as to the future, he acts towards me in a way that makes me think perhaps the boldness of my course does not suit his narrow mind."[5] Six months later, Fuller sailed for Europe, where she would spend the last four years of her life. No other American edition of her book was published in her lifetime. In 1855 a heavily edited and "improved" version of the book was pub-

1. Joel Myerson, *Margaret Fuller: A Descriptive Bibliography* (Pittsburgh: University of Pittsburgh Press, 1978), 20.
2. *Letters of Margaret Fuller*, 4:56.
3. Ibid., 3:242.
4. Ibid., 4:165–66.
5. Ibid., 4:187.

lished by Arthur Fuller and Horace Greeley in *Woman in the Nine-teenth Century, and Kindred Papers*, but it is corrupt and has no authority.

The first edition of *Woman in the Nineteenth Century* contains a number of errors that Fuller herself noticed. In March 1845, she wrote James Nathan that she "should sometime like to correct with my pen the little errors in the printing, of which I see too many, but hope to remove them all in another edition."[6] Fuller never performed this task, of course, but the present edition does emend the obvious typographical and punctuation errors of the first edition. The emendations made can be found in the list below, which is indebted to Joel Myerson's list of suggested emendations to the 1845 text.[7] Page and line numbers refer to this Norton Critical Edition.

3.11 even] evea
7.31 reward.] reward
14.33 We] "We
40.24 find] fiud
50.43 the first] he first
52.2 "Thus] Thus
52.7 "Having] Having
52.18 me,'] me,
52.18 'has] has
56.25 reformation.] reformation.'
67.32 reform-growth.] reform-growth,
68.21 vow."] vow.
75.43 mother.] mother,
80.22 wrong.' "] wrong."
84.8 "You] You
88.19 bases] basis
92.1 English] English,
95.2 Valkyrie] Walkyrie
95.20 Necker's] Neckar's
102.25 spot?"] spot?
103.9 employments] employements
109.31 the conspicuous] conspicuous
115.38 largest] argest
121.24 Mother] mother
125.24 Aulis] Anlis
128.6 friends."] friends.'

6. Ibid., 4:55.
7. *Woman in the Nineteenth Century*, ed. Joel Myerson (Columbia: University of South Carolina Press), 207–08.

BACKGROUNDS

The following section provides materials to help elucidate the origins and development of *Woman in the Nineteenth Century*. Four major areas receive coverage: (1) Fuller's own experiences as a woman, as revealed in her autobiographical sketch, semiautobiographical portraits of strong female figures, and her journals and poems; (2) her "conversations" with women in Boston about the topic of woman; (3) her discussions with her friends, especially Ralph Waldo Emerson, about friendship, marriage, and spiritual union; and (4) her observations on the marriages of her friends, especially the Emersons, Sam and Anna Ward, and the Hawthornes. Fuller's visits with the female convicts at Sing-Sing prison also seem significant, so letters to and about them are included. An additional background area that can be only mentioned here is her readings in Fourier, Goethe, Sand, Sedgewick, Sue, Swedenborg, and other authors, including Emerson, whose ideas informed her own and provided an intellectual context for them.

MARGARET FULLER

[Autobiographical Romance]†

Parents

My father[1] was a lawyer and a politician. He was a man largely endowed with that sagacious energy, which the state of New England society, for the last half century, has been so well fitted to develop. His father was a clergyman, settled as pastor in Princeton, Massachusetts, within the bounds of whose parish-farm was Wachuset. His means were small, and the great object of his ambition was to send his sons to college. As a boy, my father was taught to think only of preparing himself for Harvard University, and when there of preparing himself for the profession of Law. As a Lawyer, again, the ends constantly presented were to work for distinction in the community, and for the means of supporting a family. To be an honored citizen, and to have a home on earth, were made the great aims of existence. To open the deeper fountains of the soul, to regard life here as the prophetic entrance to immortality, to develop his spirit to perfection,—motives like these had never been suggested to him, either by fellow-beings or by outward circumstances. The result was a character, in its social aspect, of quite the common sort. A good son and brother, a kind neighbor, an active man of business—in all these outward relations he was but one of a class, which surrounding conditions have made the majority among us. In the more delicate and individual relations, he never approached but two mortals, my mother and myself.

'His love for my mother[2] was the green spot on which he stood apart from the common-places of a mere bread-winning, bread-bestowing existence. She was one of those fair and flower-like natures, which sometimes spring up even beside the most dusty highways of life—a creature not to be shaped into a merely useful instrument, but bound by one law with the blue sky, the dew, and the frolic birds. Of all persons whom I have known, she had in her most of the angelic,—of that spontaneous love for every living thing, for man, and beast, and tree, which restores the golden age.

---

† From *Memoirs of Margaret Fuller Ossoli*, ed. R. W. Emerson, W. H. Channing, and J. F. Clarke (Boston: Phillips, Sampson, 1852), 2:11–42. Written during 1840–41, this sketch remained unfinished and unpublished during Fuller's lifetime.
1. Timothy Fuller (1778–1835) [Editor].
2. Margarett Crane Fuller (1789–1859), who married Timothy in 1809 [Editor].

Death in the House

My earliest recollection is of a death,—the death of a sister,[3] two years younger than myself. Probably there is a sense of childish endearments, such as belong to this tie, mingled with that of loss, of wonder, and mystery; but these last are prominent in memory. I remember coming home and meeting our nursery-maid, her face streaming with tears. That strange sight of tears made an indelible impression. I realize how little I was of stature, in that I looked up to this weeping face;—and it has often seemed since, that—full-grown for the life of this earth, I have looked up just so, at times of threatening, of doubt, and distress, and that just so has some being of the next higher order of existences looked down, aware of a law unknown to me, and tenderly commiserating the pain I must endure in emerging from my ignorance.

She took me by the hand and led me into a still and dark chamber,—then drew aside the curtain and showed me my sister. I see yet that beauty of death! The highest achievements of sculpture are only the reminder of its severe sweetness. Then I remember the house all still and dark,—the people in their black clothes and dreary faces, —the scent of the newly-made coffin,—my being set up in a chair and detained by a gentle hand to hear the clergyman,—the carriages slowly going, the procession slowly doling out their steps to the grave. But I have no remembrance of what I have since been told I did,—insisting, with loud cries, that they should not put the body in the ground. I suppose that my emotion was spent at the time, and so there was nothing to fix that moment in my memory.

I did not then, nor do I now, find any beauty in these ceremonies. What had they to do with the sweet playful child? Her life and death were alike beautiful, but all this sad parade was not. Thus my first experience of life was one of death. She who would have been the companion of my life was severed from me, and I was left alone. This has made a vast difference in my lot. Her character, if that fair face promised right, would have been soft, graceful and lively; it would have tempered mine to a gentler and more gradual course.

Overwork

My father,—all whose feelings were now concentred on me,—instructed me himself. The effect of this was so far good that, not passing through the hands of many ignorant and weak persons as so many do at preparatory schools, I was put at once under discipline of considerable severity, and, at the same time, had a more than ordinarily high standard presented to me. My father was a man of business, even in literature; he had been a high scholar at college, and was warmly at-

3. Julia Adelaide Fuller (1812–1813) [Editor].

tached to all he had learned there, both from the pleasure he had derived in the exercise of his faculties and the associated memories of success and good repute. He was, beside, well read in French literature, and in English, a Queen Anne's man.[4] He hoped to make me the heir of all he knew, and of as much more as the income of his profession enabled him to give me means of acquiring. At the very beginning, he made one great mistake, more common, it is to be hoped, in the last generation, than the warnings of physiologists will permit it to be with the next. He thought to gain time, by bringing forward the intellect as early as possible. Thus I had tasks given me, as many and various as the hours would allow, and on subjects beyond my age; with the additional disadvantage of reciting to him in the evening, after he returned from his office. As he was subject to many interruptions, I was often kept up till very late; and as he was a severe teacher, both from his habits of mind and his ambition for me, my feelings were kept on the stretch till the recitations were over. Thus frequently, I was sent to bed several hours too late, with nerves unnaturally stimulated. The consequence was a premature development of the brain, that made me a "youthful prodigy" by day, and by night a victim of spectral illusions, nightmare, and somnambulism,[5] which at the time prevented the harmonious development of my bodily powers and checked my growth, while, later, they induced continual headache, weakness and nervous affections, of all kinds. As these again re-acted on the brain, giving undue force to every thought and every feeling, there was finally produced a state of being both too active and too intense, which wasted my constitution, and will bring me,—even although I have learned to understand and regulate my now morbid temperament,—to a premature grave.

No one understood this subject of health then. No one knew why this child, already kept up so late, was still unwilling to retire. My aunts cried out upon the "spoiled child, the most unreasonable child that ever was,—if brother could but open his eyes to see it,—who was never willing to go to bed." They did not know that, so soon as the light was taken away, she seemed to see colossal faces advancing slowly towards her, the eyes dilating, and each feature swelling loathsomely as they came, till at last, when they were about to close upon her, she started up with a shriek which drove them away, but only to return when she lay down again. They did not know that, when at last she went to sleep, it was to dream of horses trampling over her, and to awake once more in fright; or, as she had just read in her Virgil, of being among trees that dripped with blood, where she walked and walked and could not

---

4. An admirer of authors such as Jonathan Swift (1667–1745), Joseph Addison (1672–1719), Richard Steele (1672–1729), and Alexander Pope (1688–1744), who wrote during Queen Anne's reign, (1702–14) [Editor].
5. Sleepwalking [Editor].

get out, while the blood became a pool and plashed over her feet, and rose higher and higher, till soon she dreamed it would reach her lips. No wonder the child arose and walked in her sleep, moaning all over the house, till once, when they heard her, and came and waked her, and she told what she had dreamed, her father sharply bid her "leave off thinking of such nonsense, or she would be crazy,"—never knowing that he was himself the cause of all these horrors of the night. Often she dreamed of following to the grave the body of her mother, as she had done that of her sister, and woke to find the pillow drenched in tears. These dreams softened her heart too much, and cast a deep shadow over her young days; for then, and later, the life of dreams,— probably because there was in it less to distract the mind from its own earnestness,—has often seemed to her more real, and been remembered with more interest, than that of waking hours.

Poor child! Far remote in time, in thought, from that period, I look back on these glooms and terrors, wherein I was enveloped, and perceive that I had no natural childhood.

Books

Thus passed my first years. My mother was in delicate health, and much absorbed in the care of her younger children. In the house was neither dog nor bird, nor any graceful animated form of existence. I saw no persons who took my fancy, and real life offered no attraction. Thus my already over-excited mind found no relief from without, and was driven for refuge from itself to the world of books. I was taught Latin and English grammar at the same time, and began to read Latin at six years old, after which, for some years, I read it daily. In this branch of study, first by my father, and afterwards by a tutor, I was trained to quite a high degree of precision. I was expected to understand the mechanism of the language thoroughly, and in translating to give the thoughts in as few well-arranged words as possible, and without breaks or hesitation,—for with these my father had absolutely no patience.

Indeed, he demanded accuracy and clearness in everything: you must not speak, unless you can make your meaning perfectly intelligible to the person addressed; must not express a thought, unless you can give a reason for it, if required; must not make a statement, unless sure of all particulars—such were his rules. "But," "if," "unless," "I am mistaken," and "it may be so," were words and phrases excluded from the province where he held sway. Trained to great dexterity in artificial methods, accurate, ready, with entire command of his resources, he had no belief in minds that listen, wait, and receive. He had no conception of the subtle and indirect motions of imagination and feeling. His influence on me was great, and opposed to the natural unfolding of my character, which was fervent, of strong grasp, and disposed to infatuation, and self-forgetfulness. He made the common prose world so present to me, that my natural bias was controlled. I did not go mad, as many would do, at being continually roused from my dreams. I had too much strength to be crushed,—and since I must put on the fetters, could not submit to let them impede my motions. My own world sank deep within, away from the surface of my life; in what I did and said I learned to have reference to other minds. But my true life was only the dearer that it was secluded and veiled over by a thick curtain of available intellect, and that coarse, but wearable stuff woven by the ages,—Common Sense.

In accordance with this discipline in heroic common sense, was the influence of those great Romans, whose thoughts and lives were my daily food during those plastic years. The genius of Rome displayed itself in Character, and scarcely needed an occasional wave of the torch of thought to show its lineaments, so marble strong they gleamed in every light. Who, that has lived with those men, but admires the plain force of fact, of thought passed into action? They take up things with their naked hands. There is just the man, and the block he casts before you,—no divinity, no demon, no unfulfilled aim, but just the man and Rome, and what he did for Rome. Everything turns your attention to what a man can become, not by yielding himself freely to impressions, not by letting nature play freely through him, but by a single thought, an earnest purpose, an indomitable will, by hardihood, self-command, and force of expression. Architecture was the art in which Rome excelled, and this corresponds with the feeling these men of Rome excite. They did not grow,—they built themselves up, or were built up by the fate of Rome, as a temple for Jupiter Stator.[6] The ruined Roman sits among the ruins; he flies to no green garden; he does not look to heaven; if his intent is defeated, if he is less than he meant to be, he lives no more. The names which end in "us," seem to speak with lyric cadence. That measured cadence,—that tramp and march,—which are not stilted, because they indicate real force, yet which seem so when compared with any other language,—make Latin a study in itself of mighty influence. The language alone, without the literature, would give one the *thought* of Rome. Man present in nature, commanding nature too sternly to be inspired by it, standing like the rock amid the sea, or moving like the fire over the land, either impassive, or irresistible; knowing not the soft mediums or fine flights of life, but by the force which he expresses, piercing to the centre.

We are never better understood than when we speak of a "Roman virtue," a "Roman outline." There is somewhat indefinite, somewhat yet unfulfilled in the thought of Greece, of Spain, of modern Italy; but ROME! it stands by itself, a clear Word. The power of will, the dignity

6. The supreme Roman god, Jupiter, in his role as stayer of defeat [Editor].

of a fixed purpose is what it utters. Every Roman was an emperor. It is
well that the infallible church should have been founded on this rock,
that the presumptuous Peter should hold the keys, as the conquering
Jove did before his thunderbolts, to be seen of all the world. The Apollo
tends flocks with Admetus; Christ teaches by the lonely lake, or plucks
wheat as he wanders through the fields some Sabbath morning. They
never come to this stronghold; they could not have breathed freely
where all became stone as soon as spoken, where divine youth found
no horizon for its all-promising glance, but every thought put on, before
it dared issue to the day in action, its *toga virilis*.[7]

Suckled by this wolf,[8] man gains a different complexion from that
which is fed by the Greek honey. He takes a noble bronze in camps
and battle-fields; the wrinkles of council well beseem his brow, and the
eye cuts its way like the sword. The Eagle should never have been used
as a symbol by any other nation: it belonged to Rome.

The history of Rome abides in mind, of course, more than the literature. It was degeneracy for a Roman to use the pen; his life was in
the day. The "vaunting" of Rome, like that of the North American
Indians, is her proper literature. A man rises; he tells who he is, and
what he has done; he speaks of his country and her brave men; he
knows that a conquering god is there whose agent is his own right hand;
and he should end like the Indian, "I have no more to say."

It never shocks us that the Roman is self-conscious. One wants no
universal truths from him, no philosophy, no creation, but only his life,
his Roman life felt in every pulse, realized in every gesture. The universal heaven takes in the Roman only to make us feel his individuality
the more. The Will, the Resolve of Man!—it has been expressed,—fully
expressed!

I steadily loved this ideal in my childhood, and this is the cause,
probably, why I have always felt that man must know how to stand firm
on the ground, before he can fly. In vain for me are men more, if they
are less, than Romans. Dante was far greater than any Roman, yet I
feel he was right to take the Mantuan[9] as his guide through hell, and
to heaven.

Horace[1] was a great deal to me then, and is so still. Though his
words do not abide in memory, his presence does: serene, courtly, of
darting hazel eye, a self-sufficient grace, and an appreciation of the
world of stern realities, sometimes pathetic, never tragic. He is the natural man of the world; he is what he ought to be, and his darts never
fail of their aim. There is a perfume and raciness, too, which makes

7. The white toga signifying manhood (Latin) [Editor].
8. Fuller alludes to the fable that the founders of Rome, Romulus and Remus, were raised by
   a mother wolf [Editor].
9. Virgil (70–19 B.C.), the Roman poet, born in a village near Mantua and known as the Mantuan, appears as Dante's guide in the *Divine Comedy* [Editor].
1. Quintus Horatius Flaccus (65–8 B.C.), Roman poet [Editor].

life a banquet, where the wit sparkles no less that the viands were bought with blood.

Ovid gave me not Rome, nor himself, but a view into the enchanted gardens of the Greek mythology. This path I followed, have been following ever since; and now, life half over, it seems to me, as in my childhood, that every thought of which man is susceptible, is intimated there. In those young years, indeed, I did not see what I now see, but loved to creep from amid the Roman pikes to lie beneath this great vine, and see the smiling and serene shapes go by, woven from the finest fibres of all the elements. I knew not why, at that time,—but I loved to get away from the hum of the forum, and the mailed clang of Roman speech, to these shifting shows of nature, these Gods and Nymphs born of the sunbeam, the wave, the shadows on the hill.

As with Rome I antedated the world of deeds, so I lived in those Greek forms the true faith of a refined and intense childhood. So great was the force of reality with which these forms impressed me, that I prayed earnestly for a sign,—that it would lighten in some particular region of the heavens, or that I might find a bunch of grapes in the path, when I went forth in the morning. But no sign was given, and I was left a waif stranded upon the shores of modern life!

Of the Greek language, I knew only enough to feel that the sounds told the same story as the mythology;—that the law of life in that land was beauty, as in Rome it was a stern composure. I wish I had learned as much of Greece as of Rome,—so freely does the mind play in her sunny waters, where there is no chill, and the restraint is from within out; for these Greeks, in an atmosphere of ample grace, could not be impetuous, or stern, but loved moderation as equable life always must, for it is the law of beauty.

With these books I passed my days. The great amount of study exacted of me soon ceased to be a burden, and reading became a habit and a passion. The force of feeling, which, under other circumstances, might have ripened thought, was turned to learn the thoughts of others. This was not a tame state, for the energies brought out by rapid acquisition gave glow enough. I thought with rapture of the all-accomplished man, him of the many talents, wide resources, clear sight, and omnipotent will. A Cæsar seemed great enough. I did not then know that such men impoverish the treasury to build the palace. I kept their statues as belonging to the hall of my ancestors, and loved to conquer obstacles, and fed my youth and strength for their sake.

Still, though this bias was so great that in earliest years I learned, in these ways, how the world takes hold of a powerful nature, I had yet other experiences. None of these were deeper than what I found in the happiest haunt of my childish years,—our little garden. Our house, though comfortable, was very ugly, and in a neighborhood which I detested,—every dwelling and its appurtenances having a *mesquin*[2] and huddled look. I liked nothing about us except the tall graceful elms before the house, and the dear little garden behind. Our back door opened on a high flight of steps, by which I went down to a green plot, much injured in my ambitious eyes by the presence of the pump and tool-house. This opened into a little garden, full of choice flowers and fruit-trees, which was my mother's delight, and was carefully kept. Here I felt at home. A gate opened thence into the fields,—a wooden gate made of boards, in a high, unpainted board wall, and embowered in the clematis creeper. This gate I used to open to see the sunset heaven; beyond this black frame I did not step, for I liked to look at the deep gold behind it. How exquisitely happy I was in its beauty, and how I loved the silvery wreaths of my protecting vine! I never would pluck one of its flowers at that time, I was so jealous of its beauty, but often since I carry off wreaths of it from the wild-wood, and it stands in nature to my mind as the emblem of domestic love.

Of late I have thankfully felt what I owe to that garden, where the best hours of my lonely childhood were spent. Within the house everything was socially utilitarian; my books told of a proud world, but in another temper were the teachings of the little garden. There my thoughts could lie callow in the nest, and only be fed and kept warm, not called to fly or sing before the time. I loved to gaze on the roses, the violets, the lilies, the pinks; my mother's hand had planted them, and they bloomed for me. I culled the most beautiful. I looked at them on every side. I kissed them, I pressed them to my bosom with passionate emotions, such as I have never dared express to any human being. An ambition swelled my heart to be as beautiful, as perfect as they. I have not kept my vow. Yet, forgive, ye wild asters, which gleam so sadly amid the fading grass; forgive me, ye golden autumn flowers, which so strive to reflect the glories of the departing distant sun; and ye silvery flowers, whose moonlight eyes I knew so well, forgive! Living and blooming in your unchecked law, ye know nothing of the blights, the distortions, which beset the human being; and which at such hours it would seem that no glories of free agency could ever repay!

There was, in the house, no apartment appropriated to the purpose of a library, but there was in my father's room a large closet filled with books, and to these I had free access when the task-work of the day was done. Its window overlooked wide fields, gentle slopes, a rich and smiling country, whose aspect pleased without much occupying the eye, while a range of blue hills, rising at about twelve miles distance, allured to reverie. "Distant mountains," says Tieck,[3] "excite the fancy, for "be-

---

2. Shabby (French) [Editor].
3. Johann Ludwig Tieck (1773–1853), German writer of fairy tales, novels, and poetic dramas [Editor].

yond them we place the scene of our Paradise." Thus, in the poems of fairy adventure, we climb the rocky barrier, pass fearless its dragon caves, and dark pine forests, and find the scene of enchantment in the vale behind. My hopes were never so definite, but my eye was constantly allured to that distant blue range, and I would sit, lost in fancies, till tears fell on my cheek. I loved this sadness; but only in later years, when the realities of life had taught me moderation, did the passionate emotions excited by seeing them again teach how glorious were the hopes that swelled my heart while gazing on them in those early days.

Melancholy attends on the best joys of a merely ideal life, else I should call most happy the hours in the garden, the hours in the book closet. Here were the best French writers of the last century; for my father had been more than half a Jacobin, in the time when the French Republic cast its glare of promise over the world. Here, too, were the Queen Anne authors, his models, and the English novelists; but among them I found none that charmed me. Smollett, Fielding,[4] and the like, deal too broadly with the coarse actualities of life. The best of their men and women—so merely natural, with the nature found every day —do not meet our hopes. Sometimes the simple picture warm with life and the light of the common sun, cannot fail to charm,—as in the wedded love of Fielding's Amelia,[5]—but it is at a later day, when the mind is trained to comparison, that we learn to prize excellence like this as it deserves. Early youth is prince-like: it will bend only to "the king, my father." Various kinds of excellence please, and leave their impression, but the most commanding, alone, is duly acknowledged at that all-exacting age.

Three great authors it was my fortune to meet at this important period,—all, though of unequal, yet congenial powers,—all of rich and wide, rather than aspiring genius,—all free to the extent of the horizon their eye took in,—all fresh with impulse, racy with experience; never to be lost sight of, or superseded, but always to be apprehended more and more.

Ever memorable is the day on which I first took a volume of SHAK-SPEARE in my hand to read. It was on a Sunday.

—This day was punctiliously set apart in our house We had family prayers, for which there was no time on other days. Our dinners were different, and our clothes We went to church. My father put some limitations on my reading, but—bless him for the gentleness which has left me a pleasant feeling for the day!—he did not prescribe what was, but only what was *not*, to be done. And the liberty this left was a large one. "You must "not read a novel, or a play;" but all other books, the worst, or the best, were open to me. The distinction was merely technical. The day was pleasing to me, as relieving me from the routine of

---

4. Tobias Smollett (1721–1771) and Henry Fielding (1707–1754) [Editor].
5. The title character of Fielding's *Amelia* (1751) [Editor].

tasks and recitations; it gave me freer play than usual, and there were fewer things occurred in its course, which reminded me of the divisions of time; still the church-going, where I heard nothing that had any connection with my inward life, and these rules, gave me associations with the day of empty formalities, and arbitrary restrictions; but though the forbidden book or walk always seemed more charming then, I was seldom tempted to disobey.—

This Sunday—I was only eight years old—I took from the book-shelf a volume lettered SHAKSPEARE. It was not the first time I had looked at it, but before I had been deterred from attempting to read, by the broken appearance along the page, and preferred smooth narrative. But this time I held in my hand "Romeo and Juliet" long enough to get my eye fastened to the page. It was a cold winter afternoon. I took the book to the parlor fire, and had there been seated an hour or two, when my father looked up and asked what I was reading so intently. "Shakspeare," replied the child, merely raising her eye from the page. "Shakspeare,—that won't do; that's no book for Sunday; go put it away and take another." I went as I was bid, but took no other. Returning to my seat, the unfinished story, the personages to whom I was but just introduced, thronged and burnt my brain. I could not bear it long; such a lure it was impossible to resist. I went and brought the book again. There were several guests present, and I had got half through the play before I again attracted attention. "What is that child about that she don't hear a word that's said to her?" quoth my aunt. "What are you reading?" said my father. "Shakspeare" was again the reply, in a clear, though somewhat impatient, tone. "How?" said my father angrily,—then restraining himself before his guests,—"Give me the book and go directly to bed."

Into my little room no care of his anger followed me. Alone, in the dark, I thought only of the scene placed by the poet before my eye, where the free flow of life, sudden and graceful dialogue, and forms, whether grotesque or fair, seen in the broad lustre of his imagination, gave just what I wanted, and brought home the life I seemed born to live. My fancies swarmed like bees, as I contrived the rest of the story: —what all would do, what say, where go. My confinement tortured me. I could not go forth from this prison to ask after these friends; I could not make my pillow of the dreams about them which yet I could not forbear to frame. Thus was I absorbed when my father entered. He felt it right, before going to rest, to reason with me about my disobedience, shown in a way, as he considered, so insolent. I listened, but could not feel interested in what he said, nor turn my mind from what engaged it. He went away really grieved at my impenitence, and quite at a loss to understand conduct in me so unusual.

—Often since I have seen the same misunderstanding between parent and child,—the parent thrusting the morale, the discipline, of life upon the child, when just engrossed by some game of real importance and great leadings to it. That is only a wooden horse to the father,— the child was careering to distant scenes of conquest and crusade, through a country of elsewhere unimagined beauty. None but poets remember their youth; but the father who does not retain poetical apprehension of the world, free and splendid as it stretches out before the child, who cannot read his natural history, and follow out its intimations with reverence, must be a tyrant in his home, and the purest intentions will not prevent his doing much to cramp him. Each new child is a new Thought, and has bearings and discernings, which the Thoughts older in date know not yet, but must learn.—

My attention thus fixed on Shakspeare, I returned to him at every hour I could command. Here was a counterpoise to my Romans, still more forcible than the little garden. My author could read the Roman nature too,—read it in the sternness of Coriolanus, and in the varied wealth of Cæsar. But he viewed these men of will as only one kind of men; he kept them in their place, and I found that he, who could understand the Roman, yet expressed in Hamlet a deeper thought.

In CERVANTES,[6] I found far less productive talent,—indeed, a far less powerful genius,—but the same wide wisdom, a discernment piercing the shows and symbols of existence, yet rejoicing in them all, both for their own life, and as signs of the unseen reality. Not that Cervantes philosophized,—his genius was too deeply philosophical for that; he took things as they came before him, and saw their actual relations and bearings. Thus the work he produced was of deep meaning, though he might never have expressed that meaning to himself. It was left implied in the whole. A Coleridge comes and calls Don Quixote the pure Reason, and Sancho the Understanding.[7] Cervantes made no such distinctions in his own mind; but he had seen and suffered enough to bring out all his faculties, and to make him comprehend the higher as well as the lower part of our nature. Sancho is too amusing and sagacious to be contemptible; the Don too noble and clear-sighted towards absolute truth, to be ridiculous. And we are pleased to see manifested in this way, how the lower must follow and serve the higher, despite its jeering mistrust and the stubborn realities which break up the plans of this pure-minded champion.

The effect produced on the mind is nowise that described by Byron:—

"Cervantes smiled Spain's chivalry away," &c.[8]

6. Miguel De Cervantes Saavedra (1547–1616), Spanish novelist and dramatist [Editor].
7. Cervantes's greatest work, *Don Quixote* (1605, 1615), features the deluded gentleman Don Quixote of La Mancha and his rustic companion Sancho Panza. Samuel Taylor Coleridge (1772–1834), English poet and critic, commented on the characters in an 1818 lecture, which was published in *The Literary Remains of Samuel Taylor Coleridge* (1836–39) [Editor].
8. From *Don Juan* 13.11 by George, Lord Byron (1788–1824) [Editor].

On the contrary, who is not conscious of a sincere reverence for the Don, prancing forth on his gaunt steed? Who would not rather be he than any of the persons who laugh at him?—Yet the one we would wish to be is thyself, Cervantes, unconquerable spirit! gaining flavor and color like wine from every change, while being carried round the world; in whose eye the serene sagacious laughter could not be dimmed by poverty, slavery, or unsuccessful authorship. Thou art to us still more the Man, though less the Genius, than Shakspeare; thou dost not evade our sight, but, holding the lamp to thine own magic shows, dost enjoy them with us.

My third friend was MOLIÉRE,[9] one very much lower, both in range and depth, than the others, but, as far as he goes, of the same character. Nothing secluded or partial is there about his genius,—a man of the world, and a man by himself, as he is. It was, indeed, only the poor social world of Paris that he saw, but he viewed it from the firm foundations of his manhood, and every lightest laugh rings from a clear perception, and teaches life anew.

These men were all alike in this,—they loved the *natural history* of man. Not what he should be, but what he is, was the favorite subject of their thought. Whenever a noble leading opened to the eye new paths of light, they rejoiced; but it was never fancy, but always fact, that inspired them. They loved a thorough penetration of the murkiest dens, and most tangled paths of nature; they did not spin from the desires of their own special natures, but reconstructed the world from materials which they collected on every side. Thus their influence upon me was not to prompt me to follow out thought in myself so much as to detect it everywhere, for each of these men is not only a nature, but a happy interpreter of many natures. They taught me to distrust all invention which is not based on a wide experience. Perhaps, too, they taught me to overvalue an outward experience at the expense of inward growth; but all this I did not appreciate till later.

It will be seen that my youth was not unfriended, since those great minds came to me in kindness. A moment of action in one's self, however, is worth an age of apprehension through others; not that our deeds are better, but that they produce a renewal of our being. I have had more productive moments and of deeper joy, but never hours of more tranquil pleasure than those in which these demi-gods visited me,—and with a smile so familiar, that I imagined the world to be full of such. They did me good, for by them a standard was early given of sight and thought, from which I could never go back, and beneath which I cannot suffer patiently my own life or that of any friend to fall. They did me harm, too, for the child fed with meat instead of milk becomes too soon mature. Expectations and desires were thus early

9. The name used by Jean Baptiste Poquelin (1622–1673), French playwright and actor, known for his comedies of character [Editor].

raised, after which I must long toil before they can be realized. How poor the scene around, how tame one's own existence, how meagre and faint every power, with these beings in my mind! Often I must cast them quite aside in order to grow in my small way, and not sink into despair. Certainly I do not wish that instead of these masters I had read baby books, written down to children, and with such ignorant dulness that they blunt the senses and corrupt the tastes of the still plastic human being. But I do wish that I had read no books at all till later, —that I had lived with toys, and played in the open air. Children should not cull the fruits of reflection and observation early, but expand in the sun, and let thoughts come to them. They should not through books antedate their actual experiences, but should take them gradually, as sympathy and interpretation are needed. With me, much of life was devoured in the bud.

First Friend

For a few months, this bookish and solitary life was invaded by interest in a living, breathing figure. At church, I used to look around with a feeling of coldness and disdain, which, though I now well understand its causes, seems to my wiser mind as odious as it was unnatural. The puny child sought everywhere for the Roman or Shakspeare figures, and she was met by the shrewd, honest eye, the homely decency, or the smartness of a New England village on Sunday. There was beauty, but I could not see it then; it was not of the kind I longed for. In the next pew sat a family who were my especial aversion. There were five daughters, the eldest not above four-and-twenty,—yet they had the old fairy, knowing look, hard, dry, dwarfed, strangers to the All-Fair,—were working-day residents in this beautiful planet. They looked as if their thoughts had never strayed beyond the jobs of the day, and they were glad of it. Their mother was one of those shrunken, faded patterns of woman who have never done anything to keep smooth the cheek and dignify the brow. The father had a Scotch look of shrewd narrowness, and entire self-complacency. I could not endure this family, whose existence contradicted all my visions; yet I could not forbear looking at them.

As my eye one day was ranging about with its accustomed coldness, and the proudly foolish sense of being in a shroud of thoughts that were not their thoughts, it was arrested by a face most fair, and well-known as it seemed at first glance,—for surely I had met her before and waited for her long. But soon I saw that she was a new apparition foreign to that scene, if not to me. Her dress,—the arrangement of her hair, which had the graceful pliancy of races highly cultivated for long,—the intelligent and full picture of her eye, whose reserve was in its self-possession, not in timidity,—all combined to make up a whole impression, which, though too young to understand, I was well prepared to feel.

How wearisome now appears that thorough-bred *millefleur*[1] beauty, the distilled result of ages of European culture! Give me rather the wild heath on the lonely hill-side, than such a rose-tree from the daintily clipped garden. But, then, I had but tasted the cup, and knew not how little it could satisfy; more, more, was all my cry; continued through years, till I had been at the very fountain. Indeed, it was a ruby-red, a perfumed draught, and I need not abuse the wine because I prefer water, but merely say I have had enough of it. Then, the first sight, the first knowledge of such a person was intoxication.

She was an English lady,[2] who, by a singular chance, was cast upon this region for a few months. Elegant and captivating, her every look and gesture was tuned to a different pitch from anything I had ever known. She was in various ways "accomplished," as it is called, though to what degree I cannot now judge. She painted in oils;—I had never before seen any one use the brush, and days would not have been too long for me to watch the pictures growing beneath her hand. She played the harp; and its tones are still to me the heralds of the promised land I saw before me then. She rose, she looked, she spoke; and the gentle swaying motion she made all through life has gladdened memory, as the stream does the woods and meadows.

As she was often at the house of one of our neighbors, and afterwards at our own, my thoughts were fixed on her with all the force of my nature. It was my first real interest in my kind, and it engrossed me wholly. I had seen her,—I should see her,—and my mind lay steeped in the visions that flowed from this source. My task-work I went through with, as I have done on similar occasions all my life, aided by pride that could not bear to fail, or be questioned. Could I cease from doing the work of the day, and hear the reason sneeringly given,—"Her head is so completely taken up with——that she can do nothing"? Impossible.

Should the first love be blighted, they say, the mind loses its sense of eternity. All forms of existence seem fragile, the prison of time real, for a god is dead. Equally true is this of friendship. I thank Heaven that this first feeling was permitted its free flow. The years that lay between the woman and the girl only brought her beauty into perspective, and enabled me to see her as I did the mountains from my window, and made her presence to me a gate of Paradise. That which she was, that which she brought, that which she might have brought, were mine, and over a whole region of new life I ruled proprietor of the soil in my own right.

Her mind was sufficiently unoccupied to delight in my warm devotion. She could not know what it was to me, but the light cast by the

1. Extracted from many flowers (French) [Editor].
2. Ellen Kilshaw, daughter of a wealthy Liverpool manufacturer [Editor].

flame through so delicate a vase cheered and charmed her. All who saw admired her in their way; but she would lightly turn her head from their hard or oppressive looks, and fix a glance of full-eyed sweetness on the child, who, from a distance, watched all her looks and motions. She did not say much to me—not much to any one; she spoke in her whole being rather than by chosen words. Indeed, her proper speech was dance or song, and what was less expressive did not greatly interest her. But she saw much, having in its perfection the woman's delicate sense for sympathies and attractions. We walked in the fields, alone. Though others were present, her eyes were gliding over all the field and plain for the objects of beauty to which she was of kin. She was not cold to her seeming companions; a sweet courtesy satisfied them, but it hung about her like her mantle that she wore without thinking of it; her thoughts were free, for these civilized beings can really live two lives at the same moment. With them she seemed to be, but her hand was given to the child at her side; others did not observe me, but to her I was the only human presence. Like a guardian spirit she led me through the fields and groves, and every tree, every bird greeted me, and said, what I felt, "She is the first angel of your life."

One time I had been passing the afternoon with her. She had been playing to me on the harp, and I sat listening in happiness almost unbearable. Some guests were announced. She went into another room to receive them, and I took up her book. It was Guy Mannering,[3] then lately published, and the first of Scott's novels I had ever seen. I opened where her mark lay, and read merely with the feeling of continuing our mutual existence by passing my eyes over the same page where hers had been. It was the description of the rocks on the sea-coast where the little Harry Bertram was lost. I had never seen such places, and my mind was vividly stirred to imagine them. The scene rose before me, very unlike reality, doubtless, but majestic and wild. I was the little Harry Bertram, and had lost her,—all I had to lose,—and sought her vainly in long dark caves that had no end, plashing through the water; while the crags beetled above, threatening to fall and crush the poor child. Absorbed in the painful vision, tears rolled down my cheeks. Just then she entered with light step, and full-beaming eye. When she saw me thus, a soft cloud stole over her face, and clothed every feature with a lovelier tenderness than I had seen there before. She did not question, but fixed on me inquiring looks of beautiful love. I laid my head against her shoulder and wept,—dimly feeling that I must lose her and all,—all who spoke to me of the same things,—that the cold wave must rush over me. She waited till my tears were spent, then rising, took from a little box a bunch of golden amaranths or everlasting flowers, and gave them to me. They were very fragrant. "They came," she said, "from

3. A novel by British author Sir Walter Scott (1771–1832), published in 1815 [Editor].

Madeira." These flowers stayed with me seventeen years. "Madeira" seemed to me the fortunate isle, apart in the blue ocean from all of ill or dread. Whenever I saw a sail passing in the distance,—if it bore itself with fulness of beautiful certainty,—I felt that it was going to Madeira. Those thoughts are all gone now. No Madeira exists for me now,—no fortunate purple isle,—and all these hopes and fancies are lifted from the sea into the sky. Yet I thank the charms that fixed them here so long,—fixed them till pèrfumes like those of the golden flowers were drawn from the earth, teaching me to know my birth-place.

I can tell little else of this time,—indeed, I remember little, except the state of feeling in which I lived. For I *lived*, and when this is the case, there is little to tell in the form of thought. We meet—at least those who are true to their instincts meet—a succession of persons through our lives, all of whom have some peculiar errand to us. There is an outer circle, whose existence we perceive, but with whom we stand in no real relation. They tell us the news, they act on us in the offices of society, they show us kindness and aversion; but their influence does not penetrate; we are nothing to them, nor they to us, except as a part of the world's furniture. Another circle, within this, are dear and near to us. We know them and of what kind they are. They are to us not mere facts, but intelligible thoughts of the divine mind. We like to see how they are unfolded; we like to meet them and part from them; we like their action upon us and the pause that succeeds and enables us to appreciate its quality. Often we leave them on our path, and return no more, but we bear them in our memory, tales which have been told, and whose meaning has been felt.

But yet a nearer group there are, beings born under the same star, and bound with us in a common destiny. These are not mere acquaintances, mere friends, but, when we meet, are sharers of our very existence. There is no separation; the same thought is given at the same moment to both,—indeed, it is born of the meeting, and would not otherwise have been called into existence at all. These not only know themselves more, but *are* more for having met, and regions of their being, which would else have laid sealed in cold obstruction, burst into leaf and bloom and song.

The times of these meetings are fated, nor will either party be able ever to meet any other person in the same way. Both seem to rise at a glance into that part of the heavens where the word can be spoken, by which they are revealed to one another and to themselves. The step in being thus gained, can never be lost, nor can it be re-trod; for neither party will be again what the other wants. They are no longer fit to interchange mutual influence, for they do not really need it, and if they think they do, it is because they weakly pine after a past pleasure.

To this inmost circle of relations but few are admitted, because some prejudice or lack of courage has prevented the many from listening to their instincts the first time they manifested themselves. If the voice is once disregarded it becomes fainter each time, till, at last, it is wholly silenced, and the man lives in this world, a stranger to its real life, deluded like the maniac who fancies he has attained his throne, while in reality he is on a bed of musty straw. Yet, if the voice finds a listener and servant the first time of speaking, it is encouraged to more and more clearness. Thus it was with me,—from no merit of mine, but because I had the good fortune to be free enough to yield to my impressions. Common ties had not bound me; there were no traditionary notions in my mind; I believed in nothing merely because others believed in it; I had taken no feelings on trust. Thus my mind was open to their sway.

This woman came to me, a star from the east, a morning star, and I worshipped her. She too was elevated by that worship, and her fairest self called out. To the mind she brought assurance that there was a region congenial with its tendencies and tastes, a region of elegant culture and intercourse, whose object, fulfilled or not, was to gratify the sense of beauty, not the mere utilities of life. In our relation she was lifted to the top of her being. She had known many celebrities, had roused to passionate desire many hearts, and became afterwards a wife; but I do not believe she ever more truly realized her best self than towards the lonely child whose heaven she was, whose eye she met, and whose possibilities she predicted. "He raised me," said a woman inspired by love, "upon the pedestal of his own high thoughts, and wings came at once, but I did not fly away. I stood there with downcast eyes worthy of his love, for he had made me so."

Thus we do always for those who inspire us to expect from them the best. That which they are able to be, they become, because we demand it of them. "We expect the impossible—and find it."

My English friend went across the sea. She passed into her former life, and into ties that engrossed her days. But she has never ceased to think of me. Her thoughts turn forcibly back to the child who was to her all she saw of the really New World. On the promised coasts she had found only cities, careful men and women, the aims and habits of ordinary life in her own land, without that elegant culture which she, probably, over-estimated, because it was her home. But in the mind of the child she found the fresh prairie, the untrodden forests for which she had longed. I saw in her the storied castles, the fair stately parks and the wind laden with tones from the past, which I desired to know. We wrote to one another for many years;—her shallow and delicate epistles did not disenchant me, nor did she fail to see something of the old poetry in my rude characters and stammering speech. But we must never meet again.

When this friend was withdrawn I fell into a profound depression. I knew not how to exert myself, but lay bound hand and foot. Melancholy enfolded me in an atmosphere, as joy had done. This suffering, too, was out of the gradual and natural course. Those who are really children could not know such love, or feel such sorrow. "I am to blame," said my father, "in keeping her at home so long merely to please myself. She needs to be with other girls, needs play and variety. She does not seem to me really sick, but dull rather. She eats nothing, you say. I see she grows thin. She ought to change the scene."

I was indeed *dull*. The books, the garden, had lost all charm. I had the excuse of headache, constantly, for not attending to my lessons. The light of life was set, and every leaf was withered. At such an early age there are no back or side scenes where the mind, weary and sorrowful, may retreat. Older, we realize the width of the world more, and it is not easy to despair on any point. The effort at thought to which we are compelled relieves and affords a dreary retreat, like hiding in a brick-kiln till the shower be over. But then all joy seemed to have departed with my friend, and the emptiness of our house stood revealed. This I had not felt while I every day expected to see or had seen her, or annoyance and dulness were unnoticed or swallowed up in the one thought that clothed my days with beauty. But now she was gone, and I was roused from habits of reading or reverie to feel the fiery temper of the soul, and to learn that it must have vent, that it would not be pacified by shadows, neither meet without consuming what lay around it. I avoided the table as much as possible, took long walks and lay in bed, or on the floor of my room. I complained of my head, and it was not wrong to do so, for a sense of dulness and suffocation, if not pain, was there constantly.

But when it was proposed that I should go to school, that was a remedy I could not listen to with patience for a moment. The peculiarity of my education had separated me entirely from the girls around, except that when they were playing at active games, I would sometimes go out and join them. I liked violent bodily exercise, which always relieved my nerves. But I had no success in associating with them beyond the mere play. Not only I was not their school-mate, but my book-life and lonely habits had given a cold aloofness to my whole expression, and veiled my manner with a hauteur which turned all hearts away. Yet, as this reserve was superficial, and rather ignorance than arrogance, it produced no deep dislike. Besides, the girls supposed me really superior to themselves, and did not hate me for feeling it, but neither did they like me, nor wish to have me with them. Indeed, I had gradually given up all such wishes myself; for they seemed to me rude, tiresome, and childish, as I did to them dull and strange. This experience had been earlier, before I was admitted to any real friendship; but now that I had been lifted into the life of mature years, and into just that atmosphere of European life to which I had before been tending, the thought of sending me to school filled me with disgust.

Yet what could I tell my father of such feelings? I resisted all I could, but in vain. He had no faith in medical aid generally, and justly saw that this was no occasion for its use. He thought I needed change of scene, and to be roused to activity by other children. "I have kept you at home," he said, "because I took such pleasure in teaching you myself, and besides I knew that you would learn faster with one who is so desirous to aid you. But you will learn fast enough wherever you are, and you ought to be more with others of your own age. I shall soon hear that you are better, I trust."

MARGARET FULLER

[Mariana]†

At the boarding-school to which I was too early sent, a fond, a proud, and timid child, I saw among the ranks of the gay and graceful, bright or earnest girls, only one who interested my fancy or touched my young heart; and this was Mariana. She was, on the father's side, of Spanish Creole blood, but had been sent to the Atlantic coast, to receive a school education under the care of her aunt, Mrs. Z.

This lady had kept her mostly at home with herself, and Mariana had gone from her house to a dayschool; but, the aunt, being absent for a time in Europe she had now been unfortunately committed for some time to the mercies of a boarding-school.

A strange bird she proved there,—a lonely swallow that could not make for itself a summer. At first, her schoolmates were captivated with her ways; her love of wild dances and sudden song, her freaks of passion and of wit. She was always new, always surprising, and, for a time, charming.

But, after awhile, they tired of her. She could never be depended on to join in their plans, yet she expected them to follow out hers with their whole strength. She was very loving, even infatuated in her own affections, and exacted from those who had professed any love for her, the devotion she was willing to bestow.

Yet there was a vein of haughty caprice in her character; a love of solitude, which made her at times wish to retire entirely, and at these times she would expect to be thoroughly understood, and let alone, yet to be welcomed back when she returned. She did not thwart others in

† From *Summer on the Lakes, in 1843* (Boston: Little and Brown, 1844). This fictionalized account of Fuller's youth draws on her experiences at Miss Prescott's Young Ladies Seminary at Groton, Massachusetts, 1824–25. In 1844, Fuller wrote her friend William H. Channing that she would always see herself as Mariana, adding, "Nobody dreams of its being like me; they all thought Miranda was, in the Great Lawsuit. People seem to think that not more than one phase of character can be shown in one life" (*Letters of Margaret Fuller,* 3:199).

their humors, but she never doubted of great indulgence from them.

Some singular habits she had which, when new, charmed, but, after acquaintance, displeased her companions. She had by nature the same habit and power of excitement that is described in the spinning dervishes of the East. Like them, she would spin until all around her were giddy, while her own brain, instead of being disturbed, was excited to great action. Pausing, she would declaim verse of others or her own; act many parts, with strange catch-words and burdens that seemed to act with mystical power on her own fancy, sometimes stimulating her to convulse the hearer with laughter, sometimes to melt him to tears. When her power began to languish, she would spin again till fired to recommence her singular drama, into which she wove figures from the scenes of her earlier childhood, her companions, and the dignitaries she sometimes saw, with fantasies unknown to life, unknown to heaven or earth.

This excitement, as may be supposed, was not good for her. It oftenest came on in the evening, and often spoiled her sleep. She would wake in the night, and cheat her restlessness by inventions that teased, while they sometimes diverted her companions.

She was also a sleep-walker; and this one trait of her case did somewhat alarm her guardians, who, otherwise, showed the same profound stupidity as to this peculiar being, usual in the overseers of the young. They consulted a physician, who said she would outgrow it, and prescribed a milk diet.

Meantime, the fever of this ardent and too early stimulated nature was constantly increased by the restraints and narrow routine of the boarding school. She was always devising means to break in upon it. She had a taste which would have seemed ludicrous to her mates, if they had not felt some awe of her, from a touch of genius and power that never left her, for costume and fancy dresses, always some sash twisted about her, some drapery, something odd in the arrangement of her hair and dress, so that the methodical preceptress dared not let her go out without a careful scrutiny and remodelling, whose soberizing effects generally disappeared the moment she was in the free air.

At last, a vent for her was found in private theatricals. Play followed play, and in these and the rehearsals she found entertainment congenial with her. The principal parts, as a matter of course, fell to her lot; most of the good suggestions and arrangements came from her, and for a time she ruled masterly and shone triumphant.

During these performances the girls had heightened their natural bloom with artificial red; this was delightful to them—it was something so out of the way. But Mariana, after the plays were over, kept her carmine saucer on the dressing-table, and put on her blushes regularly as the morning.

When stared and jeered at, she at first said she did it because she thought it made her look prettier; but, after a while, she became quite petulant about it,—would make no reply to any joke, but merely kept on doing it.

This irritated the girls, as all eccentricity does the world in general, more than vice or malignity. They talked it over among themselves, till they got wrought up to a desire of punishing, once for all, this sometimes amusing, but so often provoking nonconformist.

Having obtained the leave of the mistress, they laid, with great glee, a plan one evening, which was to be carried into execution next day at dinner.

Among Mariana's irregularities was a great aversion to the mealtime ceremonial. So long, so tiresome she found it, to be seated at a certain moment, to wait while each one was served at so large a table, and one where there was scarcely any conversation; from day to day it became more heavy to her to sit there, or go there at all. Often as possible she excused herself on the ever-convenient plea of headache, and was hardly ever ready when the dinnerbell rang.

To-day it found her on the balcony, lost in gazing on the beautiful prospect. I have heard her say afterwards, she had rarely in her life been so happy,—and she was one with whom happiness was a still rapture. It was one of the most blessed summer days; the shadows of great white clouds empurpled the distant hills for a few moments only to leave them more golden; the tall grass of the wide fields waved in the softest breeze. Pure blue were the heavens, and the same hue of pure contentment was in the heart of Mariana.

Suddenly on her bright mood jarred the dinner bell. At first rose her usual thought, I will not, cannot go; and then the must, which daily life can always enforce, even upon the butterflies and birds, came, and she walked reluctantly to her room. She merely changed her dress, and never thought of adding the artificial rose to her cheek.

When she took her seat in the dining-hall, and was asked if she would be helped, raising her eyes, she saw the person who asked her was deeply rouged, with a bright glaring spot, perfectly round, in either cheek. She looked at the next, same apparition! She then slowly passed her eyes down the whole line, and saw the same, with a suppressed smile distorting every countenance. Catching the design at once, she deliberately looked along her own side of the table, at every schoolmate in turn; every one had joined in the trick. The teachers strove to be grave, but she saw they enjoyed the joke. The servants could not suppress a titter.

When Warren Hastings stood at the bar of Westminster Hall—when the Methodist preacher walked through a line of men, each of whom greeted him with a brickbat or a rotten egg, they had some preparation for the crisis, and it might not be very difficult to meet it with an impassive brow. Our little girl was quite unprepared to find herself in the midst of a world which despised her, and triumphed in her disgrace.

She had ruled, like a queen, in the midst of her companions; she had shed her animation through their lives, and loaded them with prodigal favors, nor once suspected that a powerful favorite might not be loved. Now, she felt that she had been but a dangerous plaything in the hands of those whose hearts she never had doubted.

Yet, the occasion found her equal to it, for Mariana had the kind of spirit, which, in a better cause, had made the Roman matron truly say of her deathwound, "It is not painful, Poetus." She did not blench— she did not change countenance. She swallowed her dinner with apparent composure. She made remarks to those near her, as if she had no eyes.

The wrath of the foe of course rose higher, and the moment they were freed from the restraints of the dining-room, they all ran off, gaily calling, and sarcastically laughing, with backward glances, at Mariana, left alone.

She went alone to her room, locked the door, and threw herself on the floor in strong convulsions. These had sometimes threatened her life, as a child, but of later years, she had outgrown them. School-hours came, and she was not there. A little girl, sent to her door, could get no answer. The teachers became alarmed, and broke it open. Bitter was their penitence and that of her companions at the state in which they found her. For some hours, terrible anxiety was felt; but, at last, nature, exhausted, relieved herself by a deep slumber.

From this Mariana rose an altered being. She made no reply to the expressions of sorrow from her companions, none to the grave and kind, but undiscerning comments of her teacher. She did not name the source of her anguish, and its poisoned dart sank deeply in. It was this thought which stung her so. What, not one, not a single one, in the hour of trial, to take my part, not one who refused to take part against me. Past words of love, and caresses, little heeded at the time, rose to her memory, and gave fuel to her distempered thoughts. Beyond the sense of universal perfidy, of burning resentment, she could not get. And Mariana, born for love, now hated all the world.

The change, however, which these feelings made in her conduct and appearance bore no such construction to the careless observer. Her gay freaks were quite gone, her wildness, her invention. Her dress was uniform, her manner much subdued. Her chief interest seemed now to lie in her studies, and in music. Her companions she never sought, but they, partly from uneasy remorseful feelings, partly that they really liked her much better now that she did not oppress and puzzle them, sought her continually. And here the black shadow comes upon her life, the only stain upon the history of Mariana.

They talked to her, as girls, having few topics, naturally do, of one another. And the demon rose within her, and spontaneously, without design, generally without words of positive falsehood, she became a genius of discord among them. She fanned those flames of envy and jealousy which a wise, true word from a third will often quench forever; by a glance, or a seemingly light reply, she planted the seeds of dissension, till there was scarce a peaceful affection, or sincere intimacy in the circle where she lived, and could not but rule, for she was one whose nature was to that of the others as fire to clay.

It was at this time that I came to the school, and first saw Mariana. Me she charmed at once, for I was a sentimental child, who, in my early ill health, had been indulged in reading novels, till I had no eyes for the common greens and browns of life. The heroine of one of these, "The Bandit's Bride," I immediately saw in Mariana. Surely the Bandit's Bride had just such hair, and such strange, lively ways, and such a sudden flash of the eye. The Bandit's Bride, too, was born to be "misunderstood" by all but her lover. But Mariana, I was determined, should be more fortunate, for, until her lover appeared, I myself would be the wise and delicate being who could understand her.

It was not, however, easy to approach her for this purpose. Did I offer to run and fetch her handkerchief, she was obliged to go to her room, and would rather do it herself. She did not like to have people turn over for her the leaves of the music book as she played. Did I approach my stool to her feet, she moved away, as if to give me room. The bunch of wild flowers which I timidly laid beside her plate was left there.

After some weeks my desire to attract her notice really preyed upon me, and one day meeting her alone in the entry, I fell upon my knees, and kissing her hand, cried, "O Mariana, do let me love you, and try to love me a little." But my idol snatched away her hand, and, laughing more wildly than the Bandit's Bride was ever described to have done, ran into her room. After that day her manner to me was not only cold, but repulsive; I felt myself scorned, and became very unhappy.

Perhaps four months had passed thus, when, one afternoon; it became obvious that something more than common was brewing. Dismay and mystery were written in many faces of the older girls; much whispering was going on in corners.

In the evening, after prayers, the principal bade us stay; and, in a grave, sad voice, summoned forth Mariana to answer charges to be made against her.

Mariana came forward, and leaned against the chimney-piece. Eight of the older girls came forward, and preferred against her charges, alas, too well-founded, of calumny and falsehood.

My heart sank within me, as one after the other brought up their proofs, and I saw they were too strong to be resisted. I could not bear the thought of this second disgrace of my shining favorite. The first had been whispered to me, though the girls did not like to talk about it. I must confess, such is the charm of strength to softer natures, that neither of these crises could deprive Mariana of hers in my eyes.

At first, she defended herself with self-possession and eloquence. But when she found she could no more resist the truth, she suddenly threw herself down, dashing her head, with all her force, against the iron hearth, on which a fire was burning, and was taken up senseless.

The affright of those present was great. Now that they had perhaps killed her, they reflected it would have been as well, if they had taken warning from the former occasion, and approached very carefully a nature so capable of any extreme. After awhile she revived, with a faint groan, amid the sobs of her companions. I was on my knees by the bed, and held her cold hand. One of those most aggrieved took it from me to beg her pardon, and say it was impossible not to love her. She made no reply.

Neither that night, nor for several days, could a word be obtained from her, nor would she touch food; but, when it was presented to her, or any one drew near for any cause, she merely turned away her head, and gave no sign. The teacher saw that some terrible nervous affection had fallen upon her, that she grew more and more feverish. She knew not what to do.

Meanwhile a new revolution had taken place in the mind of the passionate, but nobly-tempered child. All these months nothing but the sense of injury had rankled in her heart. She had gone on in one mood, doing what the demon prompted, without scruple and without fear.

But, at the moment of detection, the tide ebbed, and the bottom of her soul lay revealed to her eye. How black, how stained and sad. Strange, strange that she had not seen before the baseness and cruelty of falsehood, the loveliness of truth. Now, amid the wreck, uprose the moral nature which never before had attained the ascendant. "But," she thought, "too late, sin is revealed to me in all its deformity, and, sin-defiled, I will not, cannot live. The main-spring of life is broken."

And thus passed slowly by her hours in that black despair of which only youth is capable. In older years men suffer more dull pain, as each sorrow that comes drops its leaden weight into the past, and, similar features of character bringing similar results, draws up a heavy burden buried in those depths. But only youth has energy, with fixed unwinking gaze, to contemplate grief, to hold it in the arms and to the heart, like a child which makes it wretched, yet is indubitably its own.

The lady who took charge of this sad child had never well understood her before, but had always looked on her with great tenderness. And now love seemed, when all around were in greatest distress, fearing to call in medical aid, fearing to do without it, to teach her where the only balm was to be found that could have healed this wounded spirit.

One night she came in, bringing a calming draught. Mariana was sitting, as usual, her hair loose, her dress the same robe they had put on her at first, her eyes fixed vacantly upon the whited wall. To the proffers and entreaties of her nurse she made no reply.

The lady burst into tears, but Mariana did not seem even to observe it.

The lady then said, "O my child, do not despair, do not think that one great fault can mar a whole life. Let me trust you, let me tell you the griefs of my sad life. I will tell to you, Mariana, what I never expected to impart to any one."

And so she told her tale: it was one of pain, of shame, borne, not for herself, but for one near and dear as herself. Mariana knew the lady, knew the pride and reserve of her nature; she had often admired to see how the cheek, lovely, but no longer young, mantled with the deepest blush of youth, and the blue eyes were cast down at any little emotion. She had understood the proud sensibility of the character. She fixed her eyes on those now raised to hers, bright with fast falling tears. She heard the story to the end, and then, without saying a word, stretched out her hand for the cup.

She returned to life, but it was as one who has passed through the valley of death. The heart of stone was quite broken in her. The fiery life fallen from flame to coal. When her strength was a little restored, she had all her companions summoned, and said to them; "I deserved to die, but a generous trust has called me back to life. I will be worthy of it, nor ever betray the truth, or resent injury more. Can you forgive the past?"

And they not only forgave, but, with love and earnest tears, clasped in their arms the returning sister. They vied with one another in offices of humble love to the humbled one; and, let it be recorded as an instance of the pure honor of which young hearts are capable, that these facts, known to forty persons, never, so far as I know, transpired beyond those walls.

It was not long after this that Mariana was summoned home. She went thither a wonderfully instructed being, though in ways those who had sent her forth to learn little dreamed of.

Never was forgotten the vow of the returning prodigal. Mariana could not resent, could not play false. The terrible crisis, which she so early passed through, probably prevented the world from hearing much of her. A wild fire was tamed in that hour of penitence at the boarding school, such as has oftentimes wrapped court and camp in its destructive glow.

But great were the perils she had yet to undergo, for she was one of those barks which easily get beyond soundings, and ride not lightly on the plunging billow.

MARGARET FULLER

Leila†

"In a deep vision's intellectual scene."

I have often but vainly attempted to record what I know of Leila. It is because she is a mystery, which can only be indicated by being reproduced. Had a Poet or Artist met her, each glance of her's would have suggested some form of beauty, for she is one of those rare beings who seem a key to all nature. Mostly those we know seem struggling for an individual existence. As the procession passes an observer like me, one seems a herald, another a basket-bearer, another swings a censer, and oft-times even priest and priestess suggest the ritual rather than the Divinity. Thinking of these men your mind dwells on the personalities at which they aim. But if you looked on Leila she was rather as the *fetiche*[1] which to the mere eye almost featureless, to the thought of the pious wild man suggests all the elemental powers of nature, with their regulating powers of conscience and retribution. The eye resting on Leila's eye, felt that it never reached the heart. Not as with other men did you meet a look which you could define as one of displeasure, scrutiny, or tenderness. You could not turn away, carrying with you some distinct impression, but your glance became a gaze from a perception of a boundlessness, of depth below depth, which seemed to say "in this being (couldst thou but rightly apprehend it) is the clasp to the chain of nature." Most men, as they gazed on Leila were pained; they left her at last baffled and well-nigh angry. For most men are bound in sense, time, and thought. They shrink from the overflow of the infinite; they cannot a moment abide in the coldness of abstractions; the weight of an idea is too much for their lives. They cry, "O give me a form which I may clasp to the living breast, fuel for the altars of the heart, a weapon for the hand." And who can blame them; it is almost impossible for time to bear this sense of eternity. Only the Poet, who is so happily organized as continually to relieve himself by reproduction, can bear it without falling into a kind of madness. And men called Leila mad, because they felt she made them so. But I, Leila, could look on thee;—to my restless spirit thou didst bring a kind of peace, for thou wert a bridge between me and the infinite; thou didst arrest the

† From the *Dial* (Apr. 1841): 462–67. Like Miranda and Mariana, Leila represents a phase of Fuller's character and informs her conception of woman. The name Leila especially appealed to her: "I knew, from the very look and sound, it was mine; I knew that it meant night,— night which brings out stars, as sorrow brings out truth" (*Memoirs* 1:219). For Fuller's related poem "Leila in the Arabian Zone" see p. 194.
1. Fetish (French); an object having magical potency.

168

step, and the eye as the veil hanging before the Isis. Thy nature seemed large enough for boundless suggestion. I did not love thee, Leila, but the desire for love was soothed in thy presence. I would fain have been nourished by some of thy love, but all of it I felt was only for the all.

We grew up together with name and home and parentage. Yet Leila ever seemed to me a spirit under a mask, which she might throw off at any instant. That she did not, never dimmed my perception of the unreality of her existence among us. She *knows* all, and *is* nothing. She stays here, I suppose, as a reminder to man of the temporary nature of his limitations. For she ever transcends sex, age, state, and all the barriers behind which man entrenches himself from the assaults of Spirit. You look on her, and she is the clear blue sky, cold and distant as the Pole-star; suddenly this sky opens and flows forth a mysterious wind that bears with it your last thought beyond the verge of all expectation, all association. Again, she is the mild sunset, and puts you to rest on a love-couch of rosy sadness, when on the horizon swells up a mighty sea and rushes over you till you plunge on its waves, affrighted, delighted, quite freed from earth.

When I cannot look upon her living form, I avail myself of the art magic. At the hour of high moon, in the cold silent night, I seek the centre of the park. My daring is my vow, my resolve my spell. I am a conjurer, for Leila is the vasty deep. In the centre of the park, perfectly framed in by solemn oaks and pines, lies a little lake, oval, deep, and still it looks up steadily as an eye of earth should to the ever promising heavens which are so bounteous, and love us so, yet never give themselves to us. As that lake looks at Heaven, so look I on Leila. At night I look into the lake for Leila.

If I gaze steadily and in the singleness of prayer, she rises and walks on its depths. Then know I each night a part of her life; I know where she passes the midnight hours.

In the days she lives among men; she observes their deeds, and gives them what they want of her, justice or love. She is unerring in speech or silence, for she is disinterested, a pure victim, bound to the altar's foot; God teaches her what to say.

In the night she wanders forth from her human investment, and travels amid those tribes, freer movers in the game of spirit and matter, to whom man is a supplement. I know not then whether she is what men call dreaming, but her life is true, full, and more single than by day.

I have seen her among the Sylphs'[2] faint florescent forms that hang in the edges of life's rainbows. She is very fair, thus, Leila; and I catch, though edgewise, and sharp-gleaming as a sword, that bears down my

2. Imaginary delicate beings that supposedly inhabit the air.

sight, the peculiar light which she will be when she finds the haven of herself. But sudden is it, and whether king or queen, blue or yellow, I never can remember; for Leila is too deep a being to be known in smile or tear. Ever she passes sudden again from these hasty glories and tendernesses into the back-ground of being, and should she ever be detected it will be in the central secret of law. Breathless is my ecstasy as I pursue her in this region. I grasp to detain what I love, and swoon and wake and sigh again. On all such beauty transitoriness has set its seal. This sylph nature pierces through the smile of childhood. There is a moment of frail virginity on which it has set its seal, a silver star which may at any moment withdraw and leave a furrow on the brow it decked. Men watch these slender tapers which seem as if they would burn out next moment. They say that such purity is the seal of death. It is so; the condition of this ecstasy is, that it seems to die every moment, and even Leila has not force to die often; the electricity accumulates many days before the wild one comes, which leads to these sylph nights of tearful sweetness.

After one of these, I find her always to have retreated into the secret veins of earth. Then glows through her whole being the fire that so baffles men, as she walks on the surface of earth; the blood-red, heart's-blood-red of the carbuncle.[3] She is, like it, her own light, and beats with the universal heart, with no care except to circulate as the vital fluid; it would seem waste then for her to rise to the surface. There in these secret veins of earth she thinks herself into fine gold, or aspires for her purest self, till she interlaces the soil with veins of silver. She disdains not to retire upon herself in the iron ore. She knows that fires are preparing on upper earth to temper this sternness of her silent self. I venerate her through all this in awed silence. I wait upon her steps through the mines. I light my little torch and follow her through the caves where despair clings by the roof, as she trusts herself to the cold rushing torrents, which never saw the sun nor heard of the ocean. I know if she pauses, it will be to diamond her nature, transcending generations. Leila! thou hast never yet, I believe, penetrated to the central ices, nor felt the whole weight of earth. But thou searchest and searchest. Nothing is too cold, too heavy, nor too dark for the faith of the being whose love so late smiled and wept itself into the rainbow, and was the covenant of an only hope. Am I with thee on thy hours of deepest search? I think not, for still thou art an abyss to me, and the star which glitters at the bottom, often withdraws into newer darknesses. O draw me, Star, I fear not to follow; it is my eye and not my heart which is weak. Show thyself for longer spaces. Let me gaze myself into religion, then draw me down,—down.

3. A red gemstone, especially a garnet or ruby. For Fuller, the carbuncle was her talisman, her charm, able to ward off evil and bring good fortune.

As I have wished this, most suddenly Leila bursts up again in the fire. She greets the sweet moon with a smile so haughty, that the heavenly sky grows timid, and would draw back; but then remembering that the Earth also is planetary, and bound in one music with all its spheres, it leans down again and listens softly what this new, strange voice may mean. And it seems to mean wo, wo! for, as the deep thought bursts forth, it shakes the thoughts in which time was resting; the cities fall in ruins; the hills are rent asunder; and the fertile valleys ravaged with fire and water. Wo, wo! but the moon and stars smile denial, and the echo changes the sad, deep tone into divinest music. Wait thou, O Man, and walk over the hardened lava to fresh wonders. Let the chain be riven asunder; the gods will give a pearl to clasp it again.

Since these nights, Leila, Saint of Knowledge, I have been fearless, and utterly free. There are to me no requiems more, death is a name, and the darkest seeming hours sing Te Deum.[4]

See with the word the form of earth transfused to stellar clearness, and the Angel Leila showers down on man balm and blessing. One downward glance from that God-filled eye, and violets clothe the most ungrateful soil, fruits smile healthful along the bituminous lake, and the thorn glows with a crown of amaranth. Descend, thou of the silver sandals, to thy weary son; turn hither that swan-guided car. Not mine but thine, Leila. The rivers of bliss flow forth at thy touch, and the shadow of sin falls separate from the form of light. Thou art now pure ministry, one arrow from the quiver of God; pierce to the centre of things, and slay Dagon[5] for evermore. Then shall be no more sudden smiles, nor tears, nor searchings in secret caves, nor slow growths of centuries. But floating, hovering, brooding, strong-winged bliss shall fill eternity, roots shall not be clogged with earth, but God blossom into himself for evermore.

Straight at the wish the arrows divine of my Leila ceased to pierce. Love retired back into the bosom of chaos, and the Holy Ghost descended on the globes of matter. Leila, with wild hair scattered to the wind, bare and often bleeding feet, opiates and divining rods in each over-full hand, walked amid the habitations of mortals as a Genius, visited their consciences as a Demon.

At her touch all became fluid, and the prison walls grew into Edens. Each ray of particolored light grew populous with beings struggling into divinity. The redemption of matter was interwoven into the coronal of thought, and each serpent form soared into a Phenix.[6]

Into my single life I stooped and plucked from the burning my divine children. And ever, as I bent more and more with an unwearied be-

4. A hymn of praise to God.
5. A Philistine god, destroyed by the ark of God in I Samuel 5.1–8.
6. I.e., phoenix; a legendary bird that arises reborn from its own ashes.

nignity, an elected pain, like that of her, my wild-haired Genius; more beauteous forms, unknown before to me, nay, of which the highest God had not conscience as shapes, were born from that suddenly darting flame, which had threatened to cleave the very dome of my being. And Leila, she, the moving principle; O, who can speak of the immortal births of her unshrinking love. Each surge left Venus Urania at her feet; from each abjured blame, rose floods of solemn incense, that strove in vain to waft her to the sky. And I heard her voice, which ever sang, "I shrink not from the baptism, from slavery let freedom, from parricide piety, from death let birth be known."

Could I but write this into the words of earth, the secret of moral and mental alchymy would be discovered, and all Bibles have passed into one Apocalypse; but not till it has all been lived can it be written.

Meanwhile cease not to whisper of it, ye pines, plant here the hope from age to age; blue dome, wait as tenderly as now; cease not, winds, to bear the promise from zone to zone; and thou, my life, drop the prophetic treasure from the bud of each day,—Prophecy.

Of late Leila kneels in the dust, yea, with her brow in the dust. I know the thought that is working in her being. To be a child, yea, a human child, perhaps man, perhaps woman, to bear the full weight of accident and time, to descend as low as ever the divine did, she is preparing. I also kneel. I would not avail myself of all this sight. I cast aside my necromancy, and yield all other prowess for the talisman of humility. But Leila, wondrous circle, who hast taken into thyself all my thought, shall I not meet thee on the radius of human nature? I will be thy fellow pilgrim, and we will learn together the bliss of gratitude.

Should this ever be, I shall seek the lonely lake no more, for in the eye of Leila I shall find not only the call to search, but the object sought. Thou hast taught me to recognise all powers; now let us be impersonated, and traverse the region of forms together. *Together*, CAN that be, thinks Leila, can one be with any but God? Ah! it is so, but only those who have known the one can know the two. Let us pass out into nature, and she will give us back to God yet wiser, and worthier, than when clinging to his footstool as now. "Have I ever feared," said Leila. Never! but the hour is come for still deeper trust. Arise! let us go forth!

MARGARET FULLER

From Letter to Sophia Ripley, August 27, 1839†

My dear friend:

—The advantages of a weekly meeting, for conversation, might be great enough to repay the trouble of attendance, if they consisted only in supplying a point of union to well-educated and thinking women, in a city which, with great pretensions to mental refinement, boasts, at present, nothing of the kind, and where I have heard many, of mature age, wish for some such means of stimulus and cheer, and those younger, for a place where they could state their doubts and difficulties, with a hope of gaining aid from the experience or aspirations of others. And if my office were only to suggest topics, which would lead to conversation of a better order than is usual at social meetings, and to turn back the current when digressing into personalities or common-places, so that what is valuable in the experience of each might be brought to bear upon all, I should think the object not unworthy of the effort.

But my ambition goes much further. It is to pass in review the de-partments of thought and knowledge, and endeavor to place them in due relation to one another in our minds. To systematize thought, and give a precision and clearness in which our sex are so deficient, chiefly, I think, because they have so few inducements to test and classify what they receive. To ascertain what pursuits are best suited to us, in our time and state of society, and how we may make best use of our means for building up the life of thought upon the life of action.

Could a circle be assembled in earnest, desirous to answer the questions,—What were we born to do? and how shall we do it?—which so few ever propose to themselves till their best years are gone by, I should think the undertaking a noble one, and, if my resources should prove sufficient to make me its moving spring, I should be willing to give to it a large portion of those coming years, which will, as I hope, be my best. I look upon it with no blind enthusiasm, nor unlimited faith, but with a confidence that I have attained a distinct perception of means, which, if there are persons competent to direct them, can

---

† From *Memoirs of Margaret Fuller Ossoli*, ed. R. W. Emerson, W. H. Channing, and J. F. Clarke (Boston: Phillips, Sampson, 1852), 1:324–326. Robert N. Hudspeth provides the date for this letter in his edition of *The Letters of Margaret Fuller*, 2:86. This letter, meant to be shared, advertises Fuller's plan for her "Conversations," a series of classes for women that were held in Boston each fall and spring from 1839 to 1844. Fuller's correspondent, Sophia Dana Ripley (1803–1861) of Cambridge, Massachusetts, was an independent, learned mem-ber of the transcendentalist circle. She attended the Conversations; wrote an article on the rights of woman for the January 1841 *Dial*; and with her husband, George Ripley, founded the utopian community Brook Farm (1841–47) [Editor].

supply a great want, and promote really high objects. So far as I have
tried them yet, they have met with success so much beyond my hopes,
that my faith will not easily be shaken, not my earnestness chilled.
Should I, however, be disappointed in Boston, I could hardly hope that
such a plan could be brought to bear on general society, in any other
city of the United States. But I do not fear, if a good beginning can be
made. I am confident that twenty persons cannot be brought together
from better motives than vanity or pedantry, to talk upon such subjects
as we propose, without finding in themselves great deficiencies, which
they will be very desirous to supply.

*   *   *

MARGARET FULLER

From Boston Conversations: The 1839–1840 Series†

Miss Fuller in her introductory conversation enlarged upon the topics which she touched in her letter to Mrs. Ripley.[1] She spoke of the
education of our grandmothers as healthy though confined, & said that
in what was called the improved education of the present day the
boundaries had been enlarged but not filled up faithfully—& consequently superficialness, unhealthiness, & pedantry had been
introduced— This perhaps was a necessary effect—temporarily,—of the
transition—& did not prove that an attempt at enlargement was not
legitimate— She believed that enlargement not only lawful in itself—
but inevitable— In our country women had grown to be in situations
which gave them a great deal of leisure—even discharging all their

---

† Reprinted with permission from "Margaret Fuller's Boston Conversations: The 1839–1840
Series," ed. Nancy Craig Simmons, *Studies in the American Renaissance 1994*, ed. Joel Myerson (Charlottesville: University Press of Virginia, 1994), 203–04, 214–18. According to Simmons, these transcriptions of the conversations held during Fuller's first series of 1839–40
were made by Elizabeth Palmer Peabody (1804–1894), Boston teacher, publisher, and author,
in whose parlor the conversations took place. They reveal Fuller's interest in the topic of
"woman" in the years leading up to "The Great Lawsuit" and *Woman in the Nineteenth
Century.*

1. See letter to [Sophia Ripley?], 27 August 1839, *Letters*, 2:86–89, in which Fuller describes
her "plan for the proposed conversations." The first conversation in this series was on Wednesday, 6 November 1839. Conversations 2–8 occurred without interruption at one-week intervals
(on 13, 20, and 27 November, and 4, 11, and 18 December) with the exception of Conversation 8, scheduled for Christmas Day. According to a letter quoted by Emerson in *Memoirs*,
this conversation was postponed to the following Saturday (28 December). * * * Fuller's letter
to Sarah Whitman, 21 January 1840 (*Letters*, 2:118–19), suggests that the conversation on
Poetry (including dancing) served as her transition to the new series, and that perhaps two
more classes had occurred: in the next they will discuss "Shakspeare and Burns." Thus, the
first "series" on Grecian mythology probably consisted of only eight classes (not thirteen as
Emerson asserts [*Memoirs*, 1:336]), while the second series (which may have begun on 1 or
8 January) continued at least until 18 March. The record printed here thus probably resumes
on either 12 or 19 February (Conversation 15) and continues through either 18 or 25 March
(Conversation 20). [See p. 173—*Editor.*]

domestic duties—all the duties involved in the cultivation of the affections as their especial province—they had more leisure on the whole
than the men of our country— This leisure must be employed in some
way—to employ it intellectually was on all accounts the best way—for
women were capable of intellectual improvement, & therefore designed
by God for it.—

But the attempts at intellectual cultivation involved these evils of
unhealthiness of mind—pedantry—superficialness

The question is, why is it so? Is it that there is too much intellectual
cultivation or not enough? Let us examine.____ Women now are
taught all that men are— Is it so? Or is it not that they run over su-
perficially even *more* studies—without being really taught any thing.
Thus when they come to the business of life & the application of
knowledge they find that they are *inferior*—& all their studies have not
given them that practical good sense & mother wisdom & wit which
grew up with our grandmothers at the spinning wheel. Is not the difference between [2–3 words lost] education of women & that of men
this— Men are called on from a very early period to *reproduce* all that
they learn— First their college exercises—their political duties—the exercises of professional study—the very first action of life in any
direction—calls upon them for *reproduction* of what they have learnt.
— This is what is most neglected in the education of women—they
learn without any attempt to reproduce— The little reproduction to
which they are called seems mainly for the purposes of idle display. It
is to supply this deficiency that these conversations have been planned.
Miss Fuller guarded against the idea that she was to *teach* any thing
She merely meant to be the nucleus of conversation— She had had
some experience in conducting such a conversation,—& she proposed
to be *one* to give her own best thoughts on any subject that was named,
as a means of calling out the thoughts of others. She thought it would
be a good plan to take up subjects on which we knew words—& had
impressions, & vague irregular notions, & compel ourselves to define
those words, to turn these impressions into thoughts, & to systematise
these thoughts— We should probably have to go through some morti-
fication in finding how much less we knew than we thought—& on
the other hand we should probably find ourselves encouraged by seeing
how much & how rapidly we should gain by making a simple & clear
effort for expression.

These were Miss Fuller's most important thoughts. They were expressed with much illustration—& many more ideas were mingled with
them—& all was expressed with the most captivating address & grace
—& the most beautiful modesty. The position in which she placed
herself with respect to the rest was entirely ladylike & companionable
— She said all that she intended, to express the earnest purpose with

which she came, and expected all who shared her purpose to come [—] & with great tact indicated all the things she thought might spoil the meeting.

* * *

Miss Fuller's 16th conversation took place a week ago—& I do not know whether I can remember much of it. * * * Miss Fuller asked what was the distinction of feminine & masculine when applied to character & mind. that there was such a distinction was evident or we should not say 'a masculine woman', &c. Ellen Hooper[2] thought women were instinctive—they had spontaneously what men have by study reflection & induction Another remarked that this had been said to be the distinction of poets among men. Another said that this would confirm Coleridge's remark that every man of great poetical genius had something feminine in his face.[3]

Miss Fuller thought that the man & the woman had each every faculty & element of mind—but that they were combined in different proportions. that this was proved by the praise implied in the expressions "a courageous woman—a thoughtful woman—a reasonable woman. & on the other hand by the praise which we bestowed on men who to courage—intellect &c. added tenderness &c. &c.— Could there be such a woman as Napoleon? was asked. Queen Elizabeth— Catherine II[4] & Lady Macbeth were spoken of— Maryann Jackson asked if there could be such a man as Corinne.[5] Miss F thought Tasso was such a man, & characterised him in a wonderful manner— I wish I could remember it. Ellen suggested that the ideal woman of a fine man would perhaps give us light Miss Fuller said we had these in literature, & proposed we shd. seek them out. She characterised Dante admirably, & then sketched Beatrice—

Miss Fuller's 17th conversation began with reading the articles upon the intellectual differences between men & women.— The first made the difference to consist in the fineness & delicacy of organization—the greater openness to impressions—&c. Margaret remarked that this made no essential difference—it was only more or less. Ellen Hooper asked if the difference of organization were not essential—if it did not begin in the mind—& if this was not the author's idea? Margaret looked again & thought it was—but still said that she did not find that the author made any quality belong to the one mind

---

2. Ellen Sturgis Hooper (1812–1848), poet, friend of Fuller's, wife of Dr. Robert William Hooper [Editor].
3. See H. N. Coleridge, *Specimens of the Table Talk of the Late Samuel Taylor Coleridge*, 2 vols. (New York: Harpers, 1835), 2:15–16.
4. Catherine "The Great" of Russia (1729–96).
5. Eponymous heroine of Germaine de Staël's novel *Corinne, or Italy* (1807), the passionate and idealistic Corinne, a poet, became the nineteenth-century type of the unconventional female artist. [Marianne Cabot Jackson (1820–1846) was a former student and friend of Fuller's—*Editor.*]

that did not belong to the other— Ellen asked if she thought that there was any quality in the masculine or in the feminine mind that did not belong to the other— Margaret said no—she did not—& therefore she wished to see if the others fully admitted this. because if all admitted it, it would follow of course that we should hear no more of repressing or subduing faculties because they were not fit for women to cultivate. She desired that whatever faculty we felt to be moving within us, that we should consider a principle of our perfection, & cultivate it accordingly.— & not excuse ourselves from any duty on the ground that we had not the intellectual powers for it; that it was not for women to do, *on an intellectual ground*— Some farther remarks were made on the point of the want of objectiveness of woman, as the cause of her not giving herself to the fine arts. It was also attributed to her want of isolation The physical inconveniences of sculpture, architecture & even of painting were adverted to— But why not music & poetry? Miss Fuller said it had troubled her to think there was no great musical composer among women. It is true that at the period of life when men gave themselves to their pursuit most women became mothers—but there were some women who never married. I suggested that these too often spent the rest of their lives in mourning over this fact—& society spoke so uniformly of woman as more respectable for being married—that it was long before she entirely despaired. This caused some lively talk all round—& Margaret averred that there came a time however when every one *must give up*. I might have answered that then it was but too common for youth to be past—& the mind to have wedded itself to that mediocrity, which is too commonly the result of disappointed hope, especially if hopes are not the highest.—

The second piece that was read spoke of the subtlety of woman's mind. Miss Fuller summed it up after she had finished it, with the words—Woman more pervasive—Man more prominent.—While speaking of this piece the question came up whether Brutus' great action[6] could have been performed by a woman. It was decided that if there were no doubt about the duty in Brutus' case there could be none about the duty being obligatory on a woman who had the same general office; else the moral nature could not be the same in man & woman. A great deal of talk arose here—and Margaret repelled the sentimentalism that took away woman's moral power of performing stern duty. In answer to one thing she said that as soon as we began to calculate our condition & to make allowances for it, we sank into the depths of sentimentalism. And again—Nothing I hate to hear of so much as *woman's lot*. I wish I never could hear that word *lot*. Something must be wrong where there is a universal lamentation. Youth ought not to be mourned—for it ought to be replaced with something better.—Miss F.

6. The assassination of Julius Caesar by Marcus Junius Brutus (85 B.C.–42 B.C.) in 44 B.C. was seen as a defense of Republican virtue.

then read her own piece as she said that otherwise she should say every thing that was in it, which would make it duller when it came—It was a constant contrast of man & woman—Man had more genius—woman more taste—Man more determination of purpose—woman more delicacy of rejection—Man more versatility—woman more power of adaptation. Maryann Jackson disputed the proposition that woman had less genius—*as woman*. Is it not so? said Miss Fuller—Is not man's intellect the fire caught from heaven—woman's the flower called forth from earth by the ray? Mrs Park—Anna Shaw[7]—Ellen Hooper seemed inclined also to doubt this proposition—Somewhere here Margaret defined *taste* the reasoning of beauty—& woman the interpreter of genius.

*   *   *

Miss Fuller's 18th conversation was also upon women—there not having been time enough to read all the articles before. She began with saying that she had looked over all the remaining pieces & should read a few of them. She remarked that she was delighted with the elevation of thought in all. All spoke of men & women as equally souls—none seemed to regard men as animals & women as plants. This caused a general laugh, & she repeated seriously that she constantly heard people talk as if men were only animals & women were only plants—That men were made to get a living—to eat & drink—and women to be ornaments of society—as if these were the ultimate aims of being. Parents in educating their sons had in view as the main objects, that they should be able to make money, to eat & dress with more refinement than others—& so on—& that their daughters should be graceful pretty accomplished—*& have a good time*. In neither case did we hear of the perfect unfolding of the faculties as the indispensable or primary object. She said that a lady of high cultivation whom she had known, who was 60 years old, and had lived in cultivated society, expressed to her the wish that she had not had the powers to think & feel—that she had not thought & felt. This was in her view wishing for annihilation—Because thought & feeling had given her pain, she wished not to be! She told her she thought it was the basest thing she had ever heard said—that it was denying the immortality of the Soul—or what was worse *refusing* it—it was denying Christianity—for Christianity was nothing if it did not teach that discipline to a worthy end was the final cause of thought & feeling—Views must be essentially wrong when *being* became a burden—When one could feel able to say & hope for sympathy in saying that thought & feeling were an evil. These false views haunted society with regard to women.—or else mothers & fathers would not wish to repress or annihilate faculties—as a means of making their daughters happier—a thing we constantly saw—We constantly heard

7. Anna Blake Shaw (1817–1901), was the daughter of Robert Gould and Elizabeth Parkman Shaw of Boston. According to Charles Capper, Mrs. Park may be Agnes Major Park (1782?–1857), an English woman who became the second wife of Dr. John Park of Boston [Editor].

that it was not well to cultivate this or that faculty—because in the boy's case it would not contribute especially & certainly to his worldly success—& in the girl's case because it might make her discontented as a woman.—Miss Fuller thought it *impious* thus to speak of the gifts of God—the immortal gifts of God—as if we had a right to tamper with them—as if they were not to be received gratefully—to be held as the most precious trust—& to be cultivated—Whatever worldly disadvantages—whatever temporary sufferings their cultivation might involve—

Ellen Hooper asked if she did not think that it was the duty of a man in the first place to support himself—if he ought not to be impressed with the idea from the beginning that he must make for himself a place, so far at least as not to be dependent—If this independence on outward support with respect to his physical being was not essential to our idea of a man? Miss Fuller replied that a perfect man would of course do this—but that she was struck continually with this recurring fact in society—that those who failed *in the other* were comparatively never censured—those who failed in this were irrevocably condemned—Morally speaking she should prefer to see her son unthrifty—to seeing him unspiritual She was no friend to unthrift—but if her son were a Poet —she should wish him to cultivate the divine gift though it would inevitably keep him poor always—& ever to sacrifice the outward, when one of the two was necessarily to be sacrificed—Mrs H. said she knew of a man reputed to be of the highest genius, who to indulge this, neglected & was very indifferent to the comforts of his family, who lived on charity that it was hard for his wife to receive from conscientious feelings—& who having borrowed of every body who would lend, till he was deeply in debt, yet remained insensible to debts as such, & made something of a parade of his serenity & spiritual elevation above all such things.[8]——Miss Fuller said, to be indifferent to riches, even the smallest degree, was another thing from being indifferent to debt —The case she mentioned was an instance of moral monstrosity—an absolute deficiency of the sense of Justice—Such irregular moral developments ought not to be confounded with the cases she had in view—even though they might occur in persons of genius—they occurred also in persons of no genius—

I asked Miss Fuller if she did not think there was an illusion also in the idea that women of genius suffered so out of proportion to women

---

8. Probably Mrs. Samuel Hoar of Concord; possibly Ellen Sturgis Hooper. The speaker may refer to Bronson Alcott (1799–1888). After the collapse of the Temple School (which he and Elizabeth Peabody had opened in 1834) in 1838, Alcott remained in Boston where he unsuccessfully attempted to support himself and his family by continuing to teach a diminishing number of pupils at his lodgings and by conducting conversations. His admission of a black child in June 1839 resulted in the school's closing. Friends helped the family stay afloat and in March 1840, at Emerson's instigation, the Alcotts moved to Concord where they rented a small cottage.

who were ordinary—Supposing we had the history of the latter should
we not find that *small faculties* involved evils & suffering such as we
were apt to forget—Was not Mr Emerson's expression, the "tragedy of
limitation"[9] true to experience—There might be something in that,
Miss Fuller thought—but she declared the belief that if women *wanted
to have a good time* as the *first thing*, they must ignore their higher
faculties. Thought & feeling brought exquisite pleasures—pleasures
worth infinite sacrifices—but they inevitably brought sufferings—The
Idea of Perfection in a world of Imperfection must expose the one who
had it to pain—But this pain was of value—it quickened thought &
feeling to deeper & higher discoveries—The young soul true to itself,
desired—*demanded* in its unfoldings the *Universe*—it wanted to reform
society—to know every thing—to beautify every thing & to have a perfect friend—It could not in this world have or do any of this—This it
soon began to see—& then it yielded & sunk, & assimilated itself to
what was—called the imperfect Perfect—till it lost the idea of
perfection—narrowed its desire till it believed its small circle was the
universe—*Or*—it remained faithful to itself—suffered all the pains of
deprivation—& disappointment—again & again—& for the forever of
this world—but abandoned never those innate immortal truths by
which all things were made unsatisfactory. Yet it did not mourn & weep
forever—it triumphed—it accepted the limitation & the imperfect
friend as they were, & never doubting that the first duty is to preserve
a trust in the Ideal, waited—enjoyed what there is, & trusted that it
may be what it is not—Then all the signatures of the future & immortal
will be appreciated; then that which limits & corrupts it, will not limit
or corrupt us—Then suffering itself becomes the pledge of
immortality—that word on every lip, but whose *meaning* is the rarest
thought in minds.—(These were some of her best thoughts—but imperfectly given, for they came out in conversation, not in one long
speech)—She said besides that she did not love *pain*—nor should it
ever be *coaxed*—but always triumphed over—Yet it must be acknowledged & accepted & allowed to act so as to be met by thought &
feeling—Those who had not suffered had not *lived as yet*. The happiness that was worth any thing was not that which arose out of ignorance
of evil—or of shuffling it aside or turning the back on it—but out of
looking it in the face—accepting it—suffering it—yet feeling it was *finite*
before the infinite Soul.—Much more was said——

*   *   *

9. The "tragedy of limitation" is used in Emerson's lecture "Education," delivered 5 February
1840 at the Masonic Temple, Boston, as part of the "Present Age" series (*The Early Lectures
of Ralph Waldo Emerson*, ed. Robert E. Spiller, Stephen E. Whicher, and Wallace E. Williams, 3 vols. [Cambridge: Harvard University Press, 1959–72], 3:297).

MARGARET FULLER

[From 1842 Journal]†

* * *

[August] 17th.[1]

Arriving this evening quite late, all things looked sad to me. The Concord fog shrouded every object as I approached though the afternoon had been clear and of surpassing beauty.—I went to walk with Waldo. Near the river the misty moonlight was of fairy effect. We merely told our experiences these past months: it was an interchange of facts but no conversation, yet it was pleasant to be with him again.

Thursday [August 18]

Ellery brought down Ellen's picture & put it in my room.[2] It is a hard painting, but simple and true, the upper part of the face is very like, and he has got the purity of the brow and the shape of the eyelids which are so peculiar.

* * *

Lidian came in to see me before dinner:[3] she wept for the lost child, and I was tempted to do the same, which relieved much from the oppression I have felt since I came.[4] Though I can never meet Lidian on such subjects, I felt for her today and she liked to have me.

* * *

---

† From "Margaret Fuller's 1842 Journal: At Concord with The Emersons," ed. Joel Myerson, *Harvard Library Bulletin*, 21 (1973): 332–27, 329–32, 334–35, 337–40. Reprinted by permission of the editor. Fuller met the transcendentalist philosopher Ralph Waldo Emerson (known to his friends as Waldo) in 1836 and during the next six years became intellectually intimate with him. Together they explored, in conversations and writings, topics Fuller would treat in *Woman in the Nineteenth Century*, including friendship, love, marriage, and spiritual union. During her visit to Concord in August–September 1842, Fuller gained firsthand knowledge of the marital relations of a number of her friends, especially the Emersons [Editor].

1. In the following *literatim* transcription square brackets ([]) enclose editorial insertions; angle brackets (◊) indicate cancellations in the manuscript; and slashes (//) indicate insertions or additions in the manuscript.

2. Ellery Channing had married Margaret's sister Ellen on 24 September 1841. On 11 August he arrived in Concord to seek their winter accommodations before Ellen joined him in a few weeks.

3. During this period Lidian Emerson was "suffering from a swol[le]n face the sequel of the dentist's operations," which may have affected her behavior (letter to William Emerson, 22 August, *EmL*, III, 82).

4. Emerson's first-born, Waldo, died on 27 January 1842 from scarlatina. He was only five years old. Emerson was profoundly hurt by the death, and while he later expressed his feelings in "Threnody," at the time he said, "all that is glad & festal & almost all that is social even, for me," had departed from the world. Margaret was "deeply sad at the loss of little Waldo, from whom I hoped more than from almost any living being" (letter to E.P. Peabody, 28 January, *EmL*, III, 8; February, *MemMF*, II, 62).

181

Friday [August 19]

In the evening I took a walk with W.[5] Looking at the moon in the river
he said the same thing as in his letter, how each twinkling light breaking
there summons to demand the whole secret, and how "promising,
promising nature never fulfils what she thus gives us a right to expect[.]"
I said I never could meet him here, the beauty does not stimulate me
to ask *why*?, and press to the centre, I was satisfied for the moment,
full as if my existence was filled out, for nature had said the very word
that was lying in my heart. Then we had an excellent talk: We agreed
that my god was love, his truth. W. said that these statements alternate,
of course, in every mind, the only difference was in which you were
most at home, that he liked the pure mathematics of the thing.

Saturday [August 20]

* * * Went to see the Hawthornes: it was very pleasant. The poplars
whisper so suddenly in the avenue their pleasant tale, and every where
the view is so peaceful. The house within I like, all their things are so
expressive of themselves and mix in so gracefully with the old furniture.
H. walked home with me: we stopped some time to look at the moon
[;] she was struggling with clouds. H said he should be much more
willing to die than two months ago, for he had had some real possession
in life, but still he never wished to leave this earth: it was beautiful
enough.[6] He expressed, as he always does, many fine perceptions. I like
to hear the lightest thing he says[.][7]

Wednesday [August 24]

So day after day glides on and there is too much intercourse to write
it down. It dissipates my mind, too, so that my writing thrives but ill,
though I spend the appointed time at it. But so many interesting subjects being talked over day by day I cannot bend my mind with full
force on one poor theme. Let me remember this experience & be
content when far from my friends.

Waldo and I have good meetings, though we stop at all our old
places. But my expectations are moderate now: it is his beautiful presence that I prize, far more than our intercourse.[8]

5. Emerson's account of this meeting is in *EmJMN*, VIII, 195–196.
6. Hawthorne had married Sophia Peabody on 9 July and they settled in the Old Manse at
Concord.
7. The conversation was so pleasant that Margaret forgot that she was carrying a book and left
it at Hawthorne's house (*American Notebooks*, p. 159).
8. Margaret wrote to a friend about Emerson: "After the first excitement of intimacy with him,
—when I was made so happy by his high tendency, absolute purity, the freedom and infinite
graces of an intellect cultivated much beyond any I had known,—came with me the ques-
tioning season. . . . He had faith in the Universal, but not in the Individual Man; he met
men, not as a brother, but as a critic. . . .
  "But now I am better acquainted with him. His 'accept' is true; the 'I shall learn,' with

I wish I could retain Ellery's talk last night: it was wonderful; it was about all the past experiences frozen down in the soul, & the impossibility of being penetrated by any thing. Had I met you, said he when I was young! but now, nothing can penetrate! Absurd as was what he said on one side, it was the finest poetic inspiration on the other, painting the cruel process of life, except where genius continually burns over the stubble fields. He said too the best things of William and of Ward: they were partial but admirable statements, deep insights.[9]

He said of his marriage (W. when he would not go to Nahant with them after every persuasion called at the door in a carriage with Anna & introduced E. to her.) Why did he marry a fashionable woman, older then himself. And to marry a woman that had rejected him, what nonsense! There would have been no offering or rejecting, if the thing had been right. He should have had some small light figure hovering in the back ground. I knew before and I felt when I saw her face that I would not see them together. It would make me miserable to think she was not great, unequalled when he has married her, too.[1]

*   *   *

Sunday [August 28]

We need great energy, and self-reliance to endure to day. My age may not be the best, my position may be bad, my character ill formed, but thou, Oh Spirit, hast no regard to aught but the seeking heart, and if I try to walk upright will [thou] guide me? What despair must he feel who after a whole life passed in trying to build up himself, resolves that it would have been far better, if he had kept still as the clod of the valley, or yielded easily as the leaf to every breeze. A path has been appointed me. I have walked in it as steadily as I could. "I am what I am." That which I am not, teach me in the others. I will bear the pain of imperfection, but not of doubt. Waldo must not shake me in my worldliness, nor William in the fine motion that that [sic] has given

---

which he answers every accusation, is no less true. No one can feel his limitations, in fact, more than he . . . the calm observer of the courses of things. Surely, 'he keeps true to his thought, which is the great matter.' . . . As I look at him more by his own law, I understand him better . . ." (25 August 1842, MemMF, II, 67–68).

9. William Henry Channing, Ellery's cousin and a good friend of Margaret's, was at this time drifting towards associationism. Samuel Gray Ward had introduced both Ellery and his poetry to Emerson, and would later provide the financial backing to Ellery's Poems. Ward had also been romantically involved with Margaret Fuller three years earlier.

1. Ward had married Anna Barker on 3 October 1840. Miss Barker had turned down Ward's first proposal until his plans "of a scholar's life gave way to some lucrative profession," and when Ward proposed again, he agreed that he must "satisfy not only her feelings but her tastes." Ellery felt that Ward would now "have no place or need" for him in his "affections," and Margaret, who felt that Ward had sacrificed art for business, believed that Ward had chosen Anna's beauty over her own intelligence (Ward's statement, 2 December 1843, David Baldwin, "Puritan Aristocrat in the Age of Emerson: A Study of Samuel Gray Ward," Ph.D. dissertation, University of Pennsylvania, 1961, pp. 143–144; Ward to Sanborn, 9 June 1902, F.B. Sanborn, Recollections of Seventy Years [Boston, 1909], II, 576).

me what I have of life, nor this child of genius,[2] make me lay aside the armour without which I had lain bleeding on the field long since, but if they can keep closer to Nature, and learn to interpret her as souls, also,—let me learn from them what I have not.

*   *   *

Sept [1]

This golden afternoon I walked with Waldo to the hemlocks. There we sat down and staid till near sunset. He read me verses.—Dichtung and Wahrheit is certainly the name for his life, for he does not care for facts, except so far as the immortal essence can be distilled from them.[3] He has little sympathy with mere life: does not seem to see the plants grow, merely that he may rejoice in their energy.

We got to talking, as we almost always do, on Man and Woman, and Marriage.—W. took his usual ground. Love is only phenomenal, a contrivance of nature, in her circular motion. Man, in proportion as he is completely unfolded is man and woman by turns. The soul knows nothing of marriage, in the sense of a permanent union between two personal existences. The soul is married to each new thought as it enters into it. If this thought puts on the form of man or woman[,] if it last you seventy years, what then? There is but one love, that for the Soul of all Souls, let it put on what cunning disguises it will, still at last you find yourself lonely,—*the Soul.*

There seems to be no end to these conversations: they always leave us both where they found us, but we enjoy them, for we often get a good expression. Waldo said "Ask any woman whether her aim in this union is to further the genius of her husband; and she will say yes, but her conduct will always be to claim a devotion day by day that will be injurious to him, if he yields.["] "Those who hold their heads highest," quoth he, with a satirical side glance, "would do no better, if they were tried." I made no reply, for it is not worthwhile to, in such cases, by *words.*

[September] 2d

It is a most brilliant day, & I stole the morning from my writing to take Lidian and then Mamma to ride.[4] L. has had a slow fever which has confined her to her chamber almost ever since I came, & I have not been attentive to her as I should have been, if I had thought she cared about it. I did not go into her room at all for a day or two, simply

2. Ellery Channing [Editor].
3. Goethe's autobiography was entitled *Aus meinem Leben: Dichtung und Wahrheit.* He specifically called it "poetry and truth" because "it raises itself by higher tendencies from the region of a lower Reality" (P. Hume Brown, *Life of Goethe* [London, 1920], II, 661).
4. Emerson's mother was living at his house.

because I was engaged all the time and kept expecting to see her down stairs. When I *did* go in, she burst into tears, at sight of me, but laid the blame on her nerves, having taken opium &c.[5] I felt embarrassed, & did not know whether I ought to stay or go. Presently she said something which made me suppose she thought W. passed the evenings in talking with me, & a painful feeling flashed across me, such as I have not had, all has seemed so perfectly understood between us. I said that I was with Ellery or H[enry]. T[horeau]. both of the eve gs & that W. was writing in the study.

I thought it all over a little, whether I was considerate enough. As to W. I never keep him from any such duties, any more than a book would.—He lives in his own way, & he dont soothe the illness, or morbid feelings of a friend, because he would not wish any one to do it *for him*. It is useless to expect it; what does it signify whether he is with me or at his writing. L. knows perfectly well, that he has no regard for me or any one that would make him wish to be with me, a minute longer than I could fill up the time with thoughts.

As to my being more his companion that cannot be helped, his life is /in/ the intellect not the affections. He has affection for me, but it is because I quicken his intellect.—I dismissed it all, as a mere sick moment of L's.

Yesterday she said to me, at dinner, I have not yet been out, will you be my guide for a little walk this afternoon. I said ["]I am engaged to walk with Mr E. but["]—(I was going to say, I will walk with you first,) when L. burst into tears. The family were all present, they looked at their plates. Waldo looked on the ground, but soft & serene as ever. I said "My dear Lidian, certainly I will go with you." "No!["] she said ["]I do not want you to make any sacrifice, but I do feel perfectly desolate, and forlorn, and I thought if I once got out, the fresh air would do me good, and that with you, I should have courage, but go with Mr E. I will not go[.]"

I hardly knew what to say, but I insisted on going with her, & then she insisted on going so that I might return in time for my other walk. Waldo said not a word: he retained his sweetness of look, but never offered to do the least thing. I can never admire him enough at such times; he is so true to himself. In our walk and during our ride this morn g L. talked so fully that I felt reassured except that I think she will always have these pains, because she has always a lurking hope that Waldo's character will alter, and that he will be capable of an intimate union; now I feel convinced that it will never be more perfect between them two. I do not believe it will be less: for he is sorely troubled by imperfections in the tie, because he dont believe in any thing better.—/And where he loved her first, he loves her always./ Then

5. Tincture of laudanum, a mixture of opium and water, was a common pain reliever of the day.

the influence of any one with him would be just in proportion to independence of him, combined with pure love of him for his own sake. Yet in reply to all L. said, I would not but own that though I thought it was the only way, to take him for what he is, as he wishes to be taken, and though my experience of him has been, for that very reason, so precious to me, I dont know that I could have fortitude for it in a more intimate relation. Yet nothing could be nobler, nor more consoling than to be his wife, if one's mind were only thoroughly made up to the truth.—As for myself, if I have not done as much as I ought for L. it is that her magnanimity has led her to deceive me. I have really thought that she was happy to have me in the house solely for Waldo's sake, and my own, and she is, I know, in the long account, but there are pains of every day which I am apt to neglect for others as for myself.—But Truth, spotless Truth, and Prayer and Love shall yield a talisman to teach me how to steer.

I suppose the whole amount of the feeling is that women cant bear to be left out of the question. And they dont see the whole truth about one like me, if they did they would understand why the brow of Muse or Priestess must wear a shade of sadness. On my side I dont remember them enough. They have so much that I have not, I cant conceive of their wishing for what I have. (*enjoying* is not the word: these I know are too generous for that) But when Waldo's wife, & the mother of that child that is gone thinks me the most privileged of women, & that E[lizabeth]. H[oar]. was happy because her love was snatched away for a life long separation, & thus she can know none but ideal love: it does seem a little too insulting at first blush.—And yet they are not altogether wrong.

* * *

Friday [September 9]

* * * Aft[ernoon]. Waldo came into my room to read me what he has written in his journal about marriage, & we had a long talk. He listens with a soft wistful look to what I say, but is nowise convinced. It was late in a dark afternoon, the fine light in that red room always so rich, cast a beautiful light upon him, as he read and talked. *Since* I have found in his journal two sentences that represent the two sides of his thought.

In time

"Marriage should be a covenant to secure to either party the sweetness and the handsomeness of being a calm continuing inevitable benefactor to the other."

In eternity

"Is it not enough that souls should meet in a law, in a thought, obey the same love, demonstrate the same idea. These alone are the nuptials of minds[.]

I marry you for better, not for worse, I marry impersonally."[6]

I shall write to him about it.

* * *

[Monday, September 19]

I gave the aftn & eve g to Lidian[:] she read to me of little Waldo and talked well.

She said the Angels look on what you do, perhaps with as much disdain as you and Waldo would on Mrs. Hemans.[7] Whatever has spoken to /us of/ one human heart has a right to exist.

I confess, I replied, but ever, ever we are striving to the more excellent. Forgive if we are narrow and cold on the way. Yet should we mend.

* * *

Nothing makes me so anti-Christian, & so anti-marriage as these talks with L. She lays such undue stress on the office of Jesus, & the demands of the heart. Waldo had got through with his tedious

(Wednesday) prose, & to day he got into the mood to finish his poem. Just at night he came into the red room to read the passage he had inserted. This is to me the loveliest way to live that we have. I wish it would be so always that I could live in the red room, & Waldo be stimulated /by the fine days/ to write poems & come the rainy days to read them to me. My time to go to him is late in the evening. Then I go knock at the library door, & we have ⟨yo⟩ our long word walk through the growths of things with glimmers of light from the causes of things. Afterward, W. goes out & walks beneath the stars to compose himself for his pillow, & I open the window, & sit in the great red chair to watch them. The only thing I hate is our dining together. It is never pleasant and some days I dislike it so that I go out just before dinner & stay till night in the woods, just to break the routine. I do not think a person of more complete character would feel or make the *dinner* bell such a vulgarity as W. does, but with him these feelings are inevitable[.]

* * *

Wednesday [September 21]

I dined with the Hawthornes & went with them in their boat up the North Branch. We landed on a foreign shore, but did not find much

---

6. "I marry . . . impersonally." is in *EmJMN*, VII, 336, and VIII, 144; for "Is it . . . minds." cf. *EmJMN*, VII, 532–533.
7. Felicia Hemans was the most popular female poet of the day.

to reward the discoverer. It was a sallow and sorrowful day, no insincere harbinger of winter. Hawthorne expressed his surprise at having met Lidian out at noon day, said it seemed scarce credible you could meet such a person by the light of sun. She does look very ghostly now as she glides about in her black dress, and long black veil. The other eve g I was out with her about nine o clock; it was a night of moon struggling with clouds. She asked me to go to the churchyard, & glided before me through the long wet grass, and knelt & leaned her forehead on the tomb. The moon then burst forth, and cast its light on her as she prayed. It seemed like the ghost of a mother's joys, and I have never felt that she possessed the reality. I feel that her child is far more to her in imagination than he ever was in reality. I prayed, too; it was a good moment & will not be fruitless.

*   *   *

Sunday [September 25]

All this morning I spent in reading W's journals for the last year, or rather in finishing them, for I have had them by me for weeks. This afternoon I meant to have gone into the woods and finished Ellery's book,[8] but I went into the library after dinner & staid till night: it was our last talk and my best. We talked over many things in the journal, especially a good lead was given by "Sickness is generally the coat in which genius is drest," an unusual remark for W.—We talked too of Bulwer & the people of talent,—W grows more merciful day by day. I ought to go away now these last days I have been fairly intoxicated with his mind. I am not in full possession of my own. I feel faint in in [sic] the presence of too strong a fragrance. I think, too, he will be glad to get rid of me. Farewell, dearest friend, there has been dissonance between us, & may be again, for we do not fully meet, and to me you are too much & too little by turns, yet thanks be to the Parent of Souls, that gave us to be born into the same age and the same country and to meet with so much of nobleness and sweetness as we do, & I think constantly with more and more.

Going down I had a thorough talk with Lidian. I shall never trouble myself any more: it is not just to her. But I will do more in attending to her, for I see I could be of real use. She says she feels I am always just to her, but I might be more.

8. Ellery Channing's *Poems* was published in May 1843; probably Margaret was reading a book she had borrowed from Ellery.

MARGARET FULLER

From Letter to Ralph Waldo Emerson†

Sunday 16th Oct [1842]

Dear Waldo—

I can hardly believe that it is a month this day since I passed a true Sabbath in reading your journals and Ellery's book, and talking with you in the study. I have not felt separated from you yet.—It is not yet time for me to have my dwelling near you. I get, after a while, even *intoxicated* with your mind, and do not live enough in myself. Now dont screw up your lip to an ungracious pettiness, but hear the words of frank affection as they deserve "mente cordis".¹ Let no cold breath paralyze my hope that there will yet be a noble and profound understanding between us. We have gone so far, and yet so little way. I understand the leadings of your thought better and better, and I feel a conviction that I shall be worthy of this friendship, that I shall be led day by day to purify, to harmonize my being, to enlarge my experiences, and clear the eye of intelligence till after long long patient waiting yourself shall claim a thousand years interview at least. You need not be terrified at this prophecy nor look about for the keys of your cell.— *I* shall never claim an hour I begin to understand where I am, and feel more and more unfit to be with any body. I shall no more be so ruled by the affectionate expansions of my heart but hope is great, though my daily life must be pallid and narrow.

I must not try to say to you much that has passed in my mind which I should like you to know. I find no adequate expression for it.

I do not know whether it is owing to this feeling of your mind being too near me that I have not yet been able to finish the ragged rhymes I meant for you. I got along well enough till the point of division came, where I wanted to show that the permanent marriage cannot interfere with the soul's destiny, when lo! this future which has seemed so clear, vanished and left me without a word, yet unconvinced of your way of thinking. There lies the paper, and I expect the hour may yet come when I can make out my case,² if so, it will be sent[.]

* * *

---

† From *The Letters of Margaret Fuller, Volume 3, 1842–44*, ed. Robert N. Hudspeth (Ithaca, N.Y.: Cornell University Press, 1984), 241. Originally from bMS Am 1280, reprinted by permission of the Houghton Library, Harvard University.
1. With the understanding of the heart (Latin) [Editor].
2. Fuller's "case" most likely became "The Great Lawsuit," which she would write during the winter and spring of 1843 [Editor].

RALPH WALDO EMERSON

Margaret†

A pure & purifying mind, selfpurifying also, full of faith in men, & inspiring it. Unable to find any companion great enough to receive the rich effusions of her thought, so that her riches are still unknown & seem unknowable. It is a great joy to find that we have underrated our friend, that he or she is far more excellent than we had thought. All natures seem poor beside one so rich, which pours a stream of amber over all objects clean & unclean that lie in its path, and makes that comely & presentable which was mean in itself. We are taught by her plenty how lifeless & outward we were, what poor Laplanders burrowing under the snows of prudence & pedantry. Beside her friendship, other friendships seem trade, and by the firmness with which she treads her upward path, all mortals are convinced that another road exists than that which their feet know. The wonderful generosity of her sentiments pours a contempt on books & writing at the very time when one asks how shall this fiery picture be kept in its glow & variety for other eyes. She excels other intellectual persons in this, that her sentiments are more blended with her life; so the expression of them has greater steadiness & greater clearness. I have never known any example of such steady progress from stage to stage of thought & of character. An inspirer of courage, the secret friend of all nobleness, the patient waiter for the realization of character, forgiver of injuries, gracefully waiving aside folly, & elevating lowness,—in her presence all were apprised of their fettered estate & longed for liberation, of ugliness & longed for their beauty; of meanness, & panted for grandeur.

Her growth is visible. All the persons whom we know, have reached their height, or else their growth is so nearly at the same rate with ours, that it is imperceptible, but this child[1] inspires always more faith in her. She rose before me at times into heroical & godlike regions, and I could remember no superior women, but thought of Ceres, Minerva, Proserpine, and the august ideal forms of the Foreworld. She said that no man gave such invitation to her mind as to tempt her to a full expression; that she felt a power to enrich her thought with such wealth & variety of embellishment as would no doubt be tedious to such as

---

† Reprinted by permission of the publisher from *The Journals and Miscellaneous Notebooks of Ralph Waldo Emerson*, Volume 8 *1841–1843*, ed. William H. Gilman and J. E. Parsons (Cambridge, Mass.: Harvard University Press. Copyright © 1970 by the President and Fellows of Harvard College), 368–69. Emerson made this entry in March 1843, at a time when Fuller was engaged in writing "The Great Lawsuit" and Emerson, in response, was pondering the nature of "Woman" [Editor].

1. When Emerson wrote this entry, Fuller was thirty-two; he was thirty-nine [Editor].

she conversed with. And there is no form that does seem to wait her beck,—dramatic, lyric, epic, passionate, pictorial, humourous.

She has great sincerity, force, & fluency as a writer, yet her powers of speech throw her writing into the shade. What method, what exquisite judgment, as well as energy, in the selection of her words, what character & wisdom they convey! You cannot predict her opinion. She sympathizes so fast with all forms of life, that she talks never narrowly or hostilely nor betrays, like all the rest, under a thin garb of new words, the old droning castiron opinions or notions of many years standing. What richness of experience, what newness of dress, and fast as Olympus to her principle. And a silver eloquence, which inmost Polymnia[2] taught. Meantime, all the pathos of sentiment and riches of literature & of invention and this march of character threatening to arrive presently at the shores & plunge into the sea of Buddhism & mystic trances, consists with a boundless fun & drollery, with light satire, & the most entertaining conversation in America.

Her experience contains, I know, golden moments, which, if they could be fitly narrated, would stand equally beside any histories of magnanimity which the world contains; and whilst Dante's 'Nuova Vita' is almost unique in the literature of sentiment, I have called the imperfect record she gave me of two of her days, 'Nuovissima Vita.'[3]

* * *

2. The muse of lyric poetry [Editor].
3. Dante's *Vita Nuova* (c. 1292) (Italian for "New Life"), is a collection of lyrics celebrating ideal love; by "Nuovissima Vita," Emerson intends the superlative, "Newest Life" [Editor].

MARGARET FULLER†

[*From* 1844 Journal]

* * *

18th [*Tuesday, June*][1]

At night C.[2] & I lay down on the bed, as we had done every night. We both went to sleep & kept waking now and then. It was a time of deep life, & has had permanent effect on my life. Ever since I have been soothed and still. I have slept well; the past *is* past, only to be brought up for precept or poetic suggestion.

I cannot speak of it; it could not be spoken of unless in verse. I thought of Ceres & Persephone.

---

† From " 'The Impulses of Human Nature': Margaret Fuller's Journal from June through October 1844," ed. Martha L. Berg and Alice de V. Perry, *Massachusetts Historical Society Proceedings* 102 (1990): 38–126. Reprinted by the courtesy of the Massachusetts Historical Society.

 Fuller completed her essay "The Great Lawsuit" in May 1843 and immediately left for a tour of the Great Lakes and the Wisconsin Territory with her friend Sarah Clarke. When her essay appeared in the July 1843 *Dial*, Emerson wrote to Fuller, telling her of its positive reception: " 'The Great Lawsuit' is felt by all to be a piece of life, so much better than a piece of grammar. H[enry]. D[avid]. Thoreau, who will never like anything, writes 'Miss F's is a noble piece, rich extempore writing, talking with pen in hand.' Mrs Sophia Ripley writes that 'Margaret's article is the cream of herself, a little rambling, but rich in all good things' and Ellery [Channing] testifies his approbation very distinctly & without qualification." As for his own opinion, Emerson told Fuller, "I think the piece very proper & noble, and itself quite an important fact in the history of Woman: good for its wit, excellent for its character—it wants an introduction; the subject is not quite distinctly & adequately propounded" (*Letters of Ralph Waldo Emerson*, 3:183).

 Fuller subsequently decided to expand her essay into the book *Woman in the Nineteenth Century*, and she began this task in the summer 1844 after publishing *Summer on the Lakes, 1843*. At first she made little progress, perhaps because, as Berg and Perry have suggested, she was recovering from an ill-fated love affair with William Hull Clarke of Chicago, her friend Sarah's brother, who had served as their guide in the West. As her 1844 journal shows, Fuller's friends helped her recover her spirits, and after reflecting anew on human relations and the plight of woman, she completed her book manuscript at Fishkill Landing in the fall of 1844.

 The journal edited by Berg and Perry appears to be a traced copy of a nonextant original. There is evidence to suggest that William Hull Clarke, long after Fuller's death, may have done the tracing. [Editor]

1. In editing this journal we have made few changes in Fuller's text. We have followed her spelling and have added or emended punctuation only for purposes of clarity. We have indicated those instances by using angle brackets, thus < >. We have indented paragraphs only where fuller has. We have used the following editing conventions:

  // / Manuscript page breaks.
  /#/ Pagination where indicated on manuscript pages.
  { } Additions by a hand other than Fuller's.
  [x] Editorial additions, e.g., dates.

2. Caroline (Cary) Sturgis

It seemed we might meet yet again as Elizabeth and Mary did on the hills of Judea.[3]

/7/ The days that follow generally were spent in arranging my papers, which weary task with many interruptions has occupied me till today June 21st [Friday] when I finished about 5 pm.

*   *   *

Wednesday [June 26]

Still just so lazy.

Last night, I rose, & at the moonlight window, fine thoughts occurred to me as themes for composition<.>

Preparing this morning for a workwoman took some hours: the best of the day. I read a novel by Eugene Sue. Arthur[4]—Yet it gave me great pain. Such characters exist, no doubt, and, if I have suffered so terribly from some baseness of reaction in the minds of these I have loved, what must women /15/ endure doomed to meet, to trust, to learn such a man as Arthur. They could not have great strength of feeling, or they would not survive the shock.

A letter from S. Ward[5] today, with a postscript from Anna, far from pleasing. S. is no longer my Rafaello: he has perhaps many years to pass in working out this side of his life. I do not care to know him while about it. That side I have studied: he while he breathed the golden exhalations of the dawn cheered me in it. Now it is all well that he should be geographically removed from my ken.

3. Luke 1:39–56. That this night together had deep meaning for both Fuller and Sturgis is demonstrated by an exchange of letters a year later in which Fuller, writing after a long silence, asked, "Do you remember that night last summer when we fell asleep on the bed and we were like Elizabeth and Mary. I have often wanted to express what appeared to me that night, but would not, only everyday I understand it better. I feel profou[nd]ly bound with you and hope you wear my ring" (Hudspeth, *Letters*, 4:132). Sturgis responded, "That we are to meet very deeply, I am sure, if it were only for that hour's sleep, about which I have always felt as you do, but I cannot yet always wear your ring" (Dedmond, "Letters," 243).
4. Eugène Sue (1804–1857) was a popular French writer whose novels of the sea and of Parisian life incorporated current ideas of social and democratic reform. During the time of this journal Fuller read three of his novels: *Arthur* (Paris, 1838); *La Salamandre* (Paris, 1832); and *The Wandering Jew* (Paris, 1844).
5. Samuel Gray Ward (1817–1907) had encouraged Fuller's study of art through the portfolios of engravings he had brought back from his travels in Europe. Raphael was his favorite artist, hence Raffaello, Fuller's nickname for him. Anna Hazard Barker (1813–1900), daughter of a wealthy New Orleans merchant, had spent long vacations at Newport and in Cambridge with her cousin Eliza Farrar. During the late 1830s her relationship with Fuller was emotionally intense, and Fuller's distress at Anna's involvement with Ward was only barely disguised by the effusively sentimental attitude she developed toward their Oct. 3, 1840, marriage. At Anna's urging, Ward put his artistic and literary interests in second place and took a job in her father's firm. In June 1844, Anna and Sam Ward moved from Boston to Lenox, Mass.

Thursday [June 27]

Carbuncles, says Southey[6] are male and female. The female cast out light, the male has his within himself. Mine is the male.

Wednesday [July 3]

* * * A letter from Cary tonight<.> Methinks she is sad.

I love sadness. But let it be a grand a tragic sadness. Let its tones be sweet in their bitterness.

July 4th [Thursday]

I wrote a letter to Cary & carried it with some others to the office but it was shut. I was disappointed. I hoped I might find one there that would do me good.

O I need some help. No I need a full a godlike embrace from some sufficient love. I know not why, but the wound of my heart has reopened yesterday & today. My head aches.

Last year this day was the Ganymede /26/ day.[7] The full music of soul amid that resplendent beauty of nature. I remember every one of the golden sands of that day. All its pictures of supernatural loveliness pass before my eyes.

Here all looks so mean! The air is cold, hostile. The color sharp & painful as always in these cold summer days. * * *

> Leila[8] in the Arabian zone
> Dusky, languishing and lone
> Yet full of light are her deep eyes
> And her gales are lovers sighs
>
> So in Egyptian clime
> Grows an Isis calm sublime
> Blue black is her robe of night
> But blazoned o'er with points of light
> The horns that Io's brow deform
> With Isis take a crescent form

6. Robert Southey (1774–1843), English poet, historian, biographer, and essayist, was the brother-in-law of Coleridge and Poet Laureate of England. This citation may be found in Southey's *Common-Place Book* (J.W. Warter, ed. [London, 1850], 4:47). He is quoting Camillus Leopardus, *The Mirror of Stones* (London, 1750).

7. When Fuller spent the previous Fourth of July at Oregon, Ill., where her uncle William Williams Fuller practiced law, she made an excursion to the Eagle's Nest, a bluff overlooking Rock River. There she wrote the poem "Ganymede to his Eagle," suggested by a statue of Ganymede by the Danish sculptor Bertel Thorvaldsen (1770–1844). This statue was first exhibited at the Boston Athenaeum Gallery in 1839. Fuller's poem "Ganymede to his Eagle" was published in *Summer*, 54–57.

8. The Egyptian goddess Isis and her sistrum, the rattle that symbolizes her power, were also of great importance in Fuller's mythology. She included as Appendix A to *Woman in the Nineteenth Century* Thomas Taylor's translation of the description of Isis in *The Golden Ass of Apuleius*, clearly the basis for this poem.

And as a holy moon inform.
The magic sistrum arms her hand
And at her deep eye's command
Brutes are raised to thinking men
Soul growing to her soul filled ken.

Dean of the lonely life
Hecate fed on gloom and strife
Phebe on her throne of air
Only Leila's children are.//

Patient serpent, circle round[9]
Till in death thy life is found,
Double form of godly prime
Holding the whole thought of time,
When the perfect two embrace,
Male and female, black and white
Soul is justified in space,
Dark made fruitful by the light,
And centred in the diamond Sun
Time, eternity, are one.

* * *

5th [Friday, July]

Last night I went to bed at 12, but not feeling at all like it. I felt as if
I could have gone on stringing these verses, like the dropping of sand
in an hour glass.

9. Fuller sent a sketch of this "Double Triangle, Serpent and Rays" in a letter to Emerson, July
13, 1844, and used it, slightly altered, as the frontispiece for the first edition of *Woman*.

A beggar woman came here this morning who pleased me much by her simplicity of character and dignified feeling about her own position.

* * *

Afternoon, final arranging of these not quite eternal papers.

I will copy here from a packet that I unsealed for the occasion a passage that has often more or less distinctly occurred to memory.[1]

"I feel some difficulty in speaking frankly of the ideas suggested by your letter. They brought home to my mind the reflection how widely apart are the points from which life is surveyed by those whose personal experience of passion has been thorough, and those in whom it has (though giving brightness to the fancy and earnestness to the thoughts) remained comparatively undeveloped.

X X X The thought that an attachment subsisted between Jesus and Mary sufficient to suggest to the spotless son of God the existence of a new, vast, and tumultuous class of human emotions. Your views of life and affection /43/ are perfectly true to *you*.—I, too, once knew and recognized the possibility of Platonic affection. It is possible to those who have never passed the line X X X X Before that, all the higher classes of emotion all the nobler views of life exist; but in a shape that seems sublimated and idealized to the more experienced: to those who *have* passed that line, the higher emotions and the passions are apt to be always afterward inextricably commingled."—

So writes the sentimental man of the world and he, once my Rafaello, would now write so too. I will seal up now and read not again ever perhaps.

Tuesday [July 9]

to Concord with Almira.[2] Find Sarah, and the happy pair. The little Una is a most beautiful child.[3]

/49/ While Hawthorne and I were looking at her as she lay in her basket-cradle outdoors, looking up and smiling to the whispering trees, Mr E.[4] came. He staid some time and then I went with him through

1. The following excerpt from a letter of Sam Ward's probably dates from 1839, when he was trying to extricate himself from his involvement with Fuller in order to pursue his attachment to her close friend Anna Barker.
2. Almira Cornelia Barlow (1807–1868) was an old friend of Fuller's who had separated from her husband, David Hatch Barlow, and was living at Brook Farm with her children [Editor].
3. Sophia Amelia Peabody (1809–1871), sister of Elizabeth Palmer Peabody and Mary Peabody Mann, married Nathaniel Hawthorne on July 9, 1842, at a ceremony performed by James Freeman Clarke and attended by his sister Sarah, a friend of the bride through their mutual interest in art. The Hawthornes' first home in Concord was the Old Manse, then called the Parsonage, which they rented from July 1842 to October 1845. Their first child, Una, (1844–1877), named for a Spenserian heroine, was born on Mar. 3, 1844. Hawthorne had by this time published *Grandfather's Chair*, *Twice-Told Tales*, and *Biographical Stories for Children*, all of which Fuller had reviewed for the *Dial* (1:450; 3:130–131).
4. Ralph Waldo Emerson.

Sleepy Hollow[5] to see Ellen and her little one whom they call Greta. It was a scene of distress—Then I went with him to see Lidian[6] who is momently expecting her new child. He brought the little Edith[7] in her white nightgown and pretty bare feet and put her into my lap. The child is like a seraph. Nothing can be more poetic and tender than her smile and she whispers her little thoughts rather than speaks them. She looks of too frail a beauty for this world, while Una in her noble and harmonious beauty seems as strong as sweet, as if she might stay here always.

Wednesday [July] 10th

I spent the morning with Ellen. Dim and sorrowful indeed seems the prospect that opens before her difficult path, but she will /50/ learn from each troublous day, I think. Waldo has a son, born this morning. It is a happiness to him, but we cannot help feeling that this child will be pushed into the place of our lost darling.[8]

* * *

11th [Thursday, July]

Began to copy for Sarah the 4th July poems which she likes. Went to spend the day with Waldo. Saw his baby. Little Edith kneeling on the bed to look at the baby, it was the fairest picture.

He read me his essay on Life.[9] How beautiful, and full and grand. But oh, how cold. Nothing but Truth in the Universe, no love, and no various realities.

Yet how foolish with me to be grieved at him for showing towards me what exists toward all.

Then we talked. He showed me a page from his journal which made me rather ashamed of ever exacting more. But lure me not again too

5. Sleepy Hollow was at this time a favorite wooded walking place for the residents of Concord; it was not consecrated as a cemetery until Sept. 29, 1855, when Emerson delivered the dedication address.
6. Lydia Jackson (1802–1892) had changed her name to Lidian when she became Emerson's second wife in 1835. Her relationship with Fuller, cordial but never close, was occasionally strained by Lidian's jealousy over Fuller's intellectual intimacy with Emerson.
7. Edith Emerson (1841–1929) was the third child of Lidian and Ralph Waldo Emerson. In 1865 she married William H. Forbes, a wealthy investor, who eventually became president of Bell Telephone Co.
8. Edward Waldo Emerson (1844–1930) was the Emersons' second son; their first, Waldo, was born in 1836 and died suddenly of scarlet fever in 1842. The death of this brilliant, perceptive, and charming child, Emerson's favorite, threw him into a state of benumbed grief, which he ultimately expressed in the elegy "Threnody." Edward Emerson later became a physician, practicing in Concord. After his father's death, Edward edited Emerson's correspondence.
9. "Life" and "The Lords of Life" were earlier working titles for "Experience," in *Essays: Second Series* published in Boston in Oct. 1844. The collection, which Emerson read to Fuller during this Concord visit, also includes the essays, "The Poet," "Manners," "Nature," and "Nominalist and Realist."

/5 1/ near thee, fair Greek, I must keep steadily in mind what you really are.

He seemed so happy today and made the atmosphere so serene and golden.

He went home with me and passed an hour. Then Sarah and I had a little talk before sleep, while the dark trees whispered in the dim starlight.

*   *   *

16th[1]

Waked to hear the softest fast falling rain. Am glad to be kept in where I write up this diary & also some letters this morning to S.W. & Georgiana.[2]

*   *   *

16th [Tuesday, July]

I read and sewed a little while. Then went to pass the day at Mr. E's. He read aloud great parts of "The Poet" & "Manners."

So fine a tissue full of splendid things, yet a few burning simple words would better please. More fine than searching, kept coming into my mind, though the remarks are profound each by itself. That account of the Poet as he who sees the Metamorphosis, *the flowing*, is admirable so are the two definitions of art.

[Thursday, July 18 (?)]

/6 1/ This afternoon is lustrous warm, delicious happy, tender, gently stooping clouds. I went and lay for a long time on the rock. * * *

H. came down about six and we went out on the river & staid till after sunset. We talked a great deal this time. I love him much, & love to be with him in this sweet tender homely scene. But I should like too, to be with him on the bold ocean shore.

When we came back Una was lying on the sofa all undrest. She acted like a little wild thing / / towards me, leaning towards me, stretching out her arms whenever I turned. Her mother tried to attract her attention, in vain, her father took my place, she looked on him and smiled, but discontinued this gesture, the moment I came she resumed it.

She has daily become more attached to me; she often kisses me in

1. Here Fuller miswrote the date; it was Monday, July 15.
2. S. W. is Samuel Ward. Georgianna Bruce (1818–1887), who worked at Brook Farm for her board and instruction in the community's school, met Margaret Fuller there and idolized her. In 1844 Fuller helped her get a job at the Female State Prison at Sing Sing, N. Y., under Eliza W. Farnham, its new progressive director. Later Bruce became involved in antislavery work and taught school in Missouri, New York, and Pennsylvania, finally moving in 1850 to California, where she married Richard Kirby and lived on an isolated ranch. Parts of the letter Fuller mentions here were published in Georgianna Bruce Kirby's memoir *Years of Experience* (New York, 1887), 209–210; reprinted in Hudspeth, *Letters*, 3:210–211.

her way, or nestles her head in my bosom. But her prettiest and most marked way with me is to lean her forehead upon mine. As she does this she looks into my eyes, & I into hers. This act gives me singular pleasure: it is described in no initiation. I never saw any body prompted to do it as a caress. It indicates I think great purity of relation.

I have in my mind a treasury of sweet pictures of this child. Never was lovelier or nobler little creature! Next to little Waldo I love her better than any child I ever saw. She is also the child of a /63/³ holy and equal marriage. She will have a good chance for freedom and happiness in the quiet wisdom of her father, the obedient goodness of her mother.

This night I went out and lay in the avenue for hours, looking up at the stars. How the trees whispered: How happy, even pure I felt!—

* * *

Saturday [July 20]

* * *

It will not last.—many intricate labyrinths are yet to be traversed. Many caverns dark and cold shall be my prisons for a time but the crisis abodes on these broad sunny platforms with the commanding survey are unforgot. And of these broad marbles on which I rested for a while shall be built at last my temple, my palace home.

Waldo was here three times yesterday, and sang his song of Nature. It is a delicate a various, but not a deeply penetrating music.

On his lips is the perfumed honey of Hymettus, but we can only sip, water or wine we could drink.

We had last night one of those talks which can never bring us /71/ together, yet was there in it melody which shall help to attemper either mind.

* * *

At present, it skills not, I am able to take the superior views of life, and my place in it: but I know the deep yearnings of the heart & the bafflings of time will again be felt, & then I shall long for some dear hand to hold. But I shall never forget that my curse is nothing compared with that of those who have entered into those relations but not made them real: who only *seem* husbands, wives, & friends. H.⁴ was saying as much the other evening.

* * *

3. Blank space on journal page.
4. This is the passage that Emerson copied into his Margaret Fuller notebook, changing the initial "H" in the manuscript to "W" (Gilman, *JMN*, 11:463); he used the passage in the *Memoirs* (2:292) without the final sentence.

[Wednesday, July 24 ?]

/74/ This afternoon a soft-falling shower. I sat awhile in Ellery's room and enjoyed his presence. Read Rabelais a short time. I enjoyed the richness, but was inclined to recall the address of the Western Judge to the tavern keeper. "If its just the same to you I wish you'd put the dirt on one dish and the bars-meat on another. I'm one of them that like to mix for myself."

Waldo came in & talked his transcendental fatalism a little. Then went away, declaring he should not come again till he was less stupid. I had as lief he would sit here and not say a word, but it would be impossible to make him understand *that*.

I went up to the H's with some *new potatoes* for H. & a rattle for Una: Armed with these dignified presents I found as kind a welcome as shawls & silks would have purchased from an Eastern Pacha. H. walked home with me beneath the lovely trembling—

X X X X X

Waldo came in at night. He seemed happy, had had a good day & got afloat in his oration.[5] May it prove an Oraison.

These people here in C. (not Waldo: he is an individual;) want to know whether I give the facts of Mariana's history[6] on my own knowledge— "whether there ever was such a person, for they can conceive of such an one, perfectly!"

*   *   *

[Saturday, July 27?]

Waking this morning, ill thoughts haunted me. With pain I thought of Norris's Ideal World![7] "How long, how long!"[8]* * *

Why does the heart constantly drink oblivion of the obvious rule & expect some one tie to be exempt from the universal necessity?

I will not do so any more.

O God cleanse me from egotism, day by day!

I have just been in to see Waldo a few minutes. Sweet child.—

Great /97/ Sage—Undeveloped Man!

5. On Aug. 1, 1844, Emerson delivered his first antislavery speech, "Emancipation in the British West Indies." This controversial speech was given in the courthouse auditorium, after the Concord churches had refused to let Emerson use their space.

6. In *Summer on the Lakes* Fuller published her semi-autobiographical story of Mariana, a dramatic, eccentric young woman constricted by the atmosphere of a conventional boarding school (81–102).

7. In an Aug. 30, 1844, letter Emerson told Fuller he would give her this volume from Lane's library (Rusk, *Letters of Ralph Waldo Emerson*, 3:259). John Norris (1657–1711), an English clergyman educated at Oxford, was a member of the Cambridge group of Platonic philosophers; his *Essay Towards the Theory of an Ideal and Intelligible World* (London) was published in two parts in 1702 and 1704.

8. "How long, how long!" evokes Psalm 13, "How long must I suffer anguish in my soul,/ grief in my heart day after day?"

I made some foolish critiques on his writings. What is the use? Let me get what I can from them & be thankful!

Last night in the boat I could not help thinking each has something—more all. With Waldo how impossible to enjoy this still companionship, this mutual visionary life. With William[9] even: with whom I have for moments & hours been so happy could I ever depend on his being *at leasure,* to live thus; certainly for ages I could not. But then H<.> has not the deep polished intellect of the one or the pure & passionate beauty of the other. He has his own powers: I seem to want them all: And through ages if not for ever promises & beckons the life of reception, of renunciation. Passing every 7 days from one region to the other. She grows weary of *packing her trunk* yet blesses thee. O rich God!

* * *

/101/ Thursday 1st August.

Ellery came home this morn.g. He has been on foot with H. Thoreau to the Kaatskills<.> Rather cross at first, but it wore off & there was more of genius-light & less of goblin-gleam than for long time before. But Waldo's oration, O that was great heroic, calm, sweet, fair. All aspects melted and rendered into one, an archetypal face of the affair. So beautifully spoken too! Better than he ever spoke before:
it was true happiness to hear him; tears came to my eyes. The old story of how the blacks received their emancipation: it seemed as if I had never heard before: he gave it such expression. How ashamed one felt ever to be sad, while possessing that degree of freedom which gave them such joy.
I felt excited to new life and a nobler emulation by Waldo this day. Yes: it is deeply tragic on the one side, my relation to him, but on the other, how noble how dear! If not an immortal relation, it makes me more immortal. Let me keep /102/ both sides duly balanced in my mind. Let me once know him & I shall not be disappointed.
But he is hard to know, the subtle Greek!
Cary sat by me & we passed a part of the day together. She was very sweet. At sunset I passed an hour alone in Sleepy Hollow. It was one of the finest I ever saw, such painting of the clouds with all the richest hues, and lightning flashes from their gorgeous breasts.
And that place is a temple, in late afternoon.

9. Fuller is referring here to William Hull Clarke, rather than to William Henry Channing, as has previously been assumed.

2d [Friday, August]

* * * Walk with H. in the woods long paths, dark and mystical. We
went far & it was quite dark when we returned: we lost the path & I
got wet in the long grass & had much scrambling. Yet this was pleasant
too in its way though I reached home quite "beat out" & went straight
to bed with burning headach as I did last night.
I feel more like a sister to H. or rather more that he might be a brother
to me than ever with any man before. Yet with him it is though sweet,
not deep kindred, at least, not deep yet.

3d [Saturday, August]

* * * I went to the White House. Took leave of Lidian, who, as usual,
managing to extract poison from the most /105/ healthful plants, says
she has made herself sick by W's oration, choosing to think of the stories
of Negro suffering instead of the high and deep thoughts which excused
the anguish incident to the history of man. Took leave of Edith, the
cherub, from whose head I cut a silken curl & inclosed it in a paper
of verses her father gave me. Of the elder Edith softened, half transfigured, of my Saadi[1] so soft, so sweet to day! At parting I rose: he still
sate with his eyes cast down. His hand I pressed to my heart: it was a
gentle vow. He looked like the youngest child.
Hence in a drizzling rain.[2]

6th [Friday, September]

* * * Wrote on pamphlet[3] four of[4] five hours. Three more such days
& I could finish it. But the pain says, this eve.g that I could not write
a line tomorrow so shall go to Wrentham.
A noble sunset.

8 [Sunday, September]

* * * How entirely dissimilar that boy-baby I saw yesterday, in every
act and attitude from Una and Greta.
And yet where lies this difference betwixt male and female? I cannot
trace it, more than in the plant world farther than *function*. As the two
Shephardias /123/ are the same, except that only one bears the fruit.—

1. "Saadi," Emerson's poem about the 13th-century Persian poet Sa'di (Musleh Al-Din, Shaikh)
   was published in the Oct., 1842 *Dial* (3:265–269); Fuller felt Emerson had "put more of
   himself into Saadi . . . than in any thing he has written before." (Myerson, "Margaret Fuller's
   1842 Journal," 21:338).
2. Fuller returned to her home in Cambridge on Aug. 3; her mother and her brother Richard
   were the only family members there.
3. A note added in another hand identifies this pamphlet as "Woman in XIX Century," the
   book-length expansion of Fuller's July 1843 Dial article, "The Great Lawsuit. Man *Versus*
   Men. Woman *Versus* Women" (4:1–47), published in Feb. 1845.
4. Fuller wrote "of" although she meant "or."

How all but infinite the mystery by which sex is stamped in the germ. By what modification of thought is this caused? Impossible to trace: here am I the child of masculine energy & Eugene[5] of feminine loveliness, & so in many other families.

Yes! a human birth comprises all mysteries, and a mother that attends to that in its whole progress may apprehend as much as any one on earth.

I say a human birth, because in man is comprised the sum of all Earth's doings.

Evening of the 3d [Thursday, October].

Anniversary of the most moving event of my life, when the Ideal seemed nearest an earthly realization—alas![6]

It had been pleasant here with these kind friends in this homely life, pleasant in the field, and beneath the Juniper tree.

* * *

Monday 14th[7] [October]

Visions came to haunt me. O let the past be quite past. Help me my Angel to an increasing delicacy of conscience and a stricter honor.

* * *

Cary and I went on Friday [October 25?] to N.Y.—/144/ Next morng out shopping & in the aftn to Sing Sing[8] in the Washington Irving.

* * *

The day, the Sunday [October 27], at the prison I need not remmemorate: it is all inscribed on my brain, a theme for long instruction.

* * *

---

5. Eugene Fuller (1815–1859), Fuller's oldest brother, graduated from Harvard in 1834, became a lawyer, and later a merchant in New Orleans [Editor].
6. Oct. 3, 1844, was the fourth anniversary of the wedding of Anna H. Barker and Samuel Gray Ward. Fuller's intense romantic relationships with both Sam and Anna led her to transform her jealousy into the equally intense expectation that their marriage would achieve human perfection.
7. Fuller is now writing from Fishkill Landing (today part of Beacon, New York), on the Hudson River approximately 60 miles north of New York City, where she had gone with Cary Sturgis in the first week of October for a working vacation before beginning her job at the *New-York Daily Tribune*. During her stay at Fishkill Landing, Fuller completed her book *Woman in the Nineteenth Century*.
8. Sing Sing, the New York State Penitentiary founded in 1825, is located on the Hudson River, 33 miles north of New York City, near the present town of Ossining. It had a reputation for unusual brutality to prisoners until the early 1840s, when the general spirit of reform brought in wardens who advocated rehabilitation rather than severe punishment of convicts. One of these reformers was Eliza W. Farnham, who in 1844 became matron of the Female Prison, introducing music, flowers, and books into the prisoners' lives. She hired Fuller's friend Georgianna Bruce as assistant matron and invited Fuller to speak to the female inmates. William H. Channing, a charter member of the New York Prison Association, addressed the male prisoners.

MARGARET FULLER

Letter to Elizabeth Hoar†

Oct 20 [28?] 1844

We have just been passing Sunday at Sing Sing. We went with William Channing:[1] he staid at the chaplain's we at the prison. It was a noble occasion for his eloquence and I never felt more content than when at the words "Men and Bretheren," all those faces were upturned like a sea swayed by a single wind and the Shell of brutality burst apart at the touch of love divinely human. He visited several of them in their cells and the incidents that came were moving.

On Sunday they are all confined in their cells after 12 at noon that their keepers may have rest from their weekly fatigues, but I was allowed to have some of the women out to talk with and the interview was very pleasant. They were among the so called worst, but nothing could be more decorous than their conduct, and frank too. All passed much as in one of my Boston Classes. I told them I was writing about Woman and as my path had been a favoured one I wanted to ask some information of those who had been tempted to pollution and sorrow. They seemed to reply in the same spirit in which I asked. Several however expressed a wish to see me alone, as they could then say *all*, and they could not bear to before one another: and I intend to go there again, and take time for this. It is very gratifying to see the influence these few months of gentle and intelligent treatment have had on these women: indeed it is wonderful, and even should the State change its policy, affords the needed text for treatment of the subject.

---

† From *The Letters of Margaret Fuller*, Volume 3 *1842–44*, ed. Robert N. Hudspeth (Ithaca N.Y.: Cornell University Press, 1984), 237–38. Originally from bMS Am 1280, reprinted by permission of the Houghton Library, Harvard University. Elizabeth Sherman Hoar (1814–1878) of Concord, Fuller's good friend, never married after the death of her fiancé Charles Emerson (Waldo's brother) in 1836.
1. William Henry Channing (1810–1884), Fuller's good friend, was a graduate of Harvard Divinity School; in 1843 he moved from Cincinnati to New York City where he organized the Christian Union Church and engaged in a number of reform movements on behalf of the poor and oppressed [Editor].

MARGARET FULLER

Letter to the Women Inmates at Sing Sing†

[Early November? 1844]

My friends:

After my visit, which, though short, was sufficient to inspire great interest in your welfare and hope for your improvement, I wrote to some of the ladies of Boston on your account, and they will send you books which may, I hope, encourage the taste for reading which it gave me pleasure to hear that so many of you show. Should you acquire a habit of making good books your companions they will form your minds to a love of better pleasures than you have hitherto possessed. In those cases—and they are the greater number—where a naturally good disposition has been obscured by neglect in childhood and a want of proper food for the mind and heart, the wheat will have a chance to grow up and the tares to be choked by acquaintance with pure thoughts and the better purposes for which life was intended by its Giver.

I wrote in your behalf to several of the best and loveliest women I know, for I was sure that these would be the most eager to do any thing in their power to aid their unhappy sisters. I hope you will accept these books as a token that, though on returning to the world you may have much to encounter from the prejudices of the unthinking, yet there are many who will be glad to encourage you to begin a new career, and redeem the past by living lives of wise and innocent acts, useful to your fellow-creatures and fit for beings gifted with immortal souls. Among these you may depend on

Yours with friendliest good wishes,

S. M. FULLER.

---

† From *The Letters of Margaret Fuller,* Volume 3 1842–44, ed. Robert N. Hudspeth (Ithaca N.Y.: Cornell University Press, 1984), 238.

MARGARET FULLER

From Letter to William H. Channing†

Sunday eveg
17th Novr 1844.

At last, my dear William, I have finished the pamphlet.[1] The last day
it kept spinning out beneath my hand. After taking a long walk early
on one of the most noble exhilarating sort of mornings I sat down to
write and did not put the last stroke till near nine in the evening Then
I felt a delightful glow as if I had put a good deal of my true life in it,
as if, suppose I went away now, the measure of my foot-print would be
left on the earth. That was several days ago, and I do not know how it
will look on revision, for I must leave[n] several days more between me
and it before I undertake that, but think it will be much better than if
it had been finished at Cambridge, for here has been no headach, and
leisure to choose my hours.

It will make a pamphlet rather larger than a number of the Dial,
and would take a fortnight or more to print. Therefore I am anxious to
get the matter *en train* before I come to N. Y. that I may begin the 1st
Decr for I want to have it out by Christmas. Will you then see Mr
Greeley[2] about it the latter part of this week or the beginning of next.
He is absent now, but will be back by that time and I will write to him
about it. Perhaps he will like to undertake it himself.

The estimate you sent me last summer was made expecting an edition of fifteen hundred, but I think a thousand will be enough. The
writing, though I have tried to make my meaning full and clear, requires, shall I say? too much culture in the reader[n] to be quickly or
extensively diffused. I shall be satisfied if it moves a mind here and
there and through that others; shall be well satisfied if an edition of a
thousand is disposed of in the course of two or three years

If the expense of publication should not exceed a hundred or even[n]
a hundred and fifty dollars, I should not be unwilling to undertake it,
if thought best by you and Mr G. But I suppose you would not think
that the favorable way as to securing a sale.

If given to a publisher I wish to dispose of it only for one edition. I
should hope to be able to make it constantly better while I live and

---

† From *The Letters of Margaret Fuller*, Volume 3 1842–44, ed. Robert N. Hudspeth (Ithaca
N.Y.: Cornell University Press, 1984), 241. Originally from Ms Am 1450, reprinted by courtesy
of the Trustees of the Boston Public Library.

1. The New York firm of Greeley & McElrath published *Woman in the Nineteenth Century* in
February 1845.

2. Horace Greeley (1811–1872), printer, journalist, and founder in 1841 of the *New-York Daily
Tribune*, for whom Fuller went to work as a literary critic and social commentator soon after
completing *Woman in the Nineteenth Century* [Editor].

should wish to retain full command of it, in case of subsequent editions."^{* * *}

CAROLINE STURGIS

From Letter to Margaret Fuller†

March 4th, 1845
[Boston]

Thank you for the pamphlet, dear Margaret. I have read it through but the style troubles me very much.[1] I cannot free myself from a feeling of great consciousness in all you write. There is a recurrence of comparisons, illustrations, & words, which is not pleasing. There seems to be a want of vital powers as if you had gathered flowers and planted them in a garden but had left the roots in their own soil. It is full of suggestions like everything else in this age, but one living child is worth a whole series of tableaux. It is not a book to take to heart and that is what a book upon women should be. It makes me sad that it is necessary such an one should be written but since it is so it cannot but do good to lift the veil as you have done—how hard a thing to do! The book is good for me in giving me a glimpse of many things; I am like a child peeping into a confectioner's store & wishing to go in & taste all the sugar-swans & frosted cakes.

* * *

Do tell me all the good facts that you can about Mesmerism—perhaps you know some you can put into the Tribune—that is a good way of addressing all your friends;[2]—but are you not going to write me a

---

† Reprinted with permission from "The Letters of Caroline Sturgis to Margaret Fuller," ed. Francis B. Dedmond, *Studies in the American Renaissance 1988*, ed. Joel Myerson (Charlottesville: University Press of Virginia, 1988), 239.

1. The pamphlet is Fuller's *Woman in the Nineteenth Century* (New York: Greeley & McElrath, 1845). Fuller wrote William Henry Channing on Sunday, 17 November 1844, that she had finished the work; and on 26 December, she wrote Elizabeth Palmer Peabody that the book was in the press (Fuller, *Letters*, 3:241, 254). On 6 February 1845, the *Tribune* carried a story about "The Fire," which damaged much of the *Tribune* office. However, the article said, "The original work hitherto announced by us—Woman in the Nineteenth Century, by S. Margaret Fuller—was also in press in another office, and is saved, so that we shall issue it before the end of the month."

2. Shortly after going to New York, Fuller placed herself under the care of Dr. Theodore Leger, who, the next year, would publish *Animal Magnetism; or Psycodunamy* (New York: D. Appleton, 1846). Perhaps Sturgis had missed Fuller's review of J. Stanley Grimes' *Etherology; or the Philosophy of Mesmerism and Phrenology* in the *Tribune* for 17 February. Fuller in the review defined animal magnetism as a means of communicating "influence and thought" from one being to another, "independent of the usual organs." This was possible because of man's dual nature—the spiritual and the material. Fuller indicated that she had tested some of the "phenomena" of animal magnetism but was ignorant of "its law and analysis." Nonetheless, she had "no doubts on the subject." In her letter to Sturgis on 13 March, Fuller indicated that she was much entertained by Dr. Léger. She was not put into trances, "but seem to receive daily accessions of strength from the *insouciant* robust Frenchman, and his beard" (Fuller, *Letters*, 4:59). A good part of her morning was taken up in her visit to the

more private letter sometime. Is not Sam beautiful now? But he is not
our Raphael.[3] I have seen no other person except Anna & Richard[4] all
winter who is secure in every word & motion, for Waldo still wears his
golden chain, & all the others go in rags.

MARGARET FULLER

From Letter to Caroline Sturgis†

N.Y. 13th March, 1845.

Your letter, dear Carry, is but just recd, because I have been away
from home. * * *

What you say of my book is very true, mostly, especially is it true
that there ought to be no cause for writing such a thing. But that there
is cause is too evident by the ardent interest it excites in those who
have never known me. Those, you know, are the persons to whom it
is addressed, and they do feel their wounds probed, and healing promised by it. The opposition and the sympathy it excites are both great,
and you will laugh to hear that it is placarded here as "Great Book of
the Age."

Are you not inconsistent to reproach me for writing such outside
things, and then fear that I will reproduce, even in veils, what I have
known that is most interesting? Of what should I write then?

I am very glad you like Richard. And well content you should make
the distinction between us, you do.[1] Perhaps a "substantial" intercourse
may take place between you, for he is really of your kind, the simple
kind.

doctor, which she used also as a trysting place to meet her secret lover, James Nathan. Fuller
maintained that, on the subject of mesmerism, "I have as yet nothing worth your reading nor
even the reading of the readers of the Tribune but by & by, I hope—" (Fuller, *Letters*, 4:59).
At least, some of Fuller's hope was realized. Georgiana Bruce (Kirby) in her *Years of Experience* vivily describes one of the treatments Fuller received at the hand of Dr. Léger in which
"he *willed* that power should flow from him to the patient. She described the sensation as
like having a rod of iron worked into her poor spine" (p. 213). Nonetheless, after two months,
wrote Bruce, Fuller was able to walk the four miles from Greeley's place on Turtle Bay to
the doctor's office; and, after five months, she was three inches taller and her shoulders were
perfectly flat and similar.
3. Fuller had noted in her "Commonplace Book" that "S[am]. [Ward] is no longer my Rafaello." * * *
4. Anna Barker Ward and Richard Frederick Fuller (1824–1869), Fuller's favorite brother, who
had recently graduated from Harvard [Editor].
† From *The Letters of Margaret Fuller 1845–47*, Vol. 5, ed. Robert N. Hudspeth (Ithaca, N.Y.:
Cornell University Press), 58–61. Originally from bMS Am 1221, reprinted by permission of
the Houghton Library, Harvard University.
1. "I have a real respect for Richard, such as I have for very few persons," wrote Sturgis. "I find
this difference between you & him, & that when he talks to me upon any subject he presents
me with substantial food while you give me perfumes."

Yes! I have had great pleasure in seeing Sam, and with Anna. He seemed dignified in himself, and their relation more dignified. S.'s translations from Goethe have been a fine study for him as all things are, still in the Come Mair chapter, though roselights may have been let[n] through his windows, by draperies from another home. As you say the Raphael time is quite over—Let it go.

* * *

CRITICISM

Early Reviews

ORESTES A. BROWNSON

Miss Fuller and Reformers†

Miss Fuller belongs to the class described in the preceding article under the name of *Transcendentalists*, of which sect she is the chieftainess. She has a broader and richer nature than Mr. Parker,[1] greater logical ability, and deeper poetic feeling; more boldness, sincerity, and frankness, and perhaps equal literary attainments. But at bottom they are brother and sister, children of the same father, belong to the same school, and in general harmonize in their views, aims, and tendencies. Their differences are, that he is more of the theologian, she more of the poet; he more of the German in his taste, she more of the Grecian; he the more popular in his style of writing, she the more brilliant and fascinating in her conversation. In the Saint-Simonian classification of the race, he would belong to the class of *savans*, she to that of *artistes*.

But Miss Fuller is an *artiste* only in her admiration of art, for she has little artistic skill. Nothing is or can be less artistic than the book before us, which, properly speaking, is no book, but a long talk on matters and things in general, and men and women in particular. It has neither beginning, middle, nor end, and may be read backwards as well as forwards, and from the centre outwards each way, without affecting the continuity of the thought or the succession of ideas. We see no reason why it should stop where it does, or why the lady might not keep on talking in the same strain till doomsday, unless prevented by want of breath.

The title gives no clew to the character of the work; for it is no part of its design to sketch, as one would suppose, the condition of woman

† From *Brownson's Quarterly Review* 2 (Apr. 1845): 249–57. Orestes A. Brownson (1803–1876) was an outspoken New England clergyman, editor, and reformer, who often changed his religious affiliations, beginning as a Presbyterian and ending up a Roman Catholic. He attended several meetings of the Transcendental Club, but withdrew when he found it too pantheistic; in 1839 he offered to merge the proposed journal of the group with his own (the *Boston Quarterly Review*), but his offer was rejected and Fuller became editor of the *Dial* instead.

1. Theodore Parker (1810–1860), self-taught, learned, and radical Unitarian minister, was a prolific contributor to the *Dial*. In the preceding review, Brownson had characterized Parker as a dangerous infidel [Editor].

in the nineteenth century. Indeed, we do not know what is its design. We cannot make out what thesis or what theses it does or does not maintain. All is profoundly obscure, and thrown together in "glorious confusion." We can attempt no analysis of its contents. As talk, it is very well, and proves that the lady has great talkative powers, and that, in this respect at least, she is a genuine woman.

As we read along in the book, we keep constantly asking, What is the lady driving at? What does she want? But no answer comes. She does not know, herself, what she wants. She has an ugly feeling of uneasiness, that matters do not go right with her; and she firmly believes that if she had—I know not what—all would go better. She is feverish, and turns from one side of the bed to the other, but finds no relief. The evil she finds, and which all her class find, is in her, in them, and is removed by no turning or change of posture, and can be. She and they are, no doubt, to be compassionated, to be tenderly nursed and borne with, as are all sick people. It is no use attempting to reason them out of their crotchets; but well people should take care not to heed what they say, and especially not to receive the ravings of their delirium as divine inspirations.

* * *

The terrible evil here set forth Miss Fuller thinks is confined exclusively to her own sex. Men have the advantage; with them it is not so bad. There she is wrong. There are those who have beards on their faces, as well as those who have none, who have these cravings, these hearts full of love, such as it is, and an aching void in these same full hearts, because there is no one for them to love. They cannot love Bridget or Sukey, and all but the Bridgets and Sukeys are—not for them. Men are not much more easily satisfied than women; and if women are forced to take to tea, scandal, philanthropy, evening-meetings, and smelling-bottles, men are forced to take to trade, infidelity, sometimes the pistol, and even to turn *reformers*, the most desperate resort of all. All this is sad enough, and really under all this is a grievous evil, of which no serious-minded man will make light. But what is the remedy?

Miss Fuller, so far as we collect her thought from her interminable prattle, seems to think this evil is to be remedied by having it understood that woman has an immortal soul, and by securing her free scope to develope herself. But what change this implies, or would introduce, Yankee as we are, we are unable to guess. Understand that woman has an immortal soul! Why, we are far beyond that already. Read our poets, listen to our philanthropists, abolitionists, Fourierists, Saint-Simonians, dietetic reformers, and other reformers of all sorts and sizes, of all manner of things in the universe, and some others, and you shall find that she is already a divinity, and adored as such. * * *

* * *

In the distribution of the several spheres of social and domestic action, woman has assigned to her one sphere, and man another; both equally important, equally honorable. This therefore is no cause of complaint.—But who assigned her this sphere? Has she given her consent to be confined to it? Has she ever been consulted? her assent asked?—And what if not? Who assigned man his sphere? was his assent asked or obtained? Their appropriate spheres are allotted to man and woman by their Creator, and all they have to do is to submit, as quietly, and with as good a grace, as they can. Miss Fuller thinks it is man who has crowded woman one side, and refused her full scope for self-development; and although the sphere in which she moves may really be that most appropriate to her, yet man has no right to confine her to it, and forbid her to take another if she prefer it. She should be as free to decide her own destiny as man is his. All very plausible. But God, and not man, has assigned her the appropriate sphere; and, moreover, we must be ungallant enough to question Miss Fuller's leading doctrine of the perfect social and political equality of the sexes. She says man is not the head of the woman. We, on the authority of the Holy Ghost, say he is. The dominion was not given to woman, nor to man and woman conjointly, but to the man. Therefore the inspired Apostle, while he commands husbands to love and cherish their wives, commands wives to love and *obey* their husbands; and, even setting aside all considerations of divine inspiration, St. Paul's authority is, to say the least, equal to that of Miss Fuller.

Miss Fuller would have all offices, professions, callings, pursuits thrown open to woman as to man; and seems to think that the lost Eden will not be recovered till the petticoat carries it over the breeches. She is quite sure the ancient heathens understood this matter better than we do. They had a juster appreciation of the dignity of woman. Their principal divinities were goddesses, and women ministered in the fane, and gave the responses of the oracles. She is greatly taken with Isis, Sita, Egyptian Sphinx, Ceres, Proserpine. Would she recall these ancient heathen deities, their ancient worship, filled with obscene rites and frightful orgies? Would she restore the Isiac worship? revive that of Syrian Astarte? reëstablish the old custom which prevailed at Babylon, according to which every woman, on a certain festival, must prostitute herself to the first comer in honor of the goddess? readopt the old Phœnician method of obtaining marriage portions for dowerless daughters? have carried again in public procession certain pleasant images which Roman dames were eager to crown with wreaths of flowers? or reproduce the wild Bacchantes with loosened tresses and loosened robes, and lascivious satyrs? These and far worse obtained in the worship of those female divinities, and where woman served the fane, and gave the responses of the gods. Has it never occurred to our learned and philosophic lady to ask, if there was not some relation of cause and effect between the part women took in these ancient religions, and these filthy rites and shameful practices?

＊　＊　＊

But we have no room to proceed. As much as we dislike Miss Fuller's book, as pernicious as we regard the doctrines or notions it contains, as utterly as we are forced to condemn the whole race of modern reformers,—all who are seeking to recover the lost Eden on earth, from the harmonious development of nature alone,—we can still believe, without difficulty, that she may be a pure-minded woman, honestly and earnestly struggling to obtain a greater good for suffering humanity. Taking her starting-point, we should arrive at her conclusion. Believing a terrestrial paradise possible, we should strive for it; believing the free, full, and harmonious development of human nature the means and condition of obtaining it, we should protest against whatever restrains nature in woman as well as in man. We believe Miss Fuller wholly in the wrong, but we see no occasion for the kind of animadversions on her or her book, which we have noticed in some newspaper criticisms. She has done or said nothing which should be regarded as a sin by her Protestant brethren. In our remarks we have designed nothing personal against her. We are able, we trust, to distinguish between persons and doctrines. For persons, however far gone they may be in error, or even in sin, we trust we have the charity our holy religion commands, and which the recollection of our own errors and sins, equal to any we may have to deplore in others, requires us to exercise. But for erroneous doctrines we have no charity, no tolerance. Error is never harmless, and in no instance to be countenanced.

A. G. M. [ANONYMOUS]

The Condition of Woman†

＊　＊　＊

Among the reveries of the Talmudists,[1] is one which tells us that the bone of which Eve was made, was taken neither from the head nor the feet of Adam, but from his side, to indicate that woman should be the equal, and not the mistress or the slave of man. To that equality she has now been elevated in all things in which that equality was either practicable or desirable. She has been permitted, neither to command our armies nor to legislate in our senates, because for the one, she is incapacitated by her gentleness, and for the other, by her purity.

† From *Southern Quarterly Review* 10 (July 1846): 167–73.
1. Scholarly commentators on the Talmud, the Jewish oral law [Editor].

Yet have there been some aspiring spirits of her sex, who have demanded for woman a full participation in all the prerogatives of man. They have claimed an equal right of representation, insisted on a share in our legislative councils, and contended for a similar mode of education.

"We would have," says Miss Fuller, "every arbitrary barrier thrown down. We would have every path laid open to woman as freely as to man."

It is well for our sex's supremacy, that all women are not innoculated with this ambitious spirit; else, considering the excitability and enthusiasm of the female temperament, and the proneness of man to yield, rather than contend with a female antagonist, we should long since have been dethroned, and the sceptre of our sovereignty exchanged for a distaff.

Perhaps the best mode of entering upon the investigation of this much mooted question, will be to take into consideration the peculiarities of the female temperament.

The temperaments of individual woman differ, much less the one from the other, than those of men. They all incline more or less to the nervous type. And thus we may account for almost all her peculiarities of mind and disposition. Women have much more excitability and enthusiasm than men. Hence every passion which springs solely from the heart, burns in them with a brilliancy unknown to the more phlegmatic constitution of men. Love which is, but an episode with man, forms the whole story of a woman's life. She carries its feeling into every concern of life, and extends it even to her religion and her politics, and when her piety or her patriotism are excited, worships her God with more fervor, and loves her country or her party with more energy, than falls to the share of more calculating man. She has too, a nicer perception of minute circumstances, while she is often incapable of appreciating bolder and more striking points. This is well illustrated in the works of female novelists, where the writers often dwell on trifling and unimportant details, which the masculine genius of a Smollet or a Scott would have passed over in silence. Her sympathies are more lively, and hence arises the sweetest and most amiable trait in her character—her boundless humanity, her glowing compassion for the unfortunate, her unwearied attention to the sick, and her active benevolence to the destitute. The tear of pity which can scarce be extorted from the eye of man, flows unbidden down the cheek of woman, and while he doles out the meed of charity through some unfeeling steward, she becomes her own almoner, and bears to the hovel of poverty and wretchedness, not only the open purse, but the far richer gift of her kindness and consolation.

Again. In the sentiment of courage, man and woman widely differ.

That of the former is active, of the latter passive. His courage is bravery, hers is fortitude. He rushes into dangers and engages in contests, from which she shrinks with instinctive timidity; she submits to privations and endures sufferings and pain under which his impatient spirit would bend and break. The unflinching fortitude with which females undergo the severest operations is familiar to every surgeon. It has happened more than once to our own experience, to see a delicate and feeble woman endure an amputation without a murmur or a groan, while a robust sailor in submitting to the same operation has required the strength of all the assistants to repress his struggles, and copious doses of laudanum or brandy, to lull his sensibility.

Imagination reigns predominant in woman. So great is her susceptibility that she rushes with facility from one feeling to another, and the eye still humid with the tear of grief, is often brightened by the light of joy, again to be extinguished by a gush of sorrow. Hence, that caprice and coquetry, which, when not carried to excess, furnish one of her most pleasing charms.

One of the distinctive characters of the female organization is a feebleness of muscle. Hence arise many of those peculiarities which distinguish her from strong and robust man. Hence in childhood her sedentary amusements and in adolescence, her choice of unlaborious occupations. The boy trundles his hoop, and the girl dresses her doll in obedience to the law of physical organization. Compelled by the weakness of her frame to renounce those labors which require the exertion of strength, and incompetent to combat the turbulence of tumultuous crowds, she confines her attention to those employments which require only skill and taste for their accomplishment. Unfitted by the timidity of conscious weakness for popular meetings, she is never called to the discussion of public affairs, and for the energy of action and severity of reason which are there required, she substitutes a fertility of expedient and blandishment of manner with which ere now a Thais has conquered an Alexander, and a Cleopatra controlled an Anthony.[2] But of all the effects of this muscular debility, the most important is the dependence into which it throws her upon man. It is this dependence which gives her the most marked of all her sexual peculiarities, and will ever prevent her from assuming that masculine position in society which her ill-advised advocates have claimed for her. * * *

The exact measure and power of the female mind, has been made the subject of fruitful controversy by writers of both sexes, one side contending for woman's natural inferiority to man in intellect, and the other as strenuously claiming for her, an equality. But we must not

2. Cleopatra (69–30 B.C.), queen of Egypt, took the Roman triumvir Mark Antony (c. 83–30 B.C.) as her lover, apparently for political reasons, causing the Roman senate to deprive him of his powers. Thais, a Greek courtesan, accompanied Alexander the Great (356–323 B.C.) on his Asiatic campaign and supposedly persuaded him to set fire to the conquered city of Persepolis [Editor].

allow ourselves to be led into a participation in this contest. At least
not now and here. * * * All we require to know, is that as to her actual
condition, woman as a sex, is not and never has been learned; that the
few examples of her proficiency in the branches of abstruse science are
but exceptions to the general rule; and that she has always been less
remarkable for her talents and learning than for her tenderness and
timidity. Yet deficient as she is in those great attributes of mind by
which man rules the masses for evil or for good, which give the statesman his influence in the senate, and the soldier his power in the field,
which as they are directed, may produce a reformation in religion or a
revolution in politics, she is yet not without her unseen, though not
unfelt influence.

This Miss Fuller does not deny, for though she is continually com-
plaining of the illiberality of man, who grants indulgences where he
should concede rights, she is compelled to admit that woman, in a
proper condition of society, has always had her share of power.

* * *

Miss Fuller, in contending for what she supposes are the rights of
her sex, stops short of no claim which woman may make, to perfect
equality with man, in every thing which man now does.

> "But if you ask me," says she, 'what offices they may fill; I
> reply—any. I do not care what case you put; let them be sea-
> captains, if you will. I do not doubt there are women well fitted
> for such an office, and, if so, I should be glad to see them in it,
> as to welcome the maid of Saragossa, or the maid of Missolonghi,
> or the Suliote heroine, or Emily Plater."

This cannot be. We cannot give her "the armor and the javelin."
She may be worshipped as a deity, but it must not be as a Pallas.[3] If
she is to possess power, (and who shall gainsay her claim to the possession?) it must be the power of her weakness. Her whole history, her
physical and moral conformations, go to show that she can have no
part in the strength, the rudeness, the impenetrability that gives man
his domination. Endowed, like the partner of her race, with an immortal mind, an emanation of that holy original whence she sprang,
she yet differs from man in that peculiar organization and its effects,
which she owes to the immutable will of her Creator. Imaginative and
susceptible, weak, timid and dependent, she looks up to and leans upon
man, as the being who is to cherish, to support and to defend her, and
unlike the ungrateful mistletoe which robs the oak to which it clings,
of nourishment and life, she adds, by the claims of her dependence, a
charm to the existence of her protector, and by the sweet influence of
her virtues, leads him to better deeds and purer thoughts.

3. Pallas Athena, Greek goddess of war and peace, often depicted with breastplate and spear
[Editor].

Woman thus timid, gentle and dependent, must yield to man the rough and rugged paths of life. She was not made for tumultuous assemblies, for the chicanery of politics, the turbulence of public office, or the bold and factious declamation of the legislative hall. It is among the Lares and Penates[4] of her home, the domestic hearth and the household duties, that she claims our esteem and wins our love. Should she wander from this, her appointed path, she may, like some fiery and erratic comet, become the nine days wonder of the world, but it is only when revolving in her proper orbit as the obedient daughter, the affectionate mother, or the faithful wife, that she sheds around, the mild lustre of a planet which pleases by its regularity, while it charms by its beauty.

Those who would drag her from this modest retirement to which she has been appointed by the fiat of her nature, would rob her character of its fairest charm. In attempting to grasp the sceptre of an empire which her feeble strength can scarcely lift, woman loses the sovereignty of the heart where she has ever reigned with unrivalled sway. When like Omphale of old, she would don the lion's hide and wield the club of Hercules, like Omphale, her power must be based on love.

LYDIA MARIA CHILD

Woman in the Nineteenth Century†

This is the title of a book now in press in this city, which will be likely to excite a good deal of remark, for and against. It is from the pen of Margaret Fuller, a woman of more powerful intellect, comprehensive thought, and thorough education, than any other American authoress, with whose productions I am acquainted. Her style is vigorous and significant, abounding with eloquent passages, and affluent in illustration; but it is sometimes rough in construction, and its meaning is not always sufficiently clear. This does not arise from affectation, or pedantic elaboration; it is the defect of a mind that has too many thoughts for its words; an excess by no means common, either in men or women. She is a contralto voice in literature: deep, rich, and strong, rather than mellifluous and clear.

The book in question is written in a free energetic spirit. It contains a few passages that will offend the fastidiousness of some readers; for they allude to subjects which men do not wish to have discussed, and which women dare not approach. But the clean-minded will not sneer;

---

4. Roman gods of the household [Editor].
† From *Broadway Journal*, 1 (Feb. 15, 1845), 97. Lydia Maria Child (1802–1880), novelist and ardent abolitionist, had been a friend of Fuller's since the 1820s and had attended her Boston Conversations [Editor].

for they will see that the motive is pure, and the object is to ennoble human nature.

There is a great deal of unuttered thought and suppressed feeling, concerning the terrible discords of society, as it now exists. The passion of love, divorced from the pure and elevating sentiment, is felt to be unsatisfactory, as well as degrading. More and more earnestly rise the questions, "*Is* love a mockery, and marriage a sham? What is woman's true mission? What is the harmonious relation of the sexes?"

This extending murmur of the human heart, this increasing conviction that woman should be the friend, the companion, the real partner of man in all his pursuits, rather than the mere ornament of his parlor, or the servant of his senses, cannot be silenced.

The author of "Woman in the Nineteenth Century," has uttered noble aspirations on this subject, rather than definite theories. She is wise enough to see, that to purify the atmosphere will gradually affect all forms of life.

* * *

FREDERIC DAN HUNTINGTON

[Noble and Stirring Eloquence]†

On the whole, we have been disappointed in this book as we like to be disappointed. A woman here vindicates the cause of her own sex without a very large infusion of special pleading—an achievement not slightly meritorious, and deserving no small praise. We took up the volume,—we are willing to confess it candidly,—expecting to find in it a considerable amount of mannerism, affectation, eccentricity and pedantry. It gives us all the more pleasure therefore, to acknowledge that our suspicions were, to a great extent, unjust. The number of inverted sentences, *outré*[1] ideas, far-fetched comparisons and foreign idioms, is more limited than we had feared. Of pedantry, indeed, perhaps there is not an entire absence. Classical characters, and references to mythological fables, are introduced with a frequency which the best taste would hardly sanction; but the error is often committed with a gracefulness and appositeness which partially redeem it. We just notice these faults the more readily, because we believe Miss Fuller might easily be rid of them, and would gain greatly by the change. We observe that exactly in proportion as she becomes thoroughly in earnest, her style becomes straightforward and natural. An honest thinker, who occasionally wields the good Anglo-Saxon phrase so energetically, and with so

† From *Christian Examiner* 38 (May 1845): 416–17.
1. Bizarre (French) [Editor].

much directness as she, ought to abandon at once all seeking after the novel, the strange and the startling. Like the class of writers to which she belongs, much read in the authors of another nation, and much delighted with them, she sometimes puts herself under a yoke, while she longs above all things to be free; adopts a constrained air, while particularly ambitious of unrestraint; and while aiming at a healthful exercise of the faculties, falls into a habit of thought that is morbid, inharmonious, without symmetry, and so, of course, unattractive, if not disgusting. Moreover,—to finish cleanly this ungrateful work of censure,—the book lacks method sadly, and should have been relieved to the reader by the kindly intervention, here and there, of a sectional or capital division. It is rather a collection of clever sayings and bright intimations, than a logical treatise, or a profound examination of the subject it discusses.

Whether Miss Fuller's ethical code would correspond precisely with our own, we should be able to declare with more confidence if she had made it perfectly clear to us what that code is. The same may be said of her standard of manners. But of the general spirit of the essay we can, and we must, speak with sincere and hearty approbation. There is a noble and stirring eloquence in many of the passages, that no susceptible person can fail to be affected by. Great, lustrous thoughts break out from the pages, finely uttered. The pervading sentiment is humane, gentle, sympathetic. Miss Fuller says in one place, "I wish woman to live, first, for God's sake;" and she seems to be possessed by the reverential, devout feeling indicated by this remark. She casts a deserved contempt on the miserable trifling so often exhibited by men in their conversation and deportment with women, a custom that depreciates and openly insults their character. For our own part, we have often wondered at their patient toleration of the indignity, implied so palpably in this sort of bearing. Mean topics and flippant discourse are perpetually introduced in society for their entertainment, as if they were capable of comprehending nothing else. She urges in respectful terms their rights, both in property, and, as mothers, to their children, suggesting some worthy thoughts for law-makers. She would have woman respectably employed. She would elevate the purposes of their lives, and by dignifying their position and character, restore the ancient chivalrous respect paid them by every manly heart. Her notions do not seem *ultra* nor extravagant. She does not ask that woman may be thrust into man's sphere, but that she may have a right and honorable sphere of her own, whether as sister, daughter, mother, or "old maid." And, for ourselves, we admire the noble appeals, near the close of the work, in which she rebukes vice, and entreats for it a wise but prompt consideration. She has discussed a delicate topic delicately and fearlessly; without prudish folly, without timidity, as a true woman should. No tongue will dare to cavil at her. She is too evidently above all small criticism in this quarter, far up out of its reach. What she has said needed to be said, and, if the age has any necessity, needs, we firmly believe, to be repeated, felt and acted upon. The "nineteenth century" has a mission to woman, as well as she to the nineteenth century.

EDGAR A. POE

The Literati of New York City—
No. IV: Sarah Margaret Fuller†

Miss Fuller was at one time editor, or one of the editors of "The Dial," to which she contributed many of the most forcible, and certainly some of the most peculiar papers. She is known, too, by "Summer on the Lakes," a remarkable assemblage of sketches, issued in 1844 by Little & Brown, of Boston. More lately she has published "Woman in the Nineteenth Century," a work which has occasioned much discussion, having had the good fortune to be warmly abused and chivalrously defended. At present, she is assistant editor of "The New York Tribune," or rather a salaried contributor to that journal, for which she has furnished a great variety of matter, chiefly critical notices of new books, etc. etc., her articles being designated by an asterisk. Two of the best of them were a review of Professor Longfellow's late magnificent edition of his own works, (with a portrait,) and an appeal to the public in behalf of her friend Harro Harring. The review did her infinite credit; it was frank, candid, independent—in even ludicrous contrast to the usual mere glorifications of the day, giving honor *only* where honor was due, yet evincing the most thorough capacity to appreciate and the most sincere intention to place in the fairest light the real and idiosyncratic merits of the poet.

In my opinion it is one of the very few reviews of Longfellow's poems, ever published in America, of which the critics have not had abundant reason to be ashamed. Mr. Longfellow is entitled to a certain and very distinguished rank among the poets of his country, but that country is disgraced by the evident toadyism which would award to his social position and influence, to his fine paper and large type, to his morocco binding and gilt edges, to his flattering portrait of himself, and to the illustrations of his poems by Huntingdon, that amount of indiscriminate approbation which neither could nor would have been given to the poems themselves.

The defence of Harro Harring, or rather the Philippic against those who were doing him wrong, was one of the most eloquent and well-*put* articles I have ever yet seen in a newspaper.

† From *Godey's Magazine and Lady's Book* 33 (Aug. 1846), 72–75.

"Woman in the Nineteenth Century" is a book which few women in the country could have written, and no woman in the country would have published, with the exception of Miss Fuller. In the way of independence, of unmitigated radicalism, it is one of the "Curiosities of American Literature," and Doctor Griswold should include it in his book. I need scarcely say that the essay is nervous, forcible, thoughtful, suggestive, brilliant, and to a certain extent scholar-like—for all that Miss Fuller produces is entitled to these epithets—but I must say that the conclusions reached are only in part my own. Not that they are too bold, by any means—too novel, too startling, or too dangerous in their consequences, but that in their attainment too many premises have been distorted and too many analogical inferences left altogether out of sight. I mean to say that the intention of the Deity as regards sexual differences—an intention which can be distinctly comprehended only by throwing the exterior (more sensitive) portions of the mental retina *casually* over the wide field of universal *analogy*—I mean to say that this *intention* has not been sufficiently considered. Miss Fuller has erred, too, through her own excessive objectiveness. She judges *woman* by the heart and intellect of Miss Fuller, but there are not more than one or two dozen Miss Fullers on the whole face of the earth. Holding these opinions in regard to "Woman in the Nineteenth Century," I still feel myself called upon to disavow the silly, condemnatory criticism of the work which appeared in one of the earlier numbers of "The Broadway Journal." That article was *not* written by myself, and *was* written by my associate Mr. Briggs.

The most favorable estimate of Miss Fuller's genius (for high genius she unquestionably possesses) is to be obtained, perhaps, from her contributions to "The Dial," and from her "Summer on the Lakes." Many of the *descriptions* in this volume are unrivaled for *graphicality*, (why is there not such a word?) for the force with which they convey the true by the novel or unexpected, by the introduction of touches which other artists would be sure to omit as irrelevant to the subject. This faculty, too, springs from her subjectiveness, which leads her to paint a scene less by its features than by its effects.

* * *

From what I have quoted a *general* conception of the prose style of the authoress may be gathered. Her manner, however, is infinitely varied. It is always forcible—but I am not sure that it is always anything else, unless I say picturesque. It rather indicates than evinces scholarship. Perhaps only the scholastic, or, more properly, those accustomed to look narrowly at the structure of phrases, would be willing to acquit her of ignorance of grammar—would be willing to attribute her slovenliness to disregard of the shell in anxiety for the kernel; or to waywardness, or to affectation, or to blind reverence for Carlyle—would be able to detect, in her strange and continual inaccuracies, a capacity for the accurate.

"I cannot sympathize with such an apprehension: the spectacle is *capable to* swallow *up* all such objects."
"It is fearful, too, to know, as you look, that whatever has been swallowed by the cataract, is *like* to rise suddenly to light."
"I took our *mutual* friends to see her."
"It was always obvious that they had nothing in common *between them.*"
"The Indian cannot be looked at truly *except* by a poetic eye."
"McKenney's Tour to the Lakes gives some facts not to be met *with* elsewhere."
"There is that mixture of culture and rudeness in the aspect of things *as* gives a feeling of freedom," etc. etc. etc.

These are merely a few, a very few instances, taken at random from among a multitude of *wilful* murders committed by Miss Fuller on the American of President Polk. She uses, too, the word "ignore," a vulgarity adopted only of late days (and to no good purpose, since there is no necessity for it) from the barbarisms of the law, and makes no scruple of giving the Yankee interpretation to the verbs "witness" and "realize," to say nothing of "use," as in the sentence, "I used to read a short time at night." It will not do to say, in defence of such words, that in such senses they may be found in certain dictionaries—in that of Bolles', for instance;—*some* kind of "authority" may be found for *any* kind of vulgarity under the sun.

In spite of these things, however, and of her frequent unjustifiable Carlyleisms, (such as that of writing sentences which are no sentences, since, to be parsed, reference must be had to sentences preceding,) the style of Miss Fuller is one of the very best with which I am acquainted. In general effect, I know no style which surpasses it. It is singularly piquant, vivid, terse, bold, luminous—leaving details out of sight, it is everything that a style need be.

* * *

The supposition that the book of an author is a thing apart from the author's self, is, I think, ill-founded. The soul is a cypher, in the sense of a cryptograph; and the shorter a cryptograph is, the more difficulty there is in its comprehension—at a certain point of brevity it would bid defiance to an army of Champollions. And thus he who has written very little, may in that little either conceal his spirit or convey quite an erroneous idea of it—of his acquirements, talents, temper, manner, tenor and depth (or shallowness) of thought—in a word, of his character, of himself. But this is impossible with him who has written much. Of such a person we get, from his books, not merely a just, but the most just representation. Bulwer, the individual, personal man, in a green velvet waistcoat and amber gloves, is not by any means the veritable Sir Edward Lytton, who is discoverable only in "Ernest Maltravers," where his soul is deliberately and nakedly set forth. And who would ever know Dickens by looking at him or talking with him, or doing anything with him except reading his "Curiosity Shop"? What poet, in especial, but must feel at least the better portion of himself more fairly represented in even his commonest sonnet (earnestly written) than in his most elaborate or most intimate personalities?

I put all this as a general proposition, to which Miss Fuller affords a marked exception—to this extent, that her personal character and her printed book are merely one and the same thing. We get access to her soul *as* directly from the one as from the other—no *more* readily from this than from that—easily from either. Her acts are bookish, and her books are less thoughts than acts. Her literary and her conversational manner are identical. Here is a passage from her "Summer on the Lakes:"—

> "The rapids enchanted me far beyond what I expected; they are so swift that they cease to *seem* so—you can think only of their *beauty*. The fountain beyond the Moss islands I discovered for myself, and thought it for some time an *accidental* beauty which it would not do to *leave*, lest I might never see it again. After I found it *permanent*, I returned many times to watch the play of its crest." * * *

Now all this is precisely as Miss Fuller would *speak* it. She is perpetually saying just such things in just such words. To get the *conversational* woman in the mind's eye, all that is needed is to imagine her reciting the paragraph just quoted: but first let us have the *personal* woman. She is of the medium height; nothing remarkable about the figure; a profusion of lustrous light hair; eyes a bluish gray, full of fire; capacious forehead; the mouth when in repose indicates profound sensibility, capacity for affection, for love—when moved by a slight smile, it becomes even beautiful in the intensity of this expression; but the upper lip, as if impelled by the action of involuntary muscles, habitually uplifts itself, conveying the impression of a sneer. Imagine, now, a person of this description looking you at one moment earnestly in the face, at the next seeming to look only within her own spirit or at the wall; moving nervously every now and then in her chair; speaking in a high key, but musically, deliberately, (not hurriedly or loudly,) with a delicious distinctness of enunciation—speaking, I say, the paragraph in question, and emphasizing the words which I have italicized, not by impulsion of the breath, (as is usual,) but by drawing them out as long as possible, nearly closing her eyes the while—imagine all this, and we have both the woman and the authoress before us.

C[HARLES]. L[ANE].

[A Chaste and Honorable Book]†

The misfortune in almost every endeavor for Woman's enfranchisement and elevation is the sentiment, that she is to attain them somehow by the gift, or at least the sufferance of Man. Is it not sufficiently felt, that this presumption is the very evil to be cured, the very wrong to be righted; that this assumption is the root of the whole mistake. A mistake so deeply rooted that to eradicate the weed, serious fears will be excited lest the true plant suffer. We now always stand in the presence of sexual men and women, and we are to be brought to the consciousness of associate human souls. It is clear that such a state of mind involves an overthrow of the present civil system as completely as the Christian superseded the Mosaic. And in the self-same spirit too, that is to say, the law is at once fulfilled and destroyed by the gospel.

Antecedent to the Christian era, woman was the hand-maid, the vassal of man. Christ proclaimed her emancipation; at the sound of his voice, the chains should fall from her limbs. But in the sluggish conservatism of human nature, the old law still inheres in our system, and woman, though a little more, perhaps much more, decently treated, does not yet adorn creation by being in her true place. Nor can she, while she looks to man to bestow it, or even to concede it. There needs from him neither gift nor concession. All that is demanded is that he should not take away, should not assume, should not exclude. Woman should have her right place, not by a parade of man's pretended generosity, not with the idea of his permission, but she should *be* in it, unhindered, unquestioned. It should be an unmarvellous fact, like the relation of the seasons, for the growth of plants. It should happen.

Such a state of human relation, we have said would change the whole social order. It is evident that whatever touches this vital element must ramify throughout every limb of the social body. The modern family of pairs, and their offspring has not set aside ancient polygamy more certainly that the full accomplishment of the Christ life would repeal, yet do justice to, the present order. The time was ripe for *that* exchange. Happiness no more belonged to it.—Solomon, the monarch in all his glory of wives and concubines attained not to that consolation which the outcast Hebrew youth of Nazareth found in celibate reservation. Through him it was revealed that Woman is man's sister, not his slave; a spirit equal in moral beauty and religious value, not a souless

---

† From *Herald of Freedom* 11 (Sept. 5, 1845), 1. Charles Lane became good friends with Fuller in 1845 when they were both living in New York City. She found him "a charming companion," and told her brother Richard that Lane's review was "the only notice that ever appeared of the book, I thought worth keeping" (*Letters of Margaret Fuller*, 4:166) [Editor].

mortal, excommunicated by her very nature. He declared his kingdom is not of this world; it is not of this order; this plan of governing by force and cunning, by the strong arm and the quick wit; but it is the kingdom of patient labor, quiet understanding, of unfailing love. Which is now most a citizen in that kingdom. Woman or Man? Let either world answer.

It is not by inviting Woman more into the male world, to take place at elections, in political meetings, in commercial enterprizes, to become active in civil rights, now pertaining solely to men, that she can arrive at her true position.—She instinctively shrinks from all such externalities, which indeed bring more trouble than advantage to those who now interfere in them, as well as more detriment than progress to the human race. Men who would be the most unwilling to aid woman's restoration, will probably be found encouraging so mistaken a notion as this. It is not by playing more into the outer world's kingdom that her place will be found. But by passing more into the inner kingdom and living carefully a life in conformity to its laws, will she be enabled to become and to remain free and most truly to help man's freedom.

Woman's rectitude can never be dated from that ground, that nature, that system, wherein man's moral nature lies prostrate. Man, a fallen, an erring, a corrupt creature, as he confesses, is proposed to be the instrument of woman's elevation, the donor to her of goodness and purity. Monstrous absurdity. He who is so lost a being; he who enslaves black women in the field, and white women in the factory, for whom the royal palace and the peasant's cottage are alike scenes for the gratification of his lowest lust, is to bestow on woman her just rights. Cruel delusion! Rather it is to be hoped that woman, fleeing from the mockeries, tyrannies and vices of the present order, shall take her firm stand on that holy ground, where souls and not bodies are considered, and woman no longer treated as a chattel to be given away or bargained for, is 'neither married nor given in marriage.'

At all events it is probable, that woman's [responsibilities] . . . must be clearly her own act. That is to say not man's act, but woman's so far as it belongs to humanity to act. And as in this case, the act is but negative, it is quite in accordance with the idea of a spiritual, redeeming and saving operation on the soul by the supreme power.

Whatever opinions may be entertained regarding the ultimate destiny of the human race on the earth, there can be no doubt that for immediate as well as future happiness in this life it is needful there should be no more marriages than are sanctioned by celestial necessity. The purity, we might almost say the existence of the species, depends more on continence, than on marriage. When put on the truest and most serious grounds, how few are there, of either sex, who can declare their fitness for this relation. And unless we place it on the most serious grounds, what do we but permit the world to be transformed into a vast licensed harem?

Freedon, peace, salvation, cannot be expected for woman while she permits herself to be the instrument of man's lowest gratifications, and tolerates a degree of unchastity in him, which in her he would utterly condemn. It is for woman to bar the door against licentiousness, and thereby both herself and man will cease to be its victims. Self denial is the only hopeful means for any improvement, whether moral or phys-iological, and woman must not expect so great a work as her salvation to be wrought by any easier process. The talking of her redemption, the gilding of her chains by encircling marriage with new prettinesses will but prolong her suffering days and deepen her anguish and pains. This is the point where we are now to look for woman's relief, religious, social, moral, physical. Each sex must bear its own burdens, each must work out its own salvation with fear and trembling. Man cannot restore woman, though he may degrade and destroy her. He can withhold himself from further mischief and restraint is his first duty, but upon woman for woman, it mainly depends to effect her e-man-cipation.

There was a period when the present relation of the sexes, both in marriage, and out of it, afforded a life comparatively happy, but it is the common remark how that time has passed away. The waves of intellect come dashing over the shores of nature, and not a stone, nor a sand grain is left unturned. These waves can only be quelled by another air, by the austral spirit.—The wind that bloweth where it list-eth, is even now veering to a milder point, and this volume is a signal proof of the change.

Margaret Fuller has done the state—the moral state—no small ser-vice, by her courageous adventure into a field, esteemed so swampy and pathless as this of Woman's condition. The book is strengthening to candid minds, and must be formidable to the nervous conservative of old nations and hereditary lusts from its well selected array of pure and unquestionable evidence. A book on this unexcelled point of hu-manity, of more liberal scope or truer emphasis has rarely been pre-sented to the public. It is chaste and honorable, cheerful, and faithful.

Authors have ere now infused such life and energy into their writings as to quicken the reader's soul for immediate action. The Book is laid down in the idea that we can go and grasp the author by the hand, and join him in the enterprise. For the moment we would that this were such an instance. We want to see THE WOMAN. The woman who sits enthroned in the celestial garment of virgin purity, to whom all inferior and less pure spirits bow. The Queen of that world which Christ, the virgin son of a virgin mother, revealed to mankind and of which he is King. But perchance it is better as it is. Outer leadership is never so certain and so steadfast as inward growth, and submission to the universal leader. "Call no man master." Call no woman mistress. There is in this world somewhat too much of this miserable submission to the outward, and too little happy submission to the inward.

How frequently are we told to leave the subject alone, for that woman has her influences through her husband, her brother, her son. This is the very evil under which she suffers, namely that the influence on her and the influence from her must always be transmitted through man, strained through the narrow sieve of his prejudiced mind, mingled with the impurities of his spirit. It is true (and pity 'tis, 'tis true) a solitary woman can play wantonly with the interests of a whole nation as the hired companion of an absolute monarch, or become a mischievous puppet on a corrupt throne; but are these spheres for woman? are these legitimate modes for the extension of her true influences, the establishment of her holy rights?

Our authoress is sufficiently possessed by the true idea of the ground of woman's freedom to have diffused it throughout her book.

*   *   *

When the authoress observes, 'The spiritual tendency is towards the elevation of woman, but the intellectual by itself is not so,' (p 90) [p. 60 in this Norton Critical Edition] she expresses that fact which if followed through its deepest foldings would seriously aid the salvation of so intellectual a female community as that she immediately addresses. Of the worth or worthlessness of intellectual acquisitions, few females can speak more profoundly or experimentally than Margaret Fuller. And we hear her verdict. A verdict which no mere observer will gainsay, much less the soul which has sought and in its seeking found. The best element currently acknowledged in the outer world, that world where woman is allowed scarcely any place, is the intellect. And this is surely not a world desirable to draw woman deeper into. There are but three grand lines in the soul, the spiritual, the intellectual, the natural. Neither nature nor intellect can yield to woman what she needs. Nature, by affliction, has but made her more effectively the family slave. Intellect, by all its erudition, sister Margaret says, tends not in itself to woman's elevation. How should it? Human happiness, human growth, depends on the spirit. An active and commanding intellect, no more bestows moral or spiritual life than a large body ensures a large and brilliant intellect; through true spirit growth involves bright intelligence.

Here then are joyful news for woman. The customs of the world which have chained her to so much from which man has been free, have at the same time bestowed on her important immunities denied to men. Among the wealthier classes, she has been exempt from the weights of useless learning and absolute scholastics so, direfully imposed on man. In war, the very summit and totality of national vice, she has seldom actually mingled. From drunkenness, theft, and other *social* crimes, she has been comparatively free. And the only vice peculiar to her sex is, without man's more guilty aid, impossible. Had woman, then, a deeper spirit reliance, the hour of her emancipation were not so distant.

* * *

The catholic spirit in which this book is penned, the warm enlightened affection, the practical piety, which breathe in every page, may alarm the narrow, affront the selfish, disappoint the lustful; but the true Woman-Heart will rejoice that such a word has been seasonably spoken. It comes from the word which is in the beginning, and to the beginning or primary or inmost love in all hearts it cannot unsuccessfully be spoken.

ANONYMOUS

Stray Leaves from a Seamstress's Journal—No. 5†

1846.—Last night I sat up all night, to read a new book, "Woman in the Nineteenth Century, by Miss Fuller."

Mrs. W. came in to direct about her work, she held this book in her hand; I cast upon it many a longing look; perhaps she saw this, and purposely left it for me. I did not ask for it; not once in my four year's struggle with the world have I asked a favor, for well I know the distrust and coldness with which we are looked upon; but oh! this hungering and thirsting for reading, for knowledge of what is going on in the world, it is becoming irrepressible.

This book marks an era in my life. It is as though on its journey I had set up a white stone, to signify a night of rest, a day of thought, a glimpse of the divine life.

I shall never know the author of this work, but she is interested for women, and is groping to the light, that she may aid them, may do them good.

She is the child of genius, and as such must be an idealist; a veil is between her and the rude, practical, every-day working world. She may write, and teach, and call herself a laborer, but this brings her only into distant relationship with us.

Oh! if she would but come into our attics, our cheerless comfortless homes, where there is nothing beautiful, where the pure air of heaven visits us but scantily, and the sun only glances in to make our poverty the more apparent; if she would see us toiling fourteen and sixteen hours out of the twenty-four, and living on, with no hope for the future, combatting hand to hand, with our destiny; if she would look into the eyes, and down into the souls of the hundreds of pure young girls, that

† From *The Una*, 1 (Oct. 1853), 150.

thirst for the bread and water of life that the heart demands, she would find an inspiration for her genius which would give it untold power. She would then realize how difficult, how almost impossible is self development, where there is only the means of keeping soul and body together.

Ah! would that in her picture gallery there were a niche filled with the sewing girl, pale and thin, her throbbing head and trembling heart, with its seed of death fast germinating, sitting alone, grief stricken and sorrowing, her weary fingers plying the needle faster, and yet faster, then, then methinks, she would bend her genius to open to us some new avenue of industry, some mode in which we might have our bread made sure, without such incessant, wearying toil.

This book is for the educated few, it is rich in classic lore, and though there are many expressions of universal sympathy, it fails in practicality, and will be useful only to one class.

It is not every woman who has power, that can assert herself. This Miss Fuller sees, and demands help for such, but she points to nothing new; and we ask who will open the way for us? Who will give to those who have artists' souls, (and such there are) the means to attain? Who will, to the weak and desponding, simply point the way to what the soul craves; for even such have strength acquired in toil which could conquer mountains, if hope but beckoned them onward.

Miss Fuller claims the right for woman *to be* and *to do*, and the ability to accomplish. This may be talked a long time, but it yet remains for strong women of genius to devise the mode, and to go forward and do something which will electrify the world. Women, such as have no need to toil for their daily bread, must do this and leave open the way for others to follow.

Such women, if they ever rise, will be the benefactors of the whole human family.

* * *

GEORGE ELIOT

Margaret Fuller and Mary Wollstonecraft†

* * * Notwithstanding certain defects of taste and a sort of vague spiritualism and grandiloquence which belong to all but the very best American writers, the book [*Woman in the Nineteenth Century*] is a valuable one: it has the enthusiasm of a noble and sympathetic nature, with the moderation and breadth and large allowance of a vigorous and

---

† From *The Leader* 6 (Oct. 13, 1855): 988–89. The English novelist George Eliot (1819–1880) (whose real name was Mary Ann Evans) began her career as a translator, editor, and reviewer [Editor].

cultivated understanding. There is no exaggeration of woman's moral excellence or intellectual capabilities; no injudicious insistance on her fitness for this or that function hitherto engrossed by men; but a calm plea for the removal of unjust laws and articifial restrictions, so that the possibilities of her nature may have room for full development, a wisely stated demand to disencumber her of the

> Parasitic forms
> That seem to keep her up, but drag her down—
> And leave her field to burgeon and to bloom
> From all within her, make herself her own
> To give or keep, to live and learn and be
> All that not harms distinctive womanhood.[1]

It is interesting to compare this essay of Margaret Fuller's published in its earliest form in 1843, with a work on the position of woman, written between sixty and seventy years ago—we mean Mary Wollstonecraft's *Rights of Woman*.[2] The latter work was not continued beyond the first volume; but so far as this carries the subject, the comparison, at least in relation to strong sense and loftiness of moral tone, is not at all disadvantageous to the woman of the last century. There is in some quarters a vague prejudice against the *Rights of Woman* as in some way or other a reprehensible book, but readers who go to it with this impression will be surprised to find it eminently serious, severely moral, and withal rather heavy—the true reason, perhaps, that no edition has been published since 1796, and that it is now rather scarce. There are several points of resemblance, as well as of striking difference, between the two books. A strong understanding is present in both; but Margaret Fuller's mind was like some regions of her own American continent, where you are constantly stepping from the sunny "clearings" into the mysterious twilight of the tangled forest—she often passes in one breath from forcible reasoning to dreamy vagueness; moreover, her unusually varied culture gives her great command of illustration. Mary Wollstonecraft, on the other hand, is nothing if not rational; she has no erudition, and her grave pages are lit up by no ray of fancy. In both writers, we discern, under the brave bearing of a strong and truthful nature, the beating of a loving woman's heart, which teaches them not to undervalue the smallest offices of domestic care of kindliness. But Margaret Fuller, with all her passionate sensibility, is more of the literary woman, who would not have been satisfied without intellectual production; Mary Wollstonecraft, we imagine, wrote not at all for writing's sake, but from the pressure of other motives. So far as the difference of date allows, there is a striking coincidence in their trains of thought; indeed, every important idea in the *Rights of Woman*,

1. From *The Princess*, by Alfred, Lord Tennyson, 7.253–58 [Editor].
2. Wollstonecraft's *A Vindication of the Rights of Woman* was published in 1792 [Editor].

except the combination of home education with a common day-school for boys and girls, reappears in Margaret Fuller's essay.

One point on which they both write forcibly is the fact that, while men have a horror of such faculty or culture in the other sex as tends to place it on a level with their own, they are really in a state of subjection to ignorant and feeble-minded women.

* * *

Some of the best things [Margaret Fuller] says are on the folly of absolute definitions of woman's nature and absolute demarcations of woman's mission. "Nature," she says, "seems to delight in varying the arrangements, as if to show that she will be fettered by no rule; and we must admit the same varieties that she admits."

* * *

On one side we hear that woman's position can never be improved until women themselves are better; and, on the other, that women can never become better until their position is improved—until the laws are made more just, and a wider field opened to feminine activity. But we constantly hear the same difficulty stated about the human race in general. There is a perpetual action and reaction between individuals and institutions; we must try and mend both by little and little—the only way in which human things can be mended. Unfortunately, many over-zealous champions of women assert their actual equality with men—nay, even their moral superiority to men—as a ground for their release from oppressive laws and restrictions. They lose strength immensely by this false position. If it were true, then there would be a case in which slavery and ignorance nourished virtue, and so far we should have an argument for the continuance of bondage. But we want freedom and culture for woman, because subjection and ignorance have debased her, and with her, Man; for—

> If she be small, slight-natured, miserable,
> How shall men grow?[3]

Both Margaret Fuller and Mary Wollstonecraft have too much sagacity to fall into this sentimental exaggeration. Their ardent hopes of what woman may become do not prevent them from seeing and painting women as they are.

* * *

3. Tennyson's *The Princess* 7.249–50 [Editor].

Recent Essays

MARGARET VANDERHAAR ALLEN

[A Classic of Feminist Literature]†

* * *

Margaret Fuller's Conversations and the book that grew out of them, *Woman in the Nineteenth Century*, were her major public contributions to the progress and emancipation of women.

> By her conversations and her writings she touched the women she knew, or who knew her through her work, and told them there was more in themselves than they had ever known, and they should dream dreams even as men did. She told them to know more, do more, expect more than their mothers had, and to take pleasure in their accomplishments. As an antidote to so much of the mentor literature of the period, preaching submission and resignation, she gave women egos and told them to enjoy them.[1]

Both book and Conversations were imbued with her humanist belief in education, her humanist love of tradition and art and Graeco-Roman civilization, her power to awaken immortal aspirations and impart the unshakable conviction that they are attainable. She influenced her contemporaries enormously. Elizabeth Cady Stanton and Susan B. Anthony said of Margaret Fuller that she "possessed more influence upon the thought of American women than any women previous to her time."[2]

In the 1840s American feminism was only beginning. During the nineteenth century, it dealt with a wide range of legal, educational, and labor issues. The right to control property and earnings, guardianship of children, the right to divorce, opportunity for education, lessening of exploitation in the labor market, and attainment of legal status came

---

† From Margaret Vanderhaar Allen, *The Achievement of Margaret Fuller* (University Park, Pa.: Pennsylvania State University Press, 1979), 139–46. © 1979 by The Pennsylvania State University. Reproduced by permission of the publisher. Norton Critical Edition page references appear in brackets.
1. Barbara Welter, *Dimity Convictions: The American Woman in the Nineteenth Century* (Athens: Ohio University Press, 1976), 146.
2. Eleanor Flexner, *A Century of Struggle* (Cambridge, Mass.: Belknap Press, 1959), p. 68.

about as a result of hard-fought battles.[3] But though the nineteenth-century feminists attacked the concept of female inferiority as perpetuated by established religion, they did not otherwise explore psychological questions nor probe the basic social structures that kept women in servitude.

Thus, when Fuller in *Woman in the Nineteenth Century* boldly dared to write of sex, prostitution, marriage, the double standard of morality, women's concepts of themselves, and men's concepts of them, she astounded her contemporaries. The book is her most radical surviving work because it examines and criticizes the root of the social and personal relations that affect women's lives.

Fuller did not stress the legal, political, and economical issues of the women's rights movement. Paradoxically, one of the first American women to earn an independent living through journalism did not discuss economic independence or legal rights, nor did she speak of organizing groups to effect change. Her intention was twofold: to show that women need and have the same right to freedom for their inner and outer development as men, and to set forth, as a goal for women's aspirations, an ideal of womanhood fundamentally different from that imposed by the culture of the time. Ranging freely if unsystematically over history, mythology, and religion, she tried to show that in all ages and societies there had been some "witness of the equality of the sexes in function, duty and hope."[4] In other words, sexual equality was not some new and dangerous notion but an old and venerable human ideal. Knowing the power of myths over the consciousness of humankind, she explored the meaning of mythological creations like Minerva or the Muse. She looked to history, to Elizabeth of England, Isabella of Spain, and Mary Stuart. Such women showed others what a women might become.

Though every age has had its stellar examples of heroic women rewarded by their societies, she protested that any woman who has heroic courage, energy, or creative genius is called "manly." When she achieves something, she is told "you have *surpassed your sex*." Women's interior and exterior development has been tragically crippled by social roles. When women like Mary Wollstonecraft or George Sand broke the bonds of the intolerably narrow place they were born into, they became outlaws. For "self-dependence . . . is deprecated as a fault in most women. They are taught to learn their rule from without, not to unfold it from within." Fuller objected strenuously to the rigid spheres and occupations assigned to one sex or the other, and she was one of the first to argue that sexual stereotyping restricted personal freedom.

3. Ibid., p. 82.
4. *Woman in the Nineteenth Century*, ed. Arthur B. Fuller (Boston, 1855; rpt. New York: Norton, 1971), p. 172 [101]. The following five quotations are on pp. 43 [23], 40 [22], 116 [69], 117 [69], and 37 [20].

Artistic creativity was one example of the divisive assigning of roles (man the poet, woman the inspiration) that Fuller questioned. Alluding to the poet Manzoni, who dedicated a poem to his wife, Fuller asked: cannot the position be reversed? the woman singing the deeds, giving voice to man's life, creating great poetic beauty? The idea was undreamed of then. She argued that women were gifted in that "unimpeded clearness of the intuitive powers" that often appeared as prophecy or poetry, and "should these faculties have free play, I believe they will open new, deeper and purer sources of joyous inspiration than have as yet refreshed the earth."

Women need as wide a range of occupations as men, instead of the dull, stifling circle of routine duties to which they were consigned. Girls who loved carpentry, she wrote, became sullen and mischievous when denied that exercise for their talents. "We would have every arbitrary barrier thrown down," she wrote. "We would have every path laid open to Woman as freely as to Man." Further, this freedom must "be acknowledged as a *right*, not yielded as a concession."

In their struggle to win this dignity, Fuller recognized that women needed self-respect and self-help. She once thought more men would help in this emancipation, since so many were unhappy with weak women. But most men simply could not comprehend woman as an independent being; not one man in a hundred million could rise above the belief that woman was made for man, she said. How then could he possibly do her justice, even when he wished to be generous? On the whole, men did not really want *women*, they wanted girls, because of their vanity, which required them to be the lord over at least one being, and because they found it impossible to feel superior to a strong woman.

The question of superiority is allied to the question of power. Fuller knew the devices used to keep women out of public life, such as the widespread assumption of their weak physical constitution. To this charge she retorted that the same persons who voiced it most loudly were those who expected pregnant black slaves to work in the fields, or washwomen and seamstresses to perform their drudgery whatever their state of health. Black leader Maria Stewart also pointed out the absurdity of that position. Fuller attacked this anomaly even more vigorously several years later:

> The rhetorical gentlemen and silken dames . . . , quite forgetting their washerwomen, their seamstresses, and the poor hirelings for the sensual pleasures of man that jostle them daily in the streets, talk as if Woman need to be fitted for no other chance than that of growing like a cherished flower in the garden of domestic love . . . I would point out as a primary source of incalculable mischief, the contradiction between her assumed and her real position, be-

tween what is called her proper sphere by the laws of God and Nature, and what has become her real sphere by the law of necessity, and through the complex relations of artificial existence. In the strong language of Carlyle I would say that 'here is a LIE, standing up in the midst of society'—I would say 'down with it, even to the ground' . . . if she be liable to be thrust from the sanctuary of home to provide for herself through the exercise of such faculties as God has given her, let her at least have fair play; let it not be avowed in the same breath that protection is necessary to her, and that it is refused to her; and while we send her forth into the desert, and bind the burthen on her back, and put the staff in her hand—let not her steps be beset, her limbs fettered, and her eyes blindfolded.[5]

Fuller was learning much about exploitation, but on the issue of power she was strangely indecisive. Several times in *Woman* she implied that woman's nature and destiny were not the public ones of power and rule, although she rejected the truism that women were satisfied to exercise power indirectly through their influence on a particular man. Anticipating John Stuart Mill's later argument that power over one man was small compensation for women's loss of freedom, Fuller said that women in their present condition of servitude too often used their power meanly and frivolously. A prey to childish vanity, ignorant of life's important purposes, women were trained to selfish coquetry and the love of petty power, the pleasure of exerting a momentary influence. Deprived of equality and freedom, "they made use of the arms of the servile,—cunning, blandishment, and unreasonable emotion."[6]

Yet Fuller did not explore how women might use power if they were freer. In fact, she thought that free women would not want public power. But her own confession, "I aspired to wield the sceptre or the lyre; for I loved with wise design and irresistible command to mould many to one purpose,"[7] admitted the desire for power over others. And, in *Woman*: "If you ask me what offices they may fill, I reply—any. . . . Let them be sea-captains if you will. I do not doubt there are women well fitted for such an office, and, if so, I should be . . . glad to see them in it."[8] Women sea captains were obviously women in positions of command, and thus at best her position is contradictory. However, our age is acutely power conscious; hers was not; and so the issue interests us more than it interested her, evidently. The fact that she used the pronouns "they . . . them" instead of "we . . . us" in the

5. "Mrs. Jameson's *Memoirs*," *New York Tribune*, 24 July 1846.
6. *Woman*, p. 172 [101].
7. *Memoirs of Margaret Fuller Ossoli*, ed. Ralph Waldo Emerson, W. H. Channing, and James Freeman Clarke, 2 vols. (Boston: 1852), 2:138.
8. *Woman*, p. 174 [102].

above passage suggests that Fuller did not think this problem pertained to her, further evidence that she had not resolved the issue of women and power. This ambivalence, I believe, had its roots in a deeply felt though ill-defined personal need to yield to superior masculine authority. The submissiveness bred into nineteenth-century women had not been wholly bred out of her. Tragically, she discovered over and over through her life that masculine authority was too often *not* superior. "The best are so unripe, the wisest so ignoble, the truest so cold," she lamented.[9] Acknowledging this fact intellectually, however, did not obliterate the psychological need.

Fuller throughout her book prepared the way for women to use their minds and talents in domains other than the home. For example, she forcefully attacked the idea so deeply embedded in conventional thinking that women were creatures who existed primarily for relations, for affections. Why should a woman any more than a man be born only for personal love? Was she not also born for truth, asked Fuller, for universal love, to use her talents? Even when she was educated, the purpose was only to make her a better companion for men and a better mother for men. The summit of ambition held out to an American woman was to be the mother of a George Washington. Fuller insisted that women's talents and intellect be allowed to develop not for a relationship but because they existed. "It is not Woman, but the law of right, the law of growth that speaks in us, and demands the perfection of each being in its kind—apple as apple, Woman as Woman."[1]

Because Fuller recognized how much women presently needed to find the sources of their own being, she advocated celibacy, at least temporarily. Women's lives have always belonged to others, to their parents or husbands or children or guests. Therefore women needed to withdraw from relations and particularly needed to put aside all thought of being led and taught by men, said Fuller. Only truth should lead a woman. "Men do. *not* look at both sides, and women must leave off asking them and being influenced by them, but retire within themselves, and explore the ground-work of life till they find their peculiar secret."[2] This call to celibacy, which was not likely to find many receptive hearers, needs to be seen in the context of nineteenth-century Puritanism. Fuller may have been partly led to that assertion by her repugnance for the degradation that sex, or rather the double standard, caused for women.

In the Victorian age women were thought to have no sexual passion. Frequently women thought so too. Queen Victoria, the mother of nine

9. Quoted in Thomas Wentworth Higginson, *Margaret Fuller Ossoli* (Boston: Houghton Mifflin, 1884), 112.
1. *Woman*, p. 177 [104].
2. Ibid., p. 121 [72].

children, abhorred as "too dreadful" what she called "the animal side of our nature,"[3] and is said to have advised one of her daughters to "think of England" during the miserable business of conception.

Women were not supposed to have passion; nor were they supposed to speak of it. When Fuller dared openly to discuss sex in a book meant for both men and women, she overstepped the bounds of propriety. She questioned why men should be less pure than women, attacked men for the existence of prostitution, and pointed out the countless contradictions in society's codes of sexual morals, so different for men and women. Women have been told for centuries that men's passions are stronger, she said, and though women were not supposed to understand those passions, they were obliged to submit to them in marriage or else wickedly risk turning their husbands' thoughts to illicit relations, "for a man is so constituted that he must indulge his passions or die!"[4] Consequently, women came to regard men as a species of wild beast, she said, and married women told the unmarried not to expect continence or self-restraint from men.

Fuller answered the double standard by expressing the wish that men might become more virtuous, not women less. She greatly admired men of pure lives, like Beethoven. Her advice about female celibacy and male purity had a practical basis, Barbara Welter points out. "Until better means of birth control were devised, the ability of a woman to achieve her goals was at least partially dependent on her ability to limit the size of her family. To do this it was necessary either to be celibate or to live with a man who accepted the principle of self-control."[5]

Fuller made herself vulnerable by advocating standards of purity and celibacy—for women and men both—that she herself later did not live up to. Perhaps this discrepancy between what she first advocated and later lived led Hawthorne to chortle over her "moral collapse" in Europe. However, at the time she wrote *Woman in the Nineteenth Century* she *was* practicing what she preached; and, during her liaison with Ossoli, she no longer discussed personal morals. At no time did she recommend chastity and live unchastely. She may have been inconsistent in not meeting her own high standards. But excessive idealism is not the same thing as hypocrisy, though it may lead to it, and at least she was not guilty of hypocrisy.

Fuller wrote:

> Those who would reform the world must show that they do not speak in the heat of wild impulse; their lives must be unstained by passionate error; they must be severe lawgivers to themselves. They must be religious students of the divine purpose with regard to man, if they would not confound the fancies of a day with the

3. Duncan Crow, *The Victorian Woman* (New York: Stein and Day, 1972), 41.
4. *Woman*, p. 150 [89].
5. Welter, p. 184.

requisitions of eternal good. Their liberty must be the liberty of law and knowledge.[6]

She knew the potency of the mixture she served up in this remarkable book. She was challenging some of the most deep-rooted and fanatically held ideas on the relation of the sexes, and she was advocating action that would change one of society's most fundamental structures, marriage. "We cannot rectify marriage because it would introduce such carnage in our social relations," Emerson once wrote. "And it seems, the most rabid radical is a good Whig in relation to the theory of marriage."[7] Fuller aimed to rectify marriage, but she understood that her ideas had no chance of being heard unless people knew that her motives were pure and lofty. If they suspected the slightest breath of self-interest or self-indulgence, they would regard her pages as tainted and every argument in the book void. Change had to be based on some higher moral imperative. Many nineteenth-century feminists—particularly American feminists like Lucretia Mott, Sarah Grimké, or Sojourner Truth—expressed their pleas for reform in religious and pious language. Feminists today use a different rhetoric, but the underlying desire for justice is the same.

Woman in the Nineteenth Century, like its author, was shaped by an era. The book exuded optimism and hope, born out of American ideals and the conditions of American life. Fuller believed that America's destiny was to elucidate a great moral law, and like no other thinker of her time, she envisioned women's part in that great unfolding. The book's "value to the women to whom it was addressed was not so much the specific means it advised but the fact that it postulated as a desirable and possible end, a human being, equal to the glories and demands of the nation, who was a woman."[8] She thought American women were more fortunate than European women; they had more time to think and reflect, fewer conventions and time-hardened customs to enchain them. In America women were better situated than men, for they were less pressured to achieve success. She felt they were generally exempt from the materialism so characteristic of American life, although "its existence, among the men, has a tendency to repress their [women's] impulses and make them doubt their instincts, thus often paralyzing their action during the best years."[9]

The better liberty is understood, wrote Fuller, the broader the protest for the rights of women. The development of men and that of women are always closely linked. Thus a new era of fulfillment for all of hu-

6. *Woman*, p. 77 [pp. 45–46].
7. *Journals of Ralph Waldo Emerson, 1820–1872*, ed. William H. Gilman, Alfred R. Ferguson, et al., 14 vols. (Cambridge: Harvard University Press, 1960–1978), 8:95.
8. Welter, p. 146.
9. *Woman*, p. 109 [65]. The following four quotations are on pp. 19 [9], 118 [70], 173 [102], and 174 [102].

manity lay close at hand: "The highest ideal Man can form of his own powers is that which he is destined to attain. Whatever the soul knows how to seek, it cannot fail to obtain. . . . Man no longer paints his proper nature in some form, and says 'Prometheus had it; it is God-like; but 'Man must have it; it is human'." But for humanity to approach its golden age at last, self-dependence must be established, the weakening habit of dependence on others must be broken. Note that Fuller is not preaching a splendid isolation; always her context is that of community. "When the same community of life and consciousness of mind begin among men, humanity will have, positively and finally, subjugated its brute elements and Titanic childhood; criticism will have perished; arbitrary limits and ignorant censure be impossible; all will have entered upon the liberty of law, and the harmony of common growth." Whitman, in *Democratic Vistas*, also envisioned law internalized in perfect freedom. Fuller had no fear of widespread misuse of freedom, should it come suddenly to women (which it was not likely to do, she knew). Though individuals might indulge in excesses, women possessed "a reverence for decorums and limits," a native love of proportion, a Greek moderation that would inherently restrain, and "would gradually establish such rules as are needed to guard, without impeding, life."

Woman in the Nineteenth Century ranges over an astonishing variety of subjects: the peculiar opposition met by women of intellect; the legal inequalities and personal abuses of women under the present system; the repulsiveness of artificial devices like corsets; the stigmas society attached to the "old maid"; the hypocrisy of much American Christianity; the merits and flaws of leading writers on the situation of women; the defects of marriage as presently constituted; and the education and psychology of women.

Infused with an internationalist consciousness, this uniquely American book is bold in its challenge, exuberant in its optimism. It does contain flaws—the hedging on the question of power, the overzealous moralism, the lack of structure, the air of improvisation that probably reflects the book's origin in the conversation classes. The pearls are flung randomly on a table, not matched and strung carefully into a necklace that might better set off their luster. Still, the book is a classic of feminist literature—and a classic of American literature as well, though an unacknowledged one.

*   *   *

DAVID M. ROBINSON

Margaret Fuller and the Transcendental Ethos: *Woman in the Nineteenth Century*†

Although V. L. Parrington found Margaret Fuller to be "the completest embodiment of the inchoate rebellions and grandiose aspirations of the age of transcendental ferment," he also emphasized a fact that has become a dominant strain in later writing about Fuller—she was thwarted by the very New England milieu she embodied.[1] Even those who knew her best during her years of close association with the transcendentalists sensed that, in Emerson's words, her "athletic soul craved a larger atmosphere than it found."[2] Fuller seems to have found such an atmosphere first in New York, where she wrote for Horace Greeley's *Tribune*, and then in Italy, where she was caught up simultaneously in a love affair and in the politics of the Italian revolution. Nevertheless, her historical reputation has rested largely on her connections with the transcendentalists, connections that most critics have regarded as so unfulfilling for her. The stress has been on her friendships with Emerson, Hedge, Clarke, W. H. Channing, and Alcott; her philosophical "Conversations" for women; her scholarly work on Goethe; and her editorship of the *Dial*. One other accomplishment, however, perhaps her most notable, is more difficult to classify. In 1845 she published *Woman in the Nineteenth Century*, a long essay on the status and prospects of women that included a ringing plea for their liberation. It has since been hailed as "one of the most important statements of feminist method and theory in history," and it gained Fuller considerable notice (and notoriety) upon its publication.[3]

Woman in the Nineteenth Century was not published until Fuller had left the Boston area for New York. In marking a new and essentially political direction for her career, the book seems to express that part of Fuller which she realized only by leaving transcendental circles. Par-

† Reprinted by permission of the Modern Language Association of America from *PMLA* 97 (1982): 83–98. Some of the author's notes have been abridged. Norton Critical Edition page references appear in brackets.
1. Vernon L. Parrington, *The Romantic Revolution in America, 1800–1860*, Vol. II of *Main Currents in American Thought* (New York: Harcourt, 1927), p. 426.
2. [R. W. Emerson, W. H. Channing, and J. F. Clarke], *Memoirs of Margaret Fuller Ossoli* (Boston: Phillips, Sampson, 1852), I, 232; hereafter cited parenthetically in the text as *Memoirs*.
3. The quotation is from Barbara Walter, *Dimity Convictions: The American Woman in the Nineteenth Century* (Athens: Ohio Univ. Press, 1976), p. 180. See also Vivian C. Hopkins, "Margaret Fuller: Pioneer Women's Liberationist," *American Transcendenial Quarterly*, No. 18 (1973), 29–35; Susan Phinney Conrad, *Perish the Thought: Intellectual Women in Romantic America, 1830–1860* (New York: Oxford Univ. Press, 1976), pp. 45–92; and Bell Gale Chevigny, "Growing Out of New England: The Emergence of Margaret Fuller's Radicalism," *Women's Studies*, 5 (1978), 65–100 (hereafter cited as "Growing"). * * *

rington labeled it "her parting shot at the world that had done its best
to stifle her" (p. 432), and although he had Puritan and conservative
New England primarily in mind, other recent students of Fuller have
not spared her friends among the transcendentalists from sharp censure
for their failures regarding her. The question of the context of *Woman
in the Nineteenth Century* thus slides quickly into the vexing problem
of Fuller's personal place among the transcendentalists, a problem that
chiefly concerns her complex and ultimately frustrating relationship
with Emerson. For this reason, the Fuller scholarship has been heavily
biographical, reflecting the general sense that Fuller's life and example
far outweigh her work in importance,[4] and aimed largely at uncovering
what Parrington and others have called the "real" woman beneath the
Margaret Fuller "myth" (p. 426). Fuller herself lent some support to
his view, often confessing impatience and frustration with her written
work and chafing at the austerity of the role of literary artist, especially
as she saw it in the rather ascetic examples of Emerson and his followers. Her own expression of this dilemma encompasses both her
ambivalence about a life of art and her sense of frustration at the con-
finements imposed on women:

> I love best to be a woman; but womanhood is at present too straitly-
> bounded to give me scope. At hours, I live truly as a woman; at
> others, I should stifle; as, on the other hand, I should palsy, when
> I would play the artist.   (*Memoirs*, I, 297)

Adding to the tendency among critics to stress Fuller's life over her
work is the often repeated complaint that her prose style is anything
but that of an artist. As Emerson quaintly puts it, in a remark that tries
to preserve the sense of her personal electricity while taking into account the failures of her writing: "Her pen was a non-conductor" (*Memoirs*, I, 294). Parrington charged that Fuller was "in no sense an artist,
scarcely a competent craftsman" (p. 426), and others have said much
the same (see Margaret Vanderhaar Allen, pp. 66–67). In defending
her, Allen admits that she lacked the discipline to produce "a body of
finished work of high artistic standards" (p. 72) but argues for her skill
in the sentence unit (pp. 73–75).[5] The fact is that Fuller was certainly
not incompetent with the pen, and she did in fact achieve a good many
high moments stylistically, although, for a number of reasons, she was
often guilty of digression and obscurity.

But *Woman in the Nineteenth Century*, despite certain aesthetic
faults in the work, remains both compelling and historically important;
it is not only a major feminist document, as recent criticism of it has

---

4. On Fuller and the transcendentalists, See Bell Gale Chevigny, *The Woman and the Myth:
   Margaret Fuller's Life and Writings* (Old Westbury, N.Y.: Feminist Press, 1976), pp. 31–32;
   Chevigny, "Growing," passim; and Allen, pp. 25–44. * * *
5. See Chevigny, *Woman and Myth*, pp. 10–11.

stressed, but also a key expression of the values of American transcendentalism. This latter claim may seem to contradict the facts concerning Fuller's frustrations as one of the transcendental circle, but those frustrations were not the result of any major intellectual rift between Fuller and the others. Such conflicts as existed were rarely over aims or the metaphysical foundations of those aims, but rather over the means of achieving them. Between Fuller and Emerson, the tensions seem to have been largely the result of differing temperaments, and, given the vastness of that temperamental difference, the two friends got along remarkably well. An entry in Emerson's journal during a visit by Fuller in 1842 suggests the genuine if not wholly successful attempt they made at intimacy:

> I would that I could, I know afar off that I cannot give the lights
> & shades, the hopes & outlooks that come to me in these strange,
> cold-warm, attractive-repelling conversations with Margaret, whom
> I always admire, most revere when I nearest see, and sometimes
> love, yet whom I freeze, & who freezes me to silence, when we
> seem to promise to come nearest.[6]

Victims of temperament and perhaps of circumstance, they were also haunted by the specter of an almost unrealizable ideal of friendship that rendered trivial what closeness they did achieve. The final truce they struck, though satisfactory to neither, was especially disappointing to Fuller.

Nevertheless, her move to New York was not an escape from intellectual Concord but rather from social Concord, and *Woman in the Nineteenth Century* was in fact far less a parting shot at the New England phase of her intellectual life than a culmination of much of her thought and activity as a transcendentalist. Fuller based the book on an essay she had published in the *Dial*, and much of the impetus for that essay in turn came from her transcendental "Conversations," a series of discussion meetings she organized in Boston for educated women. But most important, *Woman in the Nineteenth Century* uses the central intellectual commitment of the transcendental movement, the belief in the possibility of "self-culture," or the continual spiritual growth of the soul, to diagnose, and prescribe a remedy for, the condition of women.[7] The work thus stands as a translation of transcendental idealism into the social and political realm and as an exemplary bridge between romantic philosophy and social reform.

6. *The Journals and Miscellaneous Notebooks of Ralph Waldo Emerson*, ed. William H. Gilman et al (Cambridge: Harvard Univ. Press, 1960–   ), viii, 109; hereafter cited as *JMN*. * * *
7. Paul John Eakin has ably discussed Fuller's influence, as "an Emersonian seeker after self-culture, on the fiction of Hawthorne and James; he argues that self-culture was "the most important model for the conception of the inner life in nineteenth-century America" (pp. 50–51). Although I have some differences with Eakin's interpretation of self-culture (see Sec. 2), his discussion of Fuller's pursuit of it is excellent. See *The New England Girl: Cultural Ideas in Hawthorne, Stowe, Howells, and James* (Athens: Univ. of Georgia Press, 1976).

Fuller came to intellectual maturity when the dominant voice in New England was that of William Ellery Channing, whose influence was perhaps most telling on those of Fuller's generation. Though not a transcendentalist himself, he was universally revered by that group, and, as Conrad Wright puts it, he "helped to prepare the way for Transcendentalism" through his preaching and writing and, perhaps more importantly, through the example of moral aspiration that he set. Central to his message is the doctrine of self-culture, or self-cultivation, derived from a long personal struggle with Calvinism and another long polemical war against it. Finding the Calvinist doctrines of election and depravity both morally repulsive and untrue to human nature, Channing counters them with a version of human perfectibility centered around a metaphor of the soul as a dynamic organism capable of cultivation to ever-increasing harmonious growth. Like "a plant [or] an animal" the "nobler" qualities of any individual can also grow, and if that individual "does what he can to unfold all his powers and capacities, especially his nobler ones . . . [he] practices self-culture."[8]

This doctrine, of course, had enormous impact on nineteenth-century America as a whole, but it was taken up as a banner by the transcendentalists. Emerson was perhaps Channing's most direct descendant in this regard, preaching on the topic "Self-Culture" as a Unitarian minister and later offering a series of lectures entitled "Human Culture" at the height of the transcendental ferment.[9] His emphasis is essentially Channing's, for he stresses the necessity of cultivation and growth, "the principle of expansion resisting the tendency to consolidation and rest" (EL, II, 218), and he eventually incorporated the theme into his Essays. Amos Bronson Alcott's Temple School, with which Fuller and Elizabeth Peabody were associated and which had the support of Emerson and other transcendentalists, took its operating principles from Alcott's manifesto, The Doctrine and Discipline of Human Culture, and Alcott, like Emerson and Channing, stresses growth and development as the high calling of human nature: "Human Cultureis the art of revealing to a man the true Idea of his Being—his endowments—his possessions—and fitting him to use these for the growth, renewal, and perfection of his spirit."[1]

8. Conrad Wright, "William Ellery Channing," in The American Renaissance in New England, ed. Joel Myerson, Vol. I of Dictionary of Literary Biography (Detroit: Gale Research, 1978), p. 21; Channing, The Works of William Ellery Channing, D.D. (Boston: American Unitarian Assn., 1875), p. 15. Quotation is from "Self-Culture" (1838).
9. See "Self-Culture," in Emerson, Young Emerson Speaks: Unpublished Discourses on Many Subjects, ed. Arthur C. McGiffert (Boston: Houghton, 1938), pp. 99–104, hereafter cited as YES; and "Human Culture," in Emerson, The Early Lectures of Ralph Waldo Emerson, ed. Stephen E. Whicher, Robert E. Spiller, and Wallace E. Williams (Cambridge: Harvard Univ. Press, 1959–72), Vol. II of 3 vols., 205–364; hereafter cited as EL.
1. Alcott, The Doctrine and Discipline of Human Culture (Boston: James Munroe, 1836), pp. 3–4. See the facsimile reprint of this essay in Alcott, Essays on Education (1830–1862), ed. Walter Harding (Gainesville, Fla.: Scholars' Facsimiles and Reprints, 1960).

Fuller took much from Channing and Emerson, finding, as a lover of oratory, a particularly rich experience in their preaching. She records her aspiration for a "more pervading faith in the divinity of my own nature" after hearing a Channing sermon (*Memoirs*, I, 176), and she writes that the influence of Emerson's preaching "has been more beneficial to me than that of any American," adding that "from him I first learned what is meant by an inward life" (*Memoirs*, I, 194–95). These comments suggest that Fuller was seeking self-assurance and inspiration for continued self-development, and they help to explain her strong response to the doctrine of self-culture. Her friend James Freeman Clarke writes that her great "aim, from first to last, was SELF-CULTURE," and he quotes her own description of her development:

> *Very early I knew that the only object in life was to grow.* I was often false to this knowledge, in idolatries of particular objects, or impatient longings for happiness, but I have never lost sight of it, have always been controlled by it, and this first gift of thought has never been superseded by a later love.
>
> (*Memoirs*, I, 133)

This quotation reveals something of the mood of aspiration typical not only of Fuller but of the transcendentalists as a group. The idea of self-culture developed by Channing and Emerson satisfied an emotional want formed primarily by religious training, and cultivation of the self assumed major importance to Fuller's generation as traditional Christianity became correspondingly dissatisfying.

The somewhat vague emotional uplift that was part of the appeal of the doctrine had a metaphysical underpinning of some importance, however, particularly in giving moral force and credence to a philosophy focused primarily on the self. This is an important point to remember, for it serves as a corrective to Paul John Eakin's comment (not an untypical response to the doctrine of self-culture) that descriptions of self-culture by its proponents "seem designed to confer a moral sanction upon the development of character which was believed in for its own sake as an elevating experience" (p. 52). According to the transcendentalists, character needed development not for its own sake but for the sake of a divine core of identity within the individual that transcended (the term is inevitable) the self. Stress on the essentially "selfless" quality of the soul when rightly cultivated, therefore, countered the potentially egotistical and asocial tendency of the commitment to self-culture. Perhaps the best-known expression of this idea is "Self-Reliance" (1841), an essay in which Emerson gradually reveals reliance on the self to be reliance on God as self becomes "the aboriginal Self on which a universal reliance may be grounded." The career of Jones Very also illustrates this paradox. Although his apparently messianic delusions suggest the dangers of the divine self taken to extremes, Very was preaching, and attempting to practice, a form of "will-less existence" that meant completely denying the self and becoming absorbed into the larger will of God.[2] The end of self-culture, therefore, was the development of a divine will or self potentially available to every individual but usually only imperfectly realized.

Such a conception of the moral and religious life demanded imaginative embodiment, and Emerson's "Genuine Man," or "Universal Man," as he sometimes called the concept, answered the demand. Emerson posits a completely developed and exemplary ideal man behind or within every individual. The various heroes and great men of history owe their attainments to a more complete realization of the potential that this universal man symbolizes. After discussing the idea in his sermons and developing it in his lectures of the middle 1830s, Emerson gives it memorable expression in "The American Scholar" (1837) with his fable of the "One Man,—present to all particular men only partially, or through one faculty" (CW, I, 53).[3] In this instance he gives the notion a social emphasis, stressing that "you must take the whole society to find the whole man" (CW, I, 53); his attitude here reflects both his growing social consciousness and his need to place "Man Thinking" in a social context. But the doctrine of the "Genuine Man," as a corollary to self-culture, has applications to both the social and the moral realm.

Although self-culture was criticized at the time as a doctrine incapable of effecting social change, and it has been criticized since as a positive hindrance to change, the doctrine of self-culture did have a distinctly political interpretation, exemplified in the Christian socialism of William Henry Channing and the flirtation of George Ripley and others with Fourierist utopianism.[4] Fuller herself considered joining the Brook Farm experiment, but she declined on grounds similar to Emerson's. As she comments ironically in the Memoirs (II, 77), she found herself "in the amusing position of a conservative" at Brook Farm. She developed her deepest political radicalism only later, during her involvement with the Italian revolution, and in many ways she must be classed with Emerson as an upholder of the more purely individualistic side of the transcendental movement. But the very individualism that

2. See Lawrence Buell, Literary Transcendentalism: Style and Vision in the American Renaissance (Ithaca: Cornell Univ. Press, 1973), pp. 269–71; Emerson, The Collected Works of Ralph Waldo Emerson, ed. Joseph Slater, Alfred R. Ferguson, and Jean Ferguson Carr (Cambridge: Harvard Univ. Press, 1979), Vol. II of 2 vols. to date, 37 (hereafter cited parenthetically in the text as CW); and Edwin Gittleman, Jones Very: The Effective Years, 1833–1840 (New York: Columbia Univ. Press, 1967), pp. 188–95.
3. For the early development of the idea see "The Genuine Man," YES, pp. 180–90; the lecture series "Biography," EL, I, 91–201; and "The Philosophy of History," EL, II, 1–188. See also Merton M. Sealts, Jr., "Emerson on the Scholar, 1833–1837," PMLA, 85 (1970), 185–95, esp. 189–93.
4. For the critique of self-culture, see Orestes A. Brownson, "The Laboring Classes," Boston Quarterly Review, 3 (1840), 358–95, and Arthur Schlesinger, Jr., The Age of Jackson (Boston: Little, 1950), pp. 272–73.

self-culture fostered in her took on an inescapably political aspect when she applied it to the condition of women in America. What had been denied women was the opportunity for development; to pursue that opportunity now meant to eliminate the social sources of the denial:

> It is not woman, but the law of right, the law of growth, that speaks in us, and demands the perfection of each being in its kind, apple as apple, woman as woman. . . . What concerns me now is, that my life be a beautiful, powerful, in a word, a complete life in its kind.[5]

This same demand for social change was implied, though not so explicitly, in the title Fuller gave to her original *Dial* article: "The Great Lawsuit. Man versus Men. Woman versus Women." In the preface to *Woman in the Nineteenth Century*, Fuller draws attention to her original title; she laments its loss because "The Great Lawsuit" offers "larger scope" (p. 83 [5]) to her argument. The earlier title also illumines the context of the work, because it takes the Emersonian distinction between individual and universal man as crucial and expands that distinction to include women explicitly.[6] The image of the lawsuit suggests the political nature of the problem—a social wrong to be redressed through social, specifically legal, means. Moreover, the title suggests conflict, for the reader's first impulse is to assume that women bring the suit against men, whereas the battle is really one of men and women against their ideal natures. But Fuller's purpose is to show that even these social ills have moral bases and that the deepest failure has been that of individual men to their better selves and, correspondingly, of individual women to their potential achievements.

*   *   *

The ultimate sources of Fuller's feminist treatise are her many frustrating experiences with the restricted role of women in nineteenth-century society. But the first significant public expression of that feminism was the series of "Conversations" organized by Fuller in 1839 for the support of women. Her proposal for the first conversations, described by Mason Wade as "nothing less than a Feminist Manifesto" (*Writings*, p. 70), was to bring "well-educated and thinking women" together to try to answer the questions "What were we born to do?" and "How shall we do it?" (*Memoirs*, I, 324–25). Fuller's hope was that such meetings, based on the principle of shared wisdom rather than on

5. Fuller, *Woman in the Nineteenth Century* (1845), in Myerson, *Margaret Fuller: Essays*, p. 207 [104]. (See Myerson's "Textual Note," pp. 43–48.)
6. Emerson intended his term "Man" to be inclusive of both sexes, and Fuller also uses it in that sense (see Preface, *Woman in the Nineteenth Century*, p. 83 [5]). Emerson himself was groping toward a redefinition of the sexual principles of the self, as an 1842 journal entry suggests: "A highly endowed man with good intellect and good conscience is a Man-woman and does not so much need the complement ↑ of woman ↓ to his being, ⟨of woman⟩ as another" (*JMN*, VIII, 175). But see also Chevigny's comments on his "paternalistic" views of women, in "Growing," pp. 79–80.

the speaker-listener model of the classroom or lyceum, would help redress the imbalance between knowledge and expression in women. She
expresses a desire to "systematize thought, and give a precision and
clearness in which our sex are so deficient," a deficiency created because women "have so few inducements to test and classify what they
receive" (*Memoirs*, I, 325). In a period of rising educational levels and
correspondingly rising expectations—a period also rife with men's advice about women's roles—Fuller's proposal struck a responsive chord,
and the "Conversations" continued as long as she was in Boston.[7]

Fuller's concern with women's expression took an important place
in the opening conversation, as the report of one in attendance reveals:

> Women are now taught, at school, all that men are; they run over,
> superficially, even *more* studies, without being really taught any-
> thing. . . . [M]en are called on, from a very early period, to repro-
> duce all that they learn. Their college exercises, their political
> duties, their professional studies, the first actions of life in any
> direction, call on them to put to use what they have learned. But
> women learn without any attempt to reproduce. Their only repro-
> duction is for purposes of display.   (*Memoirs*, I, 329)

This contrast between the sexes clarifies Fuller's portrayal of thwarted
expression as a problem belonging uniquely to women. But what this
passage represents as a qualitative difference in the conditions of men
and women is in fact a difference in the degree of a common predic-
ament, one addressed as a central problem in transcendentalist discourse. "The man is only half himself, the other half is his expression,"
Emerson writes, lamenting that "adequate expression is rare" and that
"the great majority of men . . . cannot report the conversation they
have had with nature."[8] Given this universal condition, the added barriers of social repression make adequate expression even rarer among
women. "Expression" meant more to both Fuller and Emerson than
speech and writing, encompassing almost any human activity—artistic,
political, or religious—that brought inner resources into objective realization. With Fuller increasingly inclined toward the actual and historical in this period, her call for the expression of women's inner
resources was more than a request for mere talk. While it was igniting
others, it also began to push her more quickly toward the feminist
statement that seemed inevitable—inevitable because it was the result

7. See Nancy F. Cott, *The Bonds of Womanhood: "Woman's Sphere" in New England, 1780–
1835* (New Haven: Yale Univ. Press, 1977), p. 8, for a discussion of early nineteenth-century
theories of the female role. Mason Wade, *Margaret Fuller: Whetstone of Genius* (New York:
Viking, 1940), p. 43, discusses the influence on Fuller and others of John Neal's lecture on
women. For further background on the "Conversations," see Joel Myerson, "Mrs. Dall Edits
Miss Fuller: The Story of *Margaret and Her Friends*," *Papers of the Bibliographical Society
of America*, 72 (1978), 187–200, and Chevigny, "Growing," pp. 82–87.
8. *The Complete Works of Ralph Waldo Emerson*, ed. E. W. Emerson (Boston: Houghton, 1903),
III, 5.

of the transcendental ideal of self-culture coming face to face with the social reality of the oppression of women. Sharpened by a series of "Conversations" in 1841 about the ethical influences on "Woman" of family, school, church, society, and literature and by another "Conversation," entitled "Woman," in 1842 (*Memoirs*, I, 350), Fuller published "The Great Lawsuit" in the July 1843 number of the *Dial*, revising and expanding it into book form in late 1844, just before moving to New York.[9]

One of the germs of Fuller's feminist stance in *Woman* can be found in "Goethe," where she notes that "Goethe always represents the highest principle in the feminine form," and often assigns such figures a redemptive value (p. 26). The notion of the redemptive value of woman appealed to her, since it combined elements of universal human progress with the liberation of women. She echoes Emerson's optimism by predicting that "the highest ideal man can form of his own powers, is that which he is destined to attain" (p. 87 [9]) but adds the essential qualification that such attainment is tied to the progress of feminism, that "improvement in the daughters will best aid in the reformation of the sons of this age" (p. 90 [12]).

It should be recalled that the ultimate point of reference for "improvement" is the Emersonian universal man (or woman, as Fuller illustrated), discussed earlier. If we remember that this image of perfected virtue hovers over the discussion from the beginning, it is easier to appreciate the striking rhetorical power of Fuller's argument, especially her analogy between slavery and the woman's role. Fuller notes that the abolitionists have made "the warmest appeal in behalf of women" (p. 94 [15]), and she introduces into the text a bit of dramatic dialogue in which an "irritated trader" (slave trader, or ordinary merchant?) complains first of the demise of the "national union" because of abolitionism and then of the breakup of the "family union" because of feminist agitation by the same group (pp. 94–95 [15–16]). The notion that women are enslaved is implicit here, but Fuller makes the point explicit a few pages later: "As the friend of the negro assumes that one man cannot by right, hold another in bondage, so should the friend of woman assume that man cannot, by right, lay even well-meant restrictions on woman" (p. 100 [20]).

Fuller realized that the analogy between woman and slave would tap into the moral fervor being generated by abolitionism, but she also knew that it would generate anger and would put a somewhat heavy burden of proof on her. She fashioned the argument of *Woman* to meet this challenge, and an important first step is her critique of the prevalent notions of woman's place or sphere in society. While welcoming the attention being given to women, she recognizes that much of it is char-

9. See Myerson's discussion of the publication and reception of the book in *Margaret Fuller: Essays*, pp. 14–24.

acterized "by lectures on some model-woman of bride-like beauty and gentleness" that are intended "to mark out with precision the limits of woman's sphere, and woman's mission, to prevent other than the rightful shepherd from climbing the wall, or the flock from using any chance to go astray" (p. 96 [17]). As if this wry image of sheep and shepherds were not clear enough, Fuller dismisses most of this writing with the caustic remark that "the main bent of most of [it] . . . is to fit her [woman] to please, or, at least, not to disturb a husband" (p. 192 [93]). Perhaps the most telling proof of the failure of such a conception of woman's role, she points out, is "the ennui that haunts grown women, except where they make to themselves a serene little world by art of some kind" (p. 205 [102]). Fuller recognizes that women who are gifted both with intellect and with what she calls a "magnetic" or intuitive element "are very commonly unhappy at present": "They see too much to act in conformity with those around them, and their quick impulses seem folly to those who do not discern the motives" (p. 152 [61]). What we know from Fuller's letters and journals certainly suggests that she is writing from her own experience here, and this is one of the many passages in *Woman* that seem to merge autobiography and essay.[1]

Since Fuller understands how completely woman's sphere is tied to marriage, she devotes a lengthy discussion to the questions of what marriage is and what it ought to be. Her conviction is that feminism, far from damaging marriage, will actually make it meaningful. This argument depends, of course, on a general critique of three ultimately unsatisfactory forms of marriage: household partnership, mutual idolatry, and intellectual companionship (p. 128 [42]). Each of these kinds of marriage deflects the potential of man and woman; according to Fuller, a fully successful relation requires "religious union," a term she rather imprecisely defines as "pilgrimage towards a common shrine" (pp. 135–36 [48]). Whether or not Fuller herself was entirely sure of what she meant here, any approach to such a union would demand the full equality of woman: "We must have units before we can have union" (p. 150 [60]). The development of women as individuals—that is, their cultivation of self—therefore takes on primary importance.

Such development was important enough to Fuller to lead her to suggest that at some points it would have to exclude relations with men. As a model, Fuller offers the American Indian woman who "dreamt in youth that she was betrothed to the Sun" and therefore "built her a wigwam apart, filled it with the emblems of her alliance, and means of an independent life" (p. 150 [59]). There is again an element of religious devotion here, but the model is more striking than that of the marriage of "religious union" because it so clearly presents separation

1. See Buell's discussion of the role of autobiography in transcendentalist literature, pp. 265–83.

and celibacy as an alternative for women's self-culture. The image also suggests that women should pursue a form of guidance beyond what is normally available from social resources:

> It is therefore that I would have woman lay aside all thought, such as she habitually cherishes, of being taught and led by men. I would have her, like the Indian girl, dedicate herself to the Sun, the Sun of Truth, and go no where if his beams did not make clear the path. I would have her free from compromise, from complaisance, from helplessness, because I would have her good enough and strong enough to love one and all beings, from the fulness, not the poverty of being. (p. 164 [71])

The striking relevance of these ideas to contemporary feminist discourse may overshadow their remarkable similarity to the transcendental doctrine of self-reliance, particularly as Emerson articulated it in the essay of that name:

> Check this lying hospitality and lying affection. Live no longer to the expectation of these deceived and deceiving people with whom we converse.
>
> (CW, II, 41)

And since many of Fuller's contemporaries considered feminism a threat to the family, we should remember that Emerson follows the above remarks with a long dramatic monologue in which he confronts and defies the claims of family on the self: " 'O father, O mother, O wife, O brother, O friend, I have lived with you after appearances hitherto. Henceforward I am the truth's' " (CW, II, 41–42). That Emerson's defiance was so readily accepted into the canon of American values while Fuller's was regarded as dangerous is a measure of the opposition that her feminism generated. Nevertheless, the close similarity between her argument and Emerson's underscores their shared intellectual context.

We have thus far seen Fuller's argument largely as a plea for the removal of the social barriers inhibiting the full development of woman's nature. Behind that plea, however, is a very important theory about the nature of woman, and of man. Fuller understood, intuitively at the beginning, that the emancipation of woman depended on a redefinition of the terms "female" and "male" and a reevaluation of the bearing that both these terms had on the culture of the self. Fuller recognized that the terms had a certain expressive value as metaphorical "principles," and she made persuasive use of them in that way. But there was a thin line of demarcation between expressive description and repressive definition; ignoring that line could enormously endanger the status of women. Fuller's effort was thus directed toward the recognition of feminine and masculine principles with boundaries fluid enough to pro-

mote the cultivation of a self that incorporated them both. Her concept
has certain affinites with what has evolved in modern discourse as a
theory of androgyny, although this was not her term. Moreover, we
must keep in mind the religious grounding of her vision, for the self
that Fuller was hoping to fashion became, as it approached its goal of
divinity, somehow more than the sum total of the feminine and masculine principles. In redefining the sexual principles in the self Fuller
was attempting to break the debilitating hold of the reigning notions
about the sexual nature of men and women. Out of necessity she used
those notions, but she directed them against the conventions that nurtured them.

The attempt to formulate this redefinition was clearly a major factor
in Fuller's struggle with Goethe and his influence. It was her ambivalence toward the severe beauty of his formalism—and toward the "cold"
intellect displayed therein—that caused the struggle, and she uses much
the same set of terms in *Woman* as in her essays on Goethe, but with
"masculine" and "feminine" connotations. At one point Fuller com-
mends Plato and Swedenborg for considering "man and woman as the
two-fold expression of one thought" (p. 151 [60]), though she harshly
criticizes Plato's retreat from that position in the *Republic* and *Timaeus*.
She then follows this suggestion of the unity in diversity of the sexes
with the argument that "the intellect, cold, is ever more masculine than
feminine" (pp. 151–52 [61]), stressing the need of the intellect for com-
pletion. Its counter is the "electrical, the magnetic element in woman"
(p. 152 [61]), often a source of unhappiness, as mentioned earlier, but
ultimately a necessity for the fulfillment of woman and man. This division seems only too close to sexual stereotyping and even male supremacy, since intellect is "masculine," but Fuller needs the division
because she must first establish some realm of female identity, even a
relatively conventional one, before she can go on to augment that identity. More important, she offers these definitions in the context of a
value system weighted toward the "magnetic" as more fully human and
more positive in connotation than the intellectual. Her complaint is
that "the magnetic element in woman has not been fairly brought out
at any period. Everything might be expected from it; she has far more
of it than man" (p. 152 [61]). In the light of the conflicts she found in
Goethe between life and art, intellect and humanism, Fuller now
stresses woman's service to life:

> The especial genius of woman I believe to be electrical in move-
> ment, intuitive in function, spiritual in tendency. She excels not
> so easily in classification, or re-creation, as in an instinctive seizure
> of causes, and a simple breathing out of what she receives that has
> the singleness of life, rather than the selecting and energizing of
> art.   (p. 161 [68])

Again there may be much autobiography here (surely more of that than biology), but in the paired contrasts such as instinct versus classification and unity versus selection there is also the transcendental conception of the poet-hero—in Fuller, the poet-heroine—repressed but still very much alive in woman. While Emerson and his followers glorified reason over understanding and poetic intuition over calculating intellect, Fuller simply extended this argument by identifying exactly those more valued qualities as predominant in woman. Perhaps nowhere is the transcendental and romantic bias of her thought clearer than at this point. The culture of woman, therefore, fulfills perfectly the transcendental hopes for the progressive glorification of the race.

Yet this argument is only the basis of a further argument, which, paradoxically, reverses Fuller's line of reasoning. It is not this intuitive or magnetic element, but rather the intellectual element, that must be stressed now in woman. Here Fuller's idea of the interaction of feminine and masculine principles comes fully into play:

> Male and female represent the two sides of the great radical dualism. But, in fact, they are perpetually passing into one another. Fluid hardens into solid, solid rushes into fluid. There is no wholly masculine man, no purely feminine woman.   (p. 161 [68–69])

In this passage Fuller strains the boundary of language to make her point. "Masculine" and "feminine" are unsatisfactory terms at best, and through the quasiscientific metaphor of solids and fluids she is attempting to show the intricacies of their relation and difference. Mythology offers her the most satisfactory language, and she continues, "Man partakes of the feminine in the Apollo, woman of the masculine as Minerva" (p. 162 [69]), contrasting the intellectual element represented by Minerva with the intuitive side of woman, mythically expressed as "Muse" (p. 160 [68]). Harmonious development demands that both sides of woman and man be nurtured, and therefore Fuller argues that self-culture has a double nature:

> The growth of man is two-fold, masculine and feminine.
> As far as these two methods can be distinguished they are so as Energy and Harmony.
> Power and Beauty.
> Intellect and Love.
> Or by some such rude classification, for we have not language primitive and pure enough to express such ideas with precision.
> (p. 201 [99])

Shelley is a male example of this twofold growth, for "like all men of genius, [he] shared the feminine development, and, unlike many, knew it" (p. 160 [67]). Mary Wollstonecraft and George Sand are exemplary intellectual women (pp. 130–33 [43–46]), and Fuller herself exempli-

fies the woman who shares the "masculine" development, as the autobiographical elements in the work—most notably the "Miranda"
segment—repeatedly suggest (pp. 101–04 [21–23]).

Fuller foresees a time when a "community of life and consciousness
of mind" among men will make possible a "harmony of common
growth" (p. 163 [70]) in which all human activities can be accorded a
rightful place, but she contends that "in the present crisis . . . the
preference is given to Minerva" (p. 163 [70]). She links that intellectual
development in woman with a stance of independence from men, the
"power of continence" and "self-poise" of the Indian woman betrothed
to the sun. Through this argument she thus attempts to preserve the
ultimate primacy of intuition over rationalism and to face the immediate need to stress the intellectual potential of women. She also attempts to preserve both a vision of harmony in male-female relations
and the option of self-reliance for women.

The vision of harmony, based on the belief in the possibility of a
society that would make self-culture possible, ultimately fuels Fuller's
social criticism. The irony is that she is forced to advocate short-term
goals that appear to conflict with her long-term values: does intellectual
development mean cold lifelessness? does self-reliant autonomy pre-
clude social harmony? The demands of theory and practice, therefore,
pull her book in opposite directions, even though her concrete suggestions originate in theory. More specifically, her redefinition of self demands that women emphasize a unique identity centered around
intuitive powers and also that women separate themselves from men to
cultivate a set of nonintuitive, intellectual powers. What holds these
tensions together in the book is Fuller's vision of potential perfection,
a vision arising from transcendentalism, but also capable of being seen,
in a slightly different context, as millennial. Although recent histori-
ographers have underscored the importance of millennial thinking to
American culture, they have generally tended to link millennialism
with evangelical religion rather than with the religious liberalism of
which Fuller and the transcendentalists were a cutting edge. But that
same evangelical tendency, expressed in secular language, permeates
Woman. Fuller's millennial expectation is neither religious nor political
in the usual sense; it focuses instead on the establishment of a society
offering women full equality with men. That prospect, however, is a
change radical enough to evoke millennial language in her description
of it:

> Were this done [women granted equality] and a slight temporary
> fermentation allowed to subside, we should see crystallizations
> more pure and of more various beauty. We believe the divine
> energy would pervade nature to a degree unknown in the history

of former ages, and that no discordant collision, but ravishing harmony of the spheres would ensue.   (p. 100 [20])

It is significant that Fuller's life did take an increasingly political turn
after *Woman* was published. What may sound to a modern reader like
strained language or overblown sentiment in the above pronouncement
is in fact in line with much other writing of the 1830s and 1840s that
can be called millennial. The religious categories, and the religious
imagery, are still operative, but the thrust of the rhetoric is motivation
for political change. Fuller simply offers an example from the women's
struggle of thought that more often appeared in Fourierism or abolitionism, though such examples would be found more frequently later
in the century, as the women's movement grew. That she was an in-
novator she was painfully but proudly aware; and she did not see any
conflict between her transcendental moral idealism and her political
commitment to feminism. That conflict is partly the product of a later
epoch in history and partly the product of historiography, which inevitably falsifies as it classifies. To restore Fuller to the Concord circle is
not, therefore, to charge that she lacked historical consciousness but to
suggest, rather, that the historical consciousness of that movement
needs to be explored further. We still lack an adequate explanation for
the death by slow unraveling that the movement seems to have under-
gone in the 1840s. Fuller's development implies that the death was, in
some respects at least, a fulfillment.

*   *   *

BELL GALE CHEVIGNY

To the Edges of Ideology:
Margaret Fuller's Centrifugal Evolution†

> I find how true was the lure that always drew me towards Europe. It
> was no false instinct that said I might here find an atmosphere to
> develop me in ways I need. Had I only come ten years earlier! Now
> my life must be a failure, so much strength had been wasted on
> abstractions, which only came because I grew not in the right soil.
> —Letter to Emerson, December 20, 1847[1]

In Rome in the fall of 1847 Margaret Fuller celebrated her discovery
of the place where she felt she belonged, fearing only that she had

† From *American Quarterly* 38 (1986): 173–201. Copyright © 1986 by The Johns Hopkins
University Press. Reprinted by permission. Norton Critical Edition page references appear in
brackets. I thank Myra Jehlen for encouraging me to undertake to write this essay and Daniel
Kaiser for helping me to finish it [author's note].
1. *Memoirs of Margaret Fuller Ossoli*, ed. Ralph Waldo Emerson, W. H. Channing, and J. F.
Clarke (1884; rpt. New York: Burt Franklin, 1972) (hereafter cited as *Memoirs*), II:224–25.

found it too late. She wrote that Europe had validated her long-held "instinct" by providing at last the "atmosphere," the "right soil," in which she might uniquely grow. While the figure of the "natural" self, instinctual and organic, was shared by romantics on both sides of the Atlantic, the suggestion that self and place waited for reciprocal recognition is unmistakably American. Fuller's contemporaries, Emerson, Thoreau, and Hawthorne, had quite resoundingly located—found and installed—their unique voice and vision in the specifically American landscape. In her American years, Fuller had differed from them sharply, sharing their preference neither for nature nor for New England. The appeal for her of Europe, to be sure, lay in the social and historical rather than the natural landscape, but Fuller's sense of vocational discovery in European places was as intense as that her compatriots had felt in rural retreats. "Italy receives me as a long-lost child, and I feel myself at home here," she wrote.[2] She did not mean that she was Italian in essence; it was as an American that she felt at home in Italy.

The specific interest here of Fuller's situation is that she could approximate the American sense of place only from the far side of the Atlantic Ocean; in this way, she significantly reinterprets the "American sense" of her peers. What is more, Fuller's "American sense" could not be repatriated. Her own return was balked first by her fear of recrossing and reentry, then by the abrupt and concerted discouragement of her friends, and finally by storm and shipwreck. After Fuller's death, much was written about her, but her "American sense"—precisely what had made her feel at home in Italy—was obscured. These are facts that suggested the crucial premise of this essay: to become a more quintessentially American writer only after irrevocably leaving the United States is to embody a critique of that country, and particularly of its leading ideological constructs.

*   *   *

American women in Fuller's time lived at the crossroads of two ideological constructs confirmed and sharpened in the aftermath of the American Revolution: one concerned class and history, the other gender. The prevailing ideology of class was a simple denial of the existence of class. Middle-class ideology in Western Europe was also shaped by resistance to knowledge of class realities; but in the United States the heightened commitment to individualism elevated the notion of classlessness to an article of faith. Powerfully complementing the ideology of class was the ideology of history. The notion that America had a unique destiny to fulfill arrived with the Puritans, was tempered by Jefferson, and was "proved" when the American Revolution was taken as culmination and terminus of history. By the 1840s, however, this

2. Ibid., II:220.

twofold system had become increasingly vulnerable to assault. Move-ments like the Dorr Rebellion reopened history, while its repression and the heightened exploitation of wage laborers challenged the claim of classlessness directly. Continuing objections to the persecution or extermination of Indians, growing agitation against the enslavement of blacks, and rising consciousness of the subjugation of women all un-dermined the authority and clarity of the construct in more complex ways.

Working to obscure the subjugation of women was an ideology of gender, which both grew out of and enhanced the consolidation and growth of bourgeois capitalism. The development of a market economy in the eighteenth century had dissolved the natural and relatively egal-itarian division of labor within the home. As men were drawn from the home to sell commodities or their labor, middle-class women were decisively thrust back into a home that had become narrower. Family relations were privatized, especially in the increasingly distinct middle class, and as the home lost its productive function in the economy, a "moral" function was adduced to replace it. A monument to this new arrangement was the "cult of true womanhood" which crested during Fuller's lifetime: it taught, as Barbara Welter has shown, that women were *by nature* pious, pure, submissive, and domestic.[3] Men increas-ingly schooled in the disciplines of competitive industrial society took comfort—as the economy took strength—from the notion of women as the "better" and wholly other half. The ideology of gender not only concealed its basis in social inequity, it also contradicted the ideology of class even as it was used to support it. For only by insisting on essential *differences* in gender could men pursue supposedly *universal* values of economic freedom and individual development.

Fuller was not significantly troubled by the weaknesses in class ide-ology as long as she lived in New England, and she questioned gender ideology only fitfully until she was on the verge of leaving to live in New York. Yet her earliest psychological and intellectual experiences readied her for critical thinking. I have demonstrated elsewhere how Fuller's earliest experiences made her feel torn between terms that her society considered mutually exclusive: female and intellectual. Her par-ents seemed to divide between them the worlds of nature and culture, feeling and thought; and her father's rigorous educational methods made her seek complementary modes of apprehension.[4] Again and again she counterposed the claims of mind and of womanhood, or

---

3. Barbara Welter, "The Cult of True Womanhood," reprinted in *The American Sisterhood*, ed. Wendy Martin (New York: Harper & Row, 1972), 243–56.
4. See Bell Gale Chevigny, *The Woman and the Myth: Margaret Fuller's Life and Writings* (Old Westbury, N.Y.: Feminist Press, 1976), Part I, and "Daughters Writing: Toward a Theory of Women's Biography," *Between Women: Biographers, Novelists, Critics, Teachers and Artists Write about Their Work on Women*, ed. Carol Asher, Louise De Salvo, and Sara Ruddick (Boston: Beacon Press, 1984).

pitted the achievements of intellect against the sweetness of life, without being able to forswear either. The sense of her dilemma as division between equal and irreconcilable values seems to have fed her habit of perceiving the world in terms of opposing claims.

This fundamental feeling of division probably contributed to an intellectual style which is marked by resistance to unity or resolution, even when the desire for unity or resolution is expressed. Much of Fuller's writing in New England, private as well as public, discloses a predilection to discern duality: to balance, counter, or seek an alternative to, views she found too simple or dominating or narrow—and increasingly to conceive of progress in dialectical terms.

Fuller's enthusiastic study of many languages and literatures—Latin, Greek, French, Italian, and German—gave authority to her comparativist tendencies. She became a cultural relativist. Moreover, her habit of looking for two or more positions made her adept at discerning the edges or limits of certain judgments and sometimes at locating the value system or ideology in which they were based.[5]

While Fuller's concern with literatures was an excellent preparation for ideological analysis, it was only when she began to offer discussion classes to women and to write about them that her analytic tools were put to the test. In shifting her attention from cultural issues to social ones, she was obliged directly to confront fundamental ideological categories.

As we shall see, Fuller's experience with Transcendentalism ultimately obliged her to recognize social contradictions. It functioned at first to offer her a comfortable and even attractive way to overlook and mystify them. Fuller was drawn to Emerson in particular because he appeared to circumvent social contradictions by means of personal transcendence. Fuller wrote of Emerson, "From him I first learned what is meant by an inward life," adding that he had made her understand that "the mind is its own place."[6] Emerson intended to elude the egregious effects of industrialization—human fragmentation and reification—by becoming a whole self, a "representative" and exemplary American. The effect of his efforts was to reinforce the myths in which American ideology was grounded. He made classlessness more legitimate by updating and secularizing the myth of unique national destiny; and by insisting that individualism flourished in isolation from time, place, and social action, he drew attention away from contemporary social problems. (It is not difficult to recognize Emerson's influence in Fuller's writing about the Dorr Rebellion.)

As far as the ideology of gender was concerned, Emerson shared the

5. See Margaret V. Allen's excellent discussion in ch. 4, "Goethe and Humanism," *The Achievement of Margaret Fuller* (University Park: Penn. State Univ. Press, 1979), and Chevigny, *The Woman and the Myth*, Part III for an account of how Goethe helped Fuller identify the limitations of the perspectives of many of her Transcendentalist friends.
6. *Memoirs*, I:195.

dominant essentialist interpretation. For him "a certain falseness" inhered in the subject of "Woman . . . historically considered. . . . For me today, Woman is not a degraded person with duties forgotten, but a docile daughter of God with her face heavenward endeavoring to hear the divine word & to convey it to me."[7] His rich intellectual exchange with Fuller represented an exception to his general view of women, and it must have also functioned to conceal it from Fuller. The inclusion of Fuller at the very center of the Transcendentalist circle would have worked to minimize her awareness of her marginality as a woman. But the status of a female Transcendentalist was inherently unstable in a way that the status, say, of a female romantic in Europe might not have been. If we consider the difference, for example, between the romanticism of Blake and the young Marx, for both of whom sexuality was one of the chief figures of revolutionary vision, and the sexless romanticism of Emerson and Thoreau, the point may be clear. Her society would not let Fuller transcend sex as it did Emerson. All of the irony that surrounds the image of Fuller as a Transcendentalist stems from her being female.

Hence Fuller's decision in 1839, three years after she had met Emerson, to initiate a series of weekly "Conversations" with women, meetings in which they thought aloud together, necessarily precipitated her confrontation with dominant ideology. Emerson never took the Conversations seriously; he referred to them as Fuller's "parlatorio." Yet they represented an eminently Transcendentalist exercise in promoting self-nurture through an innovative social form. Fuller might even have seen them as an attempt to follow Emerson's exhortation at the close of "Nature": "Build therefore your own world." In 1843, she wrote a long essay on women for the *Dial*; expanded the next year into the book-length *Woman in the Nineteenth Century*, this constituted Fuller's first intellectual endeavor to build her own world.

This work is rife with unresolved issues and contradictions. Not the least of these is that it simultaneously pays tribute to Transcendentalism and signals her break with that movement.[8] For as her argument unfolds, and especially in its revisions, her encounter with the sort of

---

7. W. H. Gilman and J. E. Parsons, eds., *Journals and Miscellaneous Notebooks of Ralph Waldo Emerson* (Cambridge: Belknap Press of Harvard Univ., 1970) VIII:372.

8. In "Margaret Fuller and the Transcendental Ethos: *Woman in the Nineteenth Century*," *PMLA*, 97 (January 1982), 83–98, David M. Robinson offers a reading which registers a shift toward social reform, but his interpretation emphasizes continuity while mine emphasizes rupture. In his discussion of "transcendental politics," he recalls the following "historical consciousness within the movement" and invokes the following "complex dialectic": "the ideal demands embodiment while the process of social transformation must have the guidance of an ideal. Fuller, who embodied her ideal in the commitment to self-culture, discovered that self-culture as an end required social reform as a means, that the fulfillment of woman necessitated the concerted action of women. *Woman in the Nineteenth Century* is her monument to that discovery" (95–6). Against the simple clarity of this formula, the dialectic I attribute to Fuller's evolution in this essay may appear unnecessarily convoluted. My case against continuity will rest on my reading of the Transcendentalists' reading of Fuller, their refusal of her radical meanings, elaborated in the final section of this essay.

contradictions Emerson had dedicated himself to overcoming becomes increasingly direct.

In the opening pages of *Woman in the Nineteenth Century*, Fuller appears simply to be discussing women in Transcendentalist terms. She asserts that it is the "destiny of Man . . . to ascertain and fulfill the law of his being," that "the highest Ideal Man can form of his own powers, is that which he is destined to attain," and that goal of perfection is sanctioned by "the fact of an universal, unceasing revelation." She assures us on the first page that "by man I mean both man and woman: these are the two halves of one thought," but, as her argument unfolds, she urges that man step aside to permit woman unlimited self-culture.[9] What emerges is a revealing incoherence. While her strategy and rhetoric assume the universality of Transcendentalist claims, her need to argue it undermines that assumption. In urging that universal human truths be *extended* to women, Fuller unwittingly calls their universality into question, and discloses them to be contingent or incomplete. The same objection may be raised to her *applying* to women the universal rights announced in the Declaration of Independence (in unconscious parallel with the recently despised Dorrites). This argument from universality was never retracted by Fuller. Nor did she acknowledge that feminism was ill-reconciled with Transcendentalism. Yet, in her revision of her essay for the book-length version, she developed only the concrete arguments, as if in partial recognition that her thought was more coherent when more particular.

While the grand plan of *Woman in the Nineteenth Century* inadvertently exposes the contradiction between the ideology of class and the ideology of gender, between the bourgeois "universal" and the woman as "other," the details of her argument consciously challenge specific features of the ideology of gender. Two of the cardinal qualities of the "true woman," domesticity and submissiveness, are repeatedly assaulted. Fuller calls for women's vocational freedom ("let them be seacaptains, if you will"). She encourages women to take initiative in reform (especially in antislavery activity, public speaking, and petitioning), to cultivate the "masculine" in themselves, to represent themselves by voting and holding public office, and to learn to live independently. (Dependence on men "has led to an excessive devotion, which has cooled love, degraded marriage, and prevented either sex from being what it should be to itself or the other.")[1]

Fuller's writing is most trenchant and enduring in this uneven text when she anatomizes, or deconstructs, rationales of male dominance. She reveals the contradiction in the argument that women are "destined

9. Fuller, *Woman in the Nineteenth Century* (1845; rpt. Columbia: Univ. of South Carolina Press, 1980), v, 6 [5, 9].
1. Ibid., 59, 61 [102, 103].

by nature" for the "inner circle" rather than for political life, by naming the women suppressed in the argument:

> Those who think the physical circumstances of woman would make a part in the affairs of national government unsuitable, are by no means those who think it impossible for negresses to endure field work, even during pregnancy, or the sempstresses to go through their killing labors.[2]

Probably the most controversial aspect of the book was her discussion, as an unmarried woman, of sexuality. Fuller keeps her own counsel on women's sexual feelings. Yet she exposes the logical incoherence of arguments men use to deny women's feelings, and the cruelty to women of men's monopolization of sexual knowledge in the name of morality:

> As to marriage it has been inculcated on women for centuries, that men have not only stronger passions than they, but of a sort it would be shameful for them to share or even understand. That, therefore, they must "confide in their husbands," i.e., submit implicitly to their will. That the least appearance of coldness or withdrawal, from whatever cause, in the wife is wicked, because liable to turn her husband's thought to illicit indulgence; for a man is so constituted that he must indulge his passions or die![3]

In Europe she would go further, challenging even the "true woman's" quality of purity which is left undisturbed in *Woman*. In passages like these where Fuller adopted the vantage point of the "other," of the self necessarily excluded by ideological generalization, she developed what would become one of her chief strengths as a writer—the satiric and analytic unmasking of complacent rationalization.

Fuller's permanent gain from Transcendentalism was her commitment, which we may call radically and romantically Protestant, to the intuitive capacities and rights of individuals, groups, and nations to self-fulfillment and self-determination. This commitment came to be identical for her with the project of the new American nation. But temperamental and intellectual biases kept her from embracing Emerson's version of Transcendentalism. Her interest in opposing perspectives and in opposition itself must be distinguished from Emerson's celebrated inconsistency, which was really a way station on the road to a new unity. Fuller's impatience with unity made her joke in 1844 about Emerson's retreat: "the fates which gave this place Concord, took away the animating influences of Discord." In reviewing Emerson's second series of *Essays* in 1844, she disclosed the appeal for her of

2. Ibid., 24 [19].
3. Ibid., 137 [89].

discord and the material world. She inquires, in her typically unabashed manner, whether Emerson's rejection of the flat horizontal of his world was well-advised: "This friend raised himself too early to the perpendicular. . . . We could wish he might be thrown by conflicts on the lap of mother earth, to see if he would not rise again with added powers."[4] Newly situated in New York as she wrote this, Fuller's curiosity about the actual world had displaced her interest in building a private one. Emerson had done much for Fuller. He strengthened her self-esteem and helped her to clarify her thought and tighten her style; above all, his own sharp identity helped her to define her very different one. For the rest of her life, trusting Emerson to remain the same, Fuller used him as a touchstone. (Her letter quoted in the epigraph was written to him.) Emerson figured to the end as an interlocutor for Fuller's internal debates; as such, he helped to interrogate and name her condition as it changed.

*   *   *

JULIE ELLISON

"A Crowd of Books to Sigh Over": Fuller's Method†

The recurring clash of social experience and textual representations of the feminine takes us some way into the discursive structure of *Woman in the Nineteenth Century*. When we observe the whole range of allusive and intertextual events that constitute the book, however, their meanings alter somewhat. The energy of quotation, the urgency of manifold forms of cultural reference, and the unstoppable cataloging—*as signs*—of "signs of the times" produce writing as a "stream which is ever flowing from the heights of my thought," as Fuller describes it, a flood of cultural associations which descends on the present. Or, in a moment of understandable fatigue, not a flood, but the somewhat depressing prospect of an urban crowd, a "crowd of books." As she makes a transition "from the future to the present," she effects the less exhilarating descent from myth to book review. "It would seem as if this time [of transformation] were not very near to one fresh from books, such as I have of late been—" and here she interrupts herself to revise her phrasing—"no: *not* reading, but sighing over." From the

---

4. Thomas Wentworth Higginson, *Margaret Fuller Ossoli* (1884; rpt. New York: Chelsea House, 1981), 70; New York *Tribune*, 7 Dec. 1844; *The Writings of Margaret Fuller*, ed. Mason Wade (New York: Viking Press, 1941), 393.

† Reprinted from Julie Ellison: *Delicate Subjects: Romanticism, Gender, and the Ethics of Understanding*, pp. 277–86. Copyright (©) 1990 by Cornell University. Used by permission of the publisher, Cornell University Press. The author's notes have been omitted. Norton Critical Edition page references appear in brackets.

number of books sent to her "since my friends knew me to be engaged in this way," she concludes "that almost all that is extant of formal precept has come under my eye." Her reaction is characteristic. "Among these I select as a favorable specimen, the book I have already quoted" and which she goes on to quote some more: " 'The Study of the Life of Woman, by Madame Necker de Saussure, of Geneva, translated from the French' " (WNC 200, 192 [99, 93]).

Fuller's repetitive, accumulating, and associative style is hardly unique among romantic authors. Emerson's essays are constructed in a similar way, although their recurring episodes of transformation and collapse are quite different from Fuller's movement between allegorical allusions and multivocal performances. The status of philosophical discourse in Coleridge's prose, set against the anxiety-inducing materials of journalism and novels and the compensatory references to domestic sensation, again differs in its specific economy but is alike in the close link between its mania for quotation and its ambivalent drive for idealization. The difference is that whereas the male romantics situate the feminine over against the reading of philosophy, Fuller performs reading that generates feminism and does it in the name of philosophy or the ideal. For Coleridge, Sara Hutchinson is the emotion that abstruse research has blocked; for Fuller, abstruse research reveals the desire for the feminine soul in the founding texts of Western culture. In *Woman in the Nineteenth Century* reading opposes not feeling but masculinity. Insofar as Fuller makes oppressive masculine practices speak only in idioms that are not aesthetic or literary—if anything in this highly referential book can be called "not literary"—she relegates codes of habitual behavior and speech to the enemy while appropriating the aesthetic for woman.

The character of Fuller's protagonist, the romantic essayist who marshals such diverse materials and argues their meanings, is unusually active and self-referential. The persistent reference to her emotional imperatives as both reader and writer—in addition to the allusive redundancy such emotion generates—gives *Woman in the Nineteenth Century* its tone of urgency. The vocalized energy of association and transition, Fuller hovers on the edge of her interpolated dramas as producer, interpreter, and alter ego of the figures populating the book. As the one who brings the stories before us, she cannily declines the role of heroine. Yet as metanarrative strategist, she draws attention to her own overburdened feelings of pain and pleasure and the necessary demonstrativeness to which they lead:

Such instances count up by scores within my own memory.

I said, we will not speak of this now, yet I have spoken, for the subject makes me feel too much.

> We must insert in this connection the most beautiful picture pre-
> sented by ancient literature of wedded love. . . .

> I must quote two more short passages from Xenophon, for he is a
> writer who pleases me well.

> I could swell the catalogue of instances far beyond the reader's
> patience. (WNC 97, 138, 143, 119 [17, 50, 54, 35])

Fuller speaks as the device that turns the images stored up through
reading and social witness into texts to be witnessed by others. Quantity
signifies both politically and authorially. She chooses her anecdotes
from a crowd of instances and calls attention to the feeling of pressure
behind and within her allusions, arguing as one for whom the sublime
of multiplying references is proof of her sincerity. Retold stories thus
acquire the status of evidence that proves the legitimacy of the feminist
critique.

Fundamental to Fuller's discourse both as an explanation for the
serial construction of *Woman* and as an outlet for its semiotic excess—
its surplus of examples—is the logic of "the signs of the times":

> Under these circumstances, without attaching importance, in
> themselves, to the changes demanded by the champions of
> women, we hail them as signs of the times.

> Another sign of the times is furnished by the triumphs of female
> authorship.

> All these motions of the time, tides that betoken a waxing moon,
> overflow upon our land.

> Among the throng of symptoms which denote the present ten-
> dency to a crisis in the life of woman . . . I have attempted to
> select a few. (WNC 100, 144, 155, 165 [20, 55, 64, 72])

The basis for resemblance among such signs is an underlying law or
principle that turns the whole field of culture and events into a collection of allegories all meaning roughly the same thing. Heterogeneous
assemblages prove historical laws. By virtue of their capacity to appear
as a "throng," such signifiers can be apprehended only en masse; like
all nineteenth-century crowds, they can only "denote the . . . tendency
to crisis." But if the books, deeds, or utterances enumerated after such
statements as I have just quoted function as quantity or mass, they also
make possible other stylistic attributes. Within such a structure, for example, Fuller is bound neither by chronological sequence nor by syl-
logistic logic. She moves among "signs" and "symptoms" in a loosely

associative way, and in these associative openings her loyalties and an-
tipathies surface.

Fuller's most complex entry into her own discourse takes place when
Miranda arrives in the text of *Woman* as Fuller's half-fictive, half-
autobiographical description of what feminism looks like. Miranda is
thereby related to the series of personae related to Margaret—Mariana,
Minerva, the Muse—defined by their status as representations of female
resistance and suffering. But she alone is given a voice in which to
instruct the essayist in the grounds for pessimism about women's condition. And finally, it is "from the papers of Miranda" that Fuller has
"borrowed" the material in Appendix G on "characters of women
drawn by the Greek dramatists" (WNC 224 [123]). Postponing the
question of the appendix for the moment, we can trace, in the account
of Miranda, Fuller's tendency to approach and to avoid her master
signs. In the course of a few pages she is Miranda's biographer, interlocutor, and double—and eventually her critic.

The paragraph preceding the Miranda episode concludes, "Let us
consider what obstructions impede this good era, and what signs give
reason to hope that it draws near." Miranda then materializes in two
roles: as Fuller's collaborator in interpreting signs and as herself a sign
of hope that turns out to be cause for pessimism as well. A brief biography sets forth the reasons why Fuller "had always thought [of Mi-
randa] as an example": specifically, an example "that the restraints upon
the sex were insuperable only to those who think them so, or who
noisily strive to break them" (WNC 101–2 [21–22]).

What are the conditions, then, that enable Miranda to "speak without
heat and bitterness of the position of her sex?" That produce the ethic
of nonoppositional independence for which she stands? There are
three: the apparent absence of a mother, who is never mentioned; a
father who treated his daughter as "a living mind" and "child of the
spirit"; and an intensely feminine or "electric" temperament in which
sexuality is nonetheless muted. Miranda never possessed "those charms
which might have drawn to her bewildering flatteries." Despite the fact
that her personal magnetism attracts both men and women, she is "affectionate without passion, intellectual without coldness." In other
words, Fuller gives Miranda an idealized version of her own paternal
education and characteristic "electricity," without the fault of alternat-
ing "passion" and "coldness." At this point, then, Miranda crystallizes
as "an example" of the feminist way, the precariousness of which
emerges in Fuller's balanced phrasing: "She had taken a course of her
own, and no man stood in her way. Many of her acts had been unusual
but excited no uproar. Few helped, but none checked her, and the
many men, who knew her mind and her life, showed to her confidence
as to a brother, gentleness as to a sister. And not only refined, but very
coarse men approved and aided." Independence without opposition,

unconventionality without "uproar," self-reliance without check, brotherly and sisterly love: Miranda receives all of the benefits of feminism without any of the costs. But it is she who articulates fundamental doubts about the growth of self-reliance in women and respect for women in men. "I talked with her upon these matters, and . . . said very much what I have written," Fuller interjects. She enters as a participant to resist Miranda's pessimism (WNC 101–2 [21–22]).

Miranda is fully conscious of the paradoxical nature of her position. "This self dependence, which was honored in me, is deprecated as a fault in most women," she asserts. "This is the fault of man." Because she was able to take her stand on "self-reliance" at a very young age, she was not subjected to the "precepts" of male "guardians." Most girls, their minds "impeded by doubts . . . lose their chance of fair free proportions." Miranda has arrived at her current bleak outlook after a period of hopefulness: "Once I thought that men would help to forward this state of things more than I do now." But, she says, "early I perceived that men never, in any extreme of despair, wished to be women." Male conversation, in which "any sign of weakness" is mocked as feminine and any form of power is honored as manly, is the basis for her revised conclusions about the "rooted skepticism" of men on the subject of female equality. Miranda concludes her explanation by quoting Jonson's "On Lucy, Countess of Bedford," that "learned and . . . *manly* soul." Fuller has already quoted this passage at the head of her Preface. When she argues with Miranda here, it almost initiates a critique of her own loyalty to men's praise of women: " 'Methinks,' said I, 'you are too fastidious in objecting to this. Jonson in using the word "manly" only meant to heighten the picture of this, the true, the intelligent fate, with one of the deeper colors.' " " 'And yet,' said she," zeroing in on Fuller's vague argument about "deeper colors," "so invariable is the use of this word where a heroic quality is to be described, and I feel so sure that persistence and courage are the most womanly no less than the most manly qualities, that I would exchange these words for others of a larger sense at the risk of marring the fine tissue of the verse. Read, 'a heavenward and instructed soul,' and I should be satisfied" (WNC 104 [23]).

The Miranda episode comes to an end as Fuller shuffles between giving men the benefit of the doubt and concurring with Miranda's dim view of relations between the sexes. Whenever a woman has "nobly shone forth in any form of excellence," men have praised her. But here Fuller shifts into satire, for men's "encomiums" are "mortifying; they show too much surprise. Can this be you? he cries to the transfigured Cinderella; well I should never have thought it, but I am very glad. WE will tell every one that you have '*surpassed your sex.*' " Fuller's impatience now lights even on Schiller, in whose poem "Dignity of

Woman" she finds "only a great boy to be softened and restrained by the influence of girls." And if "Poets, the elder brothers of their race," are incapable of better, "what can you expect of every-day men?" Even Richter just wanted a wife who would "cook him something good." At this point Fuller unites with Miranda on the "delicate subject" of cooking, defending "in behalf of Miranda and myself" women who keep house (WNC 105 [24]).

In the story of Miranda, then, two unresolved issues in Fuller's writing come together: first, the possibility that women whose behavior is ethically ideal cannot bring about, by nonantagonistic means, a general change in male perceptions; and second, the possibility that alluding favorably to men's celebrations of women merely perpetuates inequality based on gender. Avoiding conflict in the name of self-sufficiency or literary tradition, Miranda implies, accomplishes nothing in either the social or the textual domain. Such an ethic makes a difference to the individual woman who lives it, but not to others.

Fuller continues to regret clashes between feminists and society and to use texts by men as incentives for women for the rest of her book's considerable length. She even makes Miranda the agent of allusion in one of the eight appendices that add thirty pages to the volume in a climactic series of extracts. Appendix G is a loosely structured critical essay cum appreciation devoted mostly to the female characters of Euripides and Sophocles, but also touching on Tennyson, James Fenimore Cooper, and Joseph Haydn. Fuller accounts for its inclusion on educational and practical grounds: since she has made "many allusions . . . in the foregoing pages to characters of women drawn by the Greek dramatists, which may not be familiar to the majority of readers," she has "borrowed from the papers of Miranda, some notes upon them." Exposure to these materials offers, she endlessly hopes, "a mental standard, as to what man and woman should be." Allusions, then, are supplemented by further allusions and by commentary on key moments of "pathos" in Greek tragedy that is *less* skeptical than Fuller's writing elsewhere in *Woman*. It is so enthusiastic, in fact, that Fuller attributes it to Miranda's juvenilia: "I trust the girlish tone of apostrophizing rapture may be excused. Miranda was very young at the time of writing, compared with her present mental age. *Now*, she would express the same feelings, but in a worthier garb—if she expressed them at all" (WNC 238, 224–25 [135, 123]). If we are to understand why the arguments vested in Miranda do not impede Fuller's habit of quotation and are even subsumed by it, why allusion does not simply represent subservience, and why Fuller is able, in fact, to write the very antagonisms she deplores, we need to go more deeply into the problem of quotation. Quotation and allusion constitute the mature public style of the heterogeneous subject whom we first encountered in Fuller's letters.

The tactics of quotation both accentuate cultural differences and create a feeling of sameness as diversity is blurred by the identical textual status of discursive bits.

As in the letters of Fuller's early adulthood, heterogeneity refers not to a random mixture of styles, but to a structured movement among certain discourses and the cultural positions associated with them. The tension between the *effect* of quotation or allusion, which makes the most ordinary utterance into a literary event, and Fuller's often strenuous reference to the literal exacerbates all the questions we have confronted previously about the politics of romantic feminism. On the surface Fuller appears to play off the glamor of literary tradition against the gritty facts of nineteenth-century behavior. But insofar as it is the *speech* of her contemporaries which she most notices, even the realistic portions of the book become theatrical as Fuller finds the legitimate style of aggression.

Fuller breaks out of the pathos of literary reference and into the realm of social satire most sharply when she focuses on the ordinary speech of Americans, especially American males, as they casually exhibit their prejudices about woman's sphere. As an example of men "under the slavery of habit" she introduces a representative anecdote:

> Once two fine figures stood before me, thus. The father of very intellectual aspect, his falcon eye softened by affection as he looked down on his fair child, she the image of himself, only more graceful and brilliant in expression. I was reminded of Southey's Kehama, when lo, the dream was rudely broken. They were talking of education, and he said,
>
> "I shall not have Maria brought too forward. If she knows too much, she will never find a husband; superior women hardly ever can."
>
> "Surely," said his wife, with a blush, "you wish Maria to be as good and wise as she can, whether it will help her to marriage or not."
>
> "No," he persisted, "I want her to have a sphere and a home, and some one to protect her when I am gone." (WNC 165 [71])

Fuller, always moved by closeness between fathers and daughters, characteristically starts to assimilate the pair to an ennobling and colorful poetic context (Southey's "Kehama"), but this impulse receives its comeuppance here. The confident banality of the father's spoken words breaks the "spell" cast by his physiognomy. The "blush" of the mother—who was not mentioned and perhaps not seen until now—enters as the mark of awareness, signifying the contradiction between the father's "intellectual aspect" and his spoken policy.

Fragments of men's derogatory but everyday comments provide Miranda with the grounds for pessimism. She is "above her sex," they say; she "makes the best she can of it"; she is "a manly woman." In her angry attack on the sexual double standard built into the marital economy, Fuller seizes the stock phrases of masculine self-justification in the pincers of feminist paraphrase:

> "You," say the men, "must frown upon vice . . . you must not submit to the will of your husband when it seems to you unworthy, but give the laws in marriage, and redeem it from its present sensual and mental pollutions."
> . . . it has been inculcated on women for centuries, that men have not only stronger passions than they, but of a sort that it would be shameful for them to share or even understand. That, therefore, they must "confide in their husbands," i.e., submit implicitly to their will. . . .
> Accordingly a great part of women look upon men as a kind of wild beasts, but "suppose they are all alike" . . . assured by the married that, "if they knew men as they do . . . they would not expect continence or self-government from them." (WNC 187 [88–89])

Fuller's elementary but effective translation of mystification into fact is contained in that "i.e.": "they must 'confide in their husbands,' i.e., submit implicitly to their will." The social rules of mutual misunderstanding, according to which women accept both the fact that they should not understand male sexuality and the fact that they themselves cannot be understood by men, are shattered by the descendental vocabulary of "i.e.," the much-repeated "suppose," "inculcate," and so on.

These little satires are structurally and thematically distinct from the literary materials that form the basis for the "mental standard" by which Fuller judges contemporary conversation. In a ten-page catalog of admirable marriages, all derived from literary or historical writings, conversation between exemplary spouses is retold by the appreciative nineteenth-century reader (WNC 136–45 [46–54]). The love of Count Zinzeldorf for his wife is followed by the Indian legend of Flying Pigeon (a paragon of Victorian womanhood, lovingly remembered by her son); this, in turn, is superseded by a veritable binge of quotations from Xenophon on the marriage of Panthea and Abradatus, plus "two more short passages . . . for he is a writer who pleases me well." The unifying "thread" of Fuller's subject, spiritual marriage, produces a selective insensibility to cultural difference and historical specificity which is reflected in her refusal to break down these writings into their constituent phrases, as she does with American speech. The tendency to lengthen quotations and to string them together reflects an inspirational urgency intimately related to the dynamics of sublimity, which in certain modes requires repetition, extension, and velocity of feeling. This is why

Fuller's quotations are voluminous when she is favorable but fragmentary when she is hostile.

At the end of *Woman in the Nineteenth Century* Fuller momentarily renounces pathos for the intense clarity of realism and the enjoyment of immediacy: "I stand in the sunny noon of life. Objects no longer glitter in the dews of morning, neither are yet softened by the shadows of evening. Every spot is seen, every chasm revealed." But it is quickly apparent that this moment of poise has not taken Fuller beyond longing. The landscape of the real becomes symbolic of the way past cultures still resonate even in the uncompromising "experience" of the literary historian sighing over her books: "Climbing the dusty hill, some fair effigies that once stood for symbols of human destiny have been broken; those I still have with me, show defects in this broad light. Yet enough is left, even by experience, to point distinctly to the glories of that destiny; faint, but not to be mistaken streaks of the future day" (WNC 207 [104]). The "glitter" and the "softened" lights of prophecy and allusion reenter in the visual effects of the "streaks of . . . day" and the "dusty" effigies. The very style of allegory that Fuller cannot resist despite its anachronism is represented as almost having outlived its inspirational power. Yet, committed to reality, she feels even *within* experience the motions of divinatory witness.

Woman in the Nineteenth Century is the product of exactly such shifts between accuracy and desire, or between idealistic pluralism and feminine psychological difference. Fuller never writes in just this way again.

*   *   *

CHRISTINA ZWARG

Fuller's Scene before the Women: *Woman in the Nineteenth Century*†

Conversational Sketches

* * * Much of *Woman in the Nineteenth Century* is given over to clarifying both the difficulty and importance of establishing a viable feminist critique. Throughout the text, Fuller exhibits a powerful tendency toward a double strategy, shifting perspectives with nearly every theme she develops. Perhaps her most obvious example of this practice appears in the series of conversational sketches throughout the body of the text. Given her long interest in conversation, it is not surprising that the basic conversational structure around which she built "The Great Lawsuit" remains largely the same in *Woman*. And because the con-

† Reprinted from Christina Zwarg: *Feminist Conversations: Fuller, Emerson, and the Play of Reading*, 175–81. Copyright © 1995 by Cornell University. Used by permission of the publisher, Cornell University Press. Norton Critical Edition page references appear in brackets.

versations invariably turn on the relationship of women with men, they consistently demonstrate the efficacy of her focus on celibacy.

"The Great Lawsuit" contains three conversational sketches, two between a man and a woman and one between two women. Fuller keeps these three sketches and adds a few more when she composes *Woman*. In the first sketch, which occurs early on in both versions, we are invited to listen in on a conversation between a husband and someone whose views are obviously similar to Fuller's.[1] The husband first tries to quell all discussion of feminist issues by insisting that he had contented his wife with "indulgences." His listener immediately inquires whether the man's wife "was satisfied with these indulgences" (WNC: 18 [15]). Pressed to admit that he had never asked his wife's opinion on the matter, the husband asserts that he would never consent to let his wife discuss such issues. Somewhat incredulous, his listener insists that it is not consent from the husband that is in question, but assent from the wife (WNC: 18 [16]). When the husband responds still more defensively by asserting his role as "head of the house," his interlocutor responds by challenging the efficacy of the paternalistic metaphors of "heart" and "head." The listener appears to have the last word in this conversational sketch, yet Fuller closes the account with the observation, "Thus vaguely are these questions proposed and discussed at present" (WNC: 19 [16]). In other words, she refuses to endorse openly the position of the voice challenging patriarchy and "family union" (WNC: 18 [15]) even as she manages to show how each conversational turn between the two voices opens a potential site for critique.

Over the course of both "Lawsuit" and *Woman*, the reader learns just how completely Fuller endorses the position of the radical questioner in the first conversation. Certainly she has no difficulty showing her position in the second conversational sketch between a man and a woman which she uses in both versions.[2] Her willingness to expose her position in the second conversation derives in part from the way in which the doubts inscribed in the first are borne out by the rest of the essay. She tells her reader that she "overheard" a husband telling his wife that their daughter should not be educated because she would then be too smart to "find a husband" to "protect her" (L: 45). For the attentive reader, a terrible cycle presents itself: a woman is caught in a double bind, first through her father's "protection," which keeps her

---

1. It is interesting to note that, of the three conversations, this is the only one Fuller refuses to call her own.
2. In "The Great Lawsuit," Fuller uses this vignette toward the close, whereas in *Woman* she follows this sketch with a series of conversations, some drawn from historical contexts. Marie Urbanski points out that she probably borrowed historical examples from Lydia Maria Child's *History of the Condition of Women in Various Ages and Nations* (Boston: Otis, Broaders, 1838). See *Margaret Fuller's "Woman in the Nineteenth Century": A Literary Study of Form and Content, of Sources and Influence* (Westport, Conn.: Greenwood Press, 1980), 87. Fuller's decision not to credit Child may have reflected a desire to distance herself from the more conservative manner in which Child presented the history of women.

from developing her skills, and then through her future husband, who will likely refuse to consent to any deviation from her prescribed role as wife and mother. Unlike the first conversation, where Fuller attempts to show her reader that she will avoid taking sides, she makes clear her conviction that the father is misguided in attempting to protect his daughter. Thus she tells her women readers to "leave off asking" men to "look at both sides." She advises instead that women "retire within themselves" to "explore the groundwork of being till they find their peculiar secret" (WNC: 108 [72]).

The importance of Fuller's advice in both versions resides in the recognition that such a strategy is far more difficult than it might at first appear. This difficulty is wonderfully demonstrated in the conversational sketch placed close to the center of "The Great Lawsuit" and elaborated in *Woman*. Though only peripheral to the other conversations, Fuller is doubly central in this debate between a woman, whom she identifies as herself, and another thinly veiled autobiographical figure named Miranda. The initial version of the conversation in "The Great Lawsuit" has an air of debate. Yet the revised conversation in *Woman* actually registers the various ideological frames through which one woman must shift in order to discover her "peculiar secret."

Fuller's character adopts something of a conservative posture and deliberately expresses surprise over some of the more radical claims put forth by Miranda. Yet her character, who also acts as a foil, enhances Miranda's position without seeming to adopt it. Miranda notes that her independence was fostered by her father's generous "bias" (L: 16) toward her, making independence a matter of good fortune, rather than —as the Fuller character suggests—of some inner resolution that "the restraints of the sex were insuperable only to those who think them so, or . . . noisily strive to break them" (L: 15).

The very fact that Fuller cannot rely on a stable and unified representation of her own experience to describe the benefits of self-reliance for women, that she relies instead on a fictional rendering of her selves, emphasizes not only the constructed nature of the self as a series of subject positions in debate, but also the peculiar agency dependent on an understanding of that construction.[3] Moreover, by inserting the di-

---

3. It appears from Emerson's journals that Fuller had already engaged him in a conversation about the difficulty that the notion of self-reliance assumed when applied to women. He wrote, "In conversing with a lady it sometimes seems a bitterness & unnecessary wound to insist as I incline to, on this self sufficiency of man. There is no society, say I; there can be none. 'Very true but mournful,' replies my friend; we talk of . . . courses of action. But to women my paths are shut up and the fine women I think of who have had genius & cultivation who have not been wives but muses have something tragic in their lot & I shun to name them. Then I say Despondency bears no fruit. We do nothing whilst we distrust. It is ignoble . . . also to owe success to the coaxing & clapping of Society, to be told by the incapable, 'That's capital. Do some more.' That only is great that is thoroughly so from the egg, a god. Therefore I think a woman does herself an injustice who likens herself to any historical woman, who thinks that because Corinna or De Stael or M.M.E. do not satisfy the imagination and the serene Themis, none can, certainly not she. It needs that she feel that a new woman has a new as yet inviolate problem to solve" (JMN 5: 410).

alogue into her text in such a way that the reader cannot really be sure when the conversation between Fuller and Miranda ends, the dialogue becomes coextensive with the larger text and argument of *Woman*. The double strategy embodied in Fuller's clever use of two versions of herself in conversation becomes the method she applies to the larger body of the essay.

The Cant of Culture

One of the most significant examples of this double method occurs in "Lawsuit," when Fuller addresses the "great moral law" that "All men are born free and equal" (L: 8). Even before her journey to the Midwest, she registered some concern about the possible corruption of this idea by writing, "We are tempted to implore these 'word-heroes' these word-Catos, word-Christs, to beware of cant above all things; to remember that hypocrisy is the most hopeless as well as the meanest of crimes" (L: 9). In so doing, she effectively locates American political rhetoric in a recognizable continuum, connecting it to Greek ("word-heroes"), Roman ("word-Catos"), and Christian ("word-Christs") doctrine. Nevertheless, she backs away from a wholesale condemnation of cant. For cant originally referred to the chant of beggars in Western civilization, the song of cultural outcasts whose ranks might well include women. With this in mind, the footnote she appends to this section is extremely suggestive: "Dr. Johnson's one piece of advice should be written on every door; 'Clear your mind of cant.' But Byron, to whom it was so acceptable, in clearing away the noxious vine, shook down the building too. Stirling's [sic] emendation is note-worthy, 'Realize your cant, not cast it off' " (L: 9). Through Sterling's insistence that we "realize [our] cant," Fuller advises her reader to be attentive to cant, not only as a defense against rhetoric, but also as a map for an important cultural dynamic. We must be wary of cant and seek its origin, read it as a poem gone bad, a political oration detached from its moral context. To "realize your cant," however, is to participate in a return to its source, to follow the chant of outcasts whose song Fuller celebrates. That women literally "can't" realize the world envisioned by the high rhetoric of the culture reveals how it is, indeed, always "cant" to them, even in its most robust formulation. Thus the imperative from Sterling recalls the imperative against Woman's participation in the social world. To conceive the pun is to send us back to a rhetorical meaning never intended, making the activity of return significant.

The conflation of cant and can't in "Lawsuit" had already sharpened Fuller's focus on the problematic if not duplicitous nature of the discourse of democracy. The cant of American culture, with its emphasis on progressive equality, had clearly created a conflict of powerful proportions. And after her trip to the Midwest, it was even more obvious to her that the inevitable aspect of "the great moral law" (L: 8) of America was leading to the inevitable demise of all those who did not fit its cultural expectation. So great was the sway of this cant that Fuller's autobiographical double in *Summer on the Lakes*, Mariana, actually finds herself succumbing to a fatal end. Because she is perceived by those around her as strange, or Other, Mariana, like the Native Americans Fuller sees around her, is doomed to perish in the narrative. But upon returning to the "Great Lawsuit" after her visit to the Midwest, Fuller embellishes the feminist conversation between her narrative self and her autobiographical double, Miranda, whose echo of Mariana is inescapable. Fuller adds certain specific statements to make the complaints of Miranda more apparent, particularly when describing how women are "overloaded with precepts by guardians, who think that nothing is so much to be dreaded for a woman as originality of thought or character" (WNC: 29 [22]). In other words, she emphasizes the dread of empowering those who are considered alien.

Another revision of this type involves the addition of a poem by Ben Jonson, whose phrase "manly soul" prompts a debate between the narrator and Miranda over its suitability in praise of women. Whereas the narrator, acting as one double for Fuller, suggests that Miranda may be "too fastidious in objecting to this," Miranda insists that *manly* is so invariably used "where a heroic quality is to be described" that she "would exchange these words for others of a larger sense" (WNC: 31 [23]). Although Fuller appears to let her reader choose sides in the debate, her decision to place Miranda's version of the poem on the frontispiece of the volume reveals her overall preference in this matter.[4]

Fuller also elaborates the little conversational scenario between Miranda and a well-meaning man, who in "The Great Lawsuit" tells Miranda that she "deserved in some star to be a man" (L: 16). In *Woman*, Fuller shows her friend's disbelief when Miranda responds that it is in fact "better now to be a woman" (W: 30 [22]): "He smiled incredulous. 'She makes the best she can of it,' thought he. 'Let Jews believe in the pride of Jewry, but I am of the better sort, and know better' " (WNC: 30 [22–23]). Fuller's decision to add the tinge of anti-Semitism to the man's response ("I am of the better sort") readily reflects how her trip to the Midwest enhanced her determination to explore the cant of culture. The man demonstrates how even sympathetic responses can depend on and promulgate hateful biases. And for Fuller the same difficulty is apparent in texts that hold themselves distinct from cant.

The additions to "The Great Lawsuit" made upon Fuller's return

4. That the same poem appears on the frontispiece of the *Memoirs of Margaret Fuller Ossoli*, with the original phrase "manly soul" restored, proves one of the productive ironies of Fuller's position.

from the Midwest elaborate on the way in which the terms of valorization, words such as *manly* and *conquest*, are clues to the very structures entrapping women. In her effort to play this out, Fuller adds many more conversational sketches, sometimes borrowing them from legends and histories, and at other times drawing from her own personal experience. Most of the sketches tend to focus on the issue of marriage because—as her opening conversational sketch reveals—the relationship between husband and wife in marriage is the most obvious site of gender prescription. For her, as for Fourier, the discourse of marriage effectively followed culture as a scene of overwhelming dominance. Yet she felt it was imperative to avoid any alliance with those who were advocating a dissolution of the bond. That she is drawn into a discussion of George Sand in the middle of her section on marriage reveals how readily the issue of marriage is nevertheless aligned in her mind with the prospect of its disruption.

Fuller's sudden imposition of the issue of silence into her discussion of marriage reveals a similar kind of recognition. In a passage that serves as an important response to her opening conversational sketch between the husband and the wife, she writes:

> I do not mean to imply that community of employment is essential to the union of husband and wife, more than to the union of friends. Harmony exists in difference, no less than in likeness, if only the same key-note govern both parts. Woman the poem, man the poet! Woman the heart, man the head! Such divisions are only important when they are never to be transcended. If nature is never bound down, nor the voice of inspiration stifled, that is enough. We are pleased that women should write and speak, if they feel need of it, from having something to tell; but silence for ages would be no misfortune, if that silence be from divine command, and not from man's tradition (WNC: 68 [47]).

Just as Fuller turns celibacy into a site of feminist resistance, a place from which to critique the overwhelming forces moving women toward a repressive and uncertain experience in marriage, she also transforms the familiar attributes of silence. Of course, her focus on silence takes into consideration the fears of her reader. An audience growing anxious over the increased noise, or cant, of feminism might take comfort in her appeals on behalf of silence. In the conversation with Miranda, the Fuller character expresses concern over those who "noisily strive to break" the restraints upon women. But in Fuller's deft handling, silence is not strictly a vehicle for feminine oblivion; rather, it emerges as a form of expression that escapes traditional channels of control. Because silence must be divinely inspired, the earlier phrase "Woman the poem, man the poet!" takes on deeper political meaning. If Man insists on being the poet, he is reduced in Fuller's reading to the noisy recorder of poetry that has its counterpart in Woman's divine but silent revelation. This formulation cuts to the most radical aspect of her treatment of silence: it is not about creating more centuries of silence, but about the generation of a reading of the silence already expressed. In this way, she quietly appropriates silence for women and promotes it as a type of reading strategy.

* * *

JEFFREY STEELE

Margaret Fuller's Rhetoric of Transformation†

I

"WORDS OF A LARGER SENSE"

Between 1840 and 1844, Margaret Fuller developed a profound rhetoric of transformation that articulated her accelerating commitment to personal and social change. Many readers have been disturbed by this difficult style. In the nineteenth century, for example, Lydia Maria Child found herself perplexed by Fuller's writing, which—to her mind—exhibited "too much *effort*." "The stream is abundant and beautiful," Child commented, "but it always seem to be *pumped*, rather than to *flow*."[1] Many twentieth-century readers have shared this concern with Fuller's stylistic difficulty, prefering the relative directness and narrative simplicity of her European dispatches over the intricacy of *Woman in the Nineteenth Century*. The book's densely textured prose, complex allusions, and many digressions seem constantly to shift its ground. Discussions of contemporary social circumstances coincide with references to classical Greek and Roman goddesses. Appeals to democratic sentiments are paired with Biblical quotations and excerpts from Shakespeare. Critics continue to wrestle with this stylistic complexity. In a recent article, Annette Kolodny addressed the charge that *Woman in the Nineteenth Century* is disordered and formless by locating the roots of Fuller's textual practice in Richard Whately's *Elements of Rhetoric*, a book that she taught in Providence. Fuller, she argued, adapted many of Whately's principles in order to capture on the printed page the "spontaneity" and "polyphony of conversation."[2] According to

† First published in this Norton Critical Edition, by permission of the author. Norton Critical Edition page references appear in brackets.
1. Lydia Maria Child, *Selected Letters, 1817–1880*, ed. Milton Meltzer and Patricia G. Holland (Amherst: Univ. of Massachusetts Press, 1982), p. 212. Although Child is referring to *Summer on the Lakes*, her remarks fit the style of *Woman in the Nineteenth Century*.
2. Annette Kolodny, "Inventing a Feminist Discourse: Rhetoric and Resistance in Margaret Fuller's *Woman in the Nineteenth Century*," *New Literary History* 25 (1994): 367.

Kolodny, Fuller's commitment to "multiple voices" prevented her from using the authoritarian "coercion" of traditional male persuasion, an aggressive pattern of argumentation founded on focussed moments of emotional climax and ethical appeals to the character of the author.[3]

While this goes a long way toward explaining the rhetorical origins of Fuller's style, it does not account for the effect of political resistance generated by her writing. Fuller, we must remember, lacked the cultural authority of Richard Whately, whose handbook on rhetoric guided instructors of male divinity students. In the terms of Rachel Blau DuPlessis, she was unable to rely on "authority of tone or stasis of position" (male privileges in the nineteenth century) and was, instead, forced "to express the struggle" with the "cultural hegemony" in which she was "immersed."[4] Fuller's struggle with the ways in which her being was scripted compelled her to pair the fluidity and heterogeneity of conversation with modes of analysis that uncovered the personal effects of contemporary gender stereotypes. Presenting herself both as inscribed object and speaking subject, she examined both women's disinheritance and their potential.[5] To read Fuller well, we need to see clearly these two sides—both the pain and the ecstasy, both the grief and the joy of newly expressed human qualities. Before she could imagine a cure for the limitations confronting American women, Fuller needed to diagnose the illness that had constricted their lives. Only after she had measured their spiritual and political disenfranchisement could she define her vision of an enlarged female being.

Taking seriously the human promise mapped by her friend Ralph Waldo Emerson, Fuller believed strongly that American women—as well as men—had the right to develop self-reliance or what she termed "self-poise." But the obstacle faced by many women, she realized, was that they were "taught to learn their rule from without, not to unfold it from within."[6] At the same time, it was impossible for most women (in contrast to men like Emerson) to escape the materialistic definition of their selves as commodities. There "exists," Fuller lamented, "in the minds of men a tone of feeling toward women as toward slaves"; it is assumed "that the infinite soul can only work through them in already ascertained limits; that the gift of reason, man's highest prerogative, is allotted to them in much lower degree" (258 [18]). The consequences of such attitudes, she saw, were insidious. Rather than being addressed as independent agents with immortal souls, women (she bitterly ob-

3. Kolodny, pp. 374–75.
4. Rachel Blau DuPlessis, *The Pink Guitar: Writing as Feminist Practice* (New York and London: Routledge, 1990), p. 13.
5. Compare Julie Ellison's assertion that Fuller "occup[ies] simultaneously the positions of the object and the agent of desire," *Delicate Subjects: Romanticism, Gender, and the Ethics of Understanding* (Ithaca and London: Cornell Univ. Press, 1990), p. 217.
6. *Woman in the Nineteenth Century*, rpt. *The Essential Margaret Fuller*, ed. Jeffrey Steele (New Brunswick, N.J.: Rutgers Univ. Press, 1992), p. 262 [22]. All subsequent, parenthetical references to Fuller's works are to this edition.

served) had been treated as "bond-maids" (338 [95]) defined in physical—rather than spiritual—terms. A wife who existed only to bear children or to labor in the house fared little better than a slave in her eyes; she had become "a work-tool, an article of property" (277 [36]). The cause of such objectification, she insisted, lay with men who viewed woman "as the tool of servile labor, or the object of voluptuous indulgence" (340 [96]), not as a "soul" with "a destiny of its own" (307 [66]).

Instead of sustaining a culture that believed men and women occupied "separate spheres," Fuller imagined a world in which independence and domesticity were both male and female qualities. Challenging the widespread nineteenth-century assumption that men and women were essentially different beings, she insisted that both sexes shared masculinity and femininity in differing proportions. "Male and female represent the two sides of the great radical dualism" she observed; ". . . they are perpetually passing into one another. Fluid hardens to solid, solid rushes to fluid. There is no wholly masculine man, no purely feminine woman" (310 [69]). Although they may seem tame to twentieth-century readers, such arguments were quite radical for her age; for they directly challenged the prevailing assumption that "male" and "female" were mutually exclusive categories. "The only way in which any good can be rendered to society," Charles Briggs wrote in his review of *Woman in the Nineteenth Century*, "is by making woman more womanly and man more manly."[7] Orestes Brownson buttressed similar views with scripture: "She says man is not the head of woman. We, on the authority of the Holy Ghost, say he is. The dominion was not given to woman, not to man and woman conjointly, but to man."[8] Fuller's sin, in the eyes of Briggs and Brownson, was that she imagined in woman an independent spiritual agency beyond the control of man. Once made aware of spiritual power within herself, Fuller realized, nineteenth-century woman would be much less likely to imitate uncritically the familiar role of "model-woman of bride-like beauty and gentleness" (257 [17]). Other roles, beyond the control of male authority, might also be possible.

The result of nineteenth-century gender divisions, Fuller insisted, was a psychological and social disharmony based upon the internalization of male authority. This misconstruction of gender had led to a society that limited woman's self-development both inside and outside the home, culminating in paternalistic conceptions of marriage, restricted roles, as well as sinister forms of sexual exploitation. The women that

7. Charles F. Briggs, review of *Woman in the Nineteenth Century* (*Broadway Journal*, March 1845); rpt. Joel Myerson ed., *Critical Essays on Margaret Fuller* (Boston: G.K. Hall, 1980), p. 11.
8. Orestes A. Brownson, "Miss Fuller and Reformers," in *Brownson's Quarterly Review* 7 (April 1845); rpt. Myerson, p. 22.

Fuller saw around her had lost "harmony" with themselves and others, because they had been "seized and carried away captive" (335 [92]) by a society whose values facilitated female dependence and passivity. "Overloaded with precepts" (262 [22]), "fed on flattery" (297 [55]), and "perverted . . . by the current of opinion" (281 [41]), they had lost the "power of self-poise" (311 [70]). In response to such bondage, Fuller hoped to transform the "many incarcerated souls, that might be freed, could the idea of religious self-dependence be established in them, could the weakening habit of dependence on others be broken up" (311 [70]).

Earlier in her career, Fuller had analyzed the effects on her own character of such cultural repression. In a fragmentary "Autobiographical Romance" (written in 1840–41), she charted the effects of her father's educational practices. Her father's study, she argued, embodied the masculine ideals of American society, epitomizing a "Roman" world dedicated to an ideal of masculine power and accomplishment. In her words, the Latin texts she translated for her father dramatized "what a *man* can become . . . by a single thought, an earnest purpose, an indomitable will, by hardihood, self-command, and force of expression" (29 [147], my italics). At least for a while, Fuller argued, she internalized these values without a complete recognition of the extent to which they alienated her from herself. But by 1840, she had become acutely aware of the disastrous effects of accepting uncritically this patriarchal realm of "Roman" power.

Significantly, Fuller's analysis of her father's pedagogical methods turned into a critique that—by negative example—began to define the new style of writing that she eventually developed in *Woman in the Nineteenth Century*. Her father's instruction in "Roman" values, she recalled, enforced a rigid literary decorum:

> he demanded accuracy and clearness in everything: you must not speak, unless you can make your meaning perfectly intelligible to the person addressed; you must not express a thought, unless you can give a reason for it, if required; must not make a statement, unless sure of all particulars—such were his rules. "But," "if," "unless," "I am mistaken," and "it may be so," were words and phrases excluded from the province where he held sway.

In Fuller's terms, this masculinist standard of expression silenced in her "the subtle and indirect motions of imagination and feeling," repressing half of her personality, which "sank deep within . . . secluded and veiled over by a thick curtain of available intellect" (28 [146–47]). Fuller's goal, over the next four years, was to lift this repressive veil. In order to do so, she needed both to diagnose the static gestures of filial obedience that had frozen her life and, then, to map for herself models of an enlarged and renewed selfhood. Challenging the gender stereotypes of her age, she attempted to "exchange" its restrictive language for a new language of being, "words . . . of a larger sense" (264 [23]).

II

THE CALL OF EURYDICE

In the years immediately preceding the composition of *Woman in the Nineteenth Century*, Fuller explored what might be called a "mother tongue"—a mystical language of female being that countered the pragmatic tones of her male-dominated society. In essays such as "The Magnolia of Lake Pontchartrain" and "Leila," she imagined a divine female power located at the center of her self. Such images of maternal energy provided the foundation for a feminist rethinking of Emersonian self-reliance, revising his contention that a divine paternal center within the self authorized each person.[9] By 1843, with the composition of "The Great Lawsuit," Fuller had reached a point in her development where she began exploring the possibility that American women might also be able to achieve self-reliance by transforming themselves. The first step toward such transformation was the articulation of grief at the damage caused by restrictive gender codes. Fuller's concern with the repressed grief of American women is reflected in her striking declaration, early in "The Great Lawsuit" (and repeated in *Woman in the Nineteenth Century*) that "the time is come when Eurydice is to call for an Orpheus, rather than Orpheus for Eurydice."[1]

Journeying into the underworld in order to rescue his beloved wife Eurydice from Death, Orpheus exhibited a bravado celebrated by male Romantic artists such as Emerson and Bronson Alcott (who published his "Orphic Sayings" in *The Dial*). Having been told by Death that he could only rescue Eurydice if he did not look back until after they returned to the world of the living, Orpheus succumbed to curiosity, only to lose her once again. As Fuller knew from her study of Ovid, the call of Orpheus, the discovery of *his* poetic vocation, resulted from the loss of Eurydice to Death.[2] In this version, the story of Orpheus popularized a model of masculine artistic creativity that found

9. The classic statement of this principle is the following passage from *Nature*: "That which intellectually considered we call Reason, considered in relation to nature, we call Spirit. Spirit is the Creator. Spirit hath life in itself. And man in all ages and countries embodies it in his language as the FATHER." *Selections from Ralph Waldo Emerson*, ed. Stephen E. Whicher (Boston: Houghton Mifflin, 1957), p. 32.

1. "The Great Lawsuit," *The Dial* 4 (July 1843): 7. For ease of reference, I have used the spelling of *Woman in the Nineteenth Century*: "Eurydice" as opposed to "Euridice."

2. In her "Autobiographical Romance," Fuller remarks that "Ovid gave me not Rome, nor himself, but a view into the enchanted gardens of the Greek mythology. This path I followed, have been following ever since . . ." (30). As further confirmation of Fuller's knowledge of Ovid, it is worth noting that she refers three times in *Woman in the Nineteenth Century* to the account of Hercules and Dejanira found in book IX of the *Metamorphoses*.

its nineteenth-century analogue in Poe's infamous assertion that "the death . . . of a beautiful woman is, unquestionably, the most poetical topic in the world."[3] Silenced and objectified by male discourse, Eurydice (as well as her silenced sisters) became the occasion of *male* artistic production—an asymmetrical literary economy that occasioned much pain for women.

But in Fuller's hands, this figure took on a complexity and irony lacking in the more celebratory allusions of male writers. In place of a passive and mute Eurydice, Orpheus' muse who occasioned an endless cycle of mourning, she imagined a female agent who escapes from an economy of grief in which woman remains the most evocative signifier. Interpreting Orpheus as a symbol of man in general, she suggested that he failed to trust Eurydice (woman) enough to raise her up to his level; instead, he left her in the underworld of a half-completed psychological process. Man's having failed to rescue woman, it was time to reverse the process and allow woman to rescue man: "Eurydice is to call for an Orpheus." Saving him from his own underworld, the chasm of patriarchal prejudice, she would raise him to a higher level of self-realization. By calling Orpheus, Eurydice inaugurates a new vocation —one in which woman finds a role as the *agent*—not just the object —of artistic production. Reversing the cultural equation, Fuller's narrative disrupts the dominant tradition of male discourse.

In order to understand the importance of mourning as a central figure in Fuller's writing, we need to consider the effect of her father's sudden death on October 1, 1835, when she was twenty-five. Fuller's reaction to Timothy Fuller's premature death from cholera was complicated and delayed. In the unconscious logic of anniversary compulsion, each subsequent autumn and winter became for her a time of isolation, depression, and sickness, as her unresolved mourning inscribed itself on her body in a succession of psychological and physical ailments.[4] For nearly ten years, until the end of 1844, she experienced what her biographer Charles Capper describes as periods of "bad health and recurrent depressions."[5] Never having completed her mourning for her father, she found herself trapped each intervening year in a wintry mood that repeated the death encrypted within her. Her writing, during this period, was marked with signs of grief that measured her entrance

---

3. "The Philosophy of Composition"; rpt. in G.R. Thompson ed., *Great Short Works of Edgar Allan Poe* (New York: Harper & Row, 1970), p. 535.

4. During the months of October and November between 1837 and 1839, for example, Fuller was "miserably unwell" (L 1: 303), so ill that she "could attend to nothing that was not absolutely necessary" (L 1: 310), convinced that "the secret of all things is pain" (L 1: 347), praying that she might find some peace in "vestal solitudes" (L 1: 351), hoping that she might recover "my natural tone of health and spirits" (L 1: 352), and the victim of a three-week long headache (L 2: 98). *The Letters of Margaret Fuller*, ed. Robert Hudspeth. 6 vols. (Ithaca: Cornell UP, 1983–94).

5. Charles Capper, *Margaret Fuller: An American Romantic Life, The Private Years* (New York & Oxford: Oxford Univ. Press, 1992), p. 160.

into seasons of deep gloom—moments of emotional "winter" when the
dominant tone became one of lament.[6] In an 1838 letter, she declared,
"We are, we shall be in this life mutilated beings, but there is in my
bosom a faith that I shall sometime see the reason."[7] A succession of
personal losses—both rejections by beloved friends and the deaths of
close relatives—exacerbated this feeling of being a wounded woman.

Ultimately, Fuller was only able to finish mourning her father when
she learned how to mourn, as well, her damaged self. Beginning to see
that the passivity of the female mourner was disabling, she recognized
that her grief should be directed toward areas of damage within her
self—not toward male images. In the process, she came to see that her
position as a wounded woman, incorporating the masculinized values
of American culture, recapitulated the dependence of women in general upon patriarchal power. Generalizing her mourning into a representative posture reflecting the "bereavement" of other women, Fuller
transformed loss into agency, grief into political sympathy. At that point,
she was able to reveal the links between her grief for herself and the
paralysis of others trapped in a similar dependency. We notice such a
link in *Woman in the Nineteenth Century*, when she observes that the
great women of the past "had much to mourn, and their great impulses
did not find due scope" (267 [26]). The clear implication is that nineteenth-century women also "had much to mourn."

Juliana Schiesari's recent study, *The Gendering of Melancholia*, underscores the important connection between the representation of wom-
en's mourning and their liberation. Male writers, she argues, have
traditionally been able to use representations of loss—such as the "discourse of melancholia"—as sources of empowerment.[8] But while men
have been provided with "the most privileged access to the display of
loss," the representation of female suffering has been denigrated to the
extent that a *female* "melancholic" may be a contradiction of terms
within patriarchal definitions. At issue is the construction of a language
enabling women to represent their sense of disempowerment. Significantly, she locates such a language in the discourse of female mourning. Women, she argues, "have . . . characteristically represented their
losses through a language that approximates a mourning for their barred
or devalued status within the symbolic," language that expresses "the
structured denial of privilege for *all* women within patriarchal societies."[9] At stake, finally, is the representation of women's losses within a
culture that has inhibited the full expression of their being.

6. Julie Ellison comments on the importance of mourning to Fuller when she observes that she
constructed her literary persona as "a representative subject whose knowledge is grounded in
pain" (p. 218).
7. *Letters* 1: 331.
8. Juliana Schiesari, *The Gendering of Melancholia: Feminism, Psychoanalysis, and the Symbolics
of Loss in Renaissance Literature* (Ithaca: Cornell Univ. Press, 1992), pp. 15, 68.
9. Schiesari, pp. 31, 75, 77.

In many ways, nineteenth-century women found their lives and self-images inextricably implicated in the mourning process. Positioned within a complicated fabric of social signification that they did not control, grieving women were transformed into powerful signifiers whose actions were defined by collective cultural expectations.[1] While "the question of men and how they mourned is little mentioned in the literature of the period," women observed a complicated set of "mourning rituals" that were "symbolic of [their] place in the world."[2] During the first half of the nineteenth century, instruction in the iconography of mourning was a standard part of women's social indoctrination. In numerous finishing schools, girls were taught how to compose mourning pictures and samplers—training that imprinted on them the image of the female mourner as the natural signifier of grief. One widespread emblem was modeled upon an engraving by James Akin and William Farrison, Jr., entitled "America Lamenting Her Loss at the Tomb of General Washington." Beneath a weeping willow, a grieving woman leans against a pyramid emblazoned with the bust of Washington.[3] Both the drapery and posture of the female mourner suggest grief but also total submission to an absent (yet omnipresent) male authority. Duplicated on numerous samplers, this popular icon represented a female abjection conjoining grief with worship of male power.

One of Fuller's most important terms for this posture of abjection is "idolatry." "I wish woman to live, *first* for God's sake," she observed in *Woman in the Nineteenth Century*; "Then she will not make an imperfect man her god, and thus sink to idolatry" (346 [103]). This discussion of female idolatry identified the culturally induced passivity of women as the occasion for a grief that must be mourned. Luce Irigaray's critique of Freud's psychoanalytic theories helps to clarify the connection between such idolatry and mourning. Commenting upon Freud's theory of female "castration," Irigaray suggests that masculinist constructions of the female self motivate a profound but unlocalized melancholy for women, who are taught that their bodies and psyches manifest a fundamental lack. As a result of such indoctrination, Irigaray argues, a woman's "ego suffers, helplessly, a defeat, a wound, whose effects are to be made out in the broad outlines of melancholia."[4] Having been "castrated" by an ideology that misconstrues her being, she

1. According to Barton Levi St. Armand: "The image of the mourning maiden had archetypal resonances for the popular culture" of mid-nineteenth-century America. *Emily Dickinson and Her Culture: The Soul's Society* (Cambridge, Eng.: Cambridge Univ. Press, 1984), p. 42.
2. Martha Pike, "In Memory Of: Artifacts Relating to Mourning in Nineteenth-Century America" in *Rituals and Ceremonies in Popular Culture*, ed. Ray B. Browne (Bowling Green, Ohio: Bowling Green Univ. Press, 1980), pp. 310, 312.
3. Betty Ring, *Let Virtue Be a Guide to Thee: Needlework in the Education of Rhode Island Women, 1730–1830* (Providence: Rhode Island Historical Society, 1983), p. 160. Numerous variations on pose are represented in Ring, pp. 171–89.
4. Luce Irigaray, *Speculum of the Other Woman*, trans. Gillian C. Gill (Ithaca: Cornell Univ. Press, 1985), p. 69.

has structured within her psyche an undefinable loss, because in melancholia "one cannot see clearly what it is that has been lost."[5] Mutilated by the ideological context that gives her the very language of selfhood, the female subject is unable to mourn her status as a wounded woman. In order to escape this disabling posture, to return to Fuller's terminology, she needs to recognize the frozen posture of idolatry that had encoded within her a vocabulary of lack.

Fuller came to realize that the circumscribed roles of conventional womanhood (reflected in the classic male narrative of Orpheus) constituted an original trauma that most of her contemporaries did not know how to heal. Internalizing the image of the Father as an icon of power and authority, most of her female contemporaries failed to recognize that the postures of conventional womanhood were fundamentally alienating. As a result, they were incapable of seeing the damage caused by the incorporation within their psyches of images of an untouchable male power. Like the mourning women memorialized on countless samplers, they were locked into gestures of abject worship— postures that replicated the gender imbalances of their society. Mourning at the grave of the Father, they kept *his* image alive—locating it in a shrine outside of their own sphere of power. They sacrificed at the shrine of the Father but failed to mourn themselves. Fuller's revision of the myth of Orpheus and Eurydice began to overcome this alienated position; for it expressed her convinction that nineteenth-century women needed to grieve for that part of their selves imprisoned with Eurydice in the underworld.

III

RECOVERING THE "IDEA OF WOMAN"

An essential part of Fuller's transformation of women's grief into victory involved her representation of what she called the "idea of woman." Defining sites of female potential, her numerous portraits in *Woman in the Nineteenth Century* of great women and powerful female types enabled her to chart undeveloped areas of female being, at the same time they demonstrated that energy and creativity were not only masculine attributes. Anticipating Emerson's *Representative Men*, they provided a gallery of "representative women" who served as ontological templates mapping different images of female being. This pantheon of representative women—historical personages, famous writers, literary characters, and goddesses—defined a wide repertoire of subject-positions, each one articulating a different model of female power. At the same time, this array of female figures fractured and multiplied the limited reflections of selfhood mirrored for American women. It em-

5. *Speculum*, p. 67. Irigaray is playing with Freud's concept of "penis envy."

bodied a 'both/and' style that countered the 'either/or' world faced Fuller's contemporaries.[6]

Multiplying sites of identification, Fuller's style overthrows dominant patterns of authority and subordination. Instead of enforcing a single center of textual authority, it provides multiple sites of readerly identification that differ markedly from identification patterns in texts by nineteenth-century male writers. For example, the rhetoric of both Emerson and Whitman depends upon the presence of a single male persona who functions as a single site of identification—what Lawrence Buell has called an "exemplary persona."[7] These personae sometimes change their dimensions; but, ultimately, there is a single male voice controlling the reader's identification. On a superficial level, the memorable figure of Miranda in *Woman in the Nineteenth Century* might seem like such an "exemplary persona" modeling the reader's transformation. But in contrast to Emerson's speakers, Miranda is not given authority over the entire text. Instead, she is contained and localized when Fuller's unnamed narrator engages her in dialogue. This surprising maneuver radically subverts Fuller's own narrative authority by distancing her from her most powerful and eloquent representative. At the same time, it decenters her text by removing its dramatic center in favor of a medley of voices that displaces any single voice from exemplary status. Instead of attracting the reader to a single center, Fuller offers a number of figures that might function as an effective node of identification. In and of itself, this decentering of authority and multiplication of female roles makes an important political statement in an age when women found their choices and their roles severely limited.

Functioning as an idealized version of her self (a kind of ego ideal), Miranda represents Fuller's best example of what contemporary American woman might accomplish. Able to take "a course of her own" in which "no man stood in her way," she exemplifies the self-culture that Fuller hopes to instill in her female readers. In an echo of Emerson's famous dictum, Miranda asserts that "the position I early was enabled to take was one of self-reliance." "And were all women as sure of their wants as I was," she continues, "the result would be the same." Unfortunately, Miranda observes, most women are "so overloaded with precepts by guardians" that "their minds are impeded by doubts" (262 [22]). In contrast to such limitation, Miranda offers her own education as a model: the "early trust" of her father, she declares, "gave the first bias," training her to be "a living mind" and a "temple of immortal intellect" (262, 261 [22, 21]). This image of paternal nurturance provides a marked contrast to Fuller's portrait of her father in the 1840 "Autobiographical Romance." Three years later in "The Great

---

6. DuPlessis argues for a "both/and vision" in "For the Etruscans," *The Pink Guitar*, p. 6.
7. Lawrence Buell, *Literary Transcendentalism: Style and Vision in the American Renaissance* (Ithaca and London: Cornell Univ. Press, 1973), p. 289.

Lawsuit," we observe, she was able to dissociate the image of Timothy Fuller from that of the destructive patriarchal Father, an identification that she had made when she identified her father's Roman character as the source of her psychological and physical suffering. Now she represented Miranda's father as a source of strength, providing the intellectual and spiritual discipline that founded her self-reliance.

Having exemplified one type of female excellence (the "idea of woman"), Fuller follows Miranda with an imposing collection of representative women. She links famous historical personages such as Countess Emily Plater and Queen Elizabeth with literary characters (for example, Shakespeare's many heroines). Biblical figures (Eve and Mary) join with a pantheon of classical goddesses (Isis, Ceres, Proserpine, Diana), each figure embodying a different facet of female being. As she continues, Fuller is careful to provide models for the different members of her audience, whatever their marital status or political persuasion. In contrast to her culture, which provides a narrow range of possible female roles, she multiplies types in a carnivalesque barrage of character sketches that, through its very excess, transcends any effort to impose arbitrary barriers on the lives of women. The transformative potential of Fuller's conversational style is evident in the way she keeps multiplying examples, in opposition to formal rules of social subordination and rhetorical development.

Fuller's catalogue of representative women leads directly into a lengthy discussion of marriage. For the married members of her audience she provides numerous examples of married excellence, at the same time she defines a scale of increasing marital perfection (ranging from the "household partnership," through "mutual idolatry" and "intellectual companionship," to the "religious" union). But distinctively, she interrupts her description of married types with a lengthy digression discussing two female "outlaws"—Mary Wolstonecraft and George Sand (Madame Dudevant). In a kind of rhetorical compensation, the representation of more traditional married women evokes its opposite —transgressive women who challenged society's norms. "Such beings as these," Fuller asserts, "ought not to find themselves, by birth, in a place so narrow, that, in breaking bonds, they become outlaws" (284 [44]). Transgressing the norms of her society, Fuller turns this process of outlawing back on itself. Refusing to "be reduced" to a set of values that would exclude such brilliant women, her representation of their exclusion "points to the place and manner of [woman's] exploitation."[8] Mentioning the unmentionable, Fuller shocks her audience into an awareness of repressive gender norms.

By deliberately transgressing her society's values, the narrator exhibits

8. Mary Jacobus, "The Question of Language: Men of Maxims and *The Mill on the Floss*," *Critical Inquiry* 8 (1981): 211.

a power akin to Miranda's "strong electric nature, which repelled those who did not belong to her, and attracted those who did" (262 [21]). Nineteenth-century mesmerists and phrenologists believed that human beings manifested an electrical magnetic aura that linked them with others—a force-field manipulated by the male physician to cure his (primarily) female patients. Reversing the polarity, Fuller asserts the ability of Miranda and her "sisters" to affect those around her. As her argument develops, Fuller's depiction of "the electrical, the magnetic element in woman" (302 [61]) begins to play an increasingly prominent part, supplementing passive female values with more active qualities. We see the embodiment of this power in Fuller's assertion that marriage is not the only possible role for women. An even more complete self-reliance, she insists, is possible for single women, "undistracted by other relationships," who gain "a closer communion with the one" (that is, with the divine center of being authorizing personal independence). Since woman, she argues, is "a being of infinite scope," she "must not be treated with an exclusive view to any one relation" (i.e., marriage) (298–99 [56]).

It is no accident that Fuller places this controversial argument *after* her discussion of more traditional female roles. Having placated her audience, she begins to define a model of female power that directly challenges nineteenth-century definitions of womanhood. Fuller's representations of a transgressive female "electricity" disturbed many contemporary readers, who found it difficult to imagine female wildness in morally neutral terms. The wild woman, in their terms, was a "fallen" woman; for it was unimaginable that a "respectable" woman would manifest an energy that was not carefully contained and culturally focussed. Fuller disrupts such stereotypes through her assertion that women embody an "electricity," a pool of volatile psychic energy that "frighten[s] those around them" (302 [62]). Through images of such uncontrollable energy, she addresses the cultural pressures that had demonized the productive power of women, excluding it from definitions of respectable society.

Many women, Fuller continues, have suffered because they have been unable to find a lifestyle that allowed the full expression of such energy. Unable to achieve a "harmony" in their lives (such as that provided by a suitable marriage), they were "*over*-flowed with thought," "over-charged" by a power that had no effective outlet (303 [62]). Such was the fate of Cassandra, whose prophetic gifts were mocked by her companions, and of the Seeress of Prevorst, a famous mesmeric medium who failed to find a world corresponding with her spiritual powers.[9] In order to realize the full potential of such women, she asserts, a

---

9. In *Summer on the Lakes*, Fuller observes that the Seeress "was obliged hourly to forsake her inner home, to provide for an outer, which did not correspond with it" (153).

new psychological language is necessary—a language that she provides in her discussion of the "the Muse and Minerva." Each mythical figure, she argues, represents a part of woman's personality, what she calls "the two aspects of woman's nature" (309 [68]): the "feminine" and "masculine," the emotional and the intellectual, the imaginative and the interpretive sides of the self.

Fuller's image of the Muse taps into, but radically expands, the familiar stereotype of the "true woman."[1] But if the "true woman" was pious, pure, domestic, and submissive, Fuller's "Muse" retains primarily vestiges of the first two—piety and purity—at the same time that she embodies a power that transcends domesticity and submissiveness. Attacking conventional stereotypes of womanhood, Fuller directly confronts those who would "mark out with precision the limits of woman's sphere" (257 [17]). Her "Muse"—like the Seeress of Prevorst and Cassandra—expresses a potentially transgressive female power. Rather than embodying a reassuring domesticity, this figure suggests that beneath the civilized veneer of female selfhood exists a powerful creative energy that has the capacity to disrupt conventional definitions of femininity. The figure of the "Muse" transforms familiar qualities of beauty, piety, and purity by associating them with what Fuller identifies as woman's "electricity," a power that shatters the attempt to idealize and contain the "lyrical" side of woman's being.

Then, by pairing the Muse with the Minerva as the two sides of female being, Fuller takes her transformative paradigm to a new level. For the act of balancing the subversive potential of the "Muse's" passionate energy against the intellectual discipline of "Minerva" comments directly upon the repressive limitations of conventional female roles. As the shadow of the Muse (linked to the "true woman"), Minerva points toward the "wild zone" of female qualities suppressed by the dominant culture. One of the most warlike of the classical goddesses, Minerva (or Athena, as she is otherwise known) embodies a fierce independence, what Fuller calls "the virgin, steadfast soul" (316 [75]). This figure evokes a set of female qualities—traits such as intelligence, strength, and will—that most nineteenth-century Americans usually gendered masculine. Then, by associating female strength with virginity, Fuller went even further, striking at the very heart of middle-class definitions of the maternal as the ideal female characteristic. Her use of the virgin as a symbol of self-reliance, reflecting the ancient ideal of virgin goddess beyond male control, defined a vision of independent womanhood so threatening that it evoked the misunderstanding and anger of many of her reviewers, who were unwilling

1. Barbara Welter, "The Cult of True Womanhood," *Dimity Convictions: The American Woman in the Nineteenth Century* (Athens: Ohio Univ. Press, 1976), p. 21.

to see the unmarried Minerva (or analogues such as an American Indian woman "betrothed to the sun") as a model of female being.[2]

Fuller's lengthy discussion of prostitution (an even more controversial element that she added in 1844 as she expanded "The Great Lawsuit" into *Woman in the Nineteenth Century*) works out the implications of asserting the independent spiritual agency of women. She rejects the view that certain women are soul-less and hence beyond redemption and insists that the spiritual dignity of all women must be recognized. By asserting that the spiritual essence is female, as well as male, Fuller removes woman from the position of being defined solely in terms of her body. At the same time, she overturns the prevailing stereotype that spirit is masculine and body or nature female. In a striking reversal of this stereotype, she defines *man* in physical terms, as a being who all-too-often fails to control his "brute nature" and who sometimes acts like a "Satyr" (322 [80]). American men, she argues, have become degraded by failing to exercise control "over the lower self" (333 [90]). Indulging their physical appetites, they have defended a self-serving double standard that allows them to seduce women and frequent prostitutes. Instead of looking at prostitution as a social evil, they defend it as a necessary sexual outlet; so that, in New York, "legislators admit that ten thousand prostitutes are a fair proportion to one city" (330 [87]).

In her concern with the plight of the poor and victimized women of New York, Fuller allied herself with the New York Female Moral Reform Society, which fought to eliminate prostitution and to assist imprisoned women.[3] Reflecting the interests of the new urban "moral reform" societies, she began to question the standards of a society that incarcerated female prostitutes and "vagrants" without addressing the social factors that contributed to their delinquency. Significantly, a number of well-known female authors were drawn in the 1840s and 1850s to the new reform movements in New York.[4] Near the end of *Woman in the Nineteenth Century*, Fuller echoes the concerns of these societies, which had established themselves as guardians of sexual pro-

2. Charles F. Briggs, for example, responded to the image of Minerva in March 1845 by attacking Fuller and her text at what seemed the most vulnerable point—her unmarried, virginal status. "Woman is nothing but as a wife," Briggs pontificates; "How, then, can she truly represent the female character who has never filled it? No woman can be a true woman, who has not been a wife and mother." Rpt. in Myerson ed., *Critical Essays on Margaret Fuller*, pp. 9–10.
3. In her chapter "Association," Barbara J. Berg provides an excellent overview of the activities of this and other female moral reform societies, *The Remembered Gate: Origins of American Feminism* (Oxford and New York: Oxford Univ. Press, 1978).
4. In 1844, two years before she published *Life in Prairie Land*, Eliza Farnham became the matron of the women's division of Sing Sing Prison in Ossining, New York. In 1848 Catharine Sedgwick, the author of *Letters from Abroad to Kindred at Home* (1841) was selected the "first director" of the Women's Prison Association. In the 1850s, Caroline Kirkland, known for *A New Home, Who'll Follow?* (1839), served on the executive committee of the Home for Discharged Female Convicts.

priety, in her advocacy of "a senate of matrons . . . who should decide what candidates were fit for admission to their houses and the society of their daughters" (332 [90]). Recognizing a bond with the "fallen" women of New York, Fuller had begun visiting female prisoners by end of 1844, as she was putting the finishing touches on *Woman in the Nineteenth Century*. Commenting near the end of her book on the need to care for these abandoned and imprisoned women of New York, she insisted that middle class American women take on responsibility for their less fortunate sisters: "Seek out these degraded women, given them tender sympathy, counsel, employment. Take the place of mothers, such as might have saved them originally" (329 [87]). Such maternal care had been the tie that bound Fuller's close circle of women's friends and which animated the "Conversations" that she organized for Boston women between 1839 and 1844. Now it became a principle of organized political action.

IV

A "WOMAN BETROTHED TO THE SUN"

This maternal strain became dominant in Fuller's writing during 1844, while she was revising and expanding "The Great Lawsuit." In one of her poems that year, "To the Face Seen in the Moon," she imagined herself as sharing maternal qualities, such as the "soft Mother's smile." Writing to her friend Caroline Sturgis, she suggested a maternal relationship to her younger brothers by observing: "I did not know then I should have such a large family of sons."[5] In a September letter to Sarah Shaw, she asserted: "If you can feel towards me as a Mother, after knowing me so long, I should not be afraid to accept the sacred trust."[6] In another letter, she compared herself to the goddess Ceres seeking for her lost child, Persephone.[7] Fuller's reference to "Ceres" corresponds to numerous passages in her 1844 poetry where she evokes powerful goddesses or archetypal female powers: the waxing moon, Virgin Mother, Leila, Diana, Hecate, Sphinx, and Isis. Fuller's actions by the end of 1844—her visits with female prisoners at Sing-Sing and her growing commitment to the plight of abandoned and imprisoned women—suggest that such goddess-figures both symbolized her own creative power and defined a relationship of maternal care toward her forgotten "sisters."

Underlying Fuller's myth of maternal care was a set of mythic images that linked her writing to powerful strains of nineteenth-century female

5. *Letters* 3: 197.
6. *Letters* 3: 225–26.
7. Commenting on the possibility that Caroline Sturgis may not be able to visit her in New York, she observes: "But if not so, Ceres is well accustomed to wander, seeking the other Magna Dea, and to be refused the cup of milk by the peasant" (*Letters* 3:220).

spirituality. Some nineteenth-century reformers, for example, produced images of "Woman-Power" and even of female messiahs.[8] In England, Joanna Southcott, "the Woman clothed with the sun," had become the focus of a cult that worshiped the image of liberated woman as the bride of Christ.[9] In America, the Shakers, who followed a female Redeemer "Mother Ann" Lee, based their alternative community upon the belief "that God had a dual nature, part male and part female."[1] Fuller's writing participated in a related culture of radical female spirituality. In 1841, her mystical sketches "The Magnolia of Lake Pontchartrain" and "Leila" both dramatized a maternal power lying outside the realm of the Father. In "The Great Lawsuit" and *Woman in the Nineteenth Century*, this maternal power manifested itself in a number of powerful images: the divine child, the "woman betrothed to the sun," and the "sacred marriage."

Fuller, at times, imagined the transformation of the self as the birth of a divine child within the soul. In the opening pages of *Woman in the Nineteenth Century*, she observed: "Could we say what we want, could we give a description of the child that is lost, he would be found" (250 [10]). We find a similar pattern in an 1840 letter to Caroline Sturgis, where she exclaimed:

> . . . I could bless myself like the holy Mother. But like her I long to be virgin. . . . Does a star point out the spot. The gifts I must receive, yet for my child, not me. I have no words, wait till he is of age, then hear *him* Oh Caroline, my soul swells with the future. . . .[2]

Longing "to be a virgin" like the "holy Mother," Fuller imagined being transformed by a divine wind analogous to the Holy Spirit impregnating Mary in the first chapter of *Luke*.[3] Depicting her psyche as a receptive womb fertilized by a divine spirit, she envisioned a spiritual insemination and pregnancy in which her "soul swells" and eventually gives birth to a divine "child" that has gestated within. In this psychological myth, the frozen condition of mourning eventually gives way to new spiritual powers imagined in her letter to Sturgis as a divine "child," "seed," and "Phenix."[4]

Fuller's imagery echoes the language of Louis Claude de Saint-Martin, an eighteenth-century French mystic later cited near the beginning of *Woman in the Nineteenth Century* as an example of "a new

---

8. Barbara Taylor, *Eve and the New Jerusalem: Socialism and Feminism in the Nineteenth Century* (New York: Pantheon, 1983), pp. 157ff.
9. Taylor, pp. 162–66.
1. Barbara Welter, "The Feminization of American Religion," in *Dimity Convictions*, p. 87.
2. *Letters* 2: 167.
3. Sandra M. Gustafson also relates this pattern to Anne Hutchinson, who described "her redeemed soul impregnated with Christ." "Margaret Fuller and the Forms of Sentiment," *American Quarterly* 47, No. 1 (March 1995), p. 51.
4. *Letters* 2: 167–69.

hour in the day of man" (250 [10]). In *Le Nouvel homme* (or *The New Man*), Saint-Martin depicted in detail the process of psychological transformation needed to make the new, spiritual man. Before "divinity penetrates us," he argued, "it must traverse us in our ignominy and in our grief."[5] After "nourishing within ourselves the . . . grief of spirit," we reach a moment of "virginity" and then "the annunciation takes place in us, and not before long we perceive that the holy conception has taken place in us as well."[6] Finally, there appears in the soul the "infant annunciated in you by the angel."[7] Esther Harding's book *Woman's Mysteries* provides a useful gloss for such evocative images of spiritual annunciation and insemination. Citing Meister Eckhart's observation that God can be "born anew within the soul," Harding interprets mythological accounts of virgin birth as symbols signalling "the birth of [a] new individuality, which replaces . . . woman's ego."[8] Fuller uses such psychological language in *Woman in the Nineteenth Century* when she argues that only through woman's "pure child, or influence, shall the new Adam, the redemption, arise" (301 [60]). Carrying to term the new self emerging within her psyche, the self-reliant woman finds growing within a divine power that Fuller links to narratives of the Virgin Mary, Joanna Southcott, and the great Mother Goddesses of classical antiquity.[9]

In Fuller's psychological mythmaking, the first stage of this process —the moment of annunciation—occurs when a woman is "betrothed to the Sun" (301 [59]). The fruit of this union is a new self that Fuller described as the "pure child." We find an early version of this model of psychic conception in Fuller's poem of January 1, 1841, where she portrayed the "wedlock" of the "all-embracing Sun and Moon," joined together in cosmic harmony (17). Fuller's reference to the "all-embracing Sun and Moon" echoes the language of one of her favorite books—Goethe's *Faust*.[1] Similarly, her vision of cosmic union recapitulates the mystical conjunction of Helen and Faust later in act three —a scene that portrays a sacred marriage within the psyche "in which the King and Queen—analogous to [the alchemical figures of] Sol and Luna—bring to birth the Divine Child."[2] Adapting such mystical figures in *Woman in the Nineteenth Century*, Fuller depicted the birth of

5. Louis Claude de Saint-Martin, *Le Nouvel homme* (1792; rpt. New York: Verlag, 1986), p. 31.
6. Saint-Martin, pp. 46–47, 32.
7. Saint-Martin, p. 89.
8. M. Esther Harding, *Woman's Mysteries: Ancient and Modern* (1971; rpt. New York: Harper & Row, 1976), pp. 153–54.
9. The pregnant Southcott became the center of a short-lived cult, after she declared that she was carrying the second Messiah—a prophecy documented in *The Book of Wonders* (1813–14).
1. *Faust*, Part II, act one. In Philip Wayne's translation, the Astrologer discusses the moment "when the Sun is married to the Moon,/ Silver with gold," *Faust, Part Two* (Harmondsworth, England & New York: Penguin Books, 1959), p. 34.
2. Alice Raphael, *Goethe and the Philosopher's Stone* (New York: Garrett, 1965), p. 188.

a new self from the conjunction of gendered opposites, the male and female qualities that her culture had kept separated.

In 1844, she portrayed a similar mystical marriage in the poem "Double Triangle, Serpent and Rays"—the text that, in her 1844 journal, glossed the alchemical emblem she printed at the opening of *Woman in the Nineteenth Century*:

> Patient serpent, circle round,
> Till in death thy life is found;
> Double form of godly prime
> Holding the whole thought of time,
> When the perfect two embrace,
> Male & female, black & white,
> Soul is justified in space,
> Dark made fruitful by the light;
> And, centred in the diamond Sun,
> Time & Eternity are one. (233 [195])

This symbol of ecstatic union between "Male and female, black & white" balances what Fuller called "the two sides of the great radical dualism."[3] It defines a symbol of psychic wholeness that resolves, at least temporarily, the contradictions of psychic existence.[4]

In another important 1844 poem, "To the Face Seen in the Moon," Fuller again described the achievement of psychological equilibrium as the balancing of the masculine and feminine sides of the psyche. This poem opens by evoking the "soft Mother's smile" of the consoling moon. But as she meditates, the Poet realizes that the maternal side of her personality has covered another face that has been partially obscured: "the male eye" that looks "So mildly, stedfastly but mournfully" (241). At the climax of this poem, the heart's crypt opens to reveal the presence of both masculine and feminine power. Both "Moon and Sun" rise together, while the Poet weds the "Man in the Moon," what she calls her "Apollo." Balancing both the masculine and feminine sides of the personality, this poem dramatizes a "union" of the self—a moment of ecstatic communion in which both King and Queen are enthroned within.

From "the union of this tragic king and queen," Fuller observed in one of her journals, "shall be born a radiant sovereign self" balancing what she termed the "Woman in me" and the "Man in me" (or what *Woman in the Nineteenth Century* labels the "Muse" and the "Minerva" sides of the female psyche).[5] At its most ecstatic, Fuller's vision

3. *The Dial* 4 (July 1843): 43.
4. In her Jungian study of Goethe, Alice Raphael argues that the carbuncle, the divine child, and this symbol of interlocking triangles are interchangeable symbols, all representing psychic totality or equilibrium (p. 175).
5. *The Memoirs of Margaret Fuller Ossoli*, ed. Ralph Waldo Emerson, James Freeman Clarke, and William Henry Channing. 2 Vols. (Boston: Phillips, Sampson & Co., 1852), 2: 136.

of this "Union in the Soul" (378 [136]) culminates in what she calls "sacred marriage" (the title of the poem concluding *Woman in the Nineteenth Century*). Embodying such psychological harmony, the dominant figure of *Woman in the Nineteenth Century* is a composite of the Madonna (272 [32]), "the betrothed of heaven" (273 [32]), and the woman of "vestal loveliness" (275 [35]) who is "betrothed to the Sun" (301 [59]). Escaping from the subordinate position of "idolatry," this figure defines a model of female selfhood that balances "masculine" and "feminine" features within the psyche, instead of subordinating woman to the male world outside of her.[6] The masculine is localized as *part* of the self; it is no longer a dominant power setting the terms of female being.

V

"SOME FAIR EFFIGIES . . . HAVE BEEN BROKEN"

Rarely does Fuller—in contrast to her prominent male contemporaries—position herself on heights or promontories commanding vistas spread out at her feet. But one such moment occurs near the end of *Woman in the Nineteenth Century*. Climbing a "dusty hill," the narrator perceives that "some fair effigies that once stood for symbols of human destiny have been broken" (348 [104]). Significantly, Fuller does not survey the docile expanse of a feminized nature; rather she situates herself—as she situates her writing—into a complicated intertextual terrain that evokes the monuments of past discourse. The brokenness of these "effigies" (as Fuller calls them) anticipates Friedrich Nietzsche's iconoclastic (literally, idol-smashing) assertion that he philosophized with a hammer; it imagines a cultural terrain in which the icons of authority have been toppled. As Margaret Fuller invented for herself a new rhetoric of transformation, she began to shatter the idols and the "idolatry" that imprisoned American women in a world of male-defined standards. Sharing Emerson's conviction that a divine center within the self had the potential to authorize independent action, she mapped in *Woman in the Nineteenth Century* a series of powerful maternal symbols. At the same time, the style and structure of this text defined a feminist response to the dominant patriarchal tongue in which Fuller and other American women had been "saturated."[7]

Searching for a terrain outside of the Father's linguistic "province," Fuller developed a conversational and intertextual style that multiplied images of potential female being. Her many representations of the "idea of woman" elide into each other in a decentered syntax that undercuts

6. Esther Harding, *Woman's Mysteries: Ancient and Modern* (New York: Harper & Row, 1976), pp. 153, 187.
7. DuPlessis, p. 26.

the Father's law and language through a movement of "ceaseless displacement."[8] The effect of this intertextual multiplication is to replace the Father's authority with a medley of voices, each of which slips from any centralized control or containment. Connection with any of these sites entails a process of transformation; for each domain offers a different style of writing the self and its relationships. This multiplication of intertexts, to use the language of Verena Conley, undoes traditional "hierarchies and oppositions" through "a braiding of voices, or multiple resonances of textual echoes."[9]

Using decentered patterns of intertextuality, Fuller "disrupts" and "rewrites" the monologic textual practice enforced in the father's study.[1] The labor of her decentered rhetoric—like that of Nietzsche's anti-Hegelian aphoristic style—was to demonstrate that the image of centralized male authority was an illusion. Drawing us away from the center into a realm of conversational excess and textual vagrancy, her writing exposes the illusion that compelled Timothy Fuller (or which might compel *any* father) to force his young daughter to stand before him and dutifully recite the catechism of Rome's imperialistic law—a literary decorum that demanded precision, accuracy, clearness (in other words, filial obedience). On the pages of *Woman in the Nineteenth Century*, we leave behind—once and for all—Timothy Fuller's study, a world where "the free flow of life" was replaced with "confinement" (34 [152]). In the end, much of the transformative potential of Fuller's rhetoric resides in its self-conscious abandonment of such a male-dominated empire of signs.

8. The phrase "ceaseless displacement" is from Hélène Cixous, "Sorties" in Hélène Cixous and Catherine Clément, *The Newly Born Woman* (Minneapolis: Univ. of Minnesota Press, 1986), p. 97.
9. Verena Andermatt Conley, "Introduction" to Hélène Cixous, *Reading with Clarice Lispector* (Minneapolis: Univ. of Minnesota Press, 1990), pp. vii, x.
1. Conley, p. viii: "*écriture féminine* disrupts social practices in the ways it both discerns and literally rewrites them."

Margaret Fuller: A Chronology

1810 May 23, Sarah Margaret Fuller is born in Cambridgeport, Massachusetts, the first child of Timothy Fuller and Margarett Crane Fuller.

1813 Death of fourteen-month-old sister, Julia Adelaide.

1818 Meets Ellen Kilshaw, British visitor, the "first friend" described in "Autobiographical Romance."

1824 Attends Miss Prescott's Young Ladies' Seminary in Groton, Massachusetts, for a year.

1831 Thanksgiving, has spiritual crisis and mystical experience.

1833 Moves with family to farm at Groton, Massachusetts. Tutors four youngest siblings; translates Goethe's *Torquato Tasso*.

1835 Makes plans to go to Europe. October 1, Timothy Fuller dies suddenly from cholera.

1836 Meets Ralph Waldo Emerson. Begins teaching at Bronson Alcott's Temple School in Boston.

1837 Joins Transcendental Club. Begins eighteen months of teaching at Greene Street School in Providence, Rhode Island.

1839 Sells farm and moves to Jamaica Plain, Massachusetts. Begins first series of "Conversations" for women in Boston, which will continue until 1844. Publishes translation of *Eckermann's Conversations with Goethe*.

1840 Begins two-year editorship of the *Dial*. Participates in intense personal relations with Emerson, Caroline Sturgis, Anna Barker, and Samuel Gray Ward. Undergoes a religious conversion experience in the fall, apparently related to the October 3 marriage of Barker and Ward, both of whom she loved.

1841 Publishes "Leila" in the *Dial*.

1842 Publishes translation of *Correspondence of Fräulein Günderode with Bettine von Arnim*. Visits with Emersons and Hawthornes in Concord.

1843 Publishes "The Great Lawsuit" in the *Dial*. Travels to the Great Lakes and Wisconsin Territory with Sarah Freeman Clarke; forms strong attachment to their young guide, William Clarke.

1844   Concludes final series of "Conversations" in Boston. Publishes *Summer on the Lakes, in 1843*. Suffers depression, apparently related to failed relationship with William Clarke. Spends summer in Concord with Emersons and Hawthornes. Goes to Fishkill Landing on the Hudson River to complete *Woman in the Nineteenth Century*. Visits female convicts in Sing-Sing prison. Moves to New York City and becomes literary editor and social critic for Horace Greeley's *New-York Tribune*.

1845   Publishes *Woman in the Nineteenth Century*. Meets and falls in love with James Nathan, a German businessman, who leaves her.

1846   Publishes *Papers on Literature and Art*. Sails for Europe with Marcus and Rebecca Spring. Serves as foreign correspondent for the *Tribune*. Visits England, Scotland, and France; meets Thomas Carlyle, Joseph Mazzini, George Sand, and Adam Mickiewicz.

1847   Leaves France for Italy. Meets Giovanni Angelo Ossoli in Rome. Travels in northern Italy and Switzerland from June to October. Returns to Rome alone. Takes Ossoli as her lover; becomes pregnant.

1848   Spring, revolutions break out throughout Europe. Leaves Rome for the mountains; September 5, son, Angelo Ossoli, is born in Rieti, Italy. Returns to Rome in November and witnesses the attack on the Quirinal Palace and Pope Pius IX's flight from the city.

1849   February, Roman Republic proclaimed. April through June, witnesses seige of Rome; nurses the wounded who fall in the defense of the city. When Roman Republic falls and French troops restore the Pope to power, moves to Florence with Ossoli and Angelo. Works on manuscript "History of the Late Revolutionary Movements in Italy."

1850   Publishes last of her European dispatches. Sails for the United States on the *Elizabeth*. July 19, drowns with Ossoli and child in a shipwreck off Fire Island, New York.

Selected Bibliography

• Bullet indicates works included in or excerpted for this Norton Critical Edition.

BIBLIOGRAPHIES

Hudspeth, Robert N. "Margaret Fuller." In *The Transcendentalists: A Review of Research and Criticism*. Ed. Joel Myerson. New York: Modern Language Association of America, 1984. 175–88.

Myerson, Joel. *Margaret Fuller: An Annotated Secondary Bibliography*. New York: Burt Franklin & Company, 1977.

Myerson, Joel. *Margaret Fuller: A Descriptive Bibliography*. Pittsburgh: University of Pittsburgh Press, 1978.

FULLER'S WRITINGS

The Essential Margaret Fuller. Ed. Jeffrey Steele. New Brunswick, N.J.: Rutgers University Press, 1992.

The Letters of Margaret Fuller. Ed. Robert N. Hudspeth. Ithaca, N.Y.: Cornell University Press, 1983–95. 6 vols.

Margaret Fuller: Essays on American Life and Letters. Ed. Joel Myerson. New Haven, Conn.: College and University Press, 1978.

Memoirs of Margaret Fuller Ossoli. Ed. R. W. Emerson, W. H. Channing, and J. F. Clarke. 1852; rpt. New York: Burt Franklin, 1972. 2 vols.

Papers on Literature and Art. New York: Wiley & Putnam, 1846. 2 vols.

The Portable Margaret Fuller. Ed. Mary Kelley. New York: Penguin Books, 1994.

Summer on the Lakes, in 1843. Ed. Susan Belasco Smith. 1844; rpt. Urbana: University of Illinois Press, 1991.

"These Sad but Glorious Days": Dispatches from Europe, 1846–1850. Ed. Larry J. Reynolds and Susan Belasco Smith. New Haven, Conn.: Yale University Press, 1992.

SECONDARY WORKS

Albert, Judith Strong. "Margaret Fuller's Row at the Greene Street School: Early Female Education in Providence, 1837–1839." *Rhode Island History* 42 (May 1983): 43–55.

Allen, Margaret Vanderhaar. "The Political and Social Criticism of Margaret Fuller." *South Atlantic Quarterly*, 72 (1973): 560–73.

• Allen, Margaret Vanderhaar. *The Achievement of Margaret Fuller*. University Park: Pennsylvania State University Press, 1979.

Berkson, Dorothy. " 'Born and Bred in Different Nations': Margaret Fuller and Ralph Waldo Emerson." In *Patrons and Protégées: Gender, Friendship, and Writing in Nineteenth-Century America*. Ed. Shirley Marchalonis. New Brunswick, N.J.: Rutgers University Press, 1988. 3–30.

Blanchard, Paula. *Margaret Fuller: From Transcendentalism to Revolution*. New York: Delacorte, 1978.

Buell, Lawrence. *Literary Transcendentalism: Style and Vision in the American Renaissance*. Ithaca, N.Y.: Cornell University Press, 1973.

Capper, Charles. "Margaret Fuller as Cultural Reformer: The Conversations in Boston." *American Quarterly* 39 (1987): 509–28.

Capper, Charles. *Margaret Fuller: An American Romantic Life*. Vol. 1. *The Private Years*. New York: Oxford University Press, 1992.

Chevigny, Bell Gale. "Growing Out of New England: The Emergence of Margaret Fuller's Radicalism." *Women's Studies* 5 (1977): 65–100.

• Chevigny, Bell Gale. "To the Edges of Ideology: Margaret Fuller's Centrifugal Evolution." *American Quarterly* 38 (1986): 173–201.

Chevigny, Bell Gale. *The Woman and the Myth: Margaret Fuller's Life and Writings.* 1976; rev. Boston: Northeastern University Press, 1994.

Conrad, Susan P. *Perish the Thought: Intellectual Women in Romantic America 1830–1860.* New York: Oxford University Press, 1976.

Cott, Nancy F. *The Bonds of Womanhood: "Woman's Sphere" in New England 1780–1835.* New Haven, Conn.: Yale University Press, 1977.

Dedmond, Francis B. "The Letters of Caroline Sturgis to Margaret Fuller." *Studies in the American Renaissance* (1988): 201–52.

Deiss, Joseph Jay. *The Roman Years of Margaret Fuller: A Biography.* New York: Thomas Crowell, 1969.

Douglas, Ann. "Margaret Fuller and the Search for History: A Biographical Study." *Women's Studies* 4 (1976): 37–86.

Douglas, Ann. *The Feminization of American Culture.* New York: Alfred Knopf, 1977.

• Ellison, Julie. *Delicate Subjects: Romanticism, Gender, and the Ethics of Understanding.* Ithaca, N.Y.: Cornell University Press, 1990.

Fergenson, Laraine R. "Margaret Fuller in the Classroom: The Providence Period." *Studies in the American Renaissance* (1987): 131–42.

Fergenson, Laraine R. "Margaret Fuller as a Teacher in Providence: The School Journal of Ann Brown." *Studies in the American Renaissance* (1991): 59–118.

Fleischmann, Fritz. "Margaret Fuller." In *Classics in Cultural Criticism.* Ed. Hartmut Heuermann. Frankfurt: Peter Lang, 1990. 2: 39–68.

Flexner, Eleanor. *Century of Struggle: The Woman's Rights Movement in the United States.* Cambridge, Mass.: Harvard University Press, 1975.

Gustafson, Sandra M. "Choosing a Medium: Margaret Fuller and the Forms of Sentiment." *American Quarterly* 47 (March 1995): 34–65.

Higginson, Thomas Wentworth. *Margaret Fuller Ossoli.* 1884; rpt. New York: Confucian Press, 1980.

Hlus, Carolyn. "Margaret Fuller, Transcendentalist: A Reassessment." *Canadian Review of American Studies* 16 (Spring 1985): 1–13.

Hopkins, Vivian C. "Margaret Fuller: Pioneer Women's Liberationist." *American Transcendental Quarterly* no. 18 (Spring 1973): 29–35.

Kearns, Francis E. "Margaret Fuller and the Abolition Movement." *Journal of the History of Ideas* 25 (January–March 1964): 120–27.

Kolodny, Annette. *The Land before Her: Fantasy and Experience of the American Frontiers, 1630–1860.* Chapel Hill: University of North Carolina Press, 1984.

Kolodny, Annette. "Inventing a Feminist Discourse: Rhetoric and Resistance in Margaret Fuller's *Woman in the Nineteenth Century.*" *New Literary History* 25 (1994): 355–82.

Kornfeld, Eve, and Melissa Marks. "Margaret Fuller: Minerva and the Muse." *Journal of American Culture* 13 (Fall 1990): 47–59.

Mitchell, Thomas R. "Julian Hawthorne and the 'Scandal' of Margaret Fuller." *American Literary History* 7 (Summer 1995): 210–33.

Myerson, Joel, ed. *Critical Essays on Margaret Fuller.* Boston: G. K. Hall, 1980.

Myerson, Joel. *The New England Transcendentalists and the "Dial": A History of the Magazine and Its Contributors.* Rutherford, N.J.: Fairleigh Dickinson University Press, 1980.

Packer, Barbara L. "The Transcendentalists." In *The Cambridge History of American Literature. Volume 2, 1820–1865.* New York: Cambridge University Press, 1995. 525–47.

Parrington, Vernon Louis. "Margaret Fuller: Rebel." In *The Romantic Revolution in America 1800–1860.* New York: Harcourt, Brace, 1927. pp. 426–34.

Reynolds, Larry J. *European Revolutions and the American Literary Renaissance.* New Haven, Conn.: Yale University Press, 1988.

Reynolds, Larry J. "From *Dial* Essay to New York Book: The Making of *Woman in the Nineteenth Century.*" In *Periodical Literature in Nineteenth-Century America.* Ed. Kenneth M. Price and Susan Belasco Smith. Charlottesville and London: University Press of Virginia, 1995. 17–34.

Richardson, Robert D., Jr. *Myth and Literature in the American Renaissance.* Bloomington: Indiana University Press, 1978.

• Robinson, David M. "Margaret Fuller and the Transcendental Ethos: *Woman in the Nineteenth Century.* PMLA 97 (January 1982): 83–98.

Rose, Anne. *Transcendentalism as a Social Movement: 1830–50.* New Haven, Conn.: Yale University Press, 1981.

Sánchez-Eppler, Karen, "Bodily Bonds: The Intersecting Rhetorics of Feminism and Abolition." *Representations* 24 (Fall 1988): 28–59.

Scheick, William J. "The Angelic Artistry of Margaret Fuller's *Woman in the Nineteenth Century.*" *Essays in Literature* 11 (Fall 1984): 293–98.

Showalter, Elaine. *Sister's Choice: Tradition and Change in American Women's Writing.* Oxford, UK: Clarendon Press, 1991.

Smith-Rosenberg, Carroll. *Disorderly Conduct: Visions of Gender in Victorian America.* New York: Oxford University Press, 1985.

Steele, Jeffrey. *The Representation of the Self in the American Renaissance.* Chapel Hill: University of North Carolina Press, 1987.

Steele, Jeffrey. "The Call of Eurydice: Mourning and Intertextuality in Margaret Fuller's Writing." In *Influence and Intertextuality in Literary History.* Ed. Eric Rothstein and Jay Clayton. Madison: University of Wisconsin Press, 1991. 271–97.

Steele, Jeffrey. "Freeing the 'Prisoned Queen': The Development of Margaret Fuller's Poetry." *Studies in the American Renaissance* (1992): 137–76.

Stern, Madeleine, "Introduction." In *Woman in the Nineteenth Century.* Ed. Joel Myerson. Columbia: University of South Carolina Press. vii–xxxix.

Stowe, William W. *Going Abroad: European Travel in Nineteenth-Century American Culture.* Princeton, N.J.: Princeton University Press, 1994.

Urbanski, Marie Mitchell Olesen. *Margaret Fuller's "Woman in the Nineteenth Century": A Literary Study of Form and Content, of Sources and Influence.* Westport, Conn.: Greenwood Press, 1980.

von Frank, Albert. *The Sacred Game: Provincialism and Frontier Consciousness in American Literature, 1630–1860.* New York: Cambridge University Press, 1985.

von Mehren, Joan. *Minerva and the Muse: A Life of Margaret Fuller.* Amherst: University of Massachusetts Press, 1994.

Welter, Barbara. *Dimity Convictions: The American Woman in the Nineteenth Century.* Athens: Ohio University Press, 1976.

Wood, Mary E. "'With Ready Eye': Margaret Fuller and Lesbianism in Nineteenth-Century American Literature." *American Literature* 65 (March 1993): 1–18.

• Zwarg, Christina. *Feminist Conversations: Fuller, Emerson, and the Play of Reading* Ithaca, N.Y.: Cornell University Press, 1995.